A Point of View

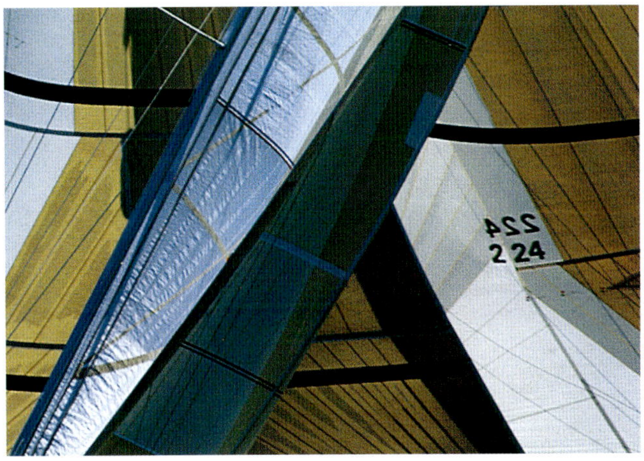

A POINT OF VIEW

PHOTOGRAPHS OF COMPETITIVE SAILING
WITH INSIGHTS INTO THE
PHOTOGRAPHER'S MIND AND EYE

Photographs and text by Stanley Rosenfeld

MYSTIC SEAPORT
THE MUSEUM
OF AMERICA
AND THE SEA

Mystic Seaport
75 Greenmanville Ave.
P.O. Box 6000
Mystic, CT 06355-0990

First Edition

Designed by Clare Cunningham

Manufactured in China

ISBN 0-939511-08-8

Mystic Seaport—The Museum of America and the Sea—is the nation's leading maritime museum, presenting the American experience from a maritime perspective.

Located along the banks of the historic Mystic River in Mystic, Connecticut, the Museum houses extensive collections representing the material culture of maritime America, and offers educational programs from preschool to postgraduate.

For more information, call us at 888-9SEAPORT, or visit us on the Web at www.mysticseaport.org

For more on Stanley Rosenfeld and the Rosenfeld Collection, visit www.rosenfeldcollection.org

Table of Contents

Introduction 10

Western Australia 13

Newport 71

Controversy and Change 105

San Diego 113

Expressions 147

Windward Passage 155

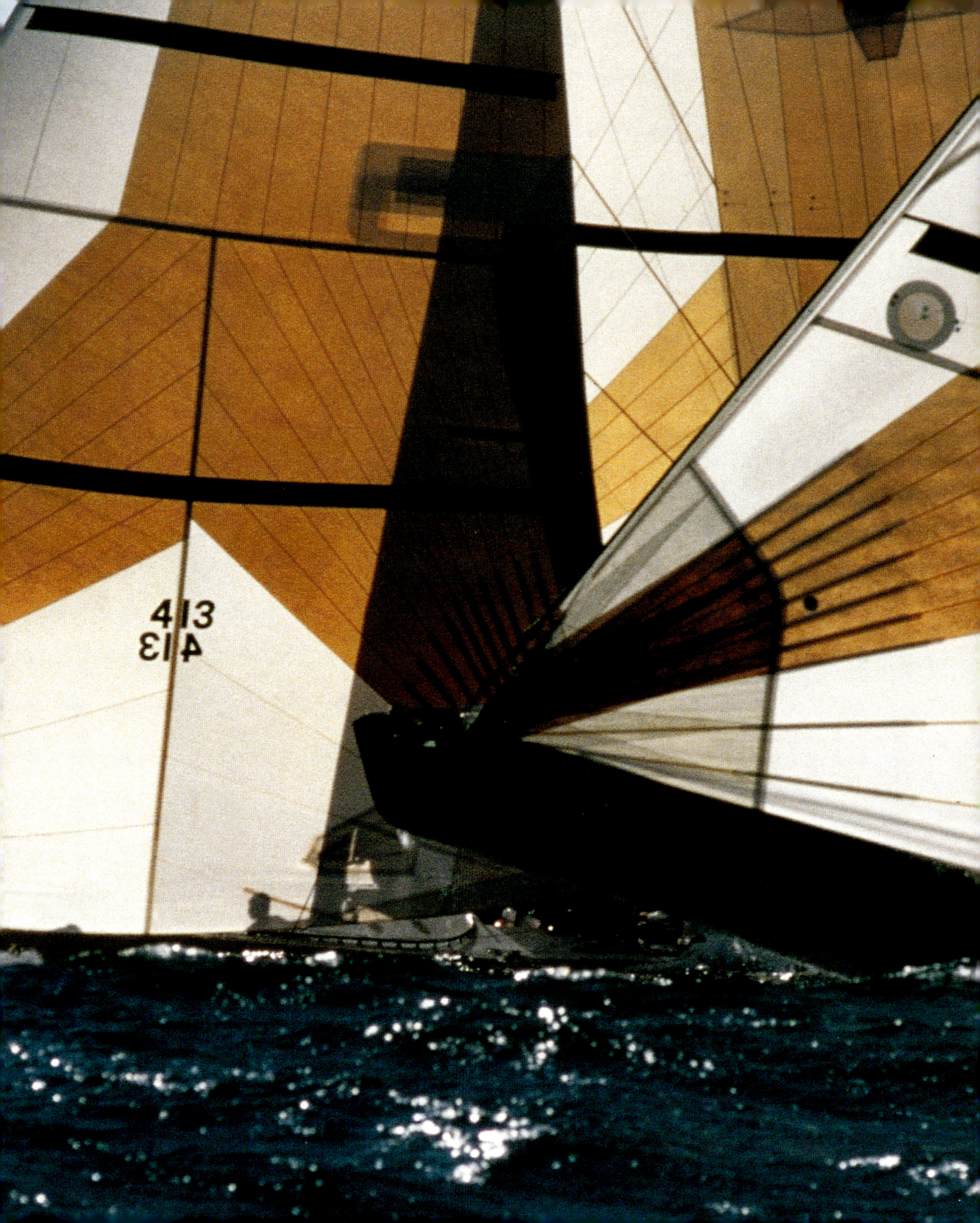
413

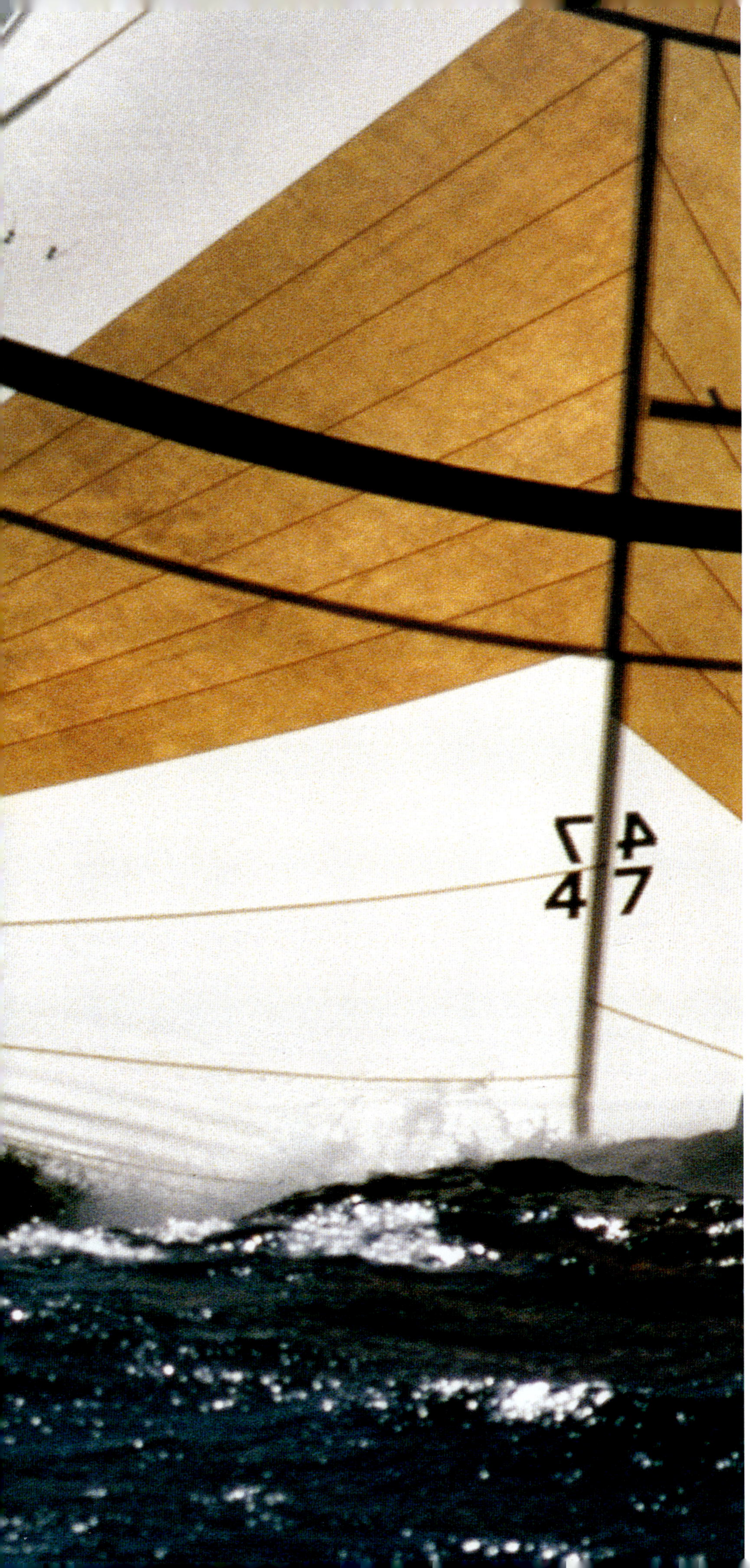

To sailors and
their craft,
who in their contest
with the sea create
images of power
and beauty

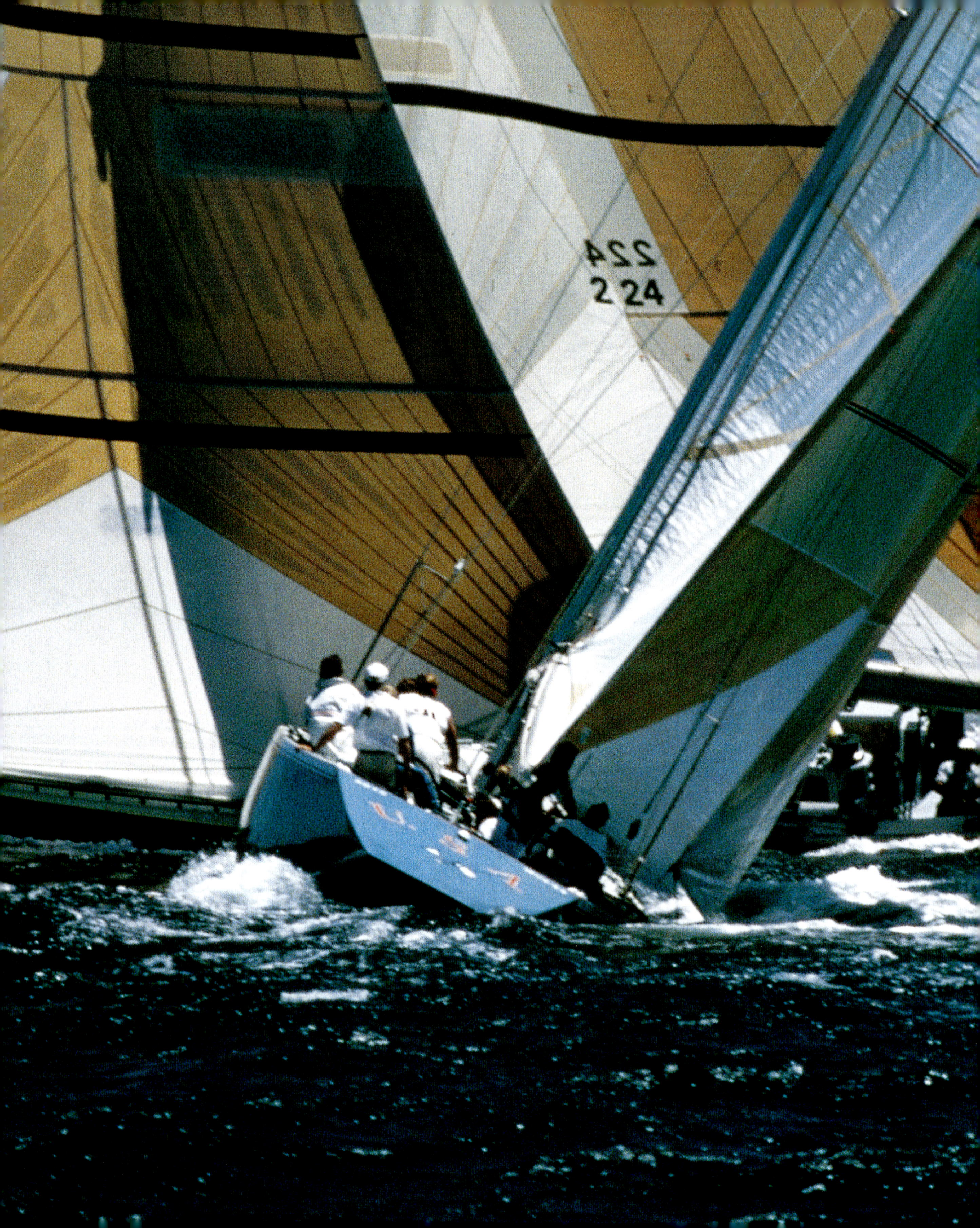
224

Acknowledgements

With appreciation and gratitude...

to Heather Hanley, who transformed
my spoken words to paper,

to Clare Cunningham, who gave form
to the words and images,

to Sally Pope, who transformed the text
to smooth-sailing prose.

INTRODUCTION

In 1984, Mystic Seaport acquired the Rosenfeld Collection of photographic prints and negatives. The negatives vary with the camera sizes that evolved from the beginnings of action photography in the early 1880s. Fast photographic emulsions were introduced then, making it possible to capture action with instantaneous exposures. My father used 8 x 10-inch glass plates until 1920, and then the negative size slowly diminished, through hundreds of thousands of plates and film, until the 35-mm camera became the standard. That small camera brought a multitude of lenses in a variety of focal lengths, making it possible to capture close-up action both from aboard a vessel and from a distance.

When I closed the Rosenfeld studio in New York and vacated my city apartment, I gathered the old cameras and lenses that had fortunately been retained and stored since the turn of the century and moved them to Mystic Seaport. The cameras ran the gamut from the 11 x 14-inch view camera, through 8 x 10-inch Graphlexes and Graphics, down to the 35-mm cameras, and included a variety of others we experimented with over the years. Subsequently, they were donated to the Rosenfeld Collection, so Mystic Seaport Museum has not only the archive of marine images spanning a century, but the cameras and lenses that made them.

For many years I had been thinking of organizing the old cameras and lenses and correlating them with the actual photographs they made. I knew in working with our file of negatives that the style of imagery changed not only with the tenets of fashion, but also with the actual cameras and lenses used. As a boy, I occasionally went along with my father when he photographed the interior of a new yacht. I observed with the taking of each photograph a ritual formula in tripod placement: the survey to establish the viewpoint; the mental estimate of the area the lens would cover; the scan to see that no salient feature was blocked; then the ceremonial setting down of the tripod. Lighting and exposure followed, but the viewpoint was literally the pivotal point of departure.

The portraits my father made in his time are very different from the ones appearing in this book. On location he used almost exclusively cameras with a normal lens, one with a focal length equivalent to the diagonal of the film size of the camera. Usually, he stood six or eight feet away from his subject, and his image very often captured the entire figure of the person. With the 35-mm camera, the portraits I made were often with lenses of a much longer focal length: from a distance, I could fill the frame with just the head of the subject. I was thus sensitized to the wide range of expressions that played over a person's features, and I looked to capture even fleeting moments that revealed inner emotions or thoughts — a more intimate interaction with the subject.

My father's vision of his subjects afloat was also very different from mine. He had come to his interest in marine photography as a lad in the 1890s as he walked along South Street in lower Manhattan, in awe and admiration of the sailing ships that were moored along the quay. The vision meant romance to him, a far-distant imagery from the teeming streets of Manhattan. I also came to the sea as a child, but my experience with it was frequently in personal contest. I handled the photo chase boats from the time I was tall enough to see over the bow, and often through the years I made lone voyages along the east coast between New York and Newport. I sensed the water and its craft not solely through observation, but also by feel and smell — the salt breeze was inside me. When I saw imagery afloat, it was not an idealized view as was my father's; it was more of a visceral perception. Happily, the 35-mm camera and lenses came at a time that made this way of thinking a photographic possibility.

As I used the cameras normal to the operation of the Rosenfeld studio and became familiar with their ungainly mass, heft, and feel, I could sense how often the type of camera or lens led toward the framing of the resulting image. In the late 1940s, I began to use the 35-mm camera more frequently and was able to take advantage of the infinite variety in images made possible by its powerful battery of lenses.

In the years just after World War II, I was more urgently concerned with rebuilding the business of the studio than in reflecting on the nature of photography. In time, as the studio became a less pressing concern, I could think again on how the experience and knowledge accumulated in years afloat had their impact on the images in my mind and how they molded the scenes I attempted with the camera.

The photographs in this book are from my mature years: the earliest was made when I was 69 and the latest in my 79th year. I have tried to give some insight into what I saw and what my mind made of the action in front of my camera. Each photograph is not just an instant out of the stream of time. It is the accumulation of a lifetime's experience afloat, reflected in the action of the passing instant.

Venice, Italy

October 1995

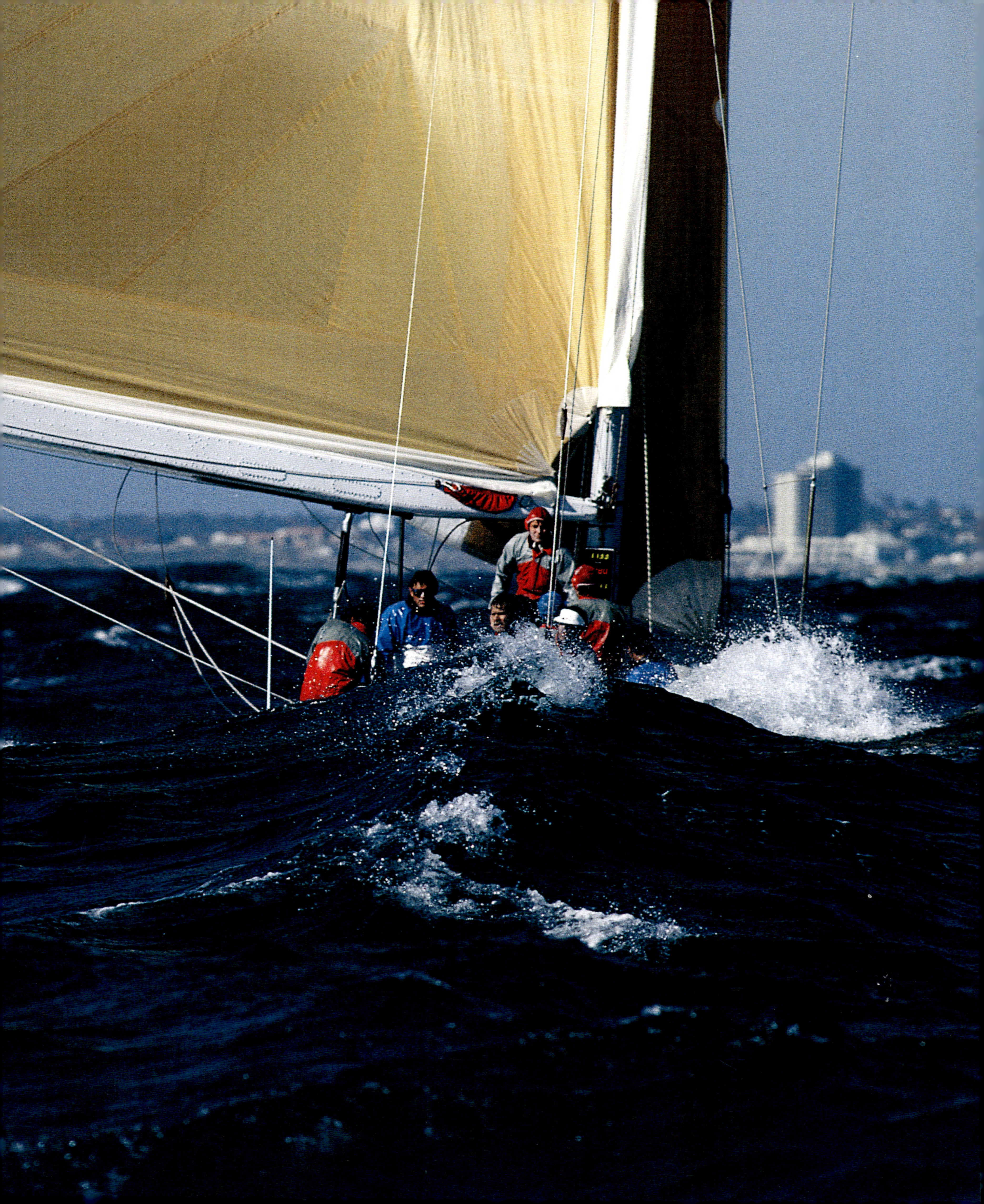

Western Australia

A season of vigorous winds,
lively seas, and sailing to test men's souls

The racecourse off Fremantle, Australia, was a venue filled with excitement. The wind blew with satisfying regularity and the machine that drove the winds, the heat of the desert, provided consistency and strength. As the wind blew up, it increased in force to a stimulating 23 knots and often settled down there. The only comparable wind condition the 12-meters had met in racing was off Porto Cervo, Sardinia, but there the mistral would spike up to more than 30 knots, an unnecessary challenge for the 12-meter craft.

The Fremantle course was in the arms of a bend in the coastline, with the water slightly over 100 feet in depth at the outside of the racing, shoaling to 30 feet inshore. This variation in depth made for deeper waves offshore. A small ring of islands lay to the southwest in the path of the prevailing breeze, while to the north the bay was open to the ocean, with a fetch that extended in a grand sweep across thousands of miles of ocean to the southern tip of Africa. Usually, a swell set in from that area of the bay at a right angle to the wind-driven waves, which brought a challenge to the sailors and action to the photographer. To me, it was the most visually exciting America's Cup racing to date.

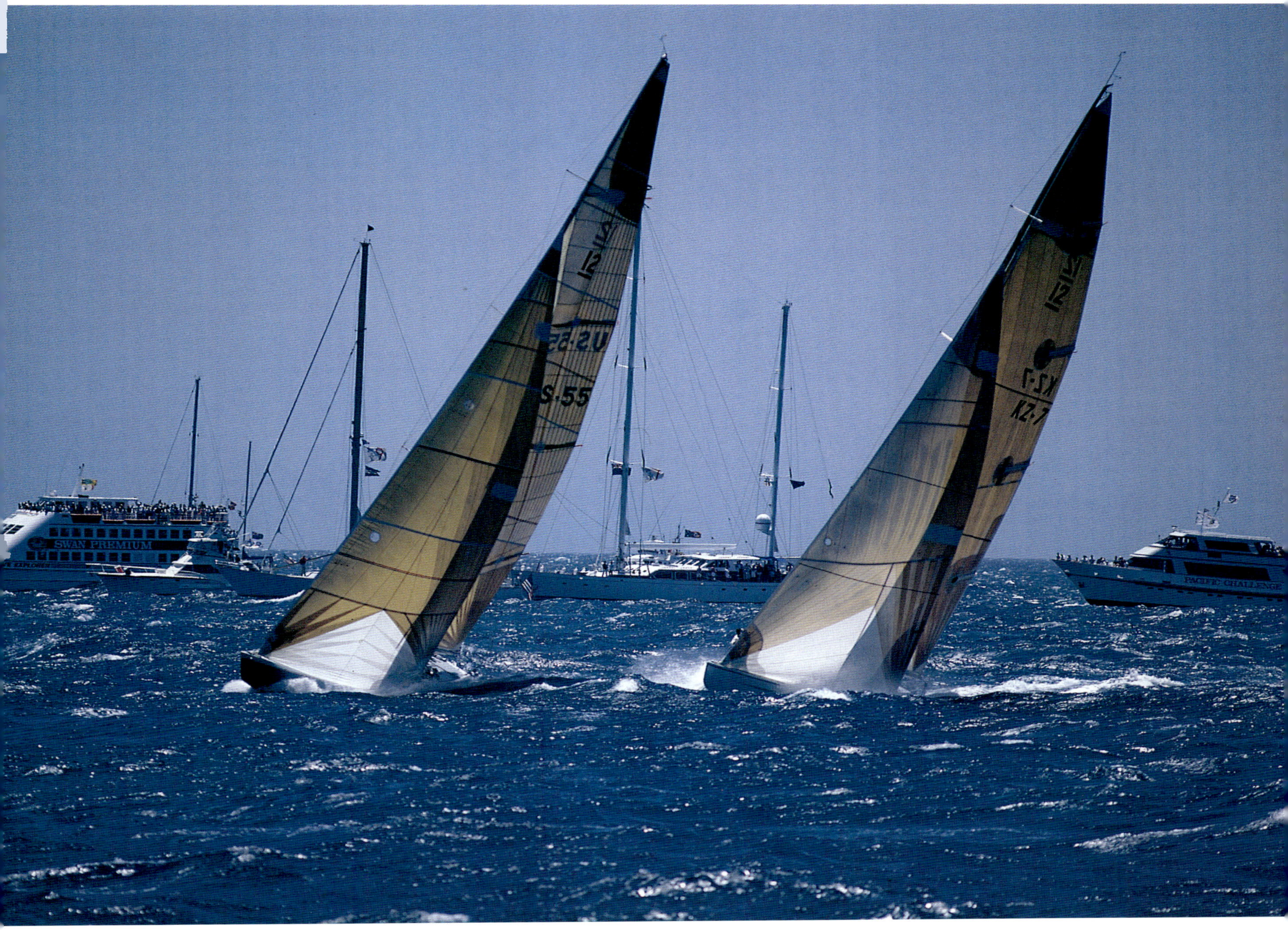

"The Fremantle Doctor"

Stars & Stripes to windward and *New Zealand* approach the starting line in the typical breeze, colloquially referred to as "The Fremantle Doctor," because, ashore, the sea breeze brought relief from the stifling temperatures that rose from the inland desert. On the racecourse, it provided stimulating sailing to 12-meters that were designed and built for the strenuous conditions they met afloat. At starting time, from the buoy end of the line, the sun came through the sails of *Stars & Stripes* and *New Zealand* as they approached on starboard tack, and the new configuration of modern sailcloth resulted in a diversity of warm colors and converging seam lines. To add to the liveliness of the tossing waves, the camera, pointed against the light, picked up the sparkle in the roiled waters. The yachts were moving slowly with genoa sheets eased, waiting for the starting gun with just a pleasant splash of spray at their bows. The triangles of mast and sail, two separate and individual centers of action, have to be tied and balanced into a single composition with a sense of imminence.

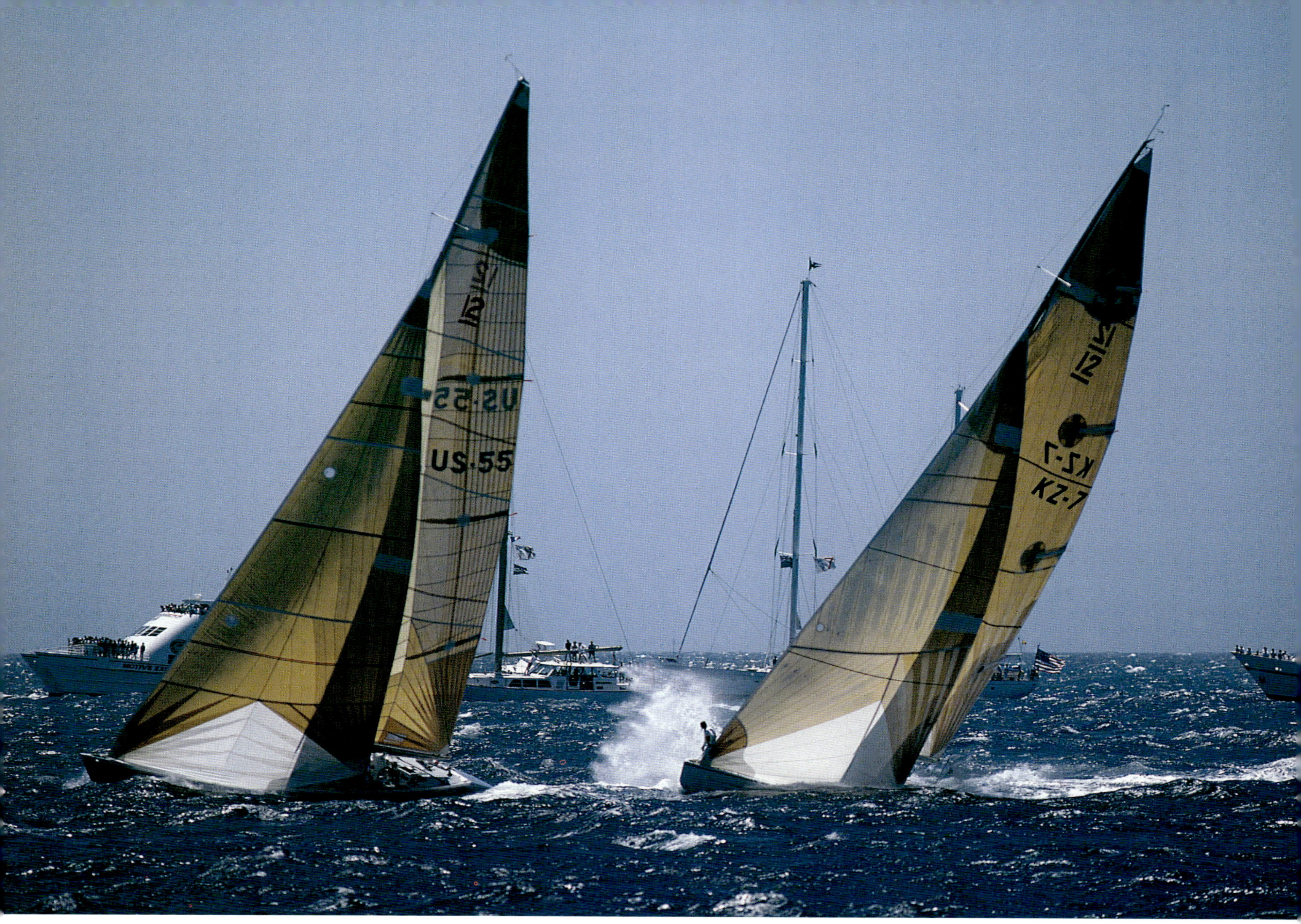

The Apex of Balance

As the yachts continue to approach the starting line, *New Zealand* has trimmed sheets, moved up, and hit one of the swells coming in at right angles to the course. Spray is thrown high in the air as she bounces through the roller that passes beneath her. The area of spray and the figure of the bowman are brought into the apex of balance in the image by the more slanting line of *New Zealand*'s mast.

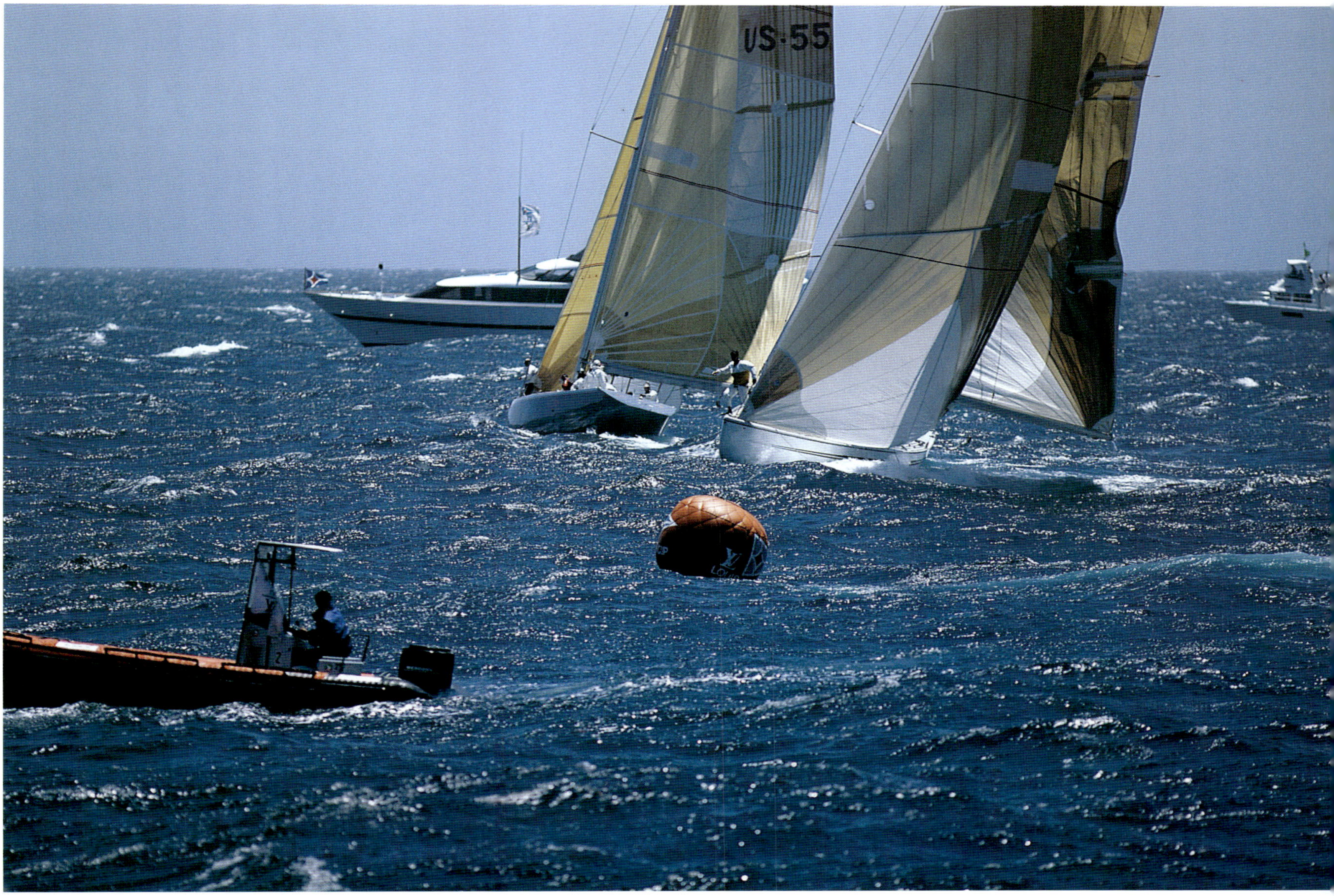

Early to the Line

The yachts are early to the line and *Stars & Stripes* tacks to port to sail across it, while *New Zealand*'s eased mainsail flaps violently to add a crescendo of sound to the tension of the start. The line is from the red buoy in the foreground to the committee boat outside. *Stars & Stripes* is heading toward the starboard side of the line and ducks into another swell moving in from there. The bowman on *New Zealand* gestures toward the starting line for the benefit of the helmsman. A vertical image might have included all the action described, but I feel that the course lies off to the left and for me, the line of action is horizontally reaching up the course and pulling that way.

The small red support boat on the left is one of the photographic hazards met on every Cup course. The boats carrying race officials, committee members, and photographers, maneuver close in to the contestants and are so often in a photographer's line of sight that shooting around them is a constant struggle and not always possible.

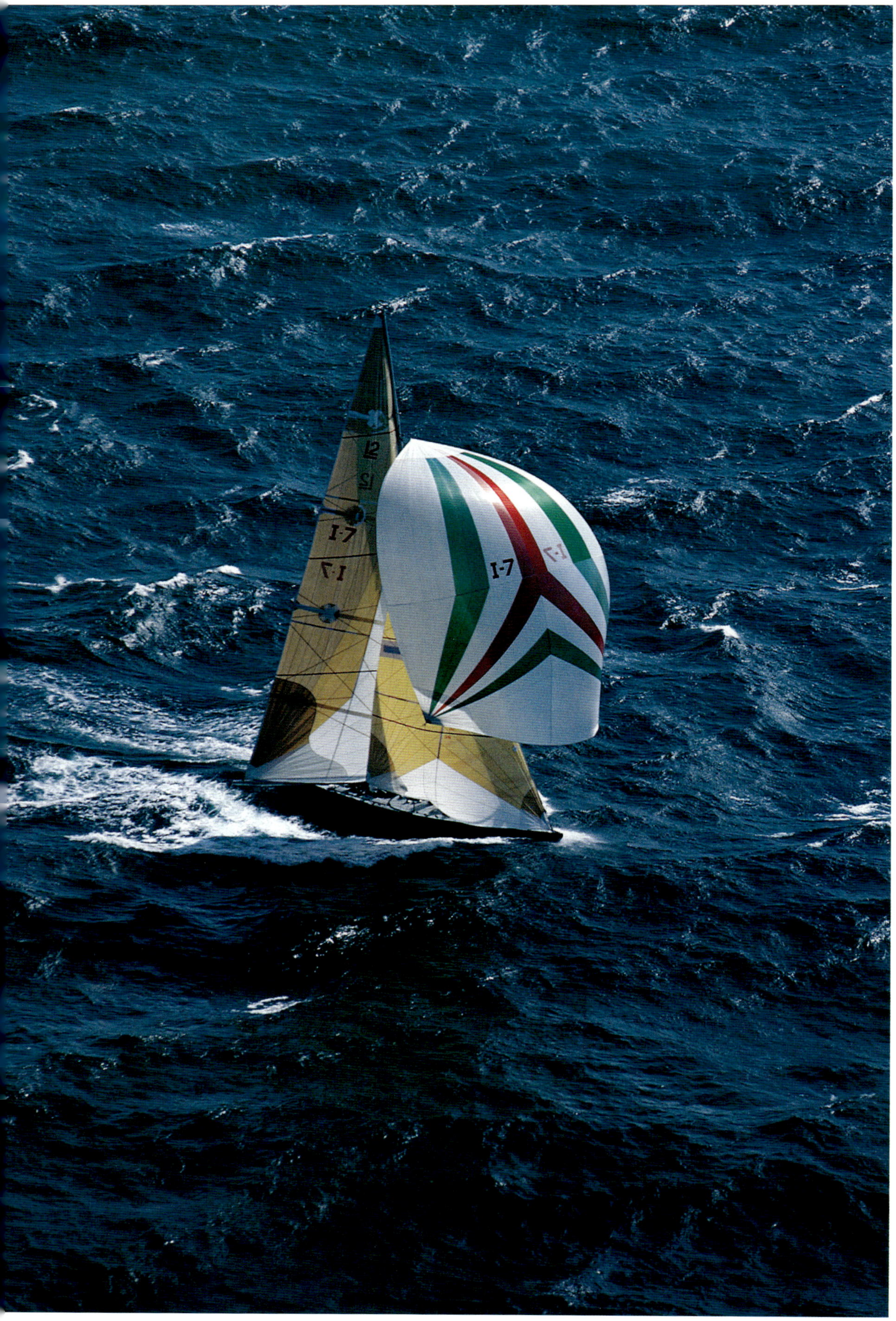

Downwind Leg

Italia is on a downwind leg, mainsheet eased and spinnaker billowing squarely ahead. The sun gleams on the rounded top of the spinnaker, backlighting the mainsail and jib. *Italia*'s bow is digging into one of the ocean swells rolling across the wind. Another swell is about a boat length nearer the camera. The swells often came across the course in pairs. At the very top of the photograph, another such swell is visible. Aerial photography over water is not one of my favorite endeavors, but this image from above does clearly show the wave pattern on the surface.

Pattern of Swells

Opposite, the pattern of swells at the top of the image shows a strong pair following closely on a third. This kind of pattern can mean a boost in speed to a vessel riding the swells downwind, but, as the following three photographs show, it can cause great discomfort to a yacht on the wind.

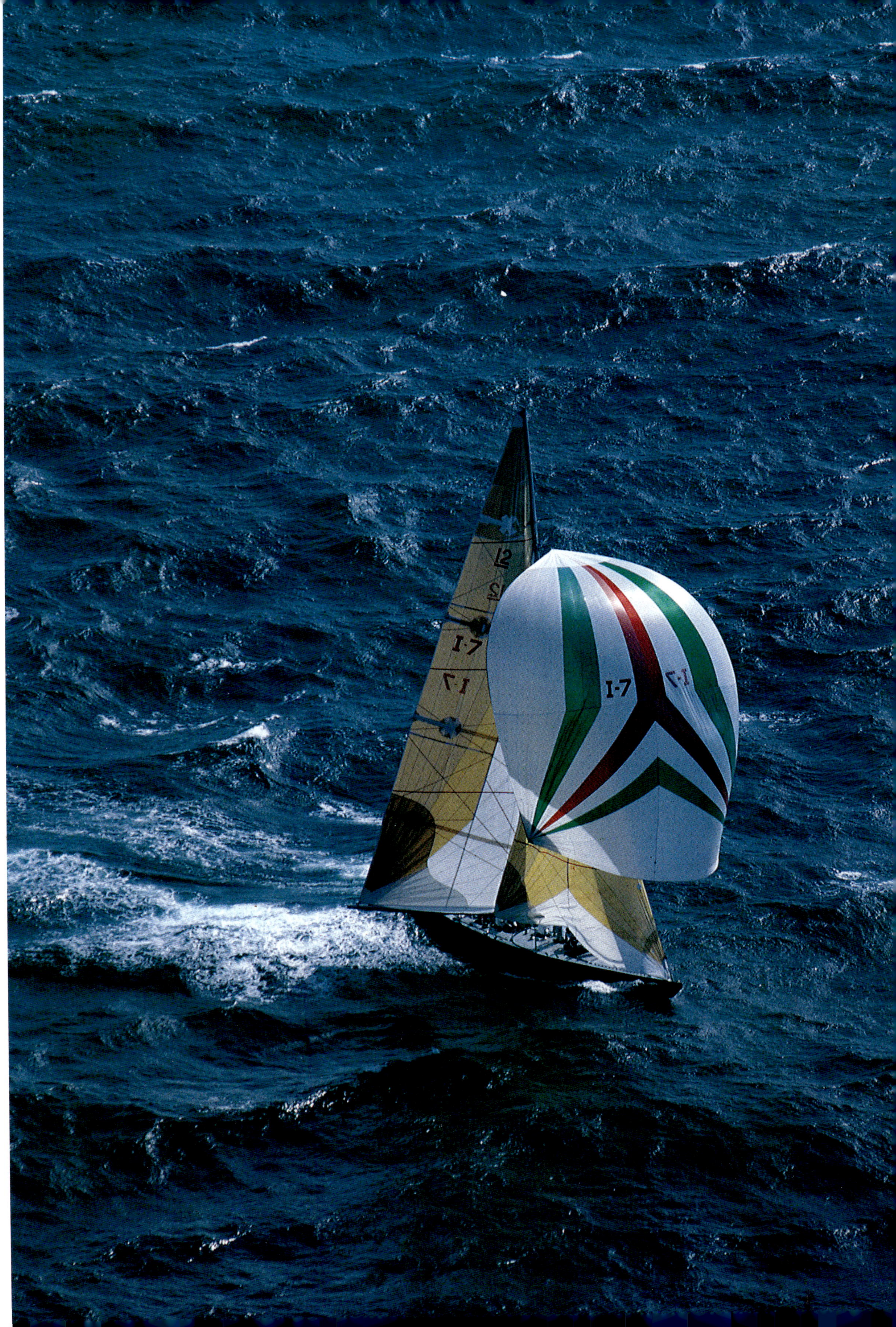
I-7
I-7
12

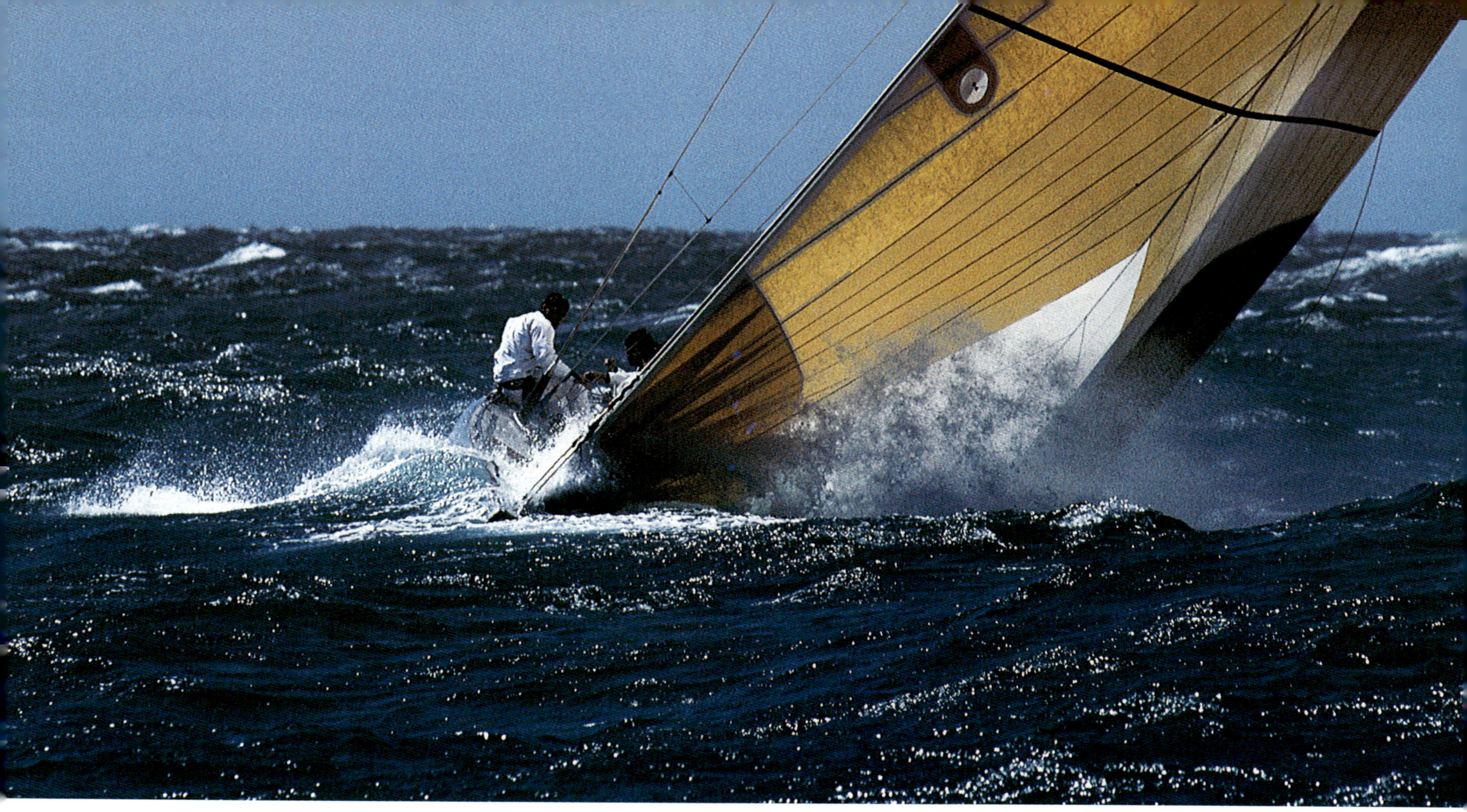

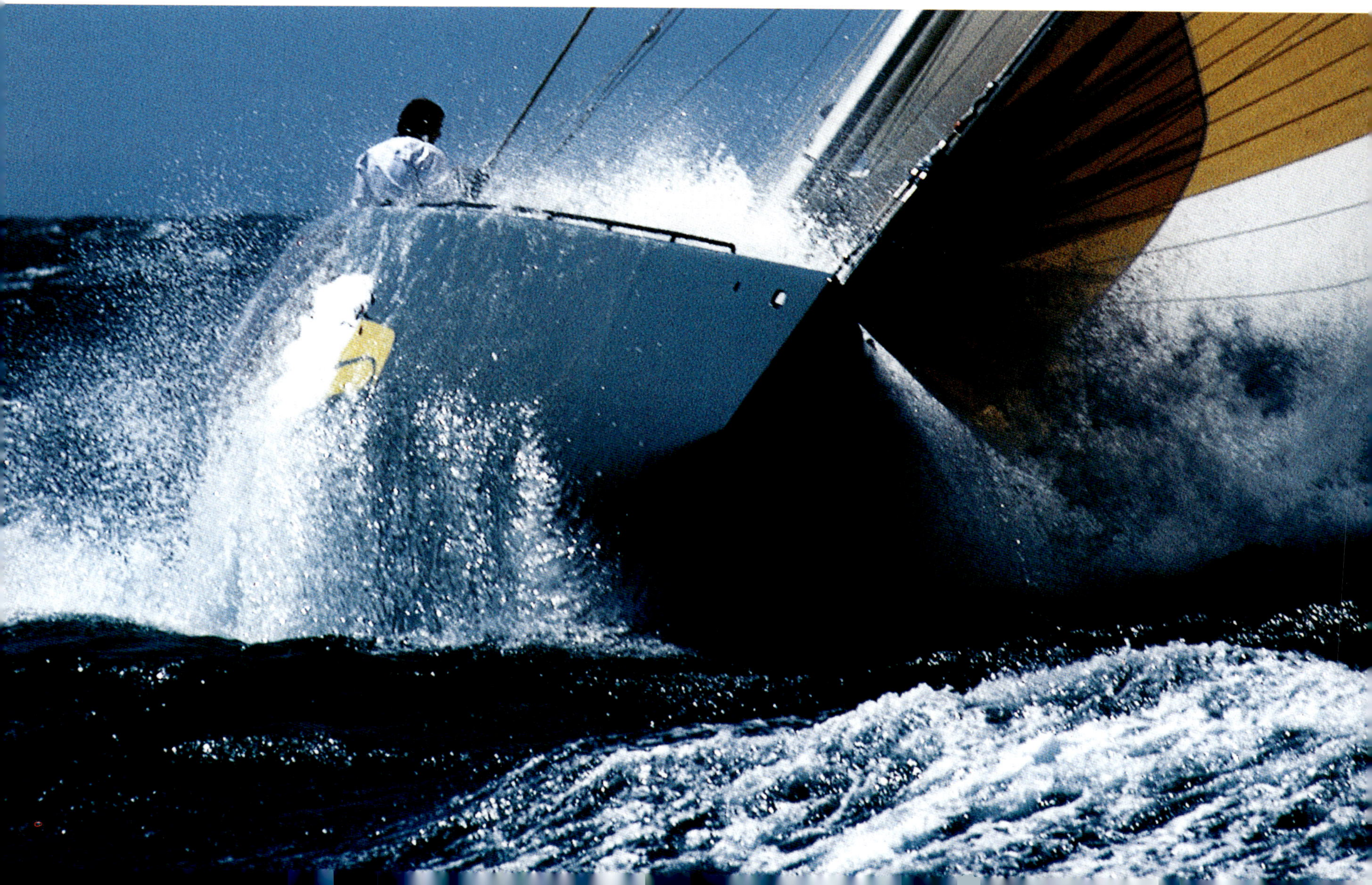

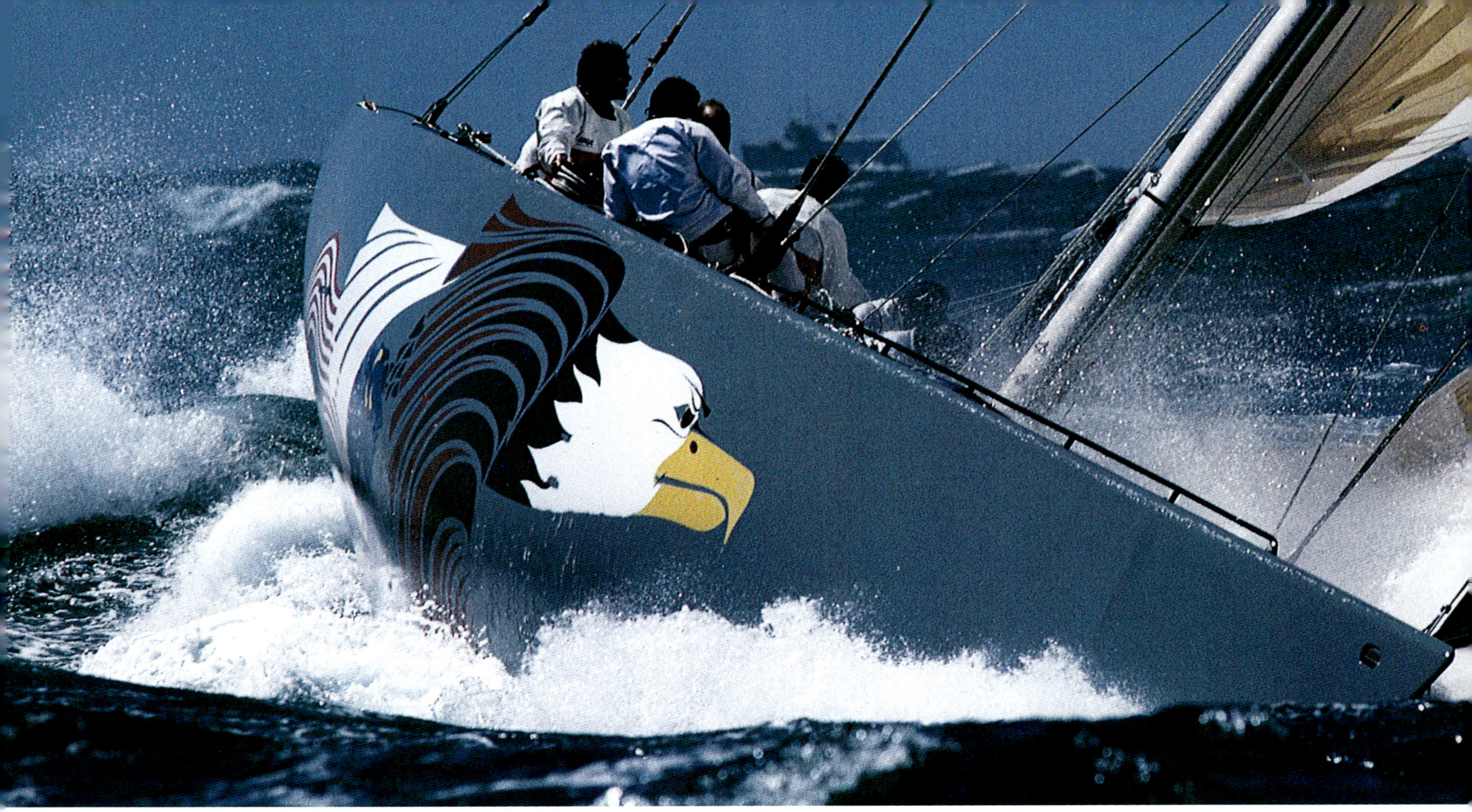

Buried Between the Crests

Opposite above, the 60-foot hull of the 12-meter *Eagle* is buried between the crests of two ocean swells as her bow digs in. A wave ominously rolls across her forward deck while, to leeward, flying spray hangs darkly against the back-lit genoa. At this moment the pervasive power of the wind-driven waves threatens and dominates the yacht.

Bursting Foam

Opposite below, a few seconds later, *Eagle*'s powerful bow breaks through, emerging in a cascade of flying spray. Bursting foam bounces over her deck and leaps under her genoa. Glistening against the hull, the iridescent streamers reflect sunlight in crystals of spray. The straight thrust of the mast is a tower of strength. Suddenly the yacht is in her element and master of the seas.

White Water Boiling

Above, seconds pass and *Eagle* is between a pair of big waves just far enough apart that one can lift her transom while her bow dives into the other. Suddenly, my mind is drawn from the aesthetics of the scene to a technical aspect that is equally fascinating. The white water boiling out underneath the feet of the eagle painted on the yacht's side is a sign that easily distracts and interests me. I wonder how much disturbance is being generated by water forced under and across the yacht's keel and what that transverse aspect of water flow and resistance costs in speed.

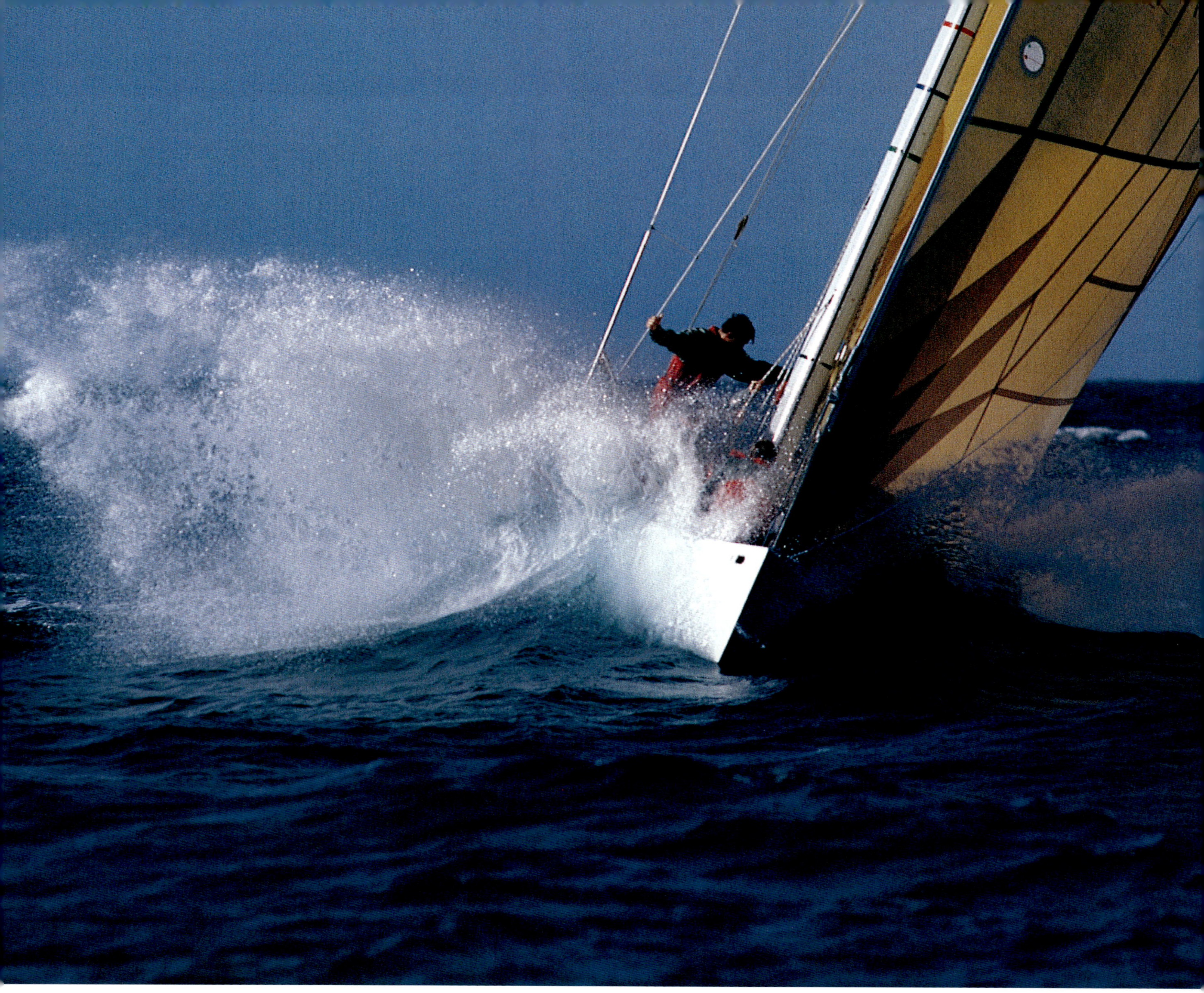

Approaching the Windward Mark

The yacht *USA* is approaching the windward mark. The weather is a very boisterous reminder that, off Fremantle, Australia's January summertime is ideal for the seagoing photographer. As *USA* drives to windward, spray from each wave is sent flying, and enough is blown aboard to drench the crew working on the foredeck. This is the instant to show drive.

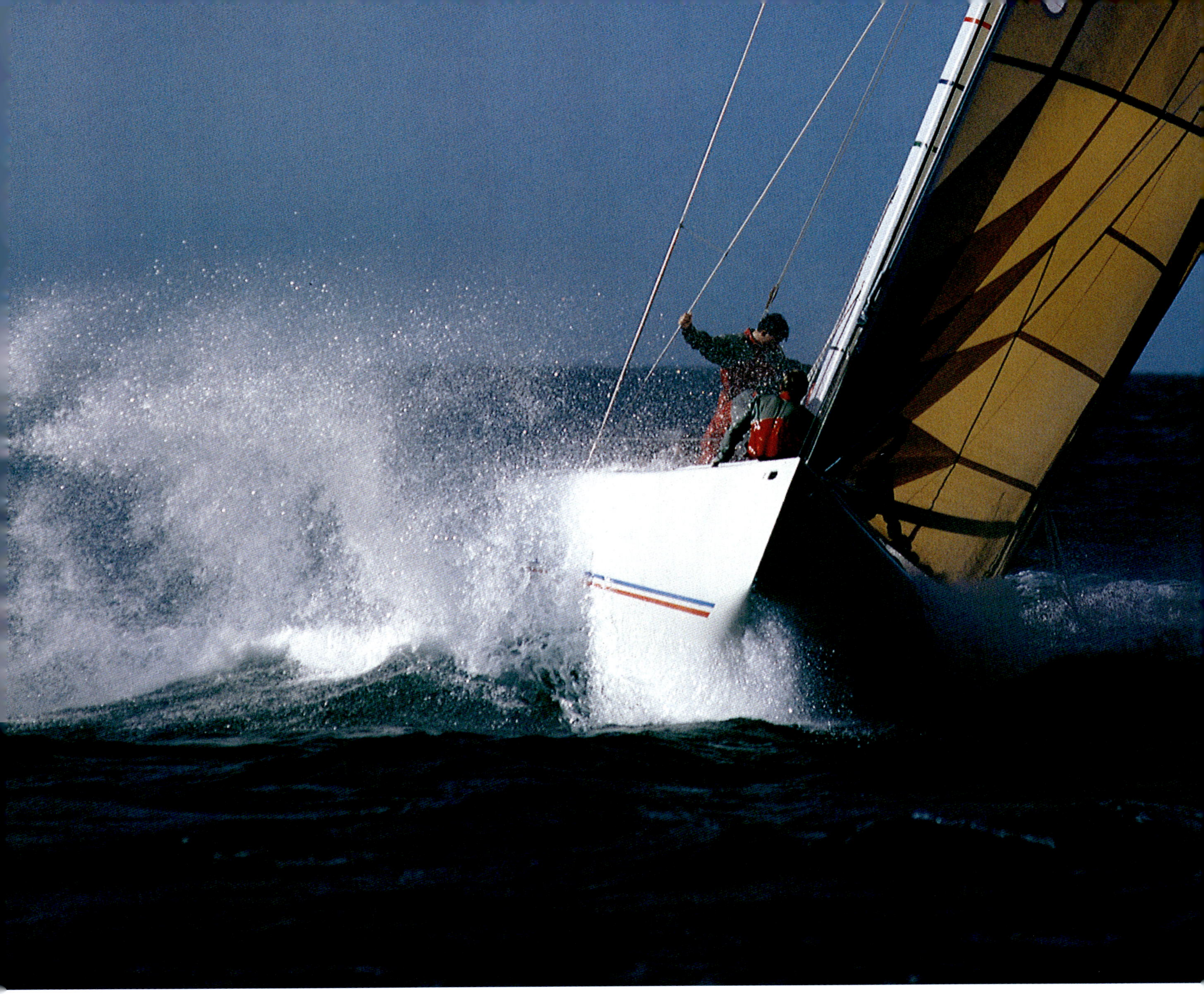

Hanging Spray

The foredeck is a place of wild gyration, flying spray, and dangerous rigging. The hull of *USA* is now lifting as spray from the last wave seems to hang in the air or pour off the deck.

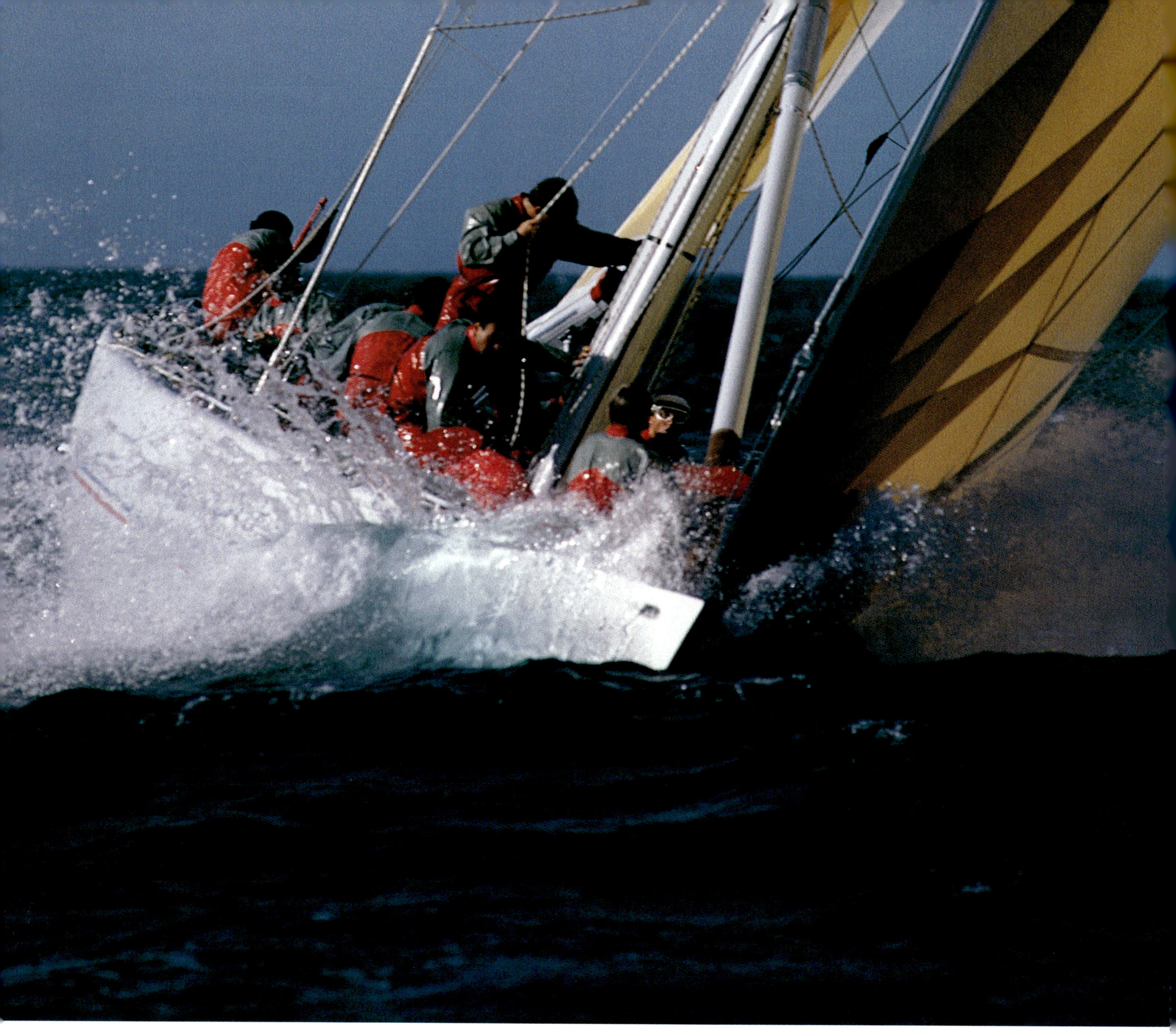

Disciplined Turmoil

As the stern of *USA* lifts and the bow dives into the sea, from my camera position on the deck of a photo boat outside the mark, the crew comes into view and gives a sense of the disciplined turmoil that accompanies a mark rounding. The spinnaker pole is being set and the crew, which appears here to be scrambling, is executing an organized series of maneuvers in anticipation of the rounding.

The flying spray in the previous three photographs of *USA* indicates that the shutter speed of the camera is not fast enough to freeze the motion of the drops of water. I usually prefer a camera speed just fast enough to stop the motion of the boat but not fast enough to freeze the motion of the spray into static little drops. The film used in these 1987 photographs was Kodachrome with an ASA of 64. The lens, a 300-mm F2 Nikon, which I used with extenders to 600 mm, was fast enough that I could have used a shutter speed that would freeze the motion of the spray had I wanted to do so.

On page 22, where *USA* was the most distant from the camera of these three photographs, the shutter speed, probably a 500th of a second, seems to stop the flying spray, but closer scrutiny will clearly show that there is motion in the droplets. On page 23, the bow is lifting and the spray is moving less rapidly, almost hovering as compared with page 22, and the droplets appear sharper. The boat is still distant from the camera lens. On page 24, the boat is much closer to the camera and motion across the lens field is more rapid. *USA* is again diving into the wave and the spray is again flung rapidly upwards and outwards. Here the same shutter speed of the camera clearly does not stop the motion of the spray, which appears as blurred streamers rather than individual droplets.

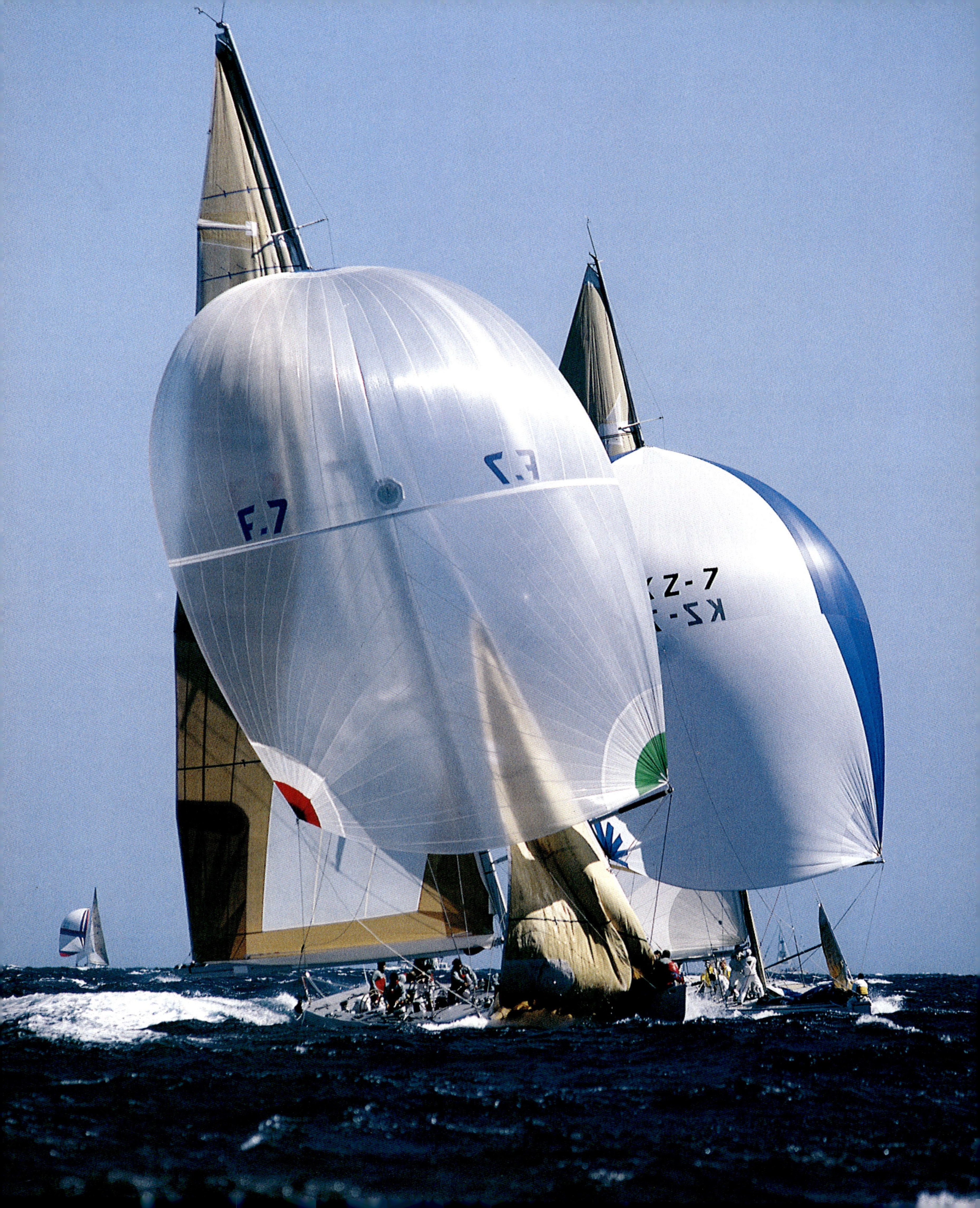
F.7
KZ-7

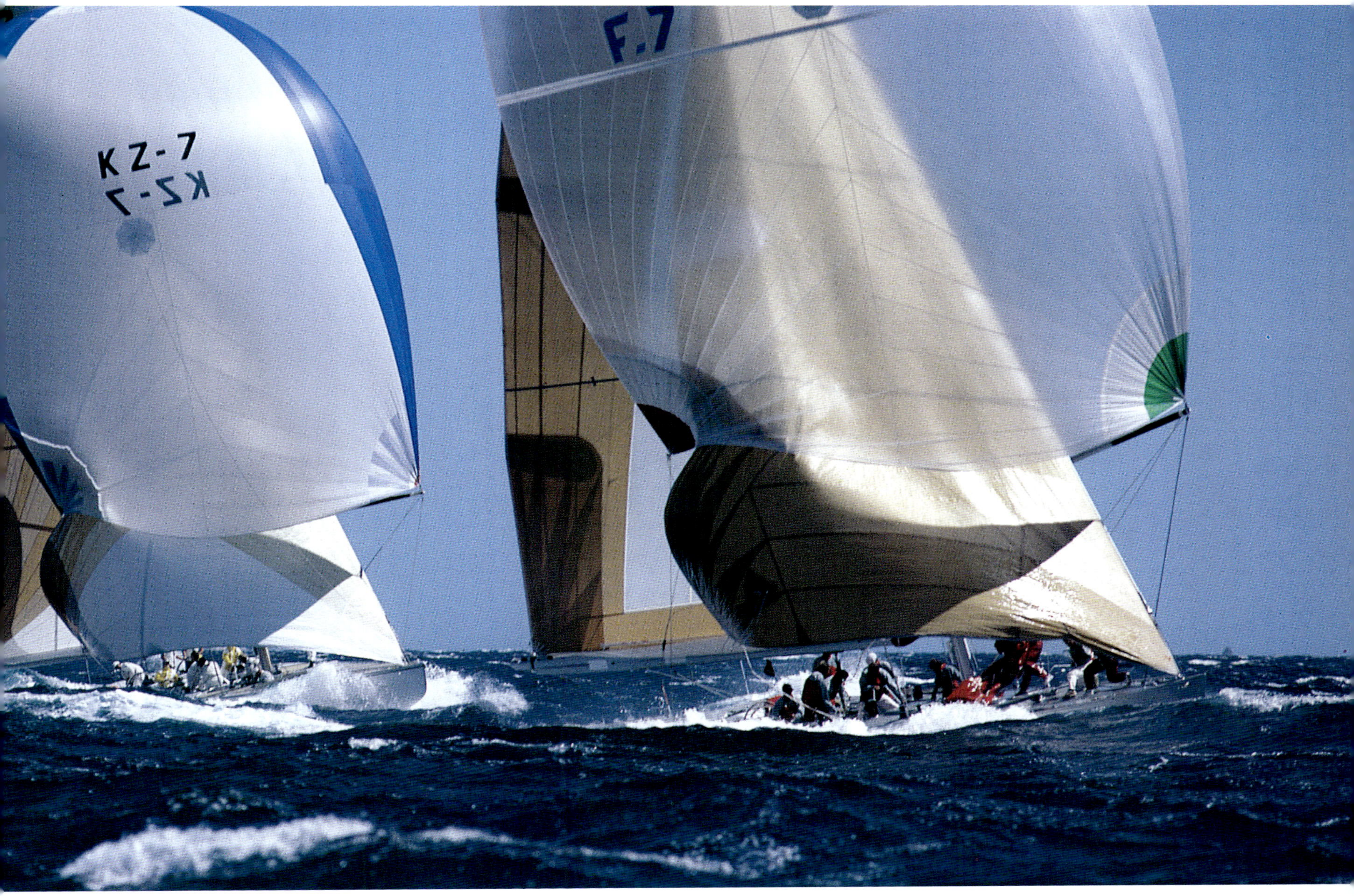

Hull Speed

Opposite, *French Kiss* and *New Zealand* approach the leeward mark with a spirited demonstration of hull speed and beautifully drawing sails. *French Kiss* flies one of the new see-through Mylar spinnakers, adding an almost iridescent transparency that belies the strength of the fabric. Our photo boat is outside the yachts' course to the mark, so they will pass between us and the turning buoy. To add to the photographic joys of their passage, they will also move through the path of the sunlight. Unfortunately, since the photo boat is standing still, as the yachts near the mark, the first will separate from the second and they will pass our cameras in file. This photograph shows the two spinnakers and hulls overlapping, the yachts pitting their strength against each other. With all their possible positions of overlap, to me this moment tells their story best. Areas of highlight and shadows of their sails interact so that the sun shines on one where the shadow falls on the other.

Controlled Power

Closer to the buoy, the hulls of *New Zealand* and *French Kiss* separate, but how boldly the spray flies as *New Zealand* drives through the sea in pursuit! This kind of photograph can be made only when the wind blows over 20 knots and the sea is comparatively smooth so that the hulls are not buried behind wavetops. The angles of the heeling yachts, the outstretched spinnaker poles, and the taut, drawn curves in the sails combine to give a sense of controlled power. Note the shadows of the spinnakers that fall on the genoas underneath. Their sharp, curved forms lend tremendous power to this image. Without those emphasizing masses, the image would lose most of its strength. It was action and light well worth the travel to far-off southwestern Australia.

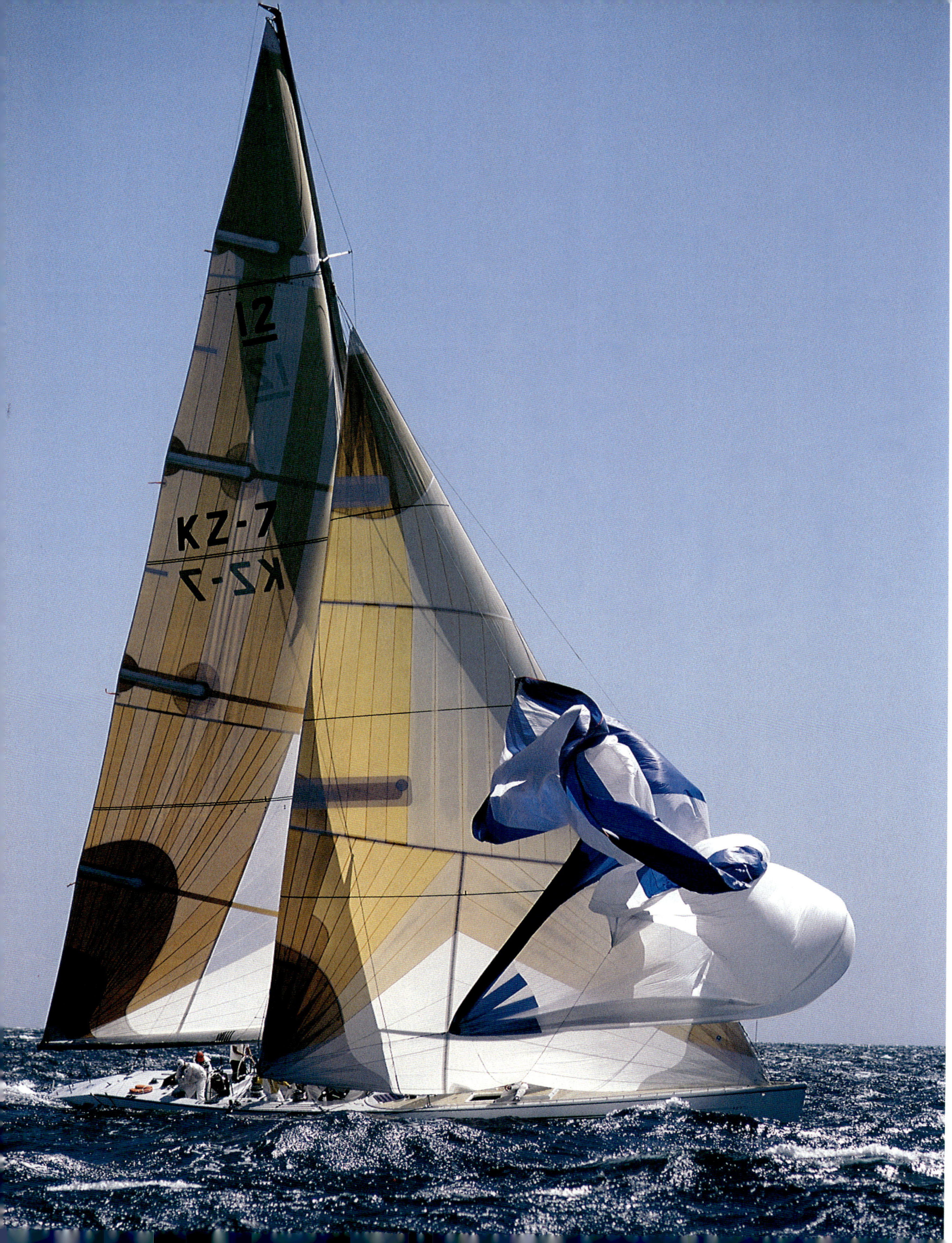
12
KZ-7

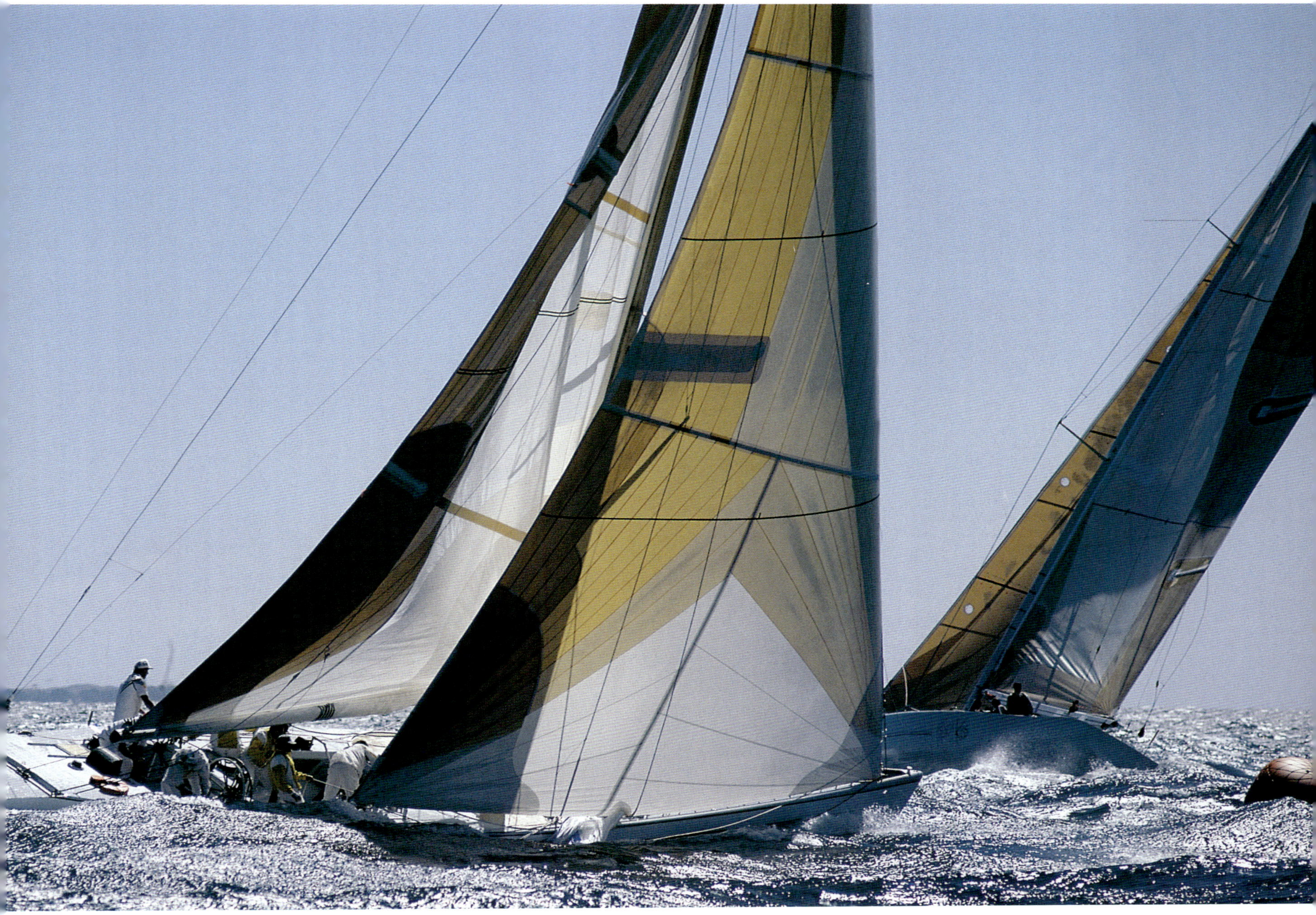

Spinnaker Drop

Opposite, *French Kiss* has passed, and *New Zealand* now drops her spinnaker and trims her genoa as she approaches the mark just off to the right. The camera has swung toward the sun; now the wind ripples on the water are burnished and the seams in the sail are dramatically drawn in backlight. The curled and falling spinnaker stands in contrast to the more rigid lines of the genoa and main.

Apparent Contact

French Kiss has rounded the mark and trimmed her sails for the windward leg as *New Zealand* approaches the turning buoy. *New Zealand*'s genoa is trimmed, ready for the next leg, though the mainsail is still eased. Photographically, the significant moment comes when the bow of *New Zealand* moves in to touch the hull of *French Kiss*. The photo acquires its primary sense of motion and tension from the action of that apparent contact and the sharp vee formed by the headstays of the two yachts. Waiting for this instant, as the photo boat rolls and pitches, my finger is poised on the shutter release and I also keep my eye on the buoy.

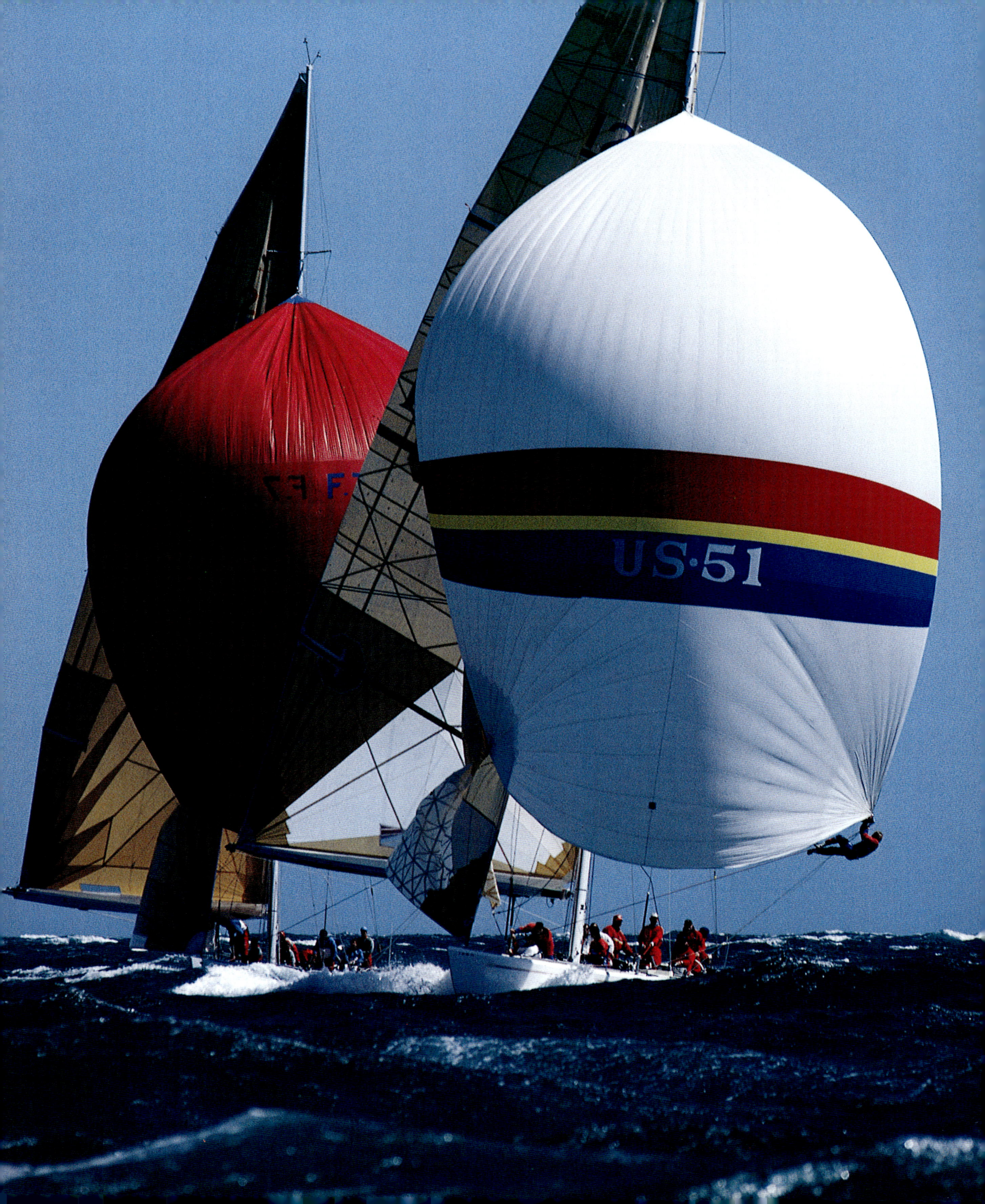
US·51

Approaching the Leeward Mark

Opposite, *Heart of America* leads *French Kiss* toward the mark, and a man hangs in horizontal equilibrium on the spinnaker pole, ready to release the sail. The jibs on both vessels are being hoisted, preparatory to rounding the mark.

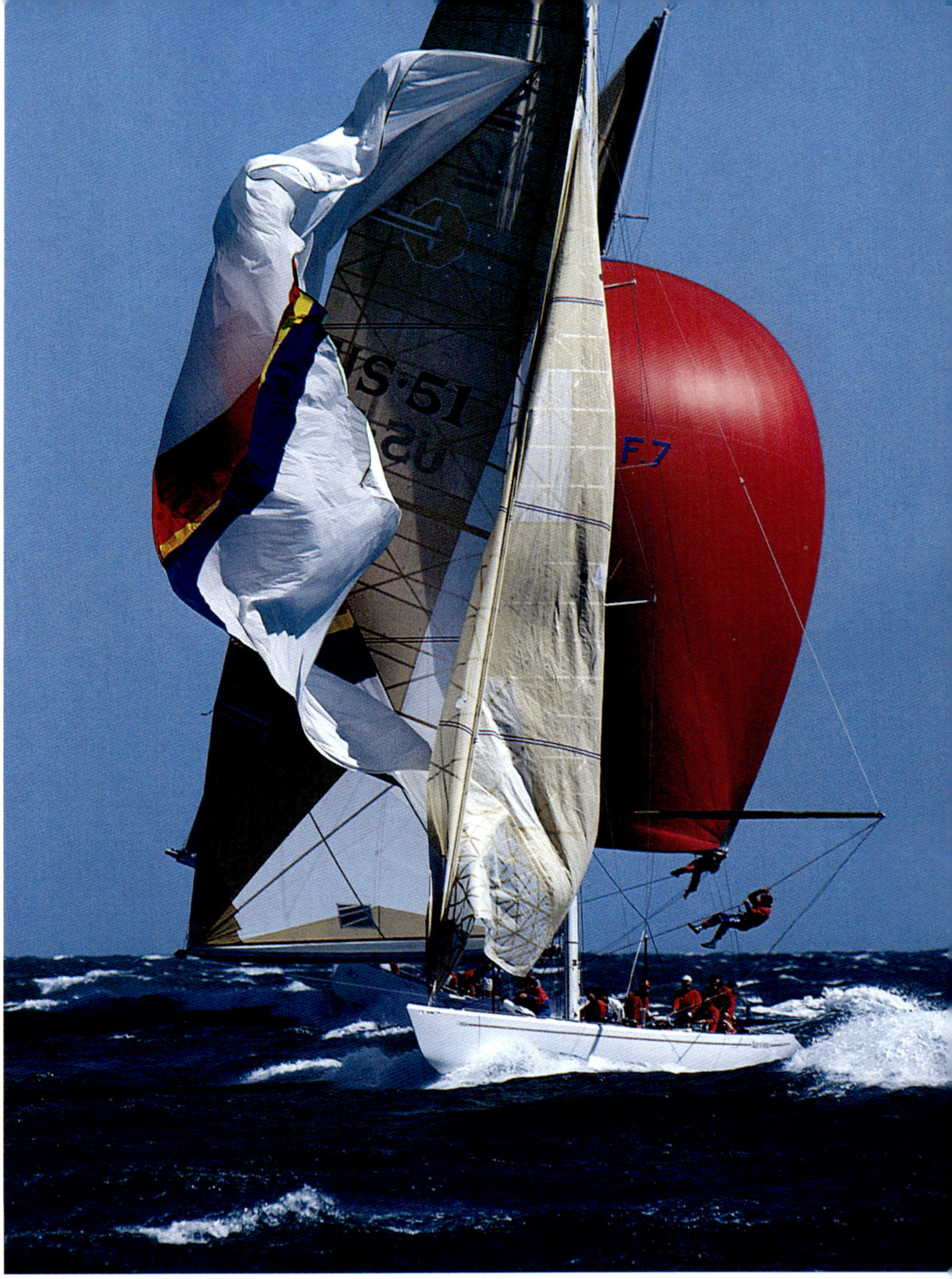

For a while in the 1987 series, the leeward mark was a place for special spinnaker-pole acrobatics as the spinnaker was released on some of the 12s by a man on the pole itself. For the photographer, this circumstance called for particular attention, as the gymnastics were not only exciting to see, but obviously potentially hazardous. In the photograph opposite, and in the following three images, the breaking waves and spume in the water indicate a wind of over 20 knots. That the spinnakers are flying so full and seemingly effortlessly is an indication that the crews have mastered their spinnaker technique to perfection.

Spinnaker Release

Heart of America's spinnaker is released and has flown up and outboard to leeward; her jib is hoisted higher up the stay. Her spinnaker release man is sliding down towards the deck, while just above him and astern, *French Kiss*'s spinnaker release man is hanging from the spinnaker pole, holding on with his right arm while his left prepares to release the billowing red spinnaker.

The strong red color of *French Kiss*'s spinnaker made a definite statement that became the dominant element of the photograph. Although it was a dramatic change in sail color, I did not keenly appreciate it because it had no translucence and little sensuousness or tactile appeal.

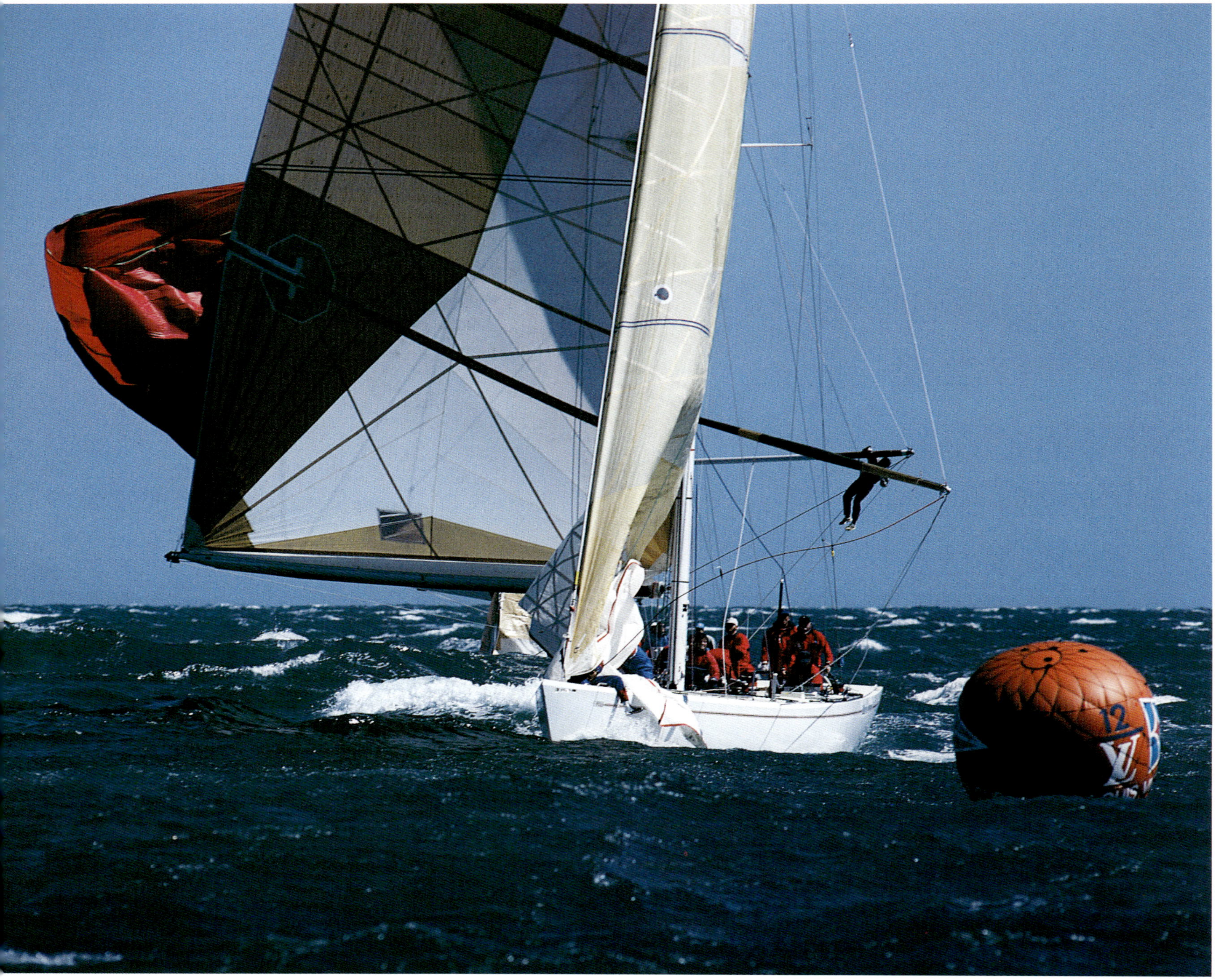

Hanging On

In the foreground, *Heart of America*'s crew has taken in most of the spinnaker and lowers the spinnaker pole toward the deck. By a happy chance, the broad dark streak running across the mainsail of *French Kiss* accentuates the mass and angle of the spinnaker pole. Behind *Heart of America*, the crewman aboard *French Kiss* hangs on to the pole with one arm while arranging his descent to the deck. The turning buoy establishes the imminence of the rounding and adds a different note of tension to the scene.

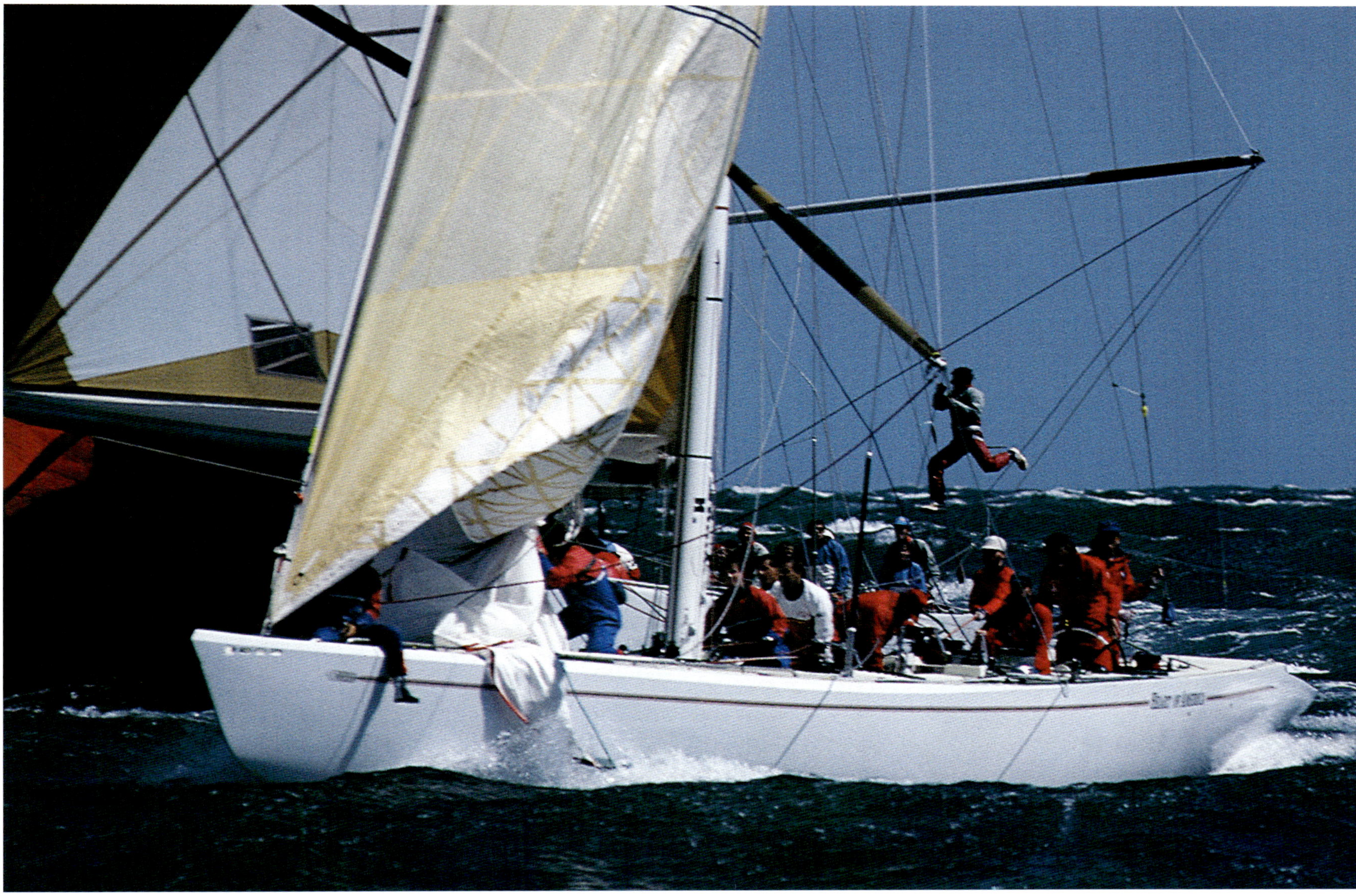

Slide to the Deck

The crewman on *French Kiss* has his descent organized and is sliding down to the deck, although his feet are spread as though he were leaping down from his lofty perch. Crewmen on both boats had performed difficult duties without fuss or mishap. These were highwire circus performances afloat.

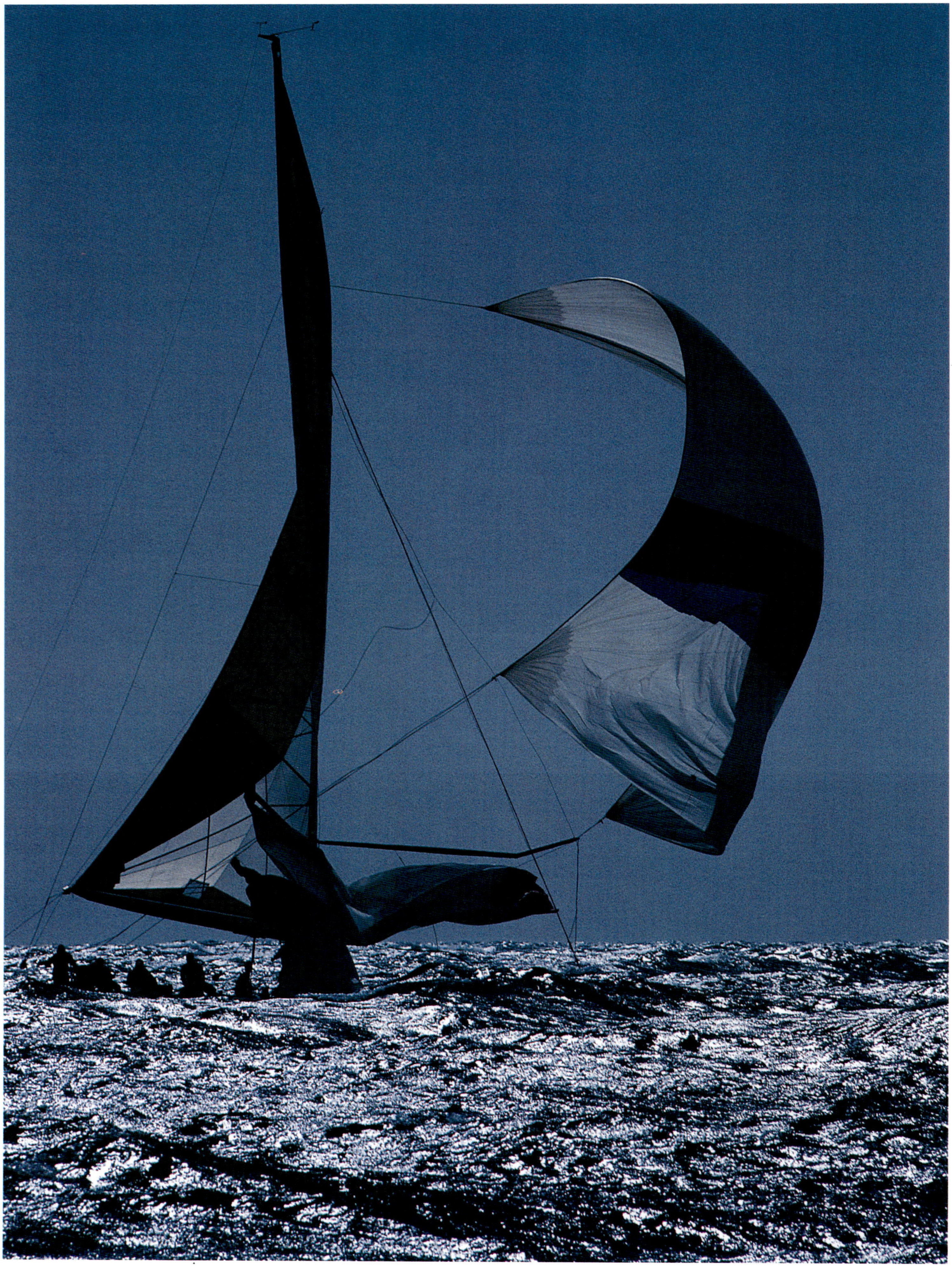

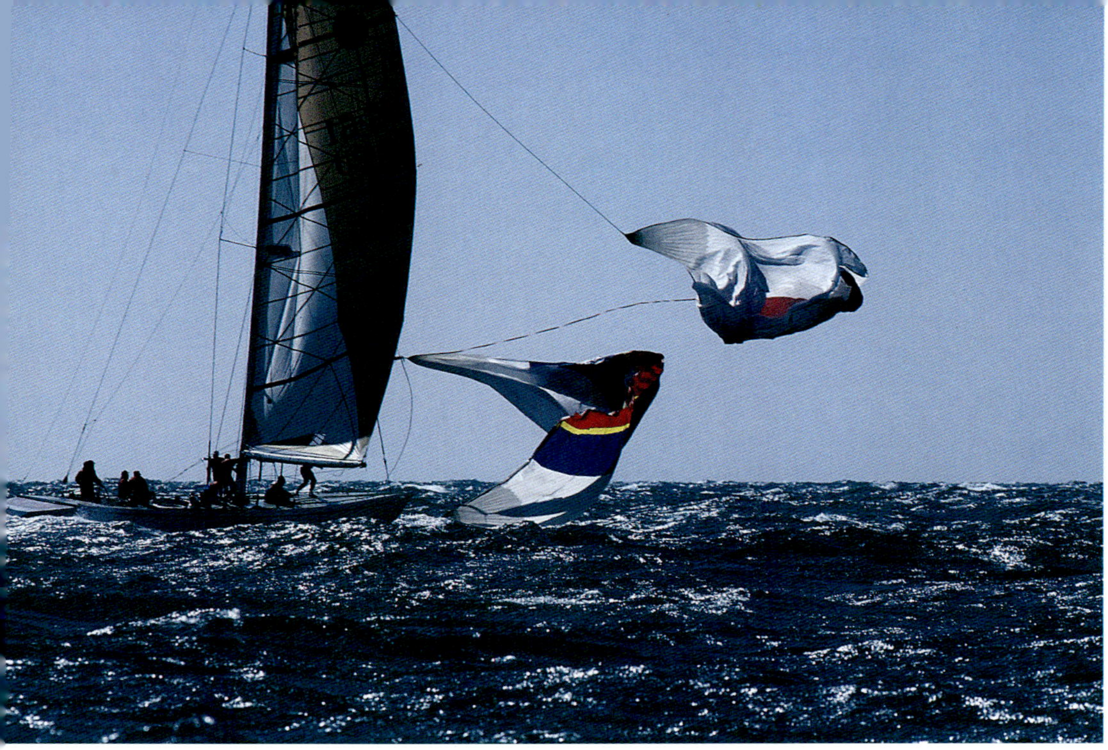

Sail Fragments

Heart of America turns to windward to get the free-flying sail fragments to fall in towards the mast.

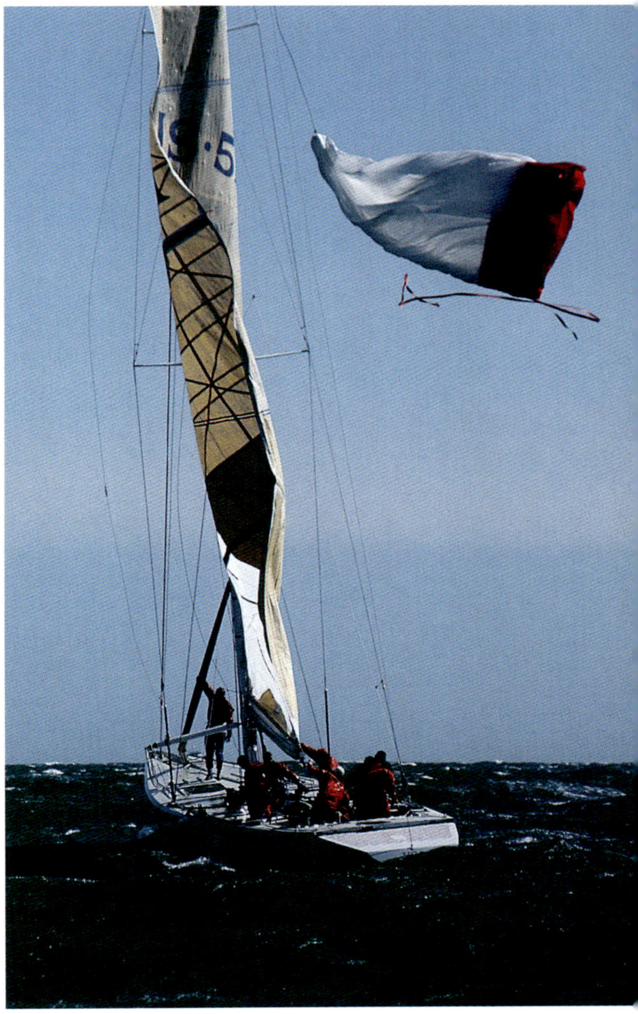

On some days during the series off Fremantle, the photo boat, because of some quirk on the racecourse, would be left following one yacht alone in a lonely sea, with no other contestant, spectator fleet, or support vessel around. On one such day, *Heart of America* met an unusual series of mishaps.

Spinnaker Problems

Opposite, *Heart of America* is sailing over the course solo, intent on finishing the race. She has blown out one spinnaker and, in the course of hoisting and setting a second, the spinnaker pole has snapped around the headstay. The pole now carries a partially hoisted new spinnaker and a still-flapping torn companion. To intensify the aesthetic depression of this image, the yacht's bow is sunk behind a wave and the sometimes-jaunty hull looks sadly ineffective. The mood was strong enough to carry over to me, for I distinctly recall, despite the action in the scene, a peculiar sense of sadness. The ocean stretched out beyond, and I knew its extent might just as well be limitless. No support vessel followed, and *Heart of America* struggled with problems she had to resolve with ingenuity and the resources on board.

Retrieving the Remnants

After the yacht has rounded up and headed into the wind, the crew has retrieved the lower fragment of sail. Now the problem is to get the rest of the free-flying sail down on deck.

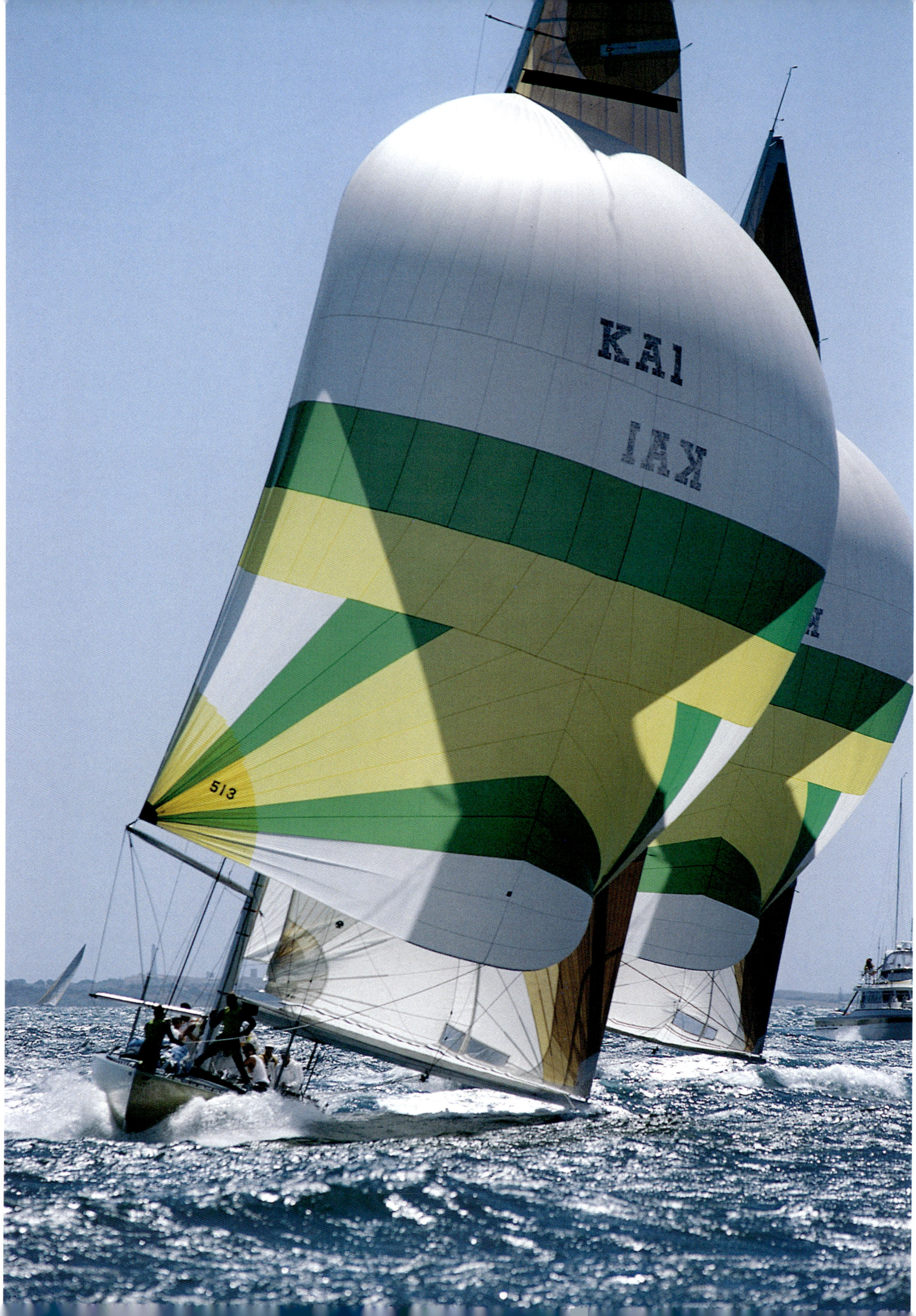
KA1
513

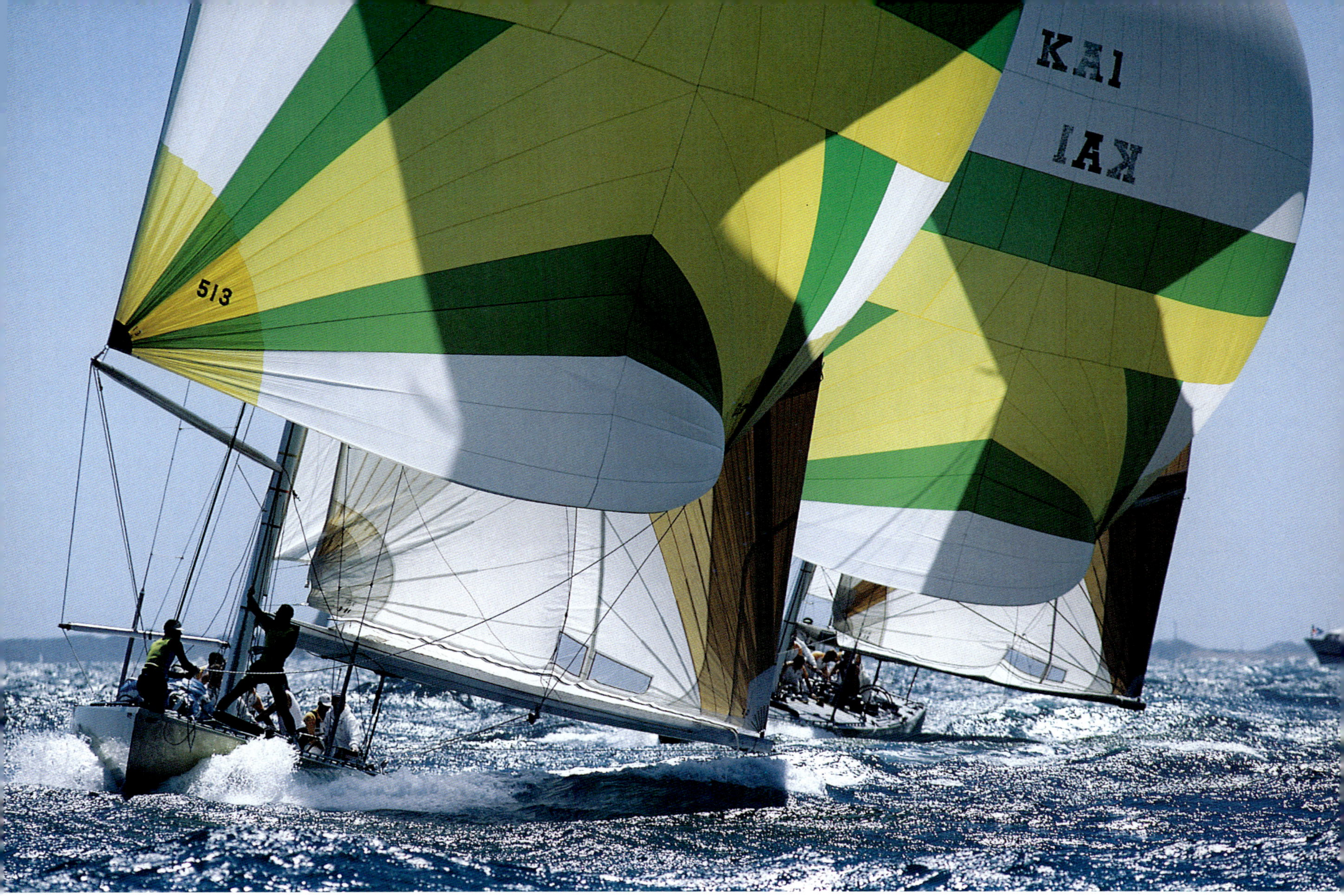

In another mark-rounding sequence, *Kookaburra III* leads *Kookaburra II* and the conditions of the light are reversed from the previous three images. The sunlight in the last sequence came from behind the camera, so the water was dark and the white hulls and sails stood out against the dark water and sky. In this sequence, I am shooting against the sun. The water is light and lively, and — as the sun comes through the sailcloth — the cloth comes alive so that one can almost feel its texture. Even better, the yachts are close together, so that they directly relate to each other and to the composition of the whole, all of which is enhanced by a lovely pattern of line and color in the billowing spinnakers.

Shadows and Highlights

Opposite, the sun shines brightly on the rounded heads of the spinnakers while the pointed darkness of the mainsails above form sharp, geometric angles. The shadows and highlights playing on the spinnakers vie with the green and yellow patterns in the sail panels, and all of the curves and darts are grounded in the diagonals of the booms, mast, and spinnaker pole. Under the strong lines and taut curves of the rigging, the surface of the water glistens with ebullient reflections, a lighthearted foil for the stress and strain in the rigging and crew.

Powerful Patterns

The yachts have separated, so both hulls are evident. The men on the deck of the forward vessel, *Kookaburra III*, though small in size, have power because their stance shows tension and effort. The lines made by the spars and the patterns of the sails are busy, but fortunately they are powerful and simple enough to give strength rather than confusion to the design.

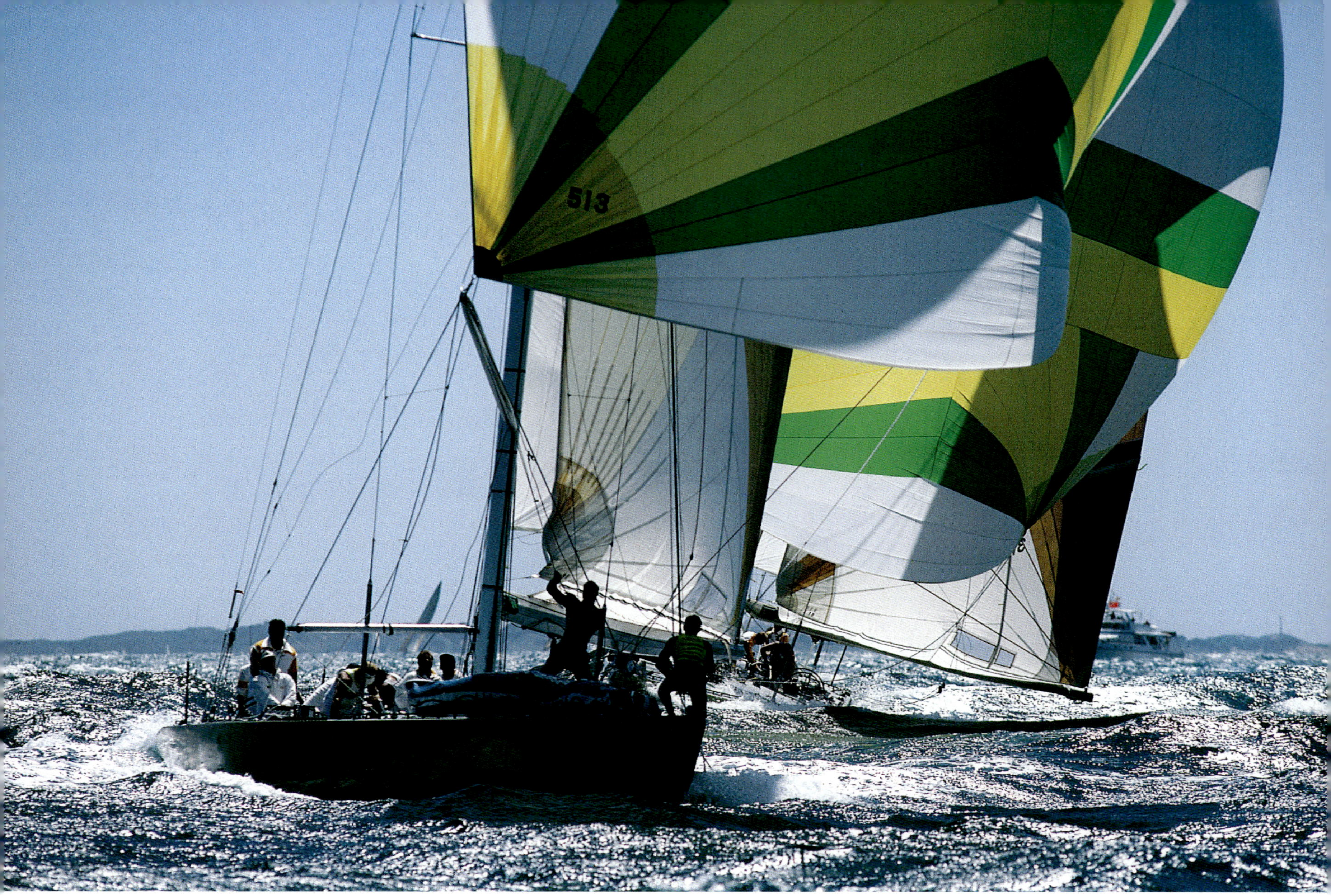

Preparing to Jibe

Kookaburra III, ahead of *Kookaburra II*, is turning toward the mark and preparing to jibe for the rounding. The difference in the directions the yachts are heading adds a new element to the composition. An alarm is ringing in my head to be aware of the turning buoy just to the right.

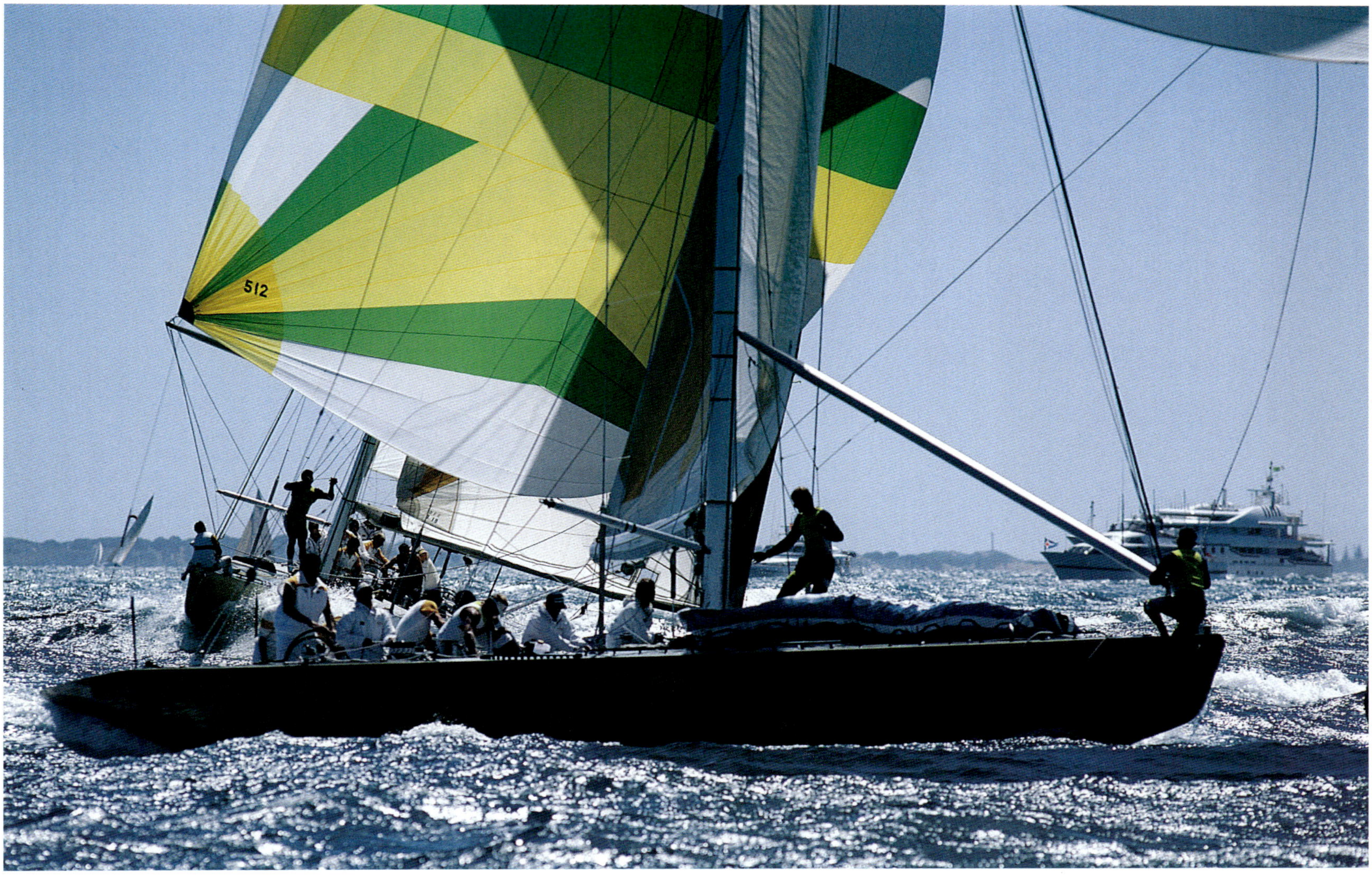

Mark Rounding

The buoy is duly recorded on the right edge of this photograph, and the spinnaker pole is just crossing the deck, lightly passing through the deft hands of the bowman. Though the image is nicely established at the critical moment of mark rounding, I am aware that the real photograph — the one I am missing — is in the area above the crew in the cockpit, where there is an action-filled vertical image with crews of both vessels straining at their tasks and the backlit spinnaker hovering over all.

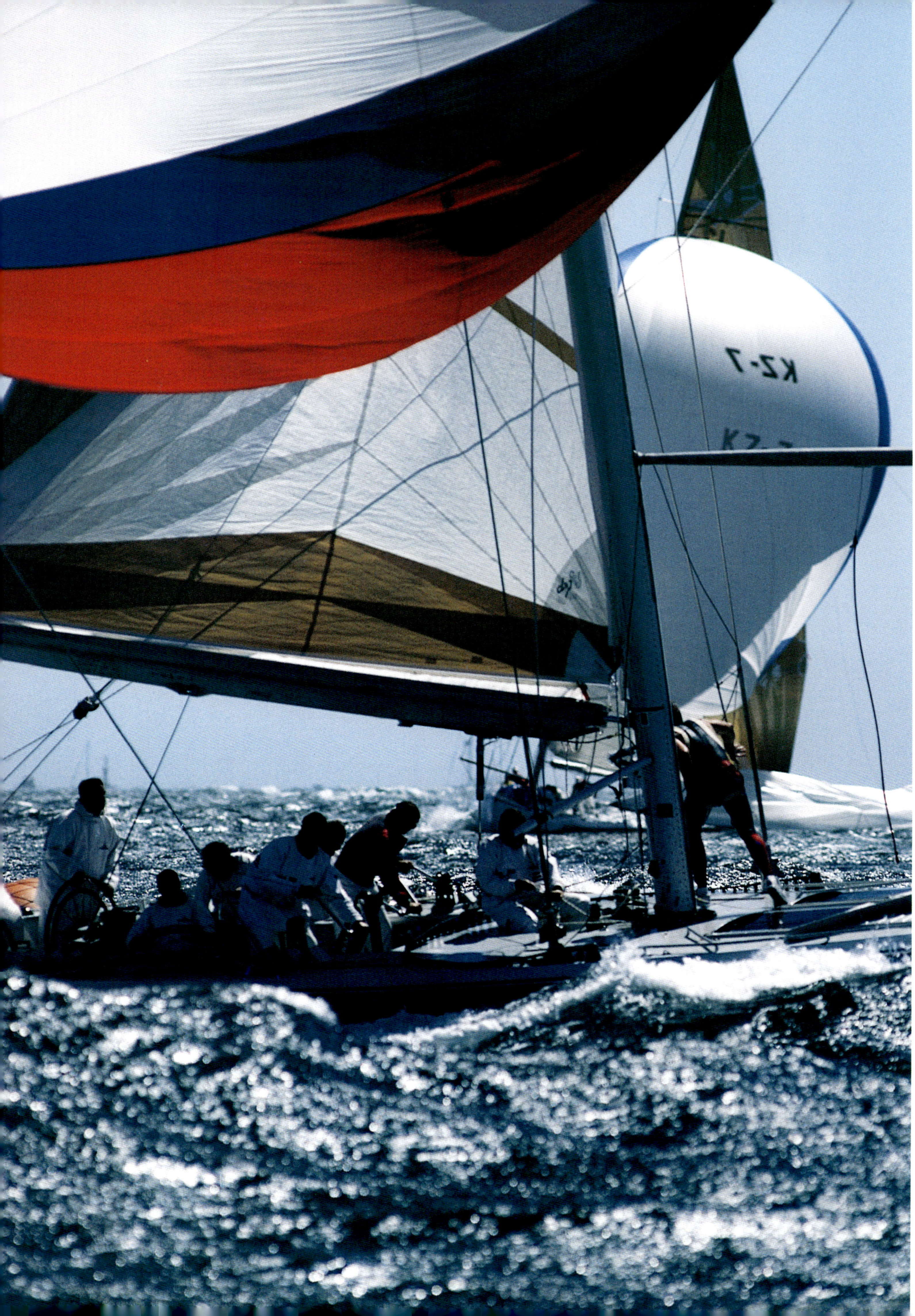
KZ-7

Holding the Eyes

If we look at the man in the blue watch cap and white foul-weather gear just astern of *Stars & Stripes*'s mast, our eyes will most likely then travel to the left, through the crew, to Dennis Conner at the wheel, over Conner's head to the boom above, and out toward the leech of the main. From there, the eyes will travel up to the foot of the spinnaker, around its red curve to the top of the mainmast of *New Zealand*, down to *New Zealand*'s spinnaker, and around and down to the white genoa dragging in the water. The eyes will hesitate here, but remain within the frame, then move back to the outstretched leg of the crewman just forward of the *Stars & Stripes* mast, and return to where we started. No angled line will drive our eyes out of the photograph: some line or curve will always draw us back in.

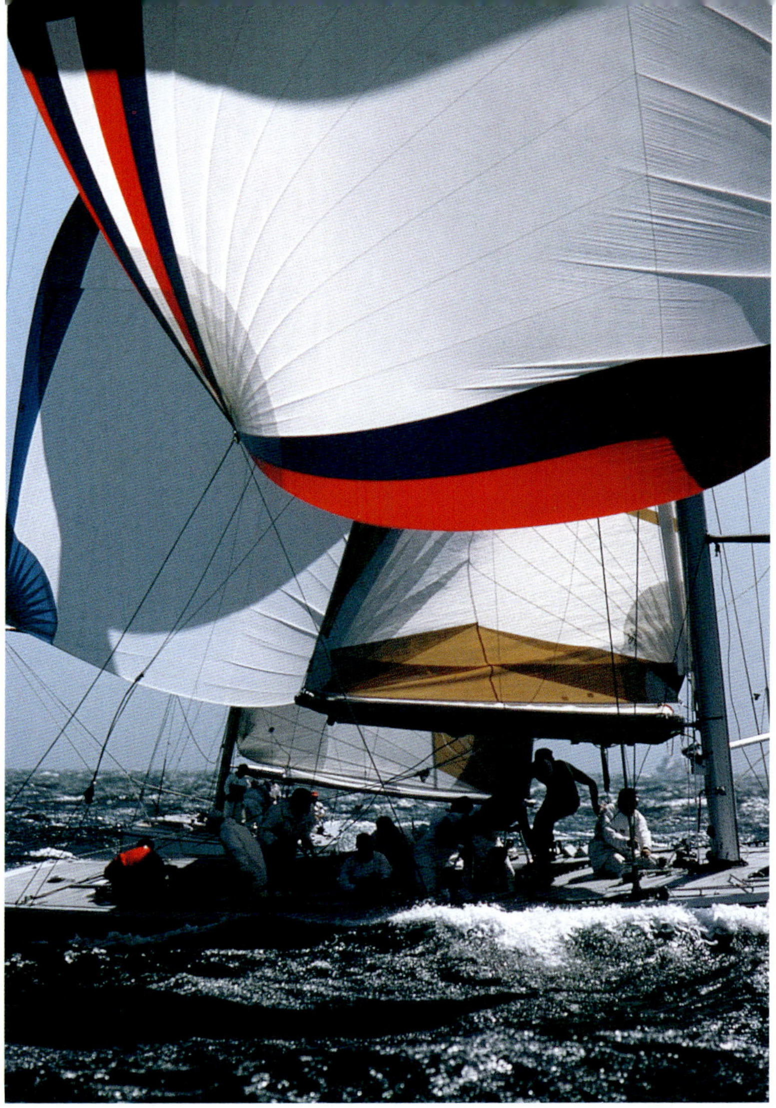

Almost a month later, I was able to capture the image I missed in the photograph on the previous page. Dennis Conner's *Stars & Stripes* was leading *New Zealand* around the mark in almost the same positions that K*ookaburra III* and *II* had held in that earlier photograph. This time the yachts were in a composition they had unwittingly made just for the photographer. Once more, I was looking against the light and wind, camera and lens ready, finger on the release button — waiting for the very instant that all the elements of sail, mast, men, and sea would combine in a composition of line, curve, light, and shadow that would hold the viewer's eyes and move them along a path within the structure of the whole image.

Crossings

When I am in position to photograph two yachts approaching on converging paths, I already hold in my mind and heart an image born of previous crossings. It is the one worthwhile image, a single photograph, that summarizes the entire crossing situation. Here, short seconds after the previous photograph, when the distant, billowing spinnaker emerges from behind the mainsail in the foreground, the sense of anticipation and the story itself are gone. The basic elements of contest and conflict are replaced by confusion.

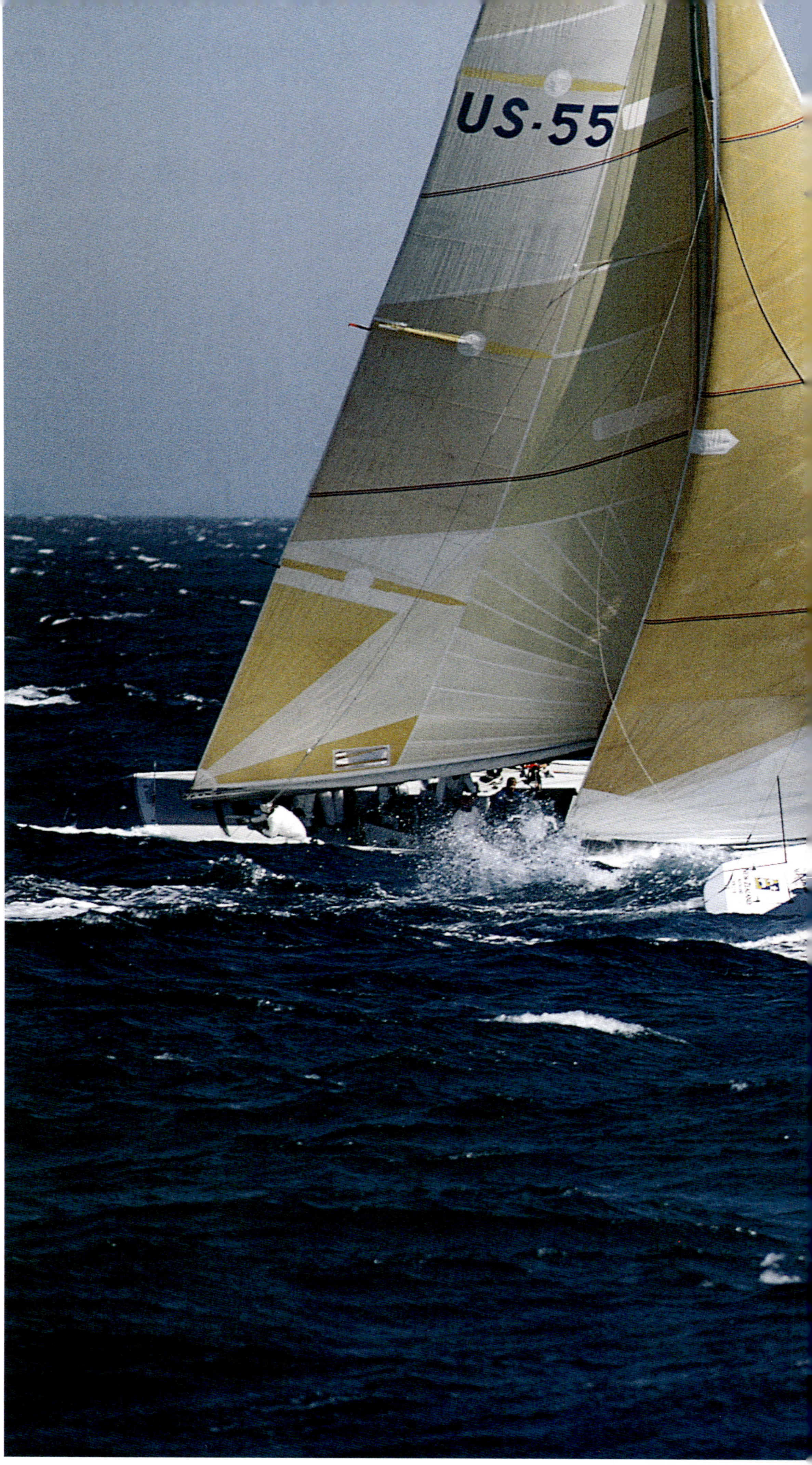

Evenly Matched

Stars & Stripes is to weather of *New Zealand* in one of the last races of the series to determine which yacht would challenge Australia for the America's Cup. Competition was fierce between these two evenly matched boats, and every race was exciting. The close-up, overlapping competition shown here on an early windward leg was characteristic of the entire race and was to culminate as the yachts rounded the seventh mark to head for the finish line. The sun is almost overhead, with less backlighting on the sails than in the previous nine photographs. Here the sails are seemingly cast of a more solid fabric.

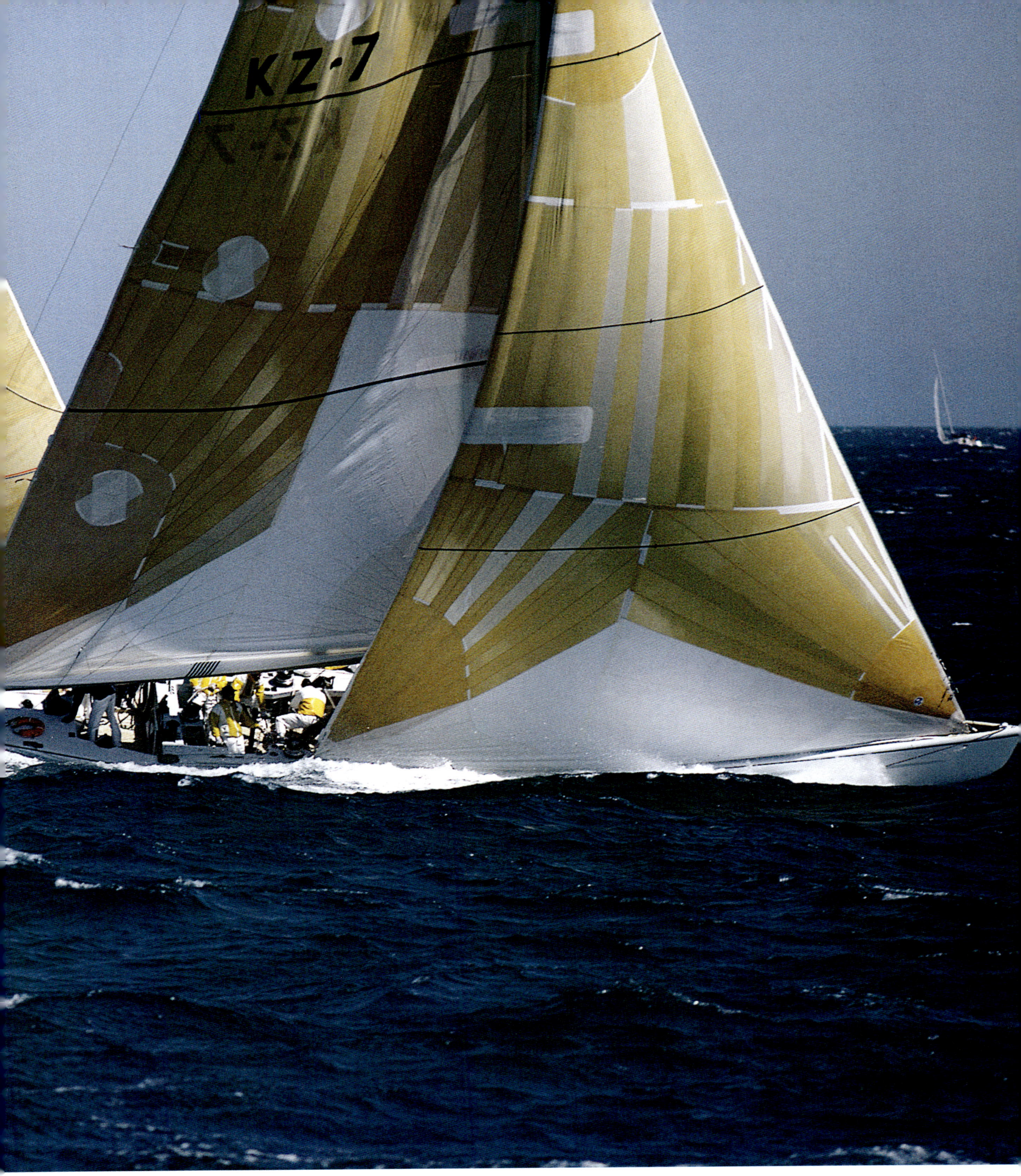
KZ-7

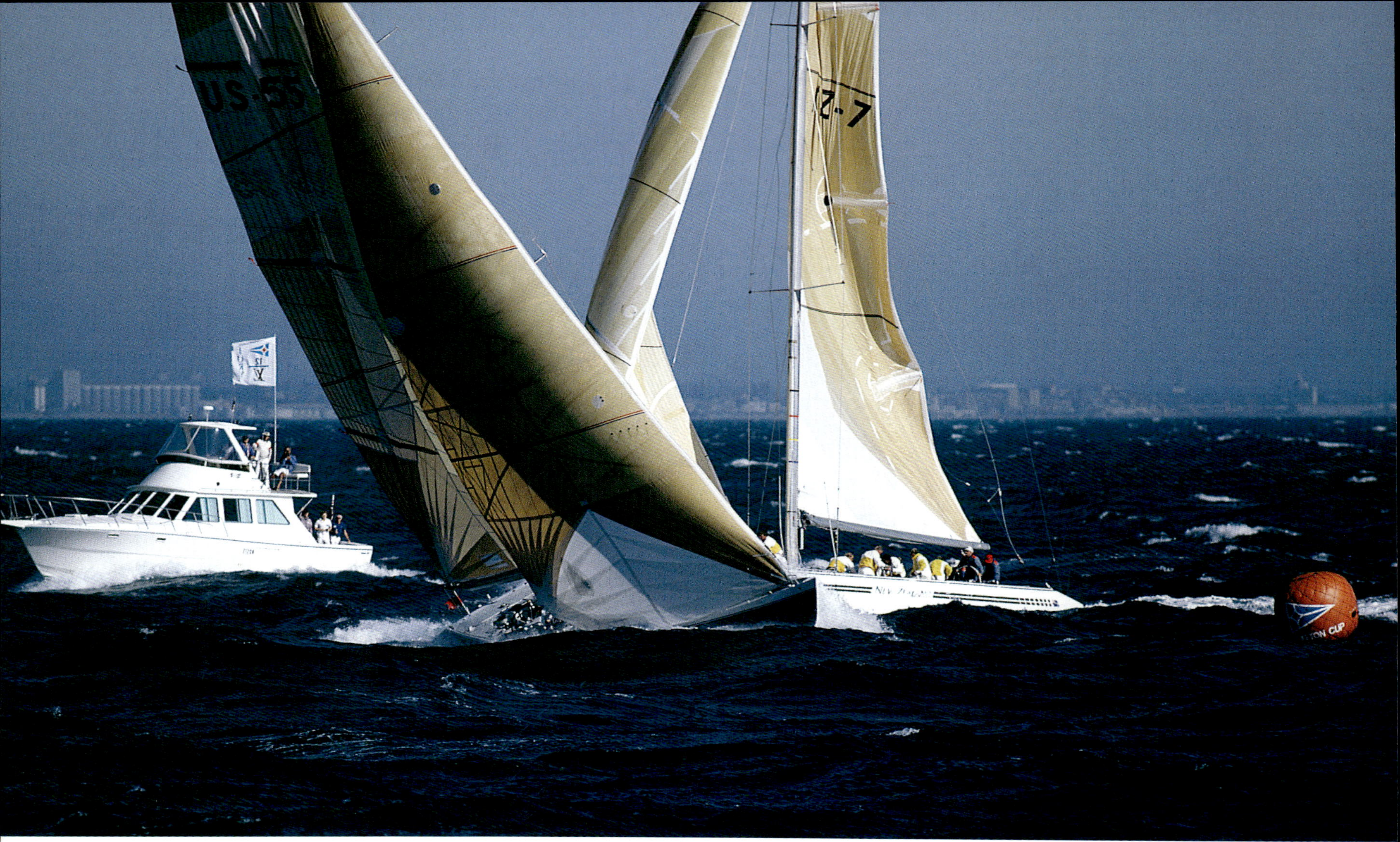
US-55

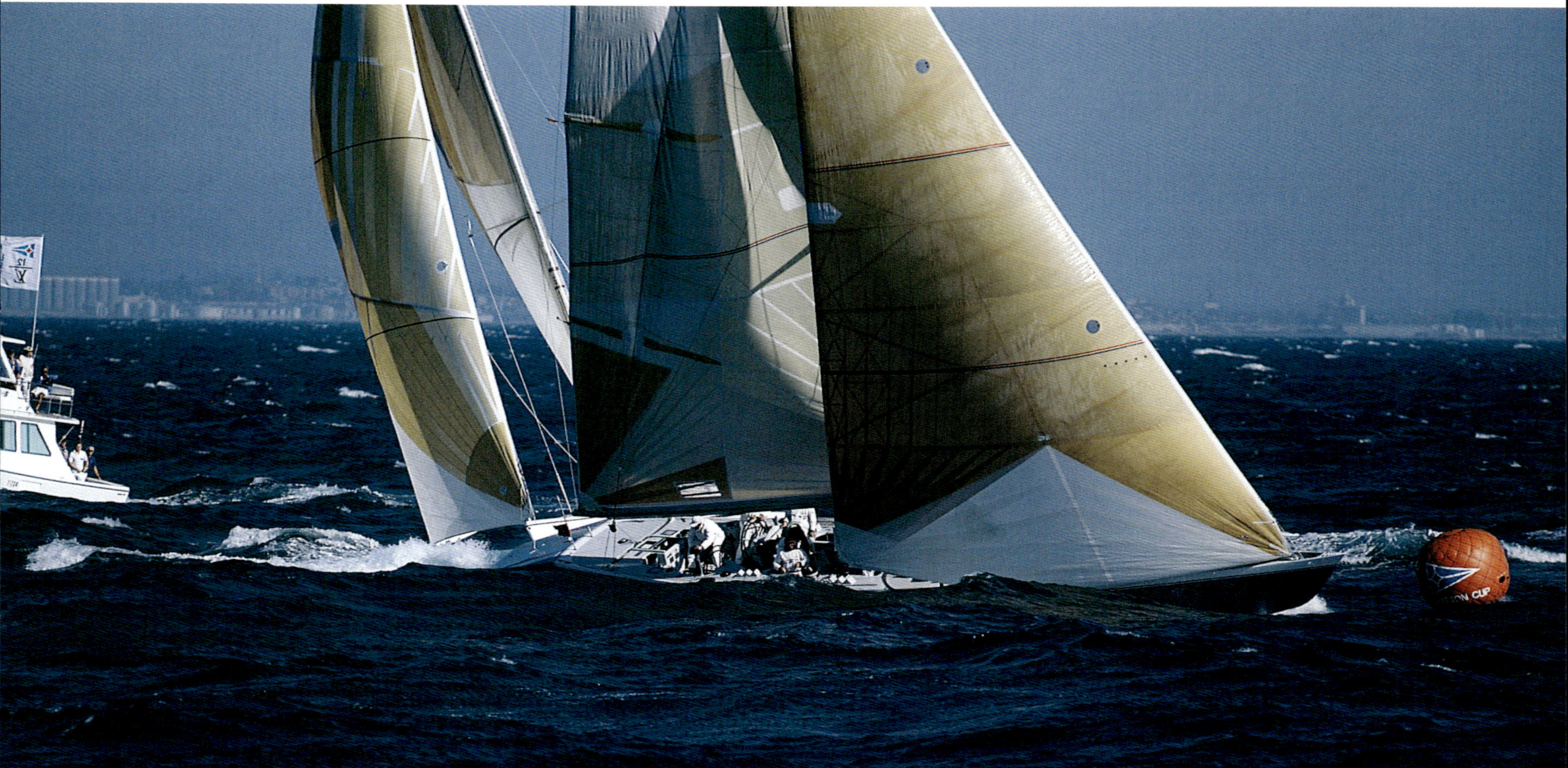

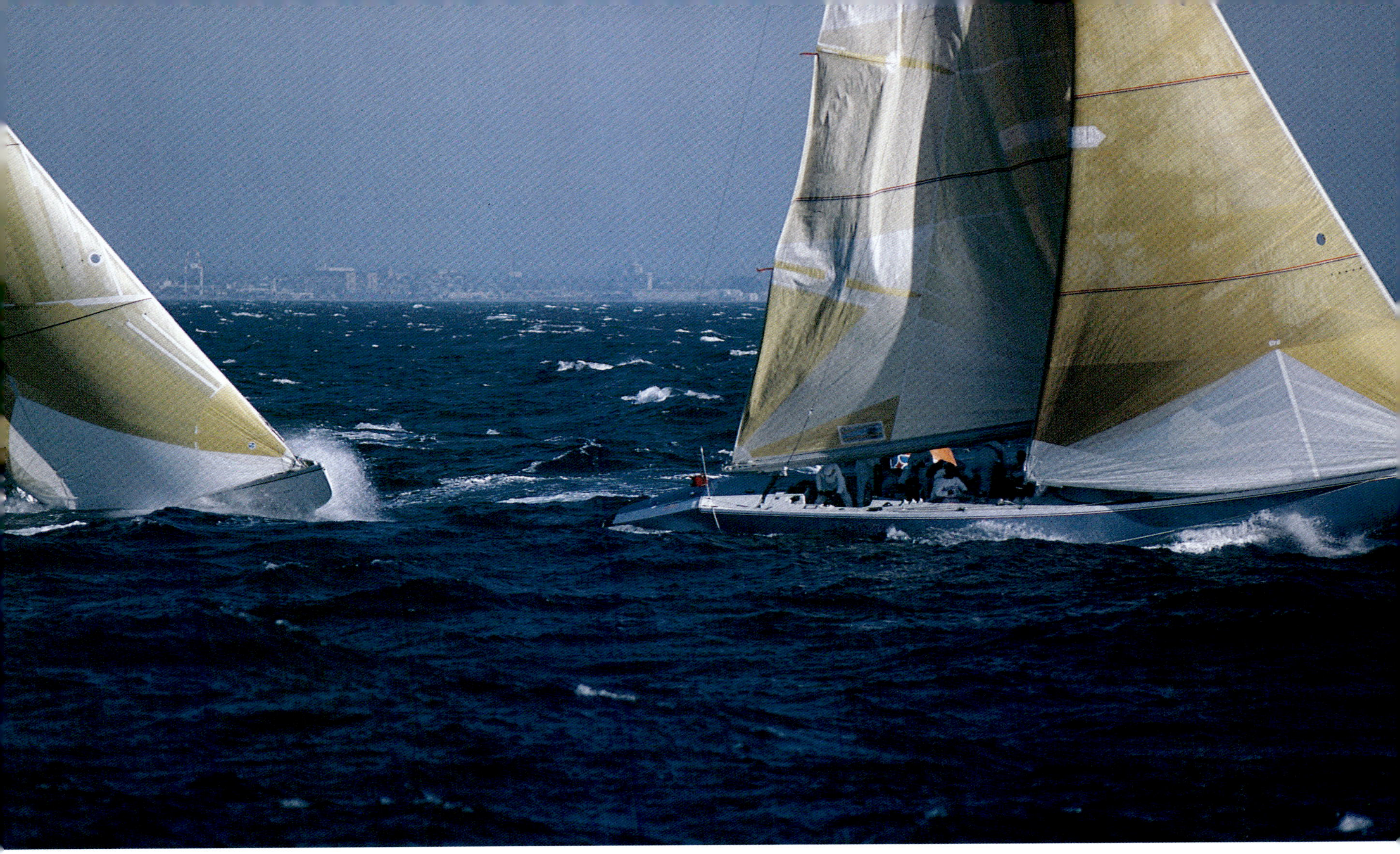

Rounding Up

Opposite above, *Stars & Stripes* has rounded up below the mark, the red ball on the right, with *New Zealand* close on her stern. Each element of the evolving mark-rounding is a story in a story. It is a wonderful, windy day — flags standing out straight, whitecaps crowning the waves, and tragedy and triumph imminent in the touch of a buoy.

A Tight Pass

Opposite below, Dennis Conner on *Stars & Stripes* now points up higher to pass the mark, obviously intending to make a tight pass alongside to port. Chris Dickson on *New Zealand* rounds up with his bow just under *Stars & Stripes*'s counter, hard on Conner's heels.

Mainsail Luffing

Above, Conner passes the mark and the red buoy can be seen over the cockpit. He is pointing high to be really close to it. Notice that the mainsail, though trimmed in, is luffing. Astern, Dickson swings *New Zealand* toward *Stars & Stripes*'s transom.

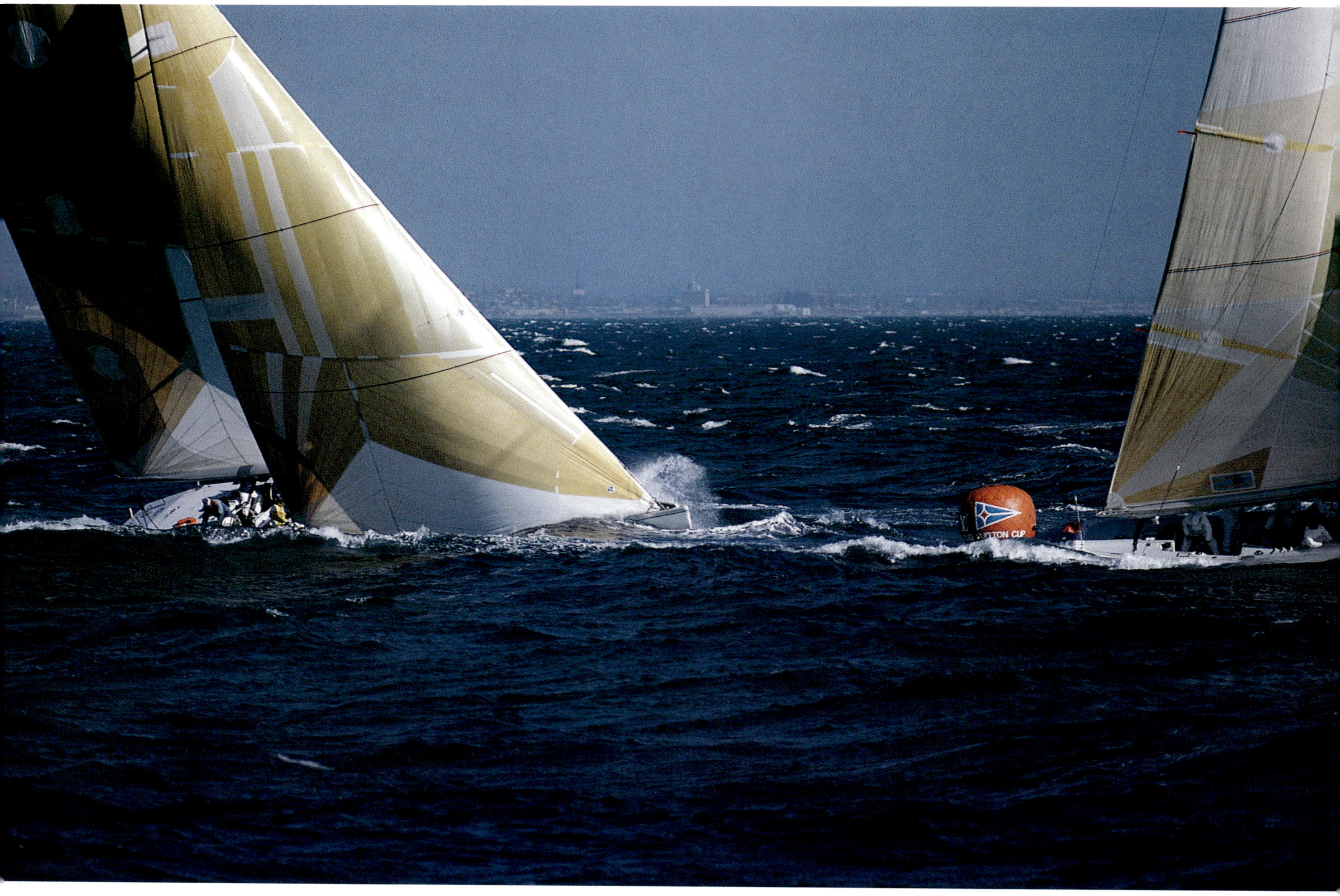

WHITE LINE

Stars & Stripes has just passed the turning mark, and her wake astern can be seen almost touching the mark. To the left, Chris Dickson pivots *New Zealand*. *New Zealand*'s bow is to windward of *Stars & Stripes*'s track on the mark side of the wake. It was probably Dickson's intention to round the mark very closely and immediately tack. Note the white line of foam circling *New Zealand*'s bow. As events evolved in the next few seconds, it seems that wind and water, in a work of fate, drew a line around the bow to emphasize its treacherous position.

Coming About

On the right, *Stars & Stripes*'s sails are filled and she is moving up the course. On the left, *New Zealand* is coming about and her white line of wake astern is touching the buoy. As she passed, she nudged the buoy with her port side. She now has tacked, and Dickson has decided to take the penalty of rounding the mark again.

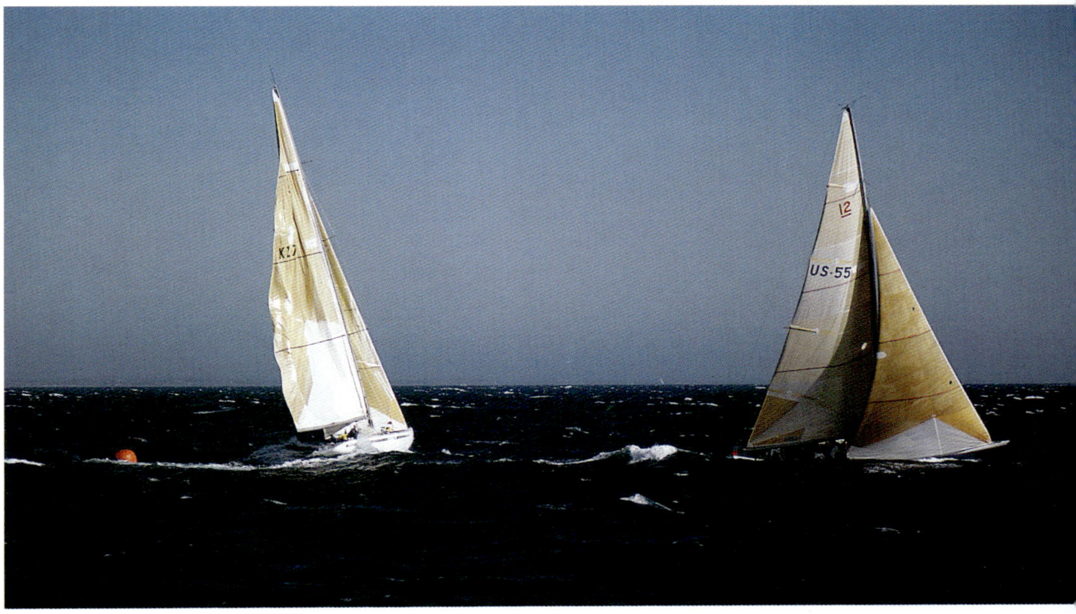

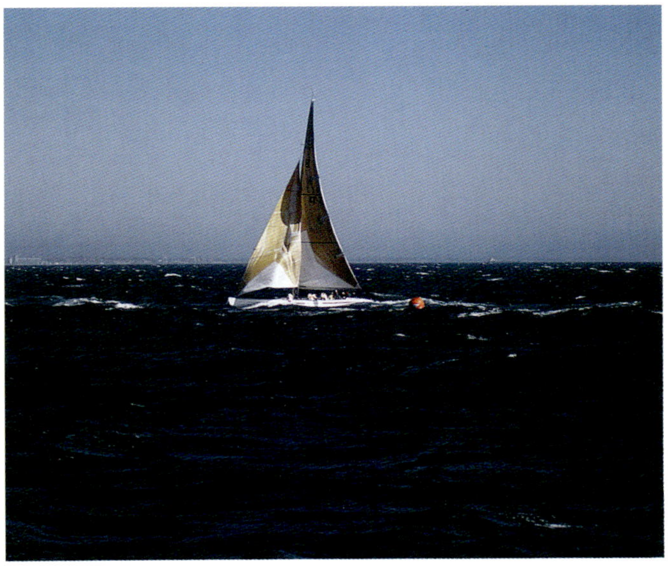

Jibe

New Zealand is about to jibe around the mark, and the track of her wake shows that this time she is giving the mark enough room. For *New Zealand*, the race is already lost. It is a moment of anguish for skipper Chris Dickson.

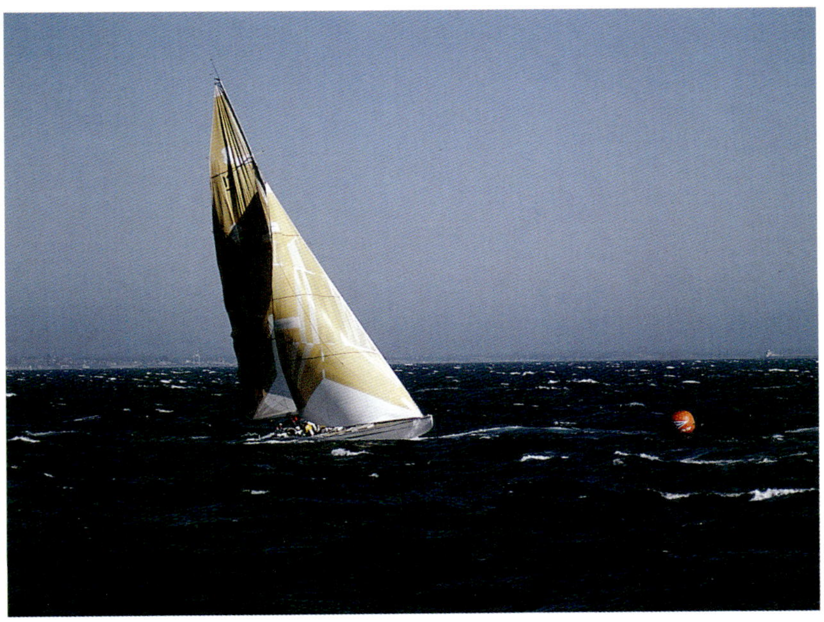

Second Pass

New Zealand has jibed and approaches the mark again to set out on the lonely beat to the finish line. Her only hope of winning is for *Stars & Stripes* to meet a disabling mishap before crossing the line.

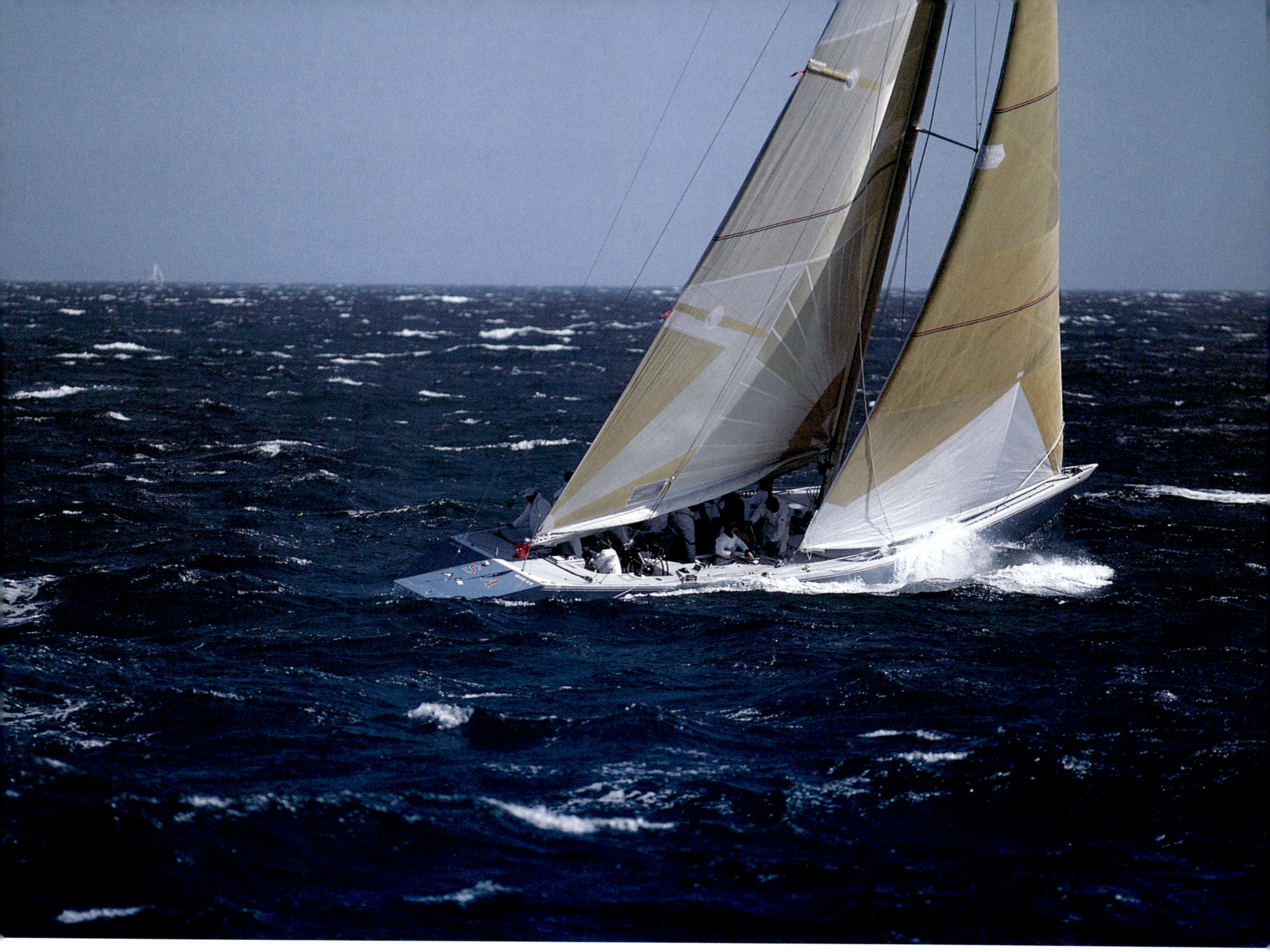

Easy to Windward

Stars & Stripes, meanwhile, has been gently working up the course toward the finish line. Her tension in the contest is over: her lead is substantial, and it should be a pleasant sail to the finish line.

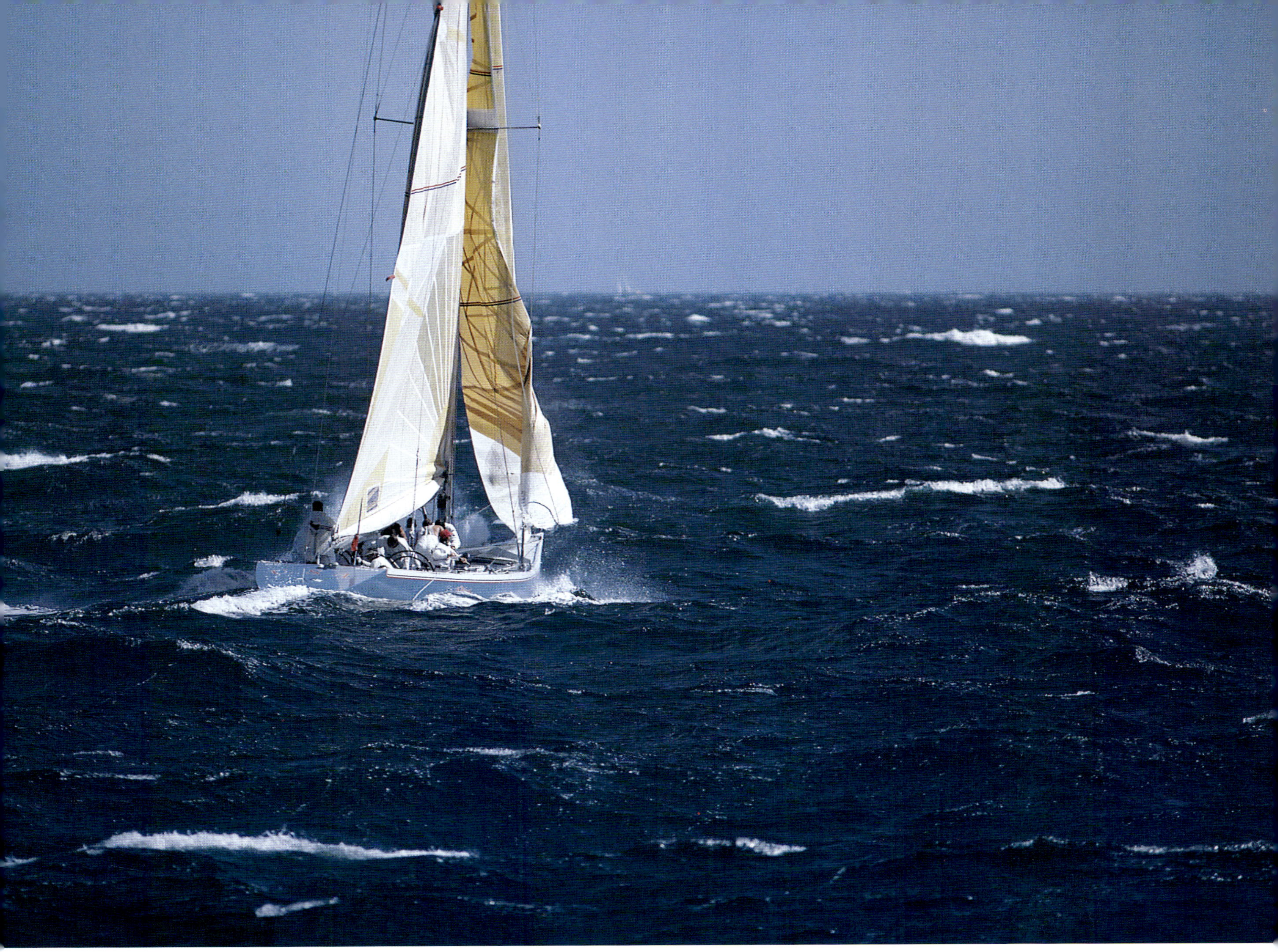

Tacking

Stars & Stripes tacks to cover *New Zealand*, for though Conner is easily ahead, he observes proper racing principles and covers *New Zealand*, now well astern.

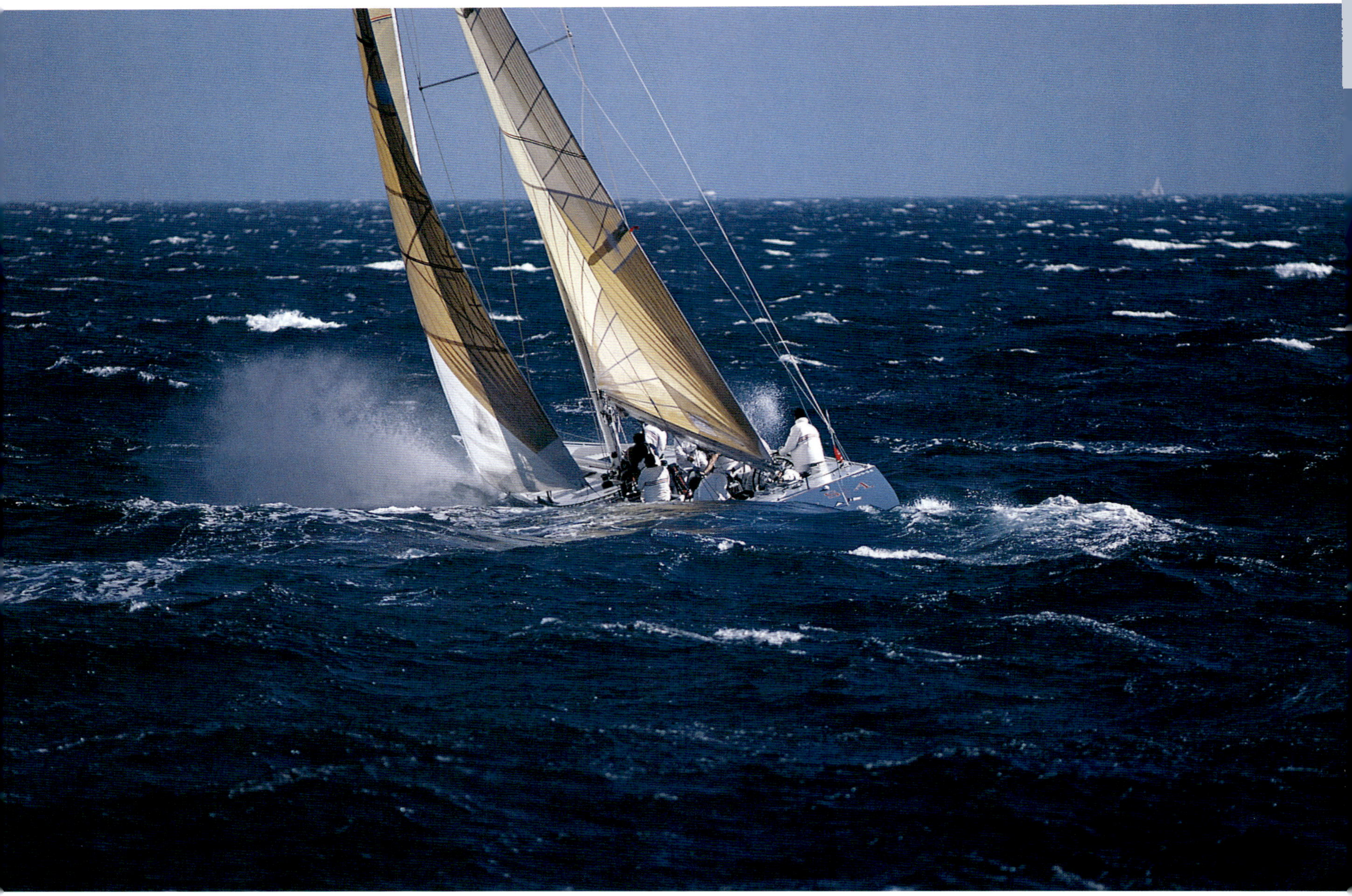

FROTHY SEAS

Stars & Stripes on the new tack trims her main and jib before hardening up. The frothy nature of the racecourse is clearly evident here.

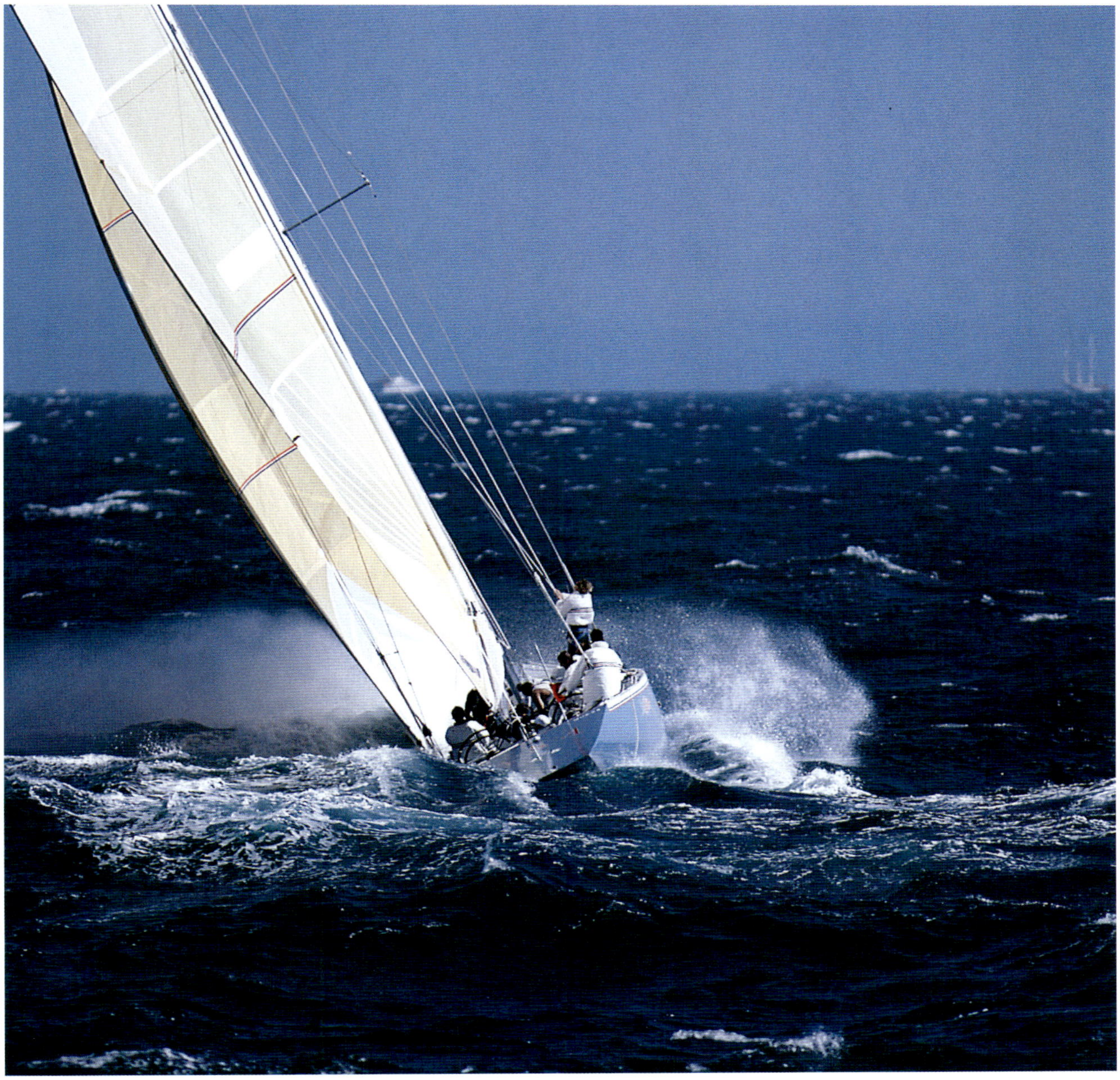

Hardened Up

Stars & Stripes has hardened up and heads up the course toward the finish line. Flying spray soaks the crew, but there could have been no complaints aboard on this winning leg of the race.

The previous 12 photographs were made from a vantage point along the rail of a large Australian catamaran, one of two used as press boats at Fremantle. It was about 100 feet long, the largest catamaran I had ever been on, and could carry more than 200 passengers. The camera angle for these photographs is higher than for any others made from shipboard in the Australian series and gives an informative perspective of the water at the inshore buoy on the course off Fremantle. The waves were not as steep here as they were at the outer buoys, but the white water at the wave crests is clearly evident on those views that look seaward.

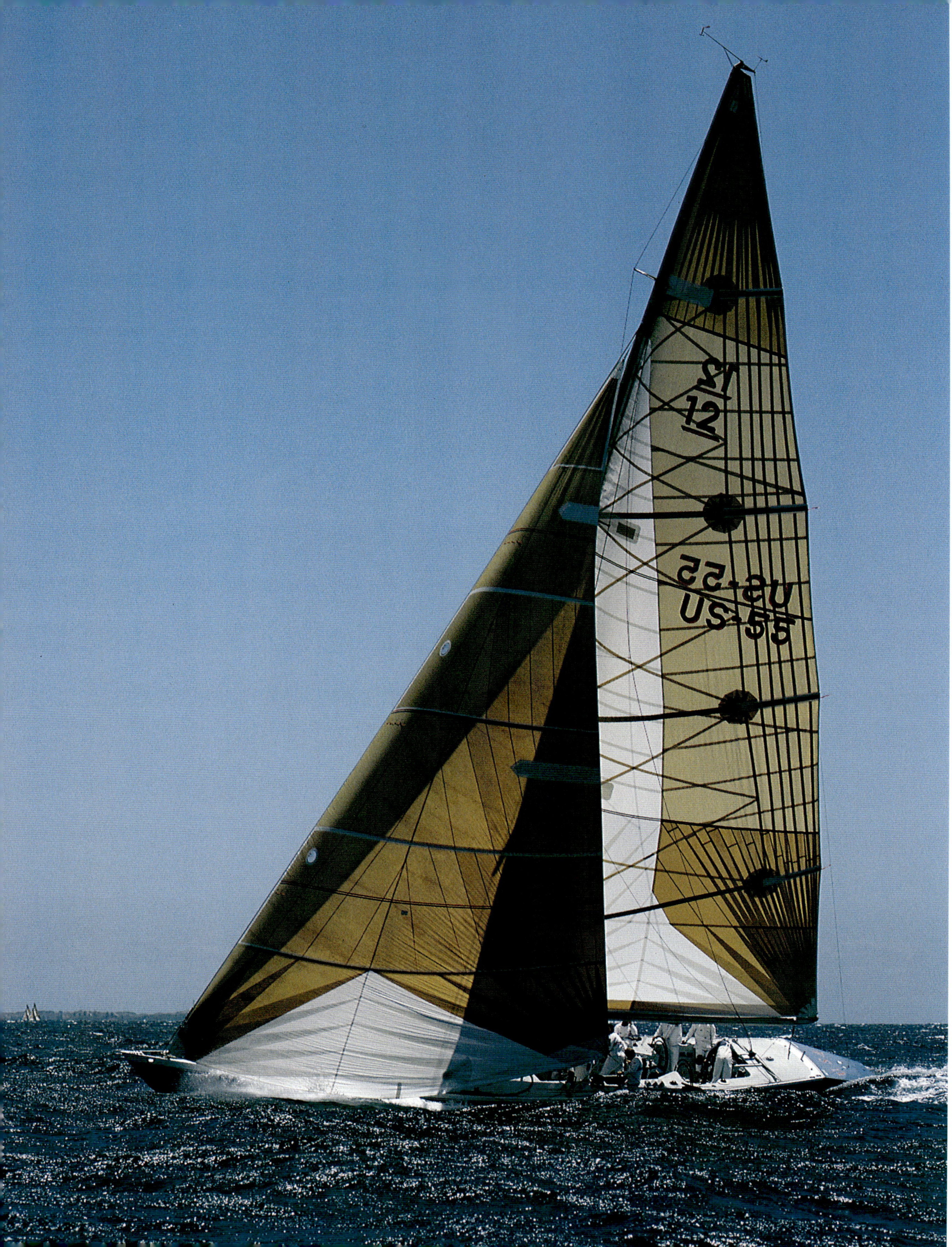
12
US-55

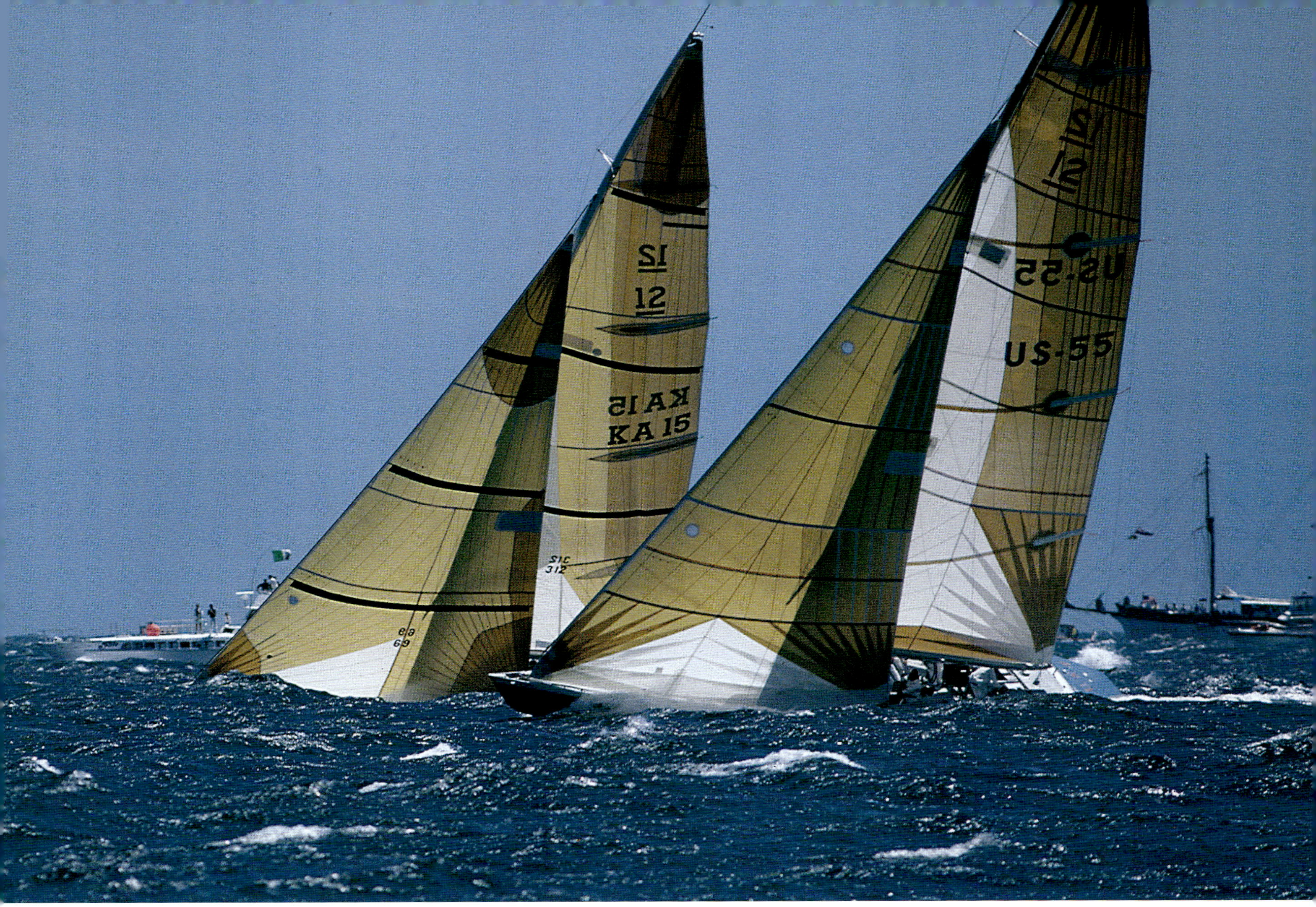

Backlighting

Stars & Stripes is sailing with the sun coming through the sails, and the backlighting graphically illuminates the texture and weave of the cloth. This series of races came at a time when sails were being radically altered in design and materials. The new materials brought an entirely different dimension to the surface of sails. Their skeletons were a new design feature in marine photography. I loved to photograph the new sails until their innocence and beauty were corrupted with the advertising logos that adorned them in later Cup contests.

Sheets Taut

Kookaburra III and *Stars & Stripes* face off at a start in the final contest for the America's Cup. *Kookaburra III* is to weather and ahead of *Stars & Stripes*, but her leading position is deceptive, for the Cup was won by *Stars & Stripes* in a clean sweep over four races. Whatever anyone's feelings about the outcome of the contest, nothing could diminish the joy of watching the two 12s cross the starting line in a burst of speed, sails taut, rigging humming, sky clear, sunshine brilliant, salt air tingling the nostrils, everything stirring the senses to the inevitable conclusion that all is right with the world.

Although I have flown over most of the America's Cup courses since the 1950s, I have never been fond of the aerial vantage point. Sometimes, however, a story can be told more vividly from this angle than any other. Flying off Fremantle was a particular adventure because my airborne seat was in a tiny two-person helicopter. I felt these little flying machines were nothing but toys and — with due respect for the ocean we were flying over — I could not convince myself that being up in a toy was logical. However, the confidence of the pilots in their noisy machines and their joy in flying over the course were both contagious and fear-dispelling. Moreover, the vantage point did provide some unforgettable images, as well as wonderfully illustrating the intricacies of water flow.

My interest in the water flow around and under a boat comes not only from reading, but from fortunate hours spent at and under the towing tank at the Stevens Institute in Hoboken. Whatever the beauty of the sky and wave surface, I think of what is happening underneath the vessel as it makes its way through the water. Each line of foam and curl of wave speak in their language of the hull's passage.

In the following three photos, made in succession over a period of a few seconds, *Eagle* — roaring along with her spinnaker pole against the headstay and the mainsail eased — slides at hull speed down a wave and dips her bow.

Note the wind pattern on the surface of the water in the foreground forward of *Eagle*. It is particularly clear in the second photo of the series. The pattern of each little finger of wind is drawn starkly in small curves that look almost like the scales of a fish.

Bow Wave

The bow wave is forming just aft of the stem, and a stream of white water extends back and out in an almost straight line until it begins to break outboard of the cockpit. At the transom to starboard, a burst of spray rises several feet into the air. Across the transom to leeward, a sharp line of wake extends out and aft. On the port side, under the spinnaker pole, a slight disturbance of white water rushes out from under the vessel. Forward of the bow, the dark line of the shadow of the spinnaker pole reaches ahead over the sparkling water toward the shadow of the spinnaker. These are aspects of the image my eye and mind were aware of as I balanced the camera in the bouncing helicopter. They were tracks the boat's hull was leaving in its course and, once photographed, signs of its passage through the water.

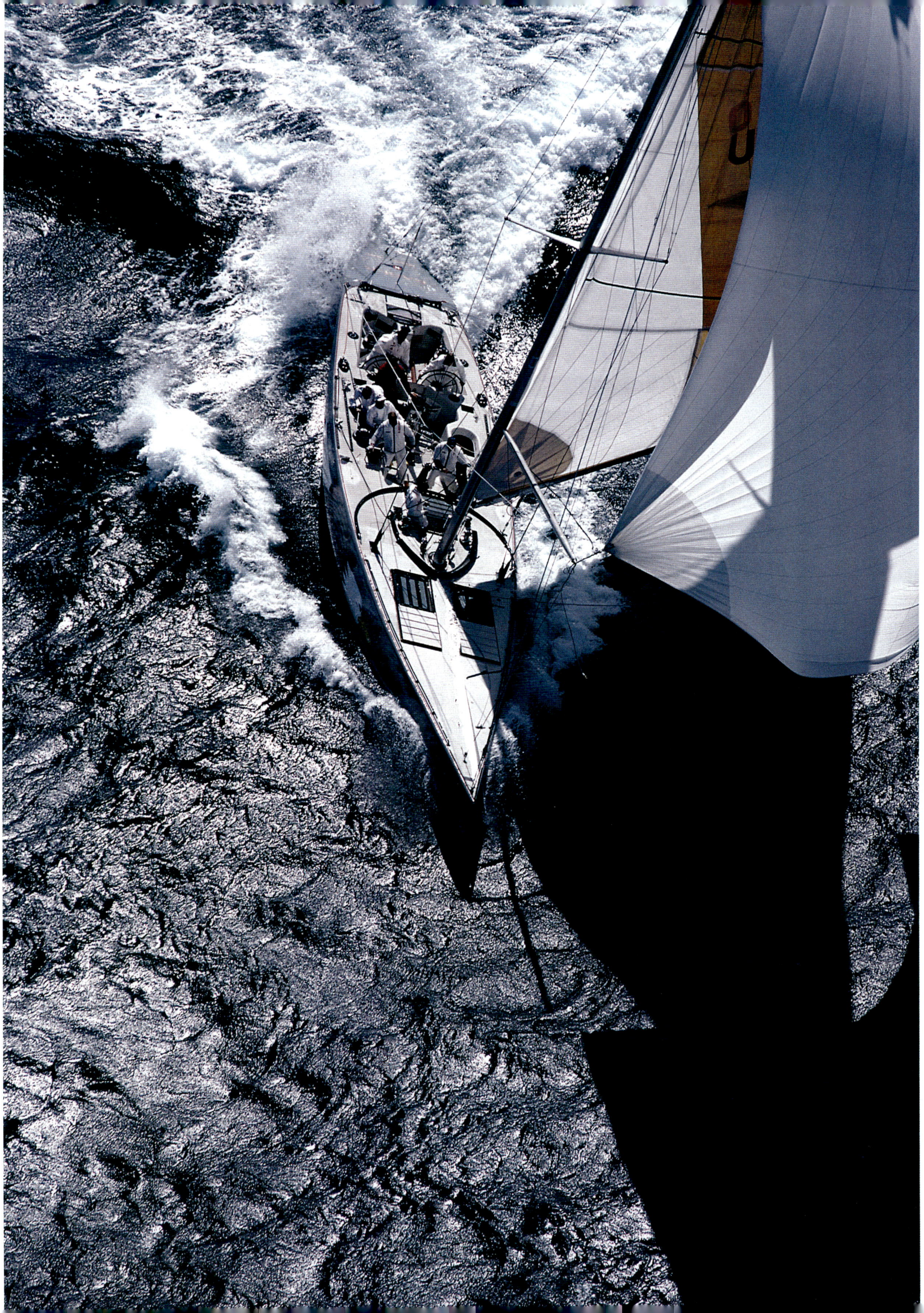

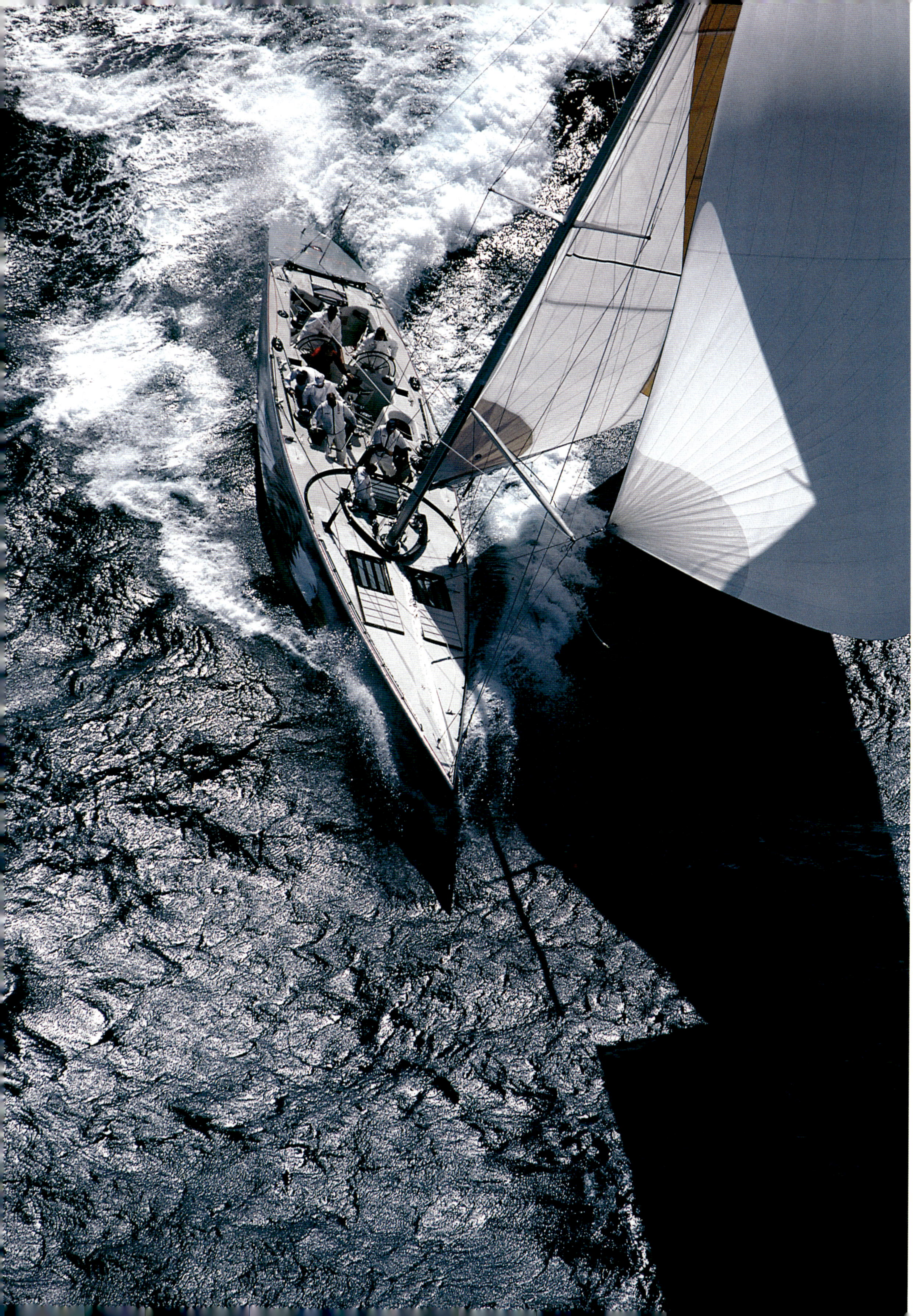

White Water

Opposite, now the bow is deeper into the wave and the curl of white water at the starboard bow curves outboard of the forward edge of the foredeck hatch. Its formation breaks down farther forward than in the previous photograph. At the starboard transom, the burst of spray that was in the air previously is collapsing. At the port transom, the wave of white water has built up strength as though the line of emerging foam was moving with more force and direction. Forward to port, alongside the hull under the spinnaker pole, a dark line of water appears where the previous photograph had light spray. The water being driven out from under the hull here has more force. Forward of the bow, the shadow of the spinnaker pole and the curve of the spinnaker are still in the frame, a triumph of camera control in my struggle against the buffeting of the helicopter.

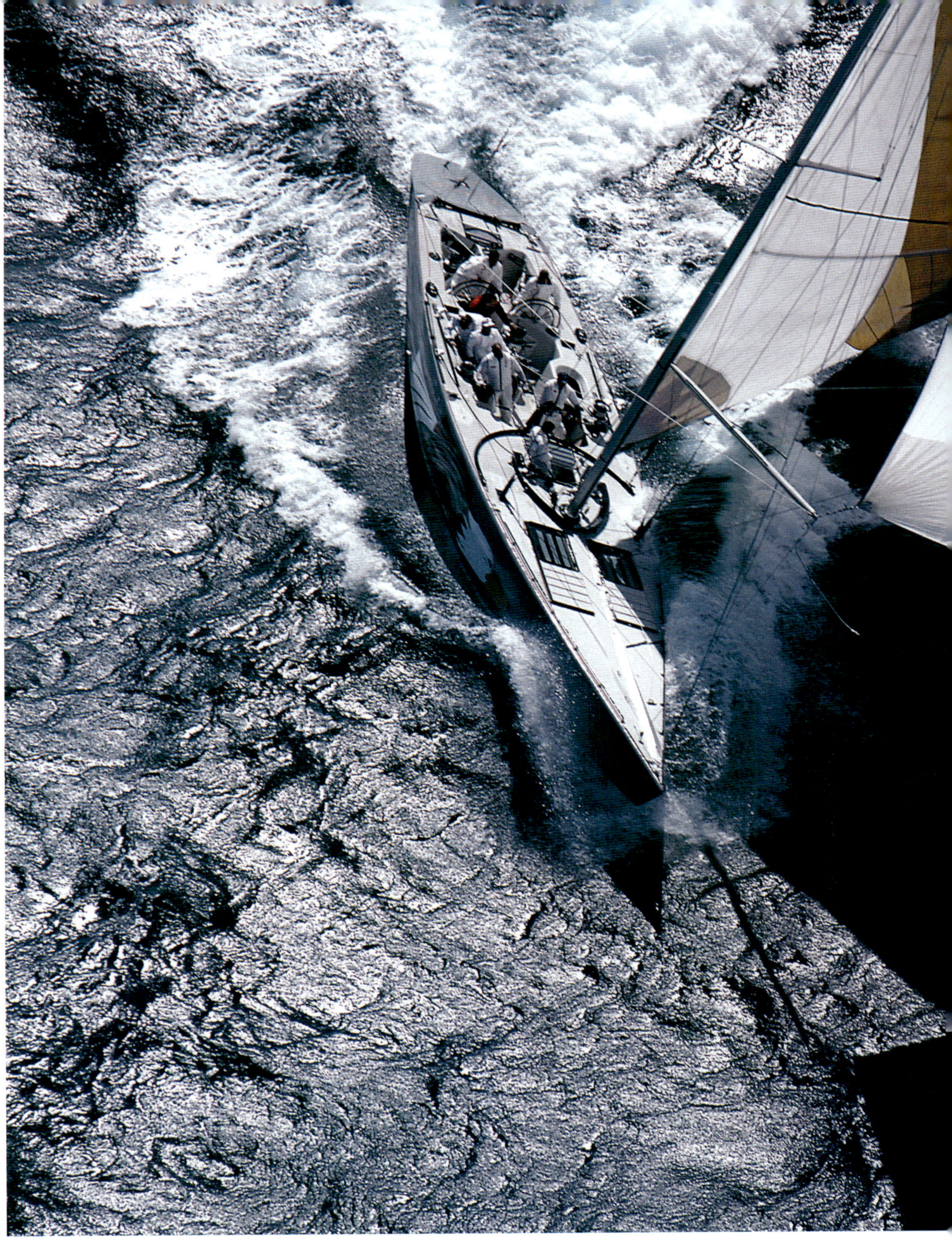

Streamers

The wake along the starboard skin of *Eagle*'s bow is now farther aft and its wave form more pronounced. The white water of this wave moves aft and outward along the hull in an almost unbroken line past the transom. To port of the transom, the wave that had seemed to cling under it is now spread out astern. Under the spinnaker pole along *Eagle*'s port side, the darkness of a wave rushes out in streamers of solid water expelled from underneath the yacht's keel and white foam crosses the deck at the chainplates. Forward along the port side toward the bow, spray is rising straight up and out from the side of the hull. Forward of the bow, I finally have lost most of the shadow of the spinnaker, either because I was bounced by the helicopter or because I concentrated too intently on the water around the hull.

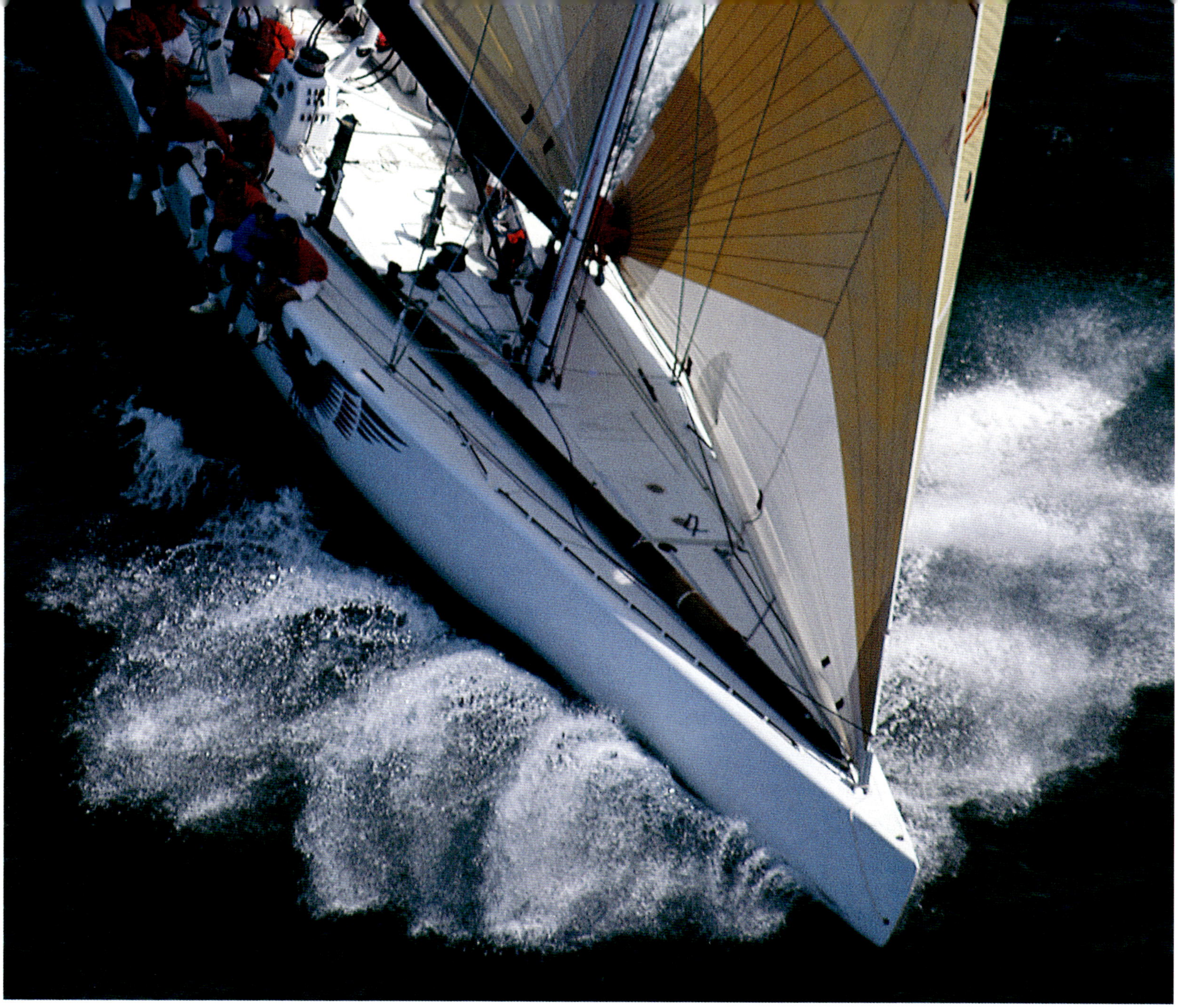

Occasionally the eye catches a situation that does not seem to be part of any developing action — an element that perhaps was not observed at the time of making the photograph.

Streamers of Spray

Here, for a fleeting second, the bow of *USA 23* slaps into a three-part (or six-part) wave so that individual streamers of spray radiate around the bow.

Sinkhole at Sea

As the hull drives along, it displaces the water that forms the pattern of wake and wave that radiates out and aft. Here a particularly fascinating pattern develops in the water to leeward of the cockpit and out about 30 feet. It looks like a sinkhole, and it might well be a nautical one.

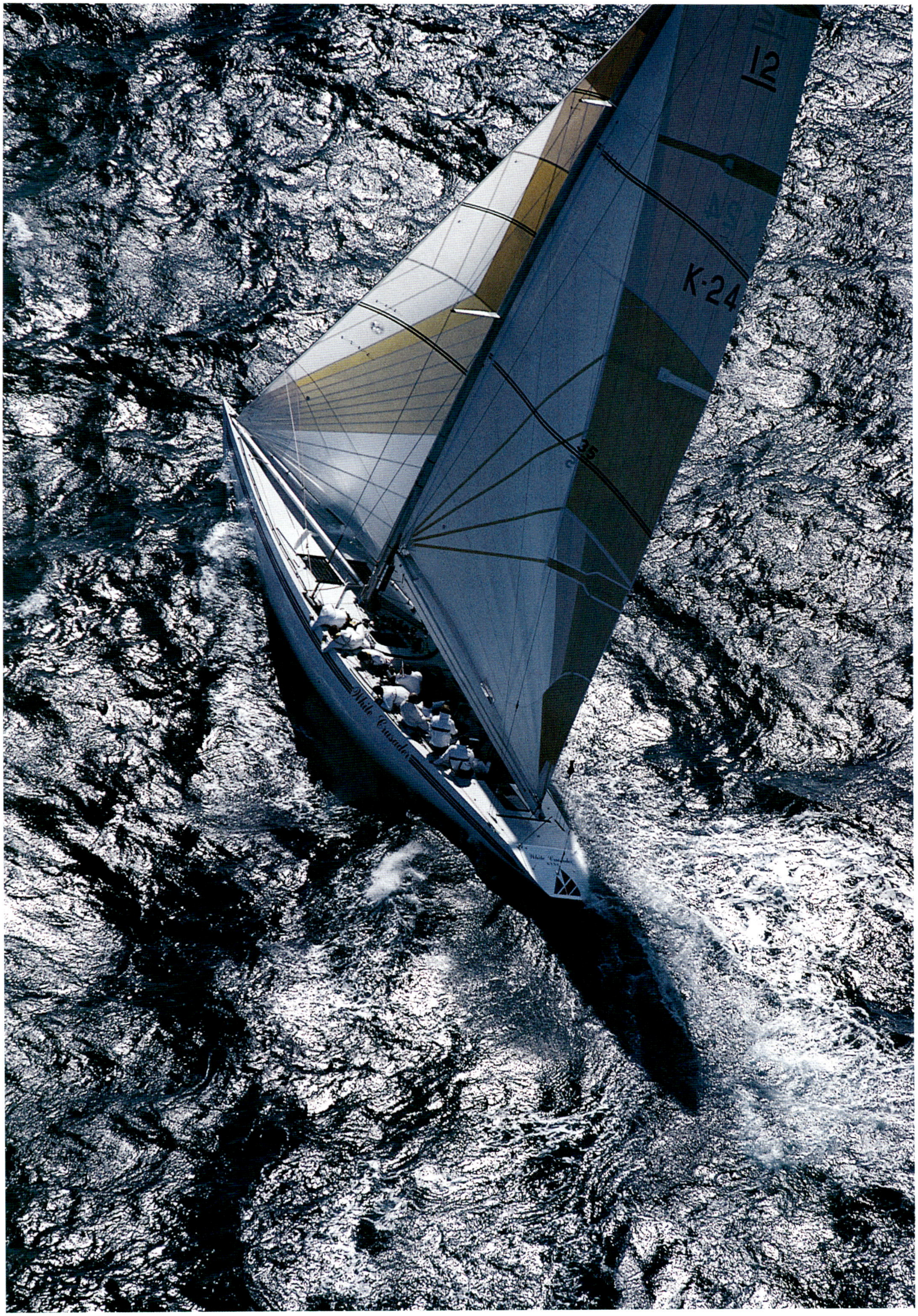
12
K-24
35

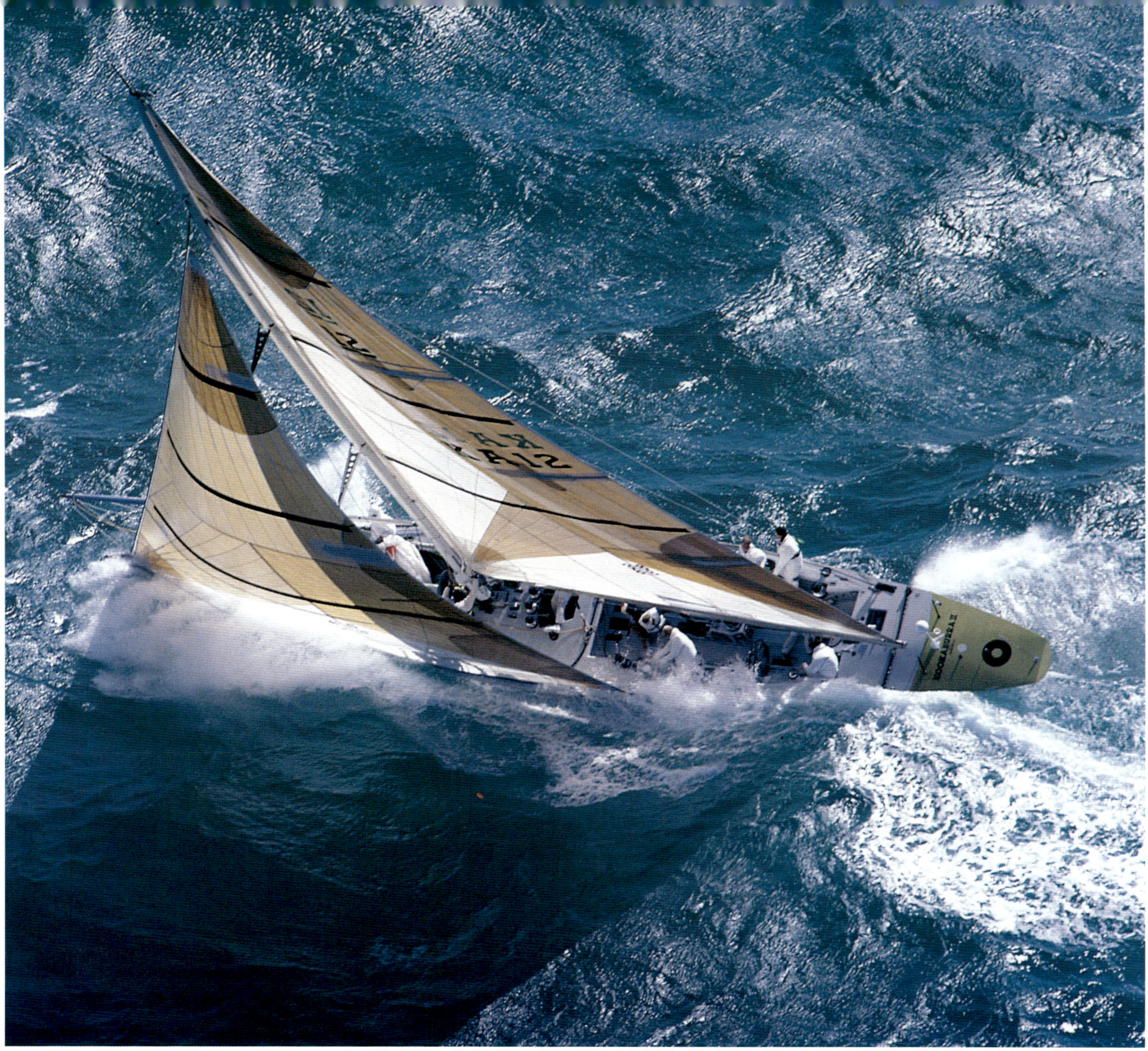

These two images clearly show how a photographer's joy in flying spray can be a crewman's nightmare.

Bursting Wake

Kookaburra II is approaching the windward mark, its spinnaker pole set, ready for the rounding. The line of wake is bursting up at the leeward edge of the cockpit, adding a lively sense of speed to the image.

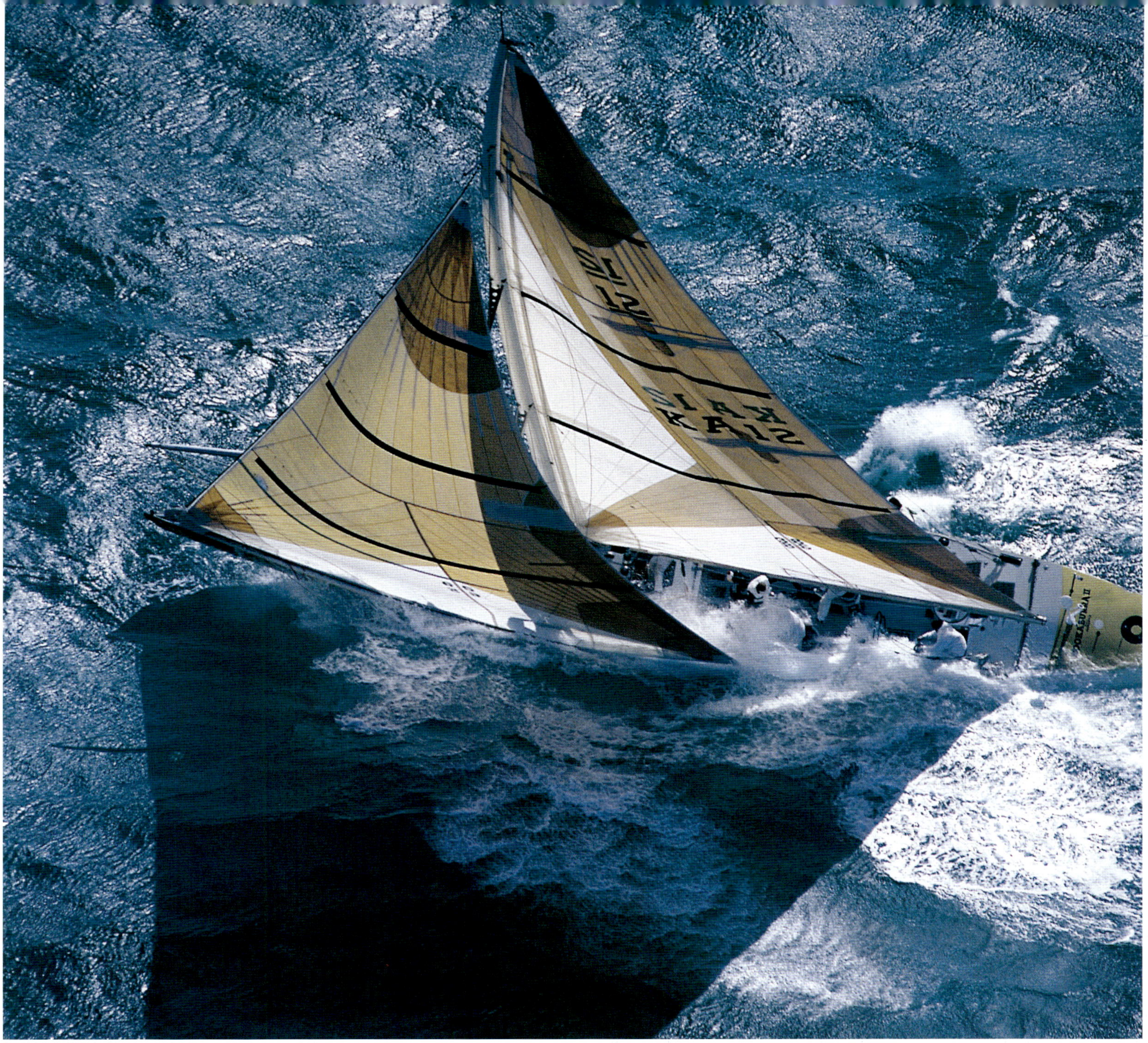

Beauty and Danger

The wake that flew up to add freshness to the image is now falling back and pouring into the cockpit and over the crew in abundance. The bilge pump was a significant feature of this spirited sailing and one that I should mention in extolling the joys of wind and wave. In this image, the sunlight through the taut sails is beautiful, the surface of the water is an exciting shimmer of reflections, the action is exhilarating, but it must not be forgotten that with this beauty comes danger.

The Burnished Sea

Overleaf: *Stars & Stripes* leads *USA* across the burnished sea, illuminated in an almost eerie stage setting. The blue clarity and piercing reality of the previous photographs have changed to an ethereal scene in which the mind could easily create magical scenarios. *Stars & Stripes*'s translucent spinnaker lends an insubstantial quality to rigging that must have been pushed to near the breaking point. The play of light coming through *USA*'s spinnaker has the sail floating in a billowing shape of light and shadow. The outreaching girders of the spinnaker poles anchor both sails to the masts and the yachts below. They neatly tie the gossamer sails to the reality of their function.

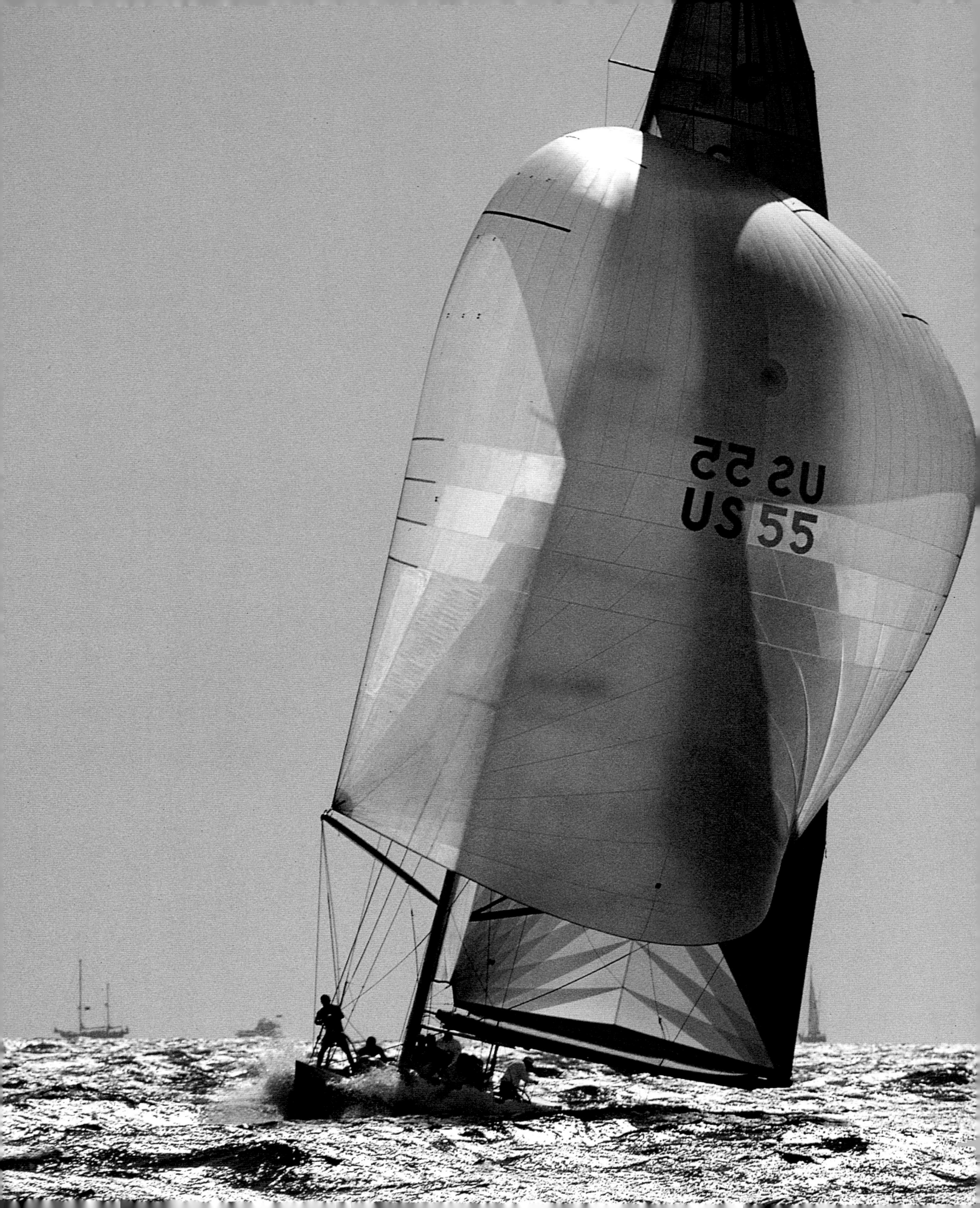
US 55

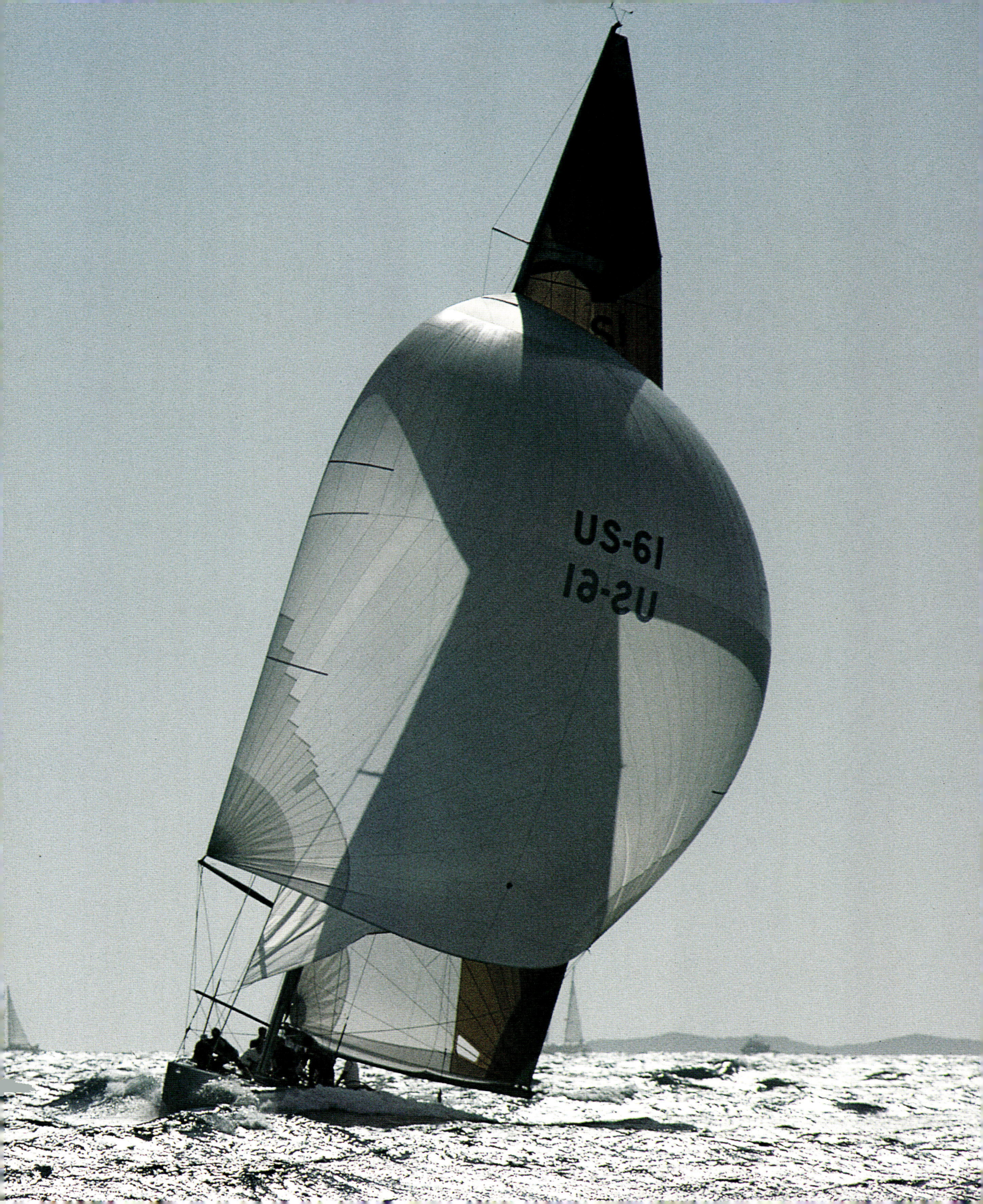
US-61

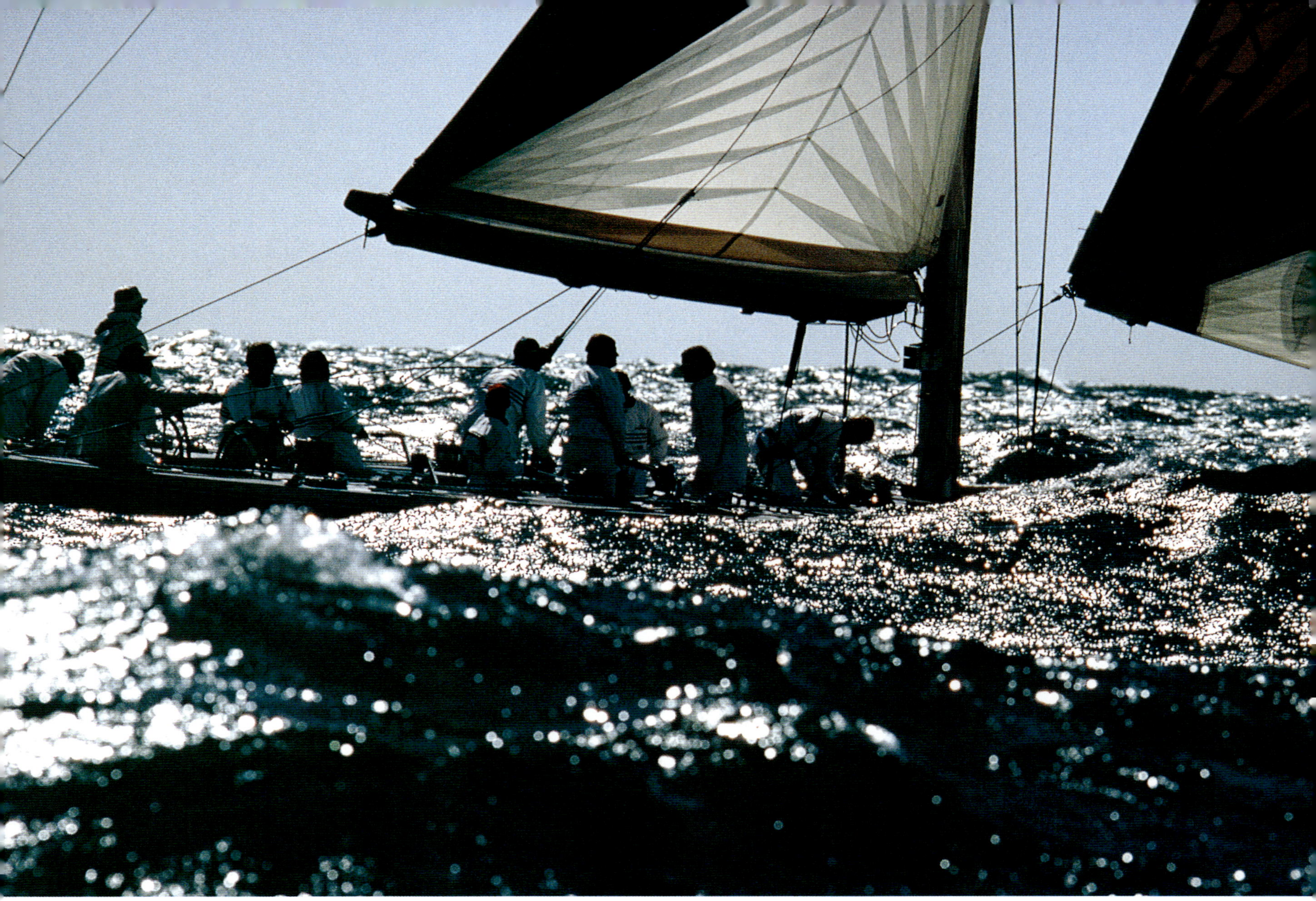

Into a Trough

Stars & Stripes off Fremantle, Western Australia, is sailing into a trough on the sun-dappled sea. A photographer has to be grateful for the circumstances that conspired to produce this effect, but particularly to the crewman forward who bends over and down in a position to emphasize the significant hull direction.

Patterns of Wake

Opposite, the giant sloop *New Zealand,* after the second and final race of her unfortunate 1988 encounter with the American catamaran defending the America's Cup, sails into San Diego harbor at about 10 knots, accompanied by a well-wishing fleet of motoryachts. Churning white patterns of wake kiss the transoms of the smaller boats and mark their paths through the water. However, no wake shows astern of the wind-driven *New Zealand,* which — with her fish-like underwater design — gracefully wends her way, all glide, no churn.

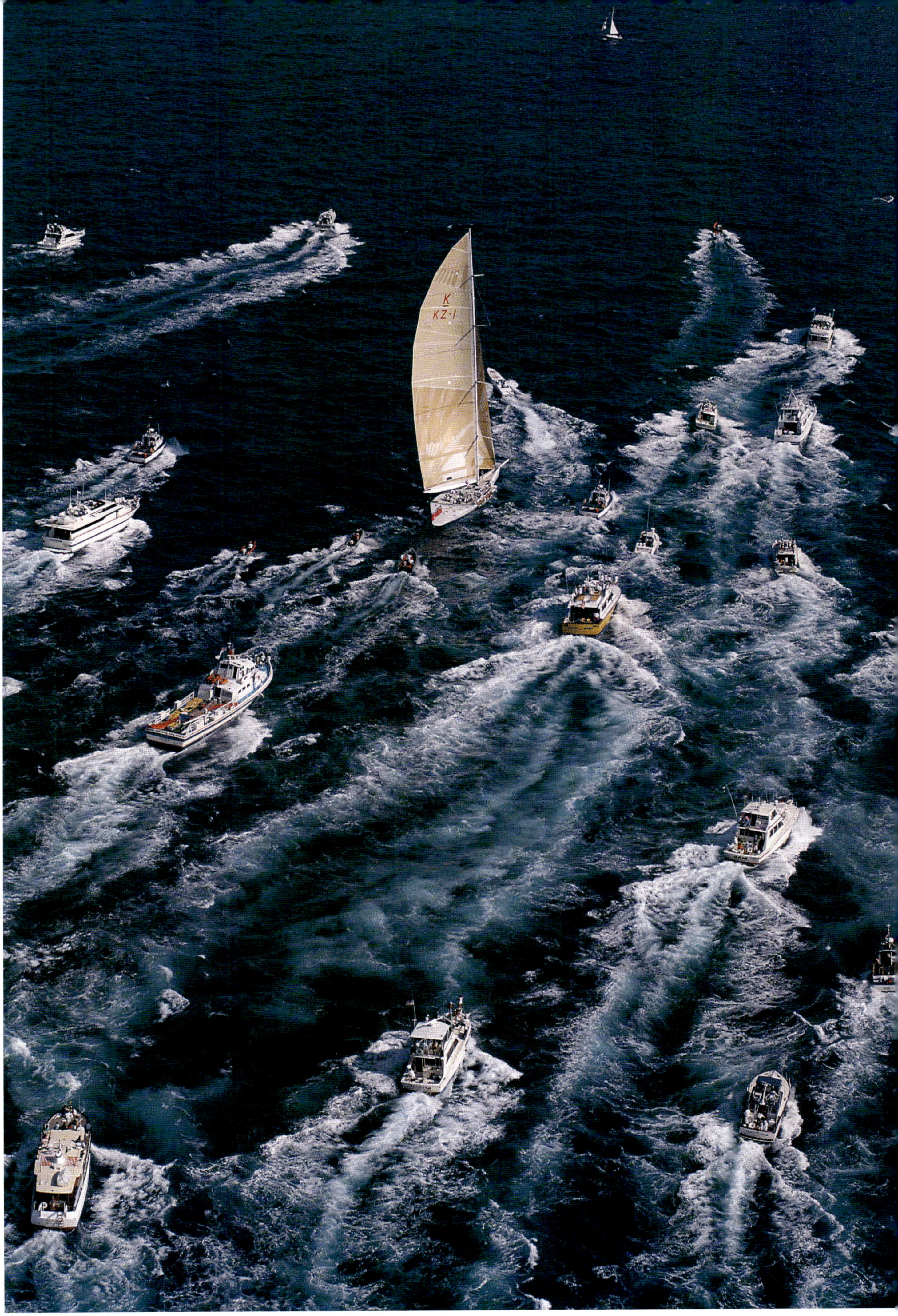
K
KZ-1

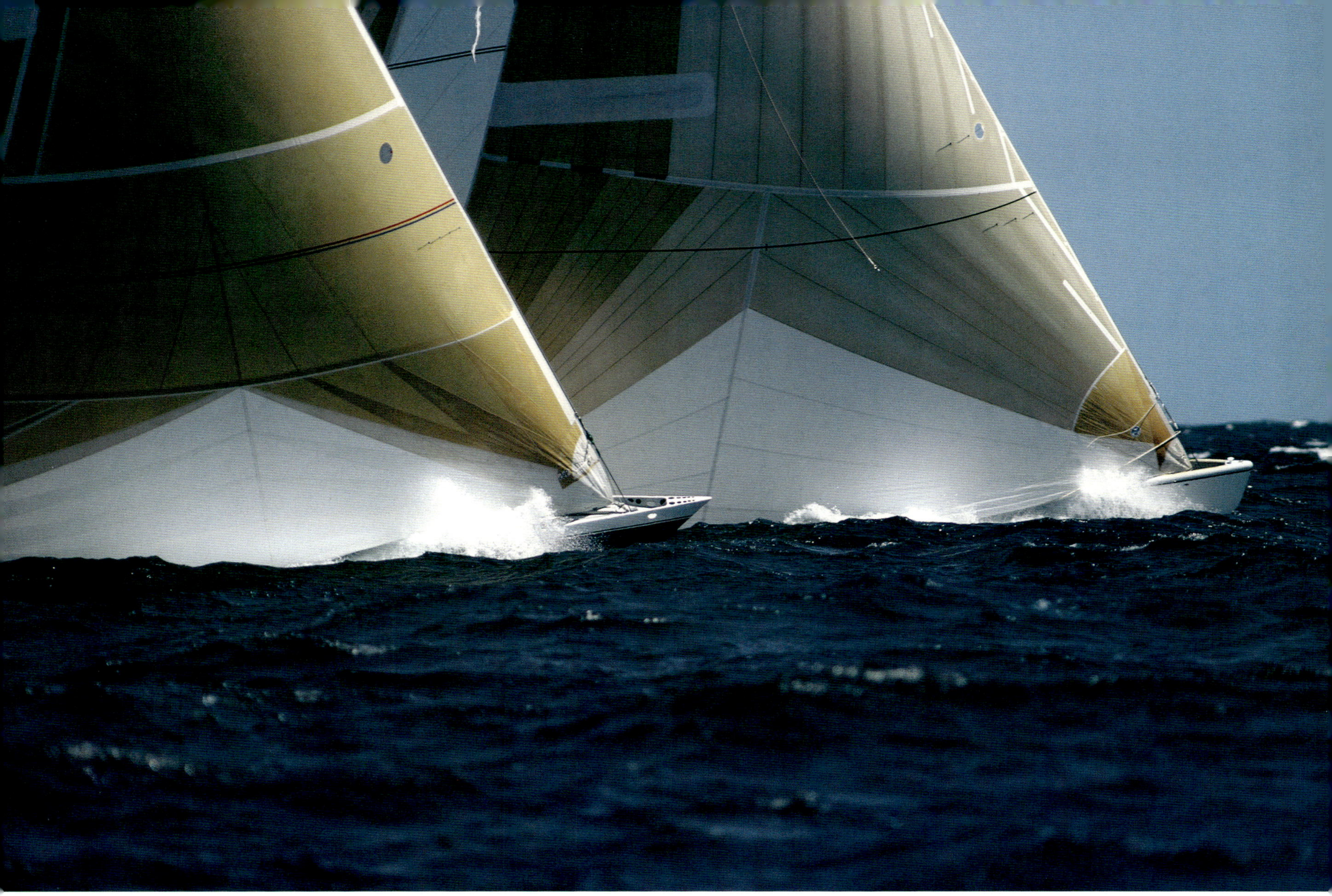

Racing in the 1987 America's Cup challenger finals between *Stars & Stripes*, skippered by the dominant Dennis Conner, and *New Zealand*, sailed by the young and rising Chris Dickson, was hard-fought and dramatic because the boats were almost evenly matched. The competition was sparked by personality clashes, caustic words, and a rising state of tension both in the press and on the racecourse. The turning point came in a few dramatic seconds at a fateful mark rounding, but before the drama of that incident, there were hours of intense competition, often in an aura of flashing line and light. The Fremantle course during this period was the venue of brilliant sailing tactics known round the world.

Feathers of Spray

New Zealand to weather leads *Stars & Stripes* in a moment symbolized by the feather of spray at their bows and the line etched by the sun on the rounded luff of their genoas. In the pattern of the seams and smoothness of their sails, the technological advances of sailcloth and sailmaking illustrate the modernity of the moment. The information can be read because the sun backlights the sails, with only a highlight of direct light along their luff.

Sun Overhead

Opposite, backlighting reveals sail structure in this vertical image which goes to the masthead. Sunlight pours through the leech area of the mainsail of *Stars & Stripes* in the foreground, so the seams of the sail are exaggerated. The same occurs at the clew of the jib. The bow of *Stars & Stripes* is lifting, and the power of the yacht rising to the lift of a wave is evident throughout its bearing. A slight lift in the attitude of the yacht does more to indicate joy and strength in the contest than a slight drooping of the bow, which implies weakness, although neither may be accurate descriptions of its state at the moment.

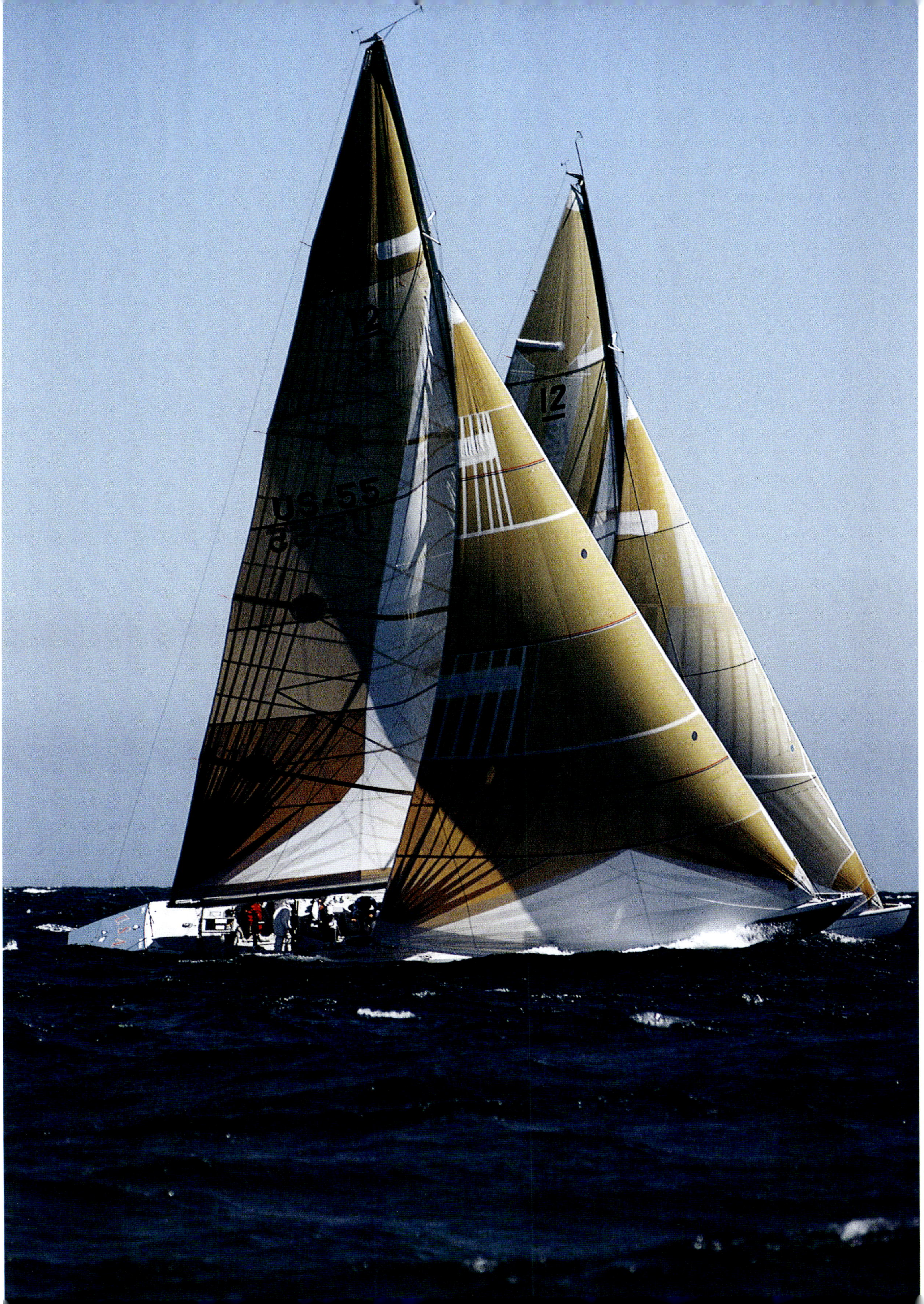

12
US-55
12

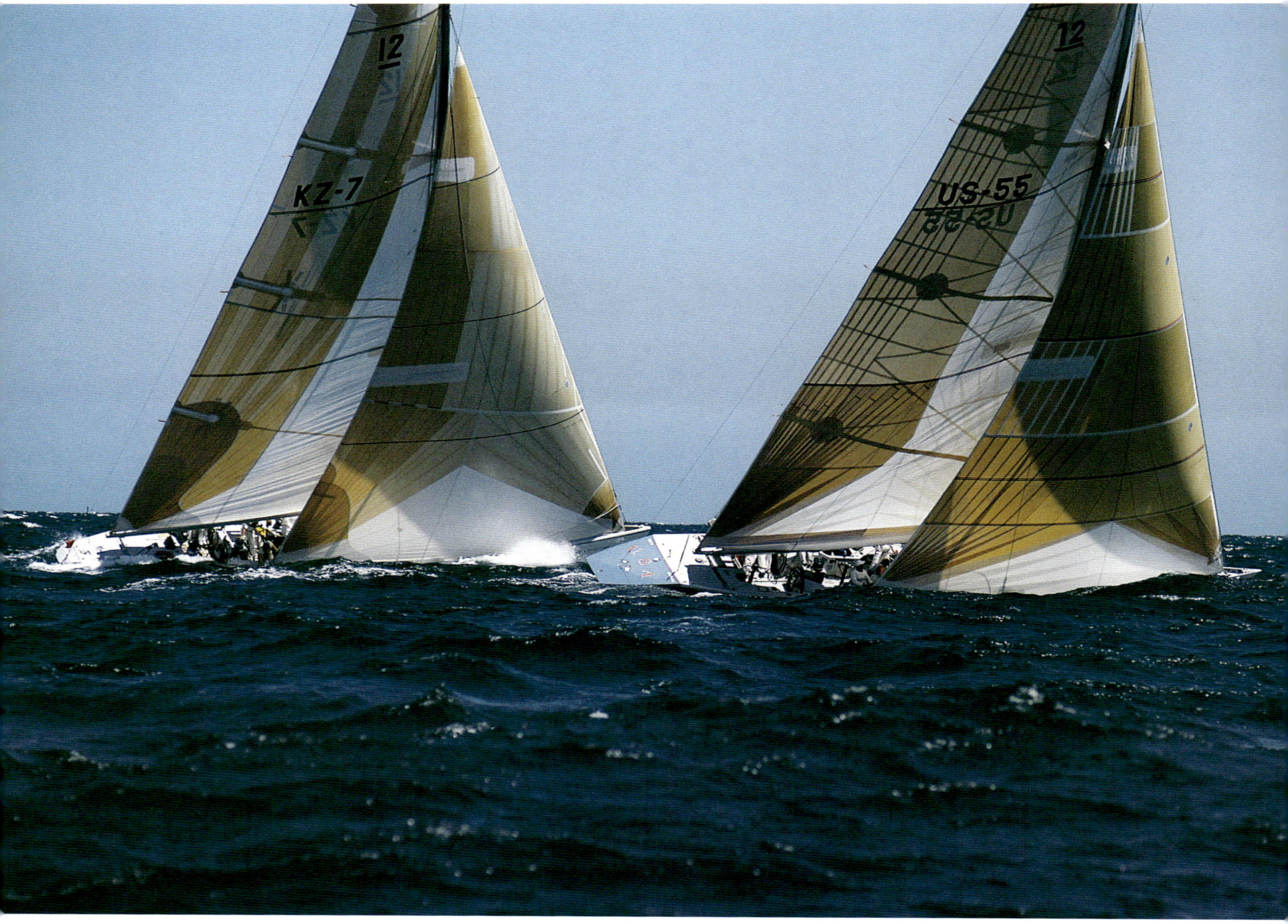

LIFTING

Here I have moved to a horizontal format, cutting the mastheads off the image. The hulls are bolder and more directly attract the eye. The yachts are leaning more than in the previous photograph and heading slightly off the wind, as indicated by the larger area of sunlight backlit on the clew of their genoas. *New Zealand*, to windward, is lifting to a wave and *Stars & Stripes* is dipping into one. Competition is the key.

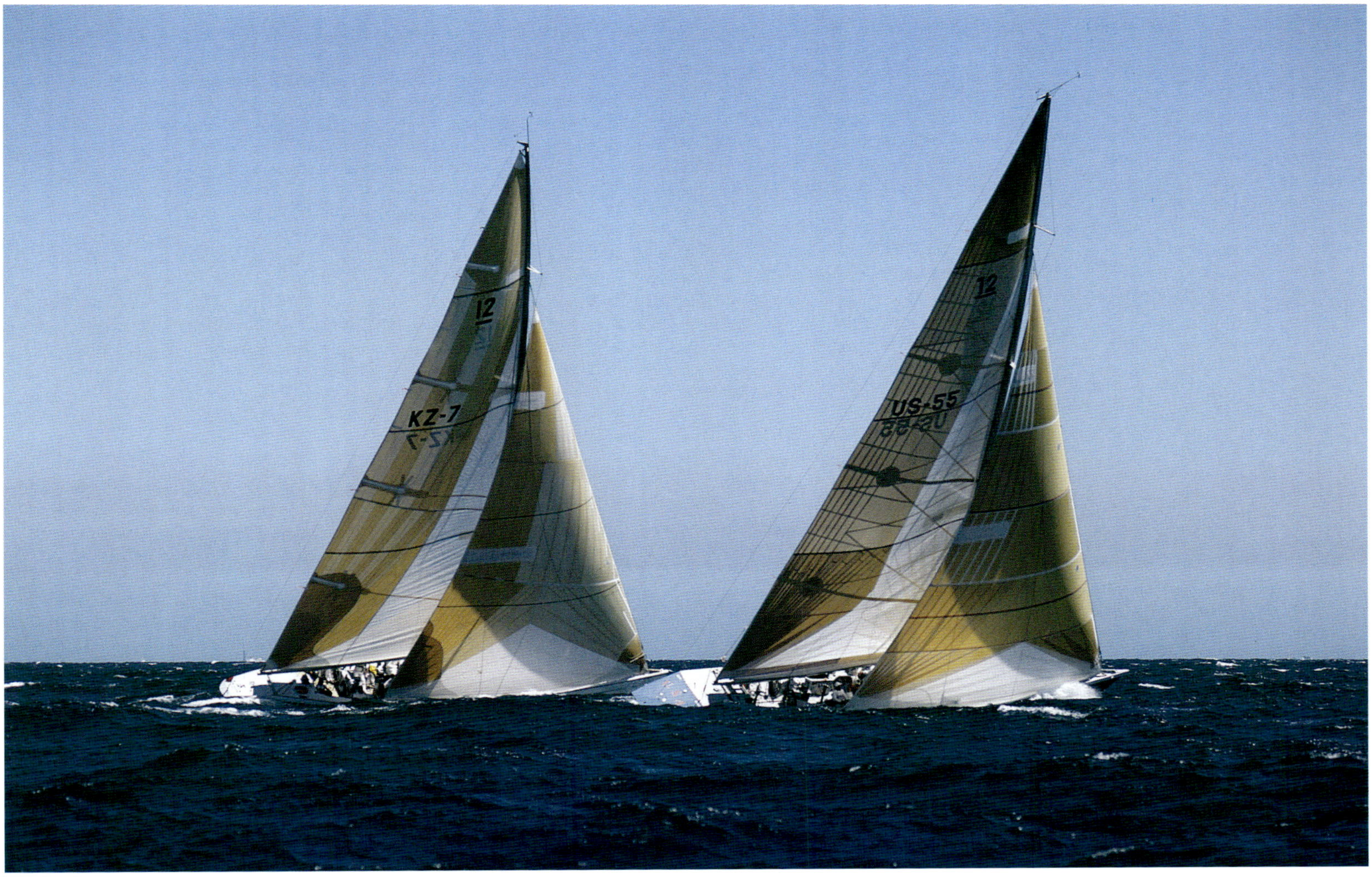

Seascape

In a more classical composition, the two yachts drive to weather, both lifting to the seas. This photograph would have made my father very happy. I think it was the way he saw images, for he constructed them in the kind of cameras he used for most of his life. They were large-format cameras, with plates of 5x7 inches or larger. The outfits of cameras, lenses, plates, and plate-holders were heavy, and he seldom had very many photographic plates with him at sea. He wanted to tell a story, and since he seldom worked from a very maneuverable photo boat in his early years, he thought primarily in a seascape frame. I came actively to photography, working from a fast, maneuverable chase boat with a smaller, more versatile camera and thus could move into the action and be closely involved with it. I saw images close up and searched for tension, though I understood the images that long ago played in my father's mind and would appreciate and capture them, even as this one.

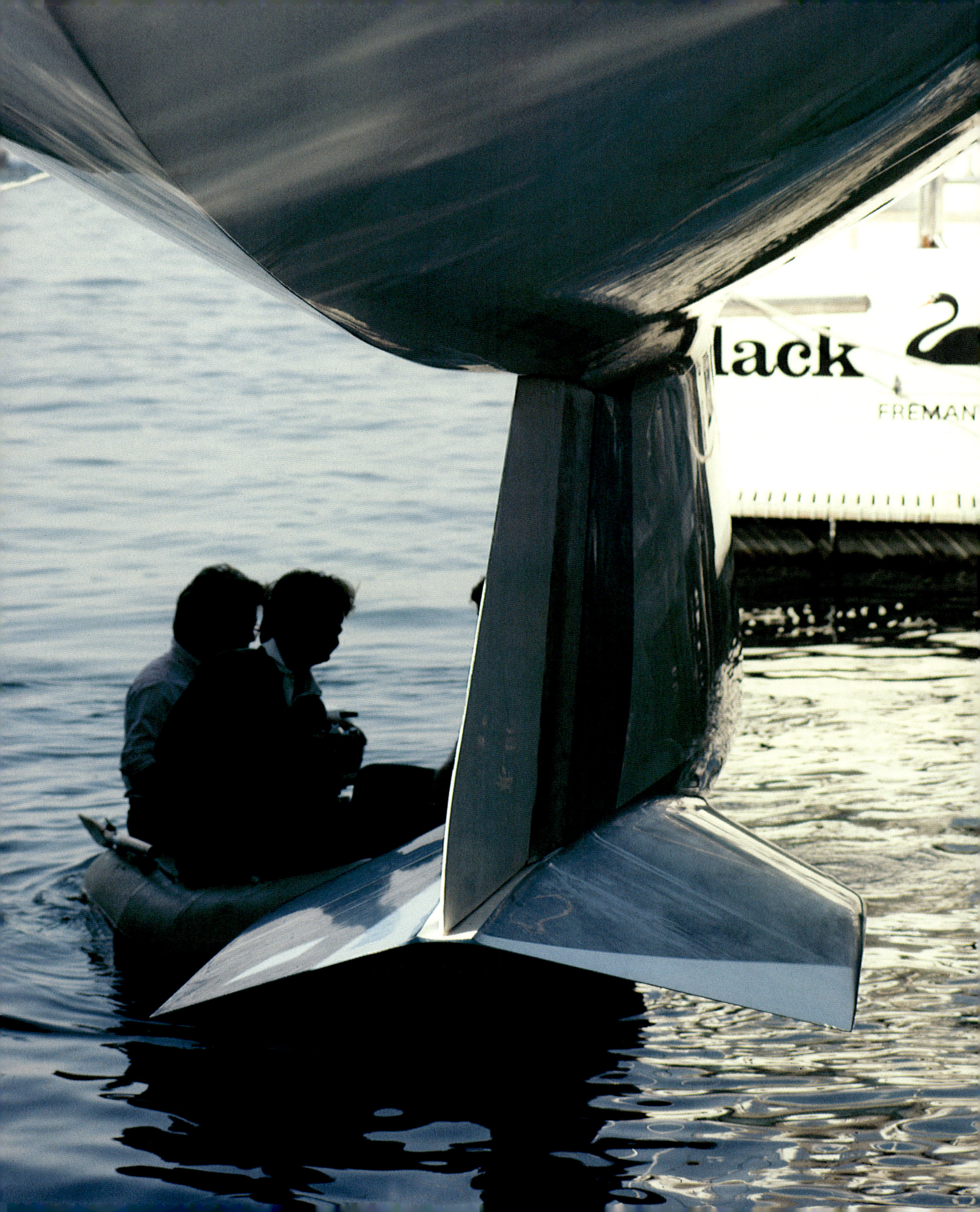

NEWPORT

Was it on wings the America's Cup flew to Australia?

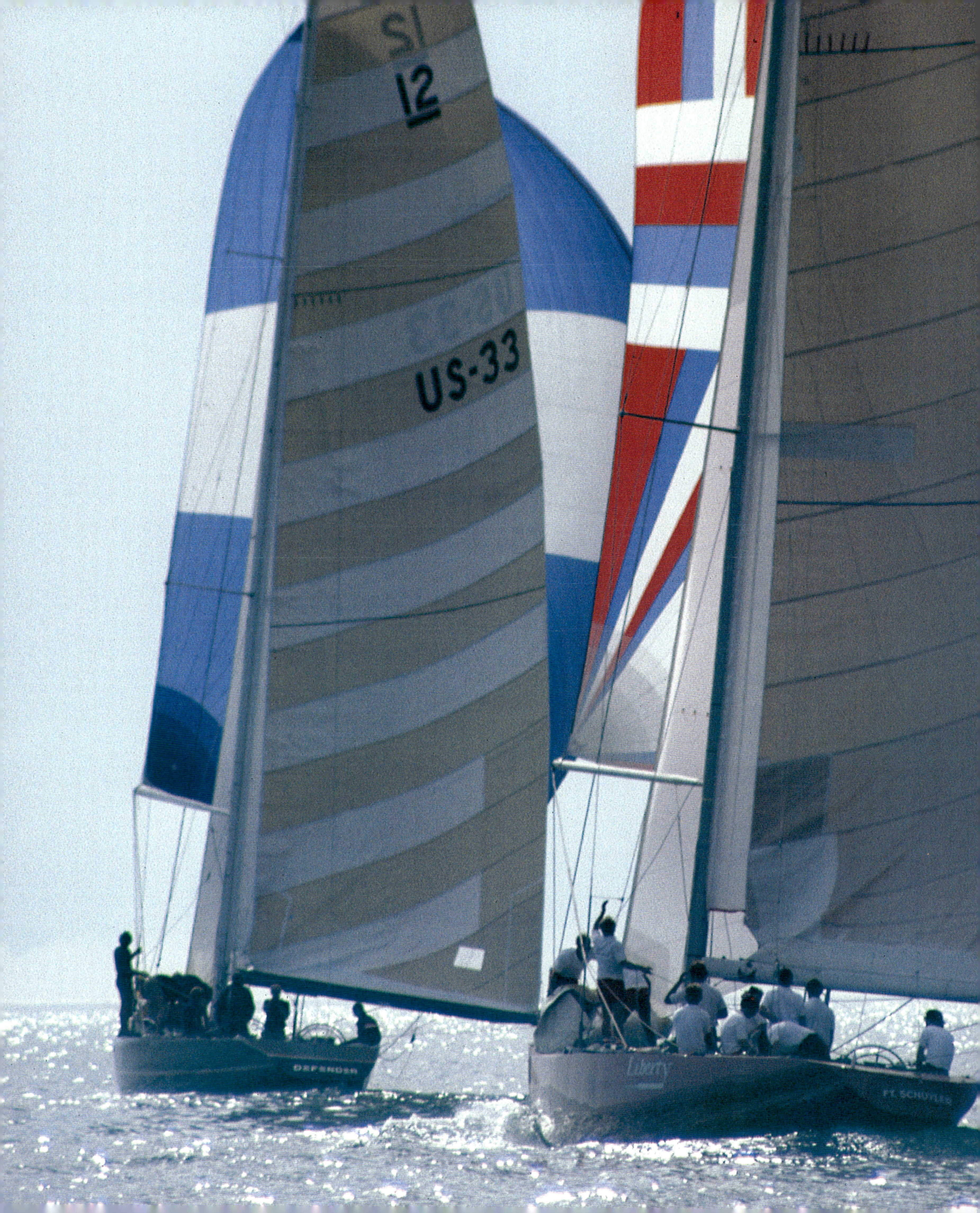
12
US-33
DEFENDER
Liberty

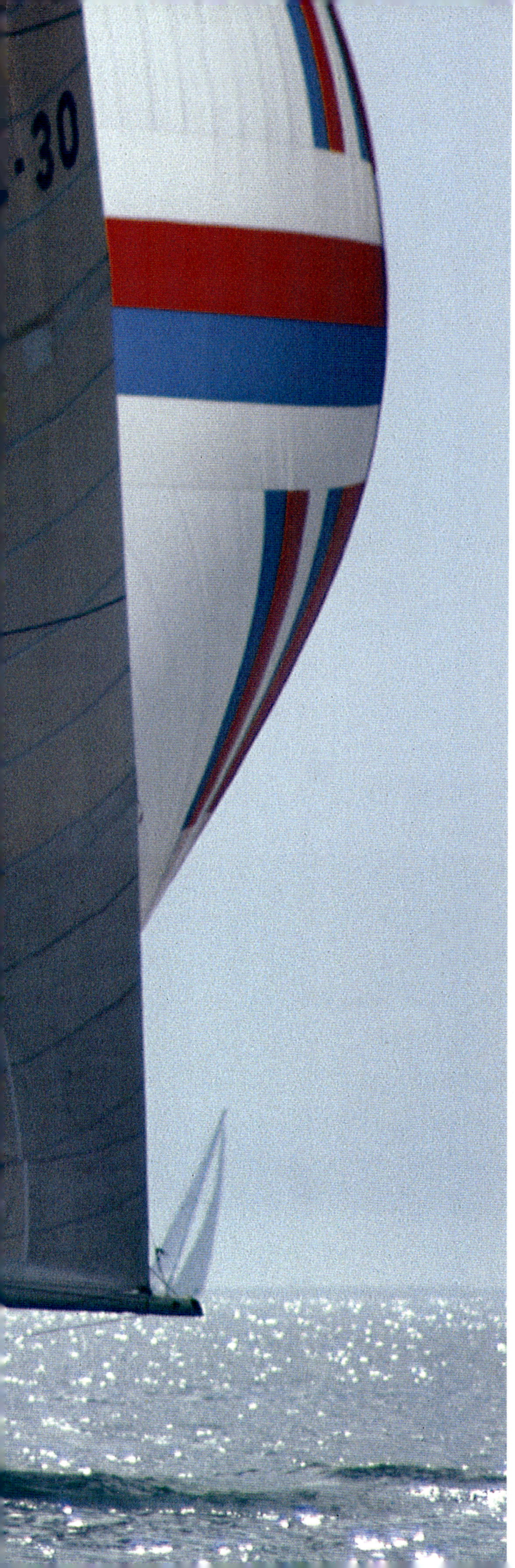

Both below and aloft, the yachts of the America's Cup were changing in the 1980s. But what a constant joy to follow them with a camera over the sometimes sparkling waters of Block Island Sound. In the following sequence of nine images made on a June day, the breeze was gentle, the sky was somewhat overcast, and time sat gently on us.

THE LIGHT

Sometimes when action on the course is not intense, I look at the yachts and wonder just where the picture is. If the word that comes to mind is not action and not technique, it sometimes is simply light.

Defender and *Liberty* under spinnaker are gliding toward the leeward mark over a flat, sun-speckled sea. My first thought as we cruised behind them was of their spinnakers, dominant in both color and form. Then I became aware that the story was not in the sails, but in the sky and sea and the light on them. In one image after another, I changed the focal length of my lens and finally moved to short, wide-angle lenses. Each step brought a different balance to sky, water, and yachts.

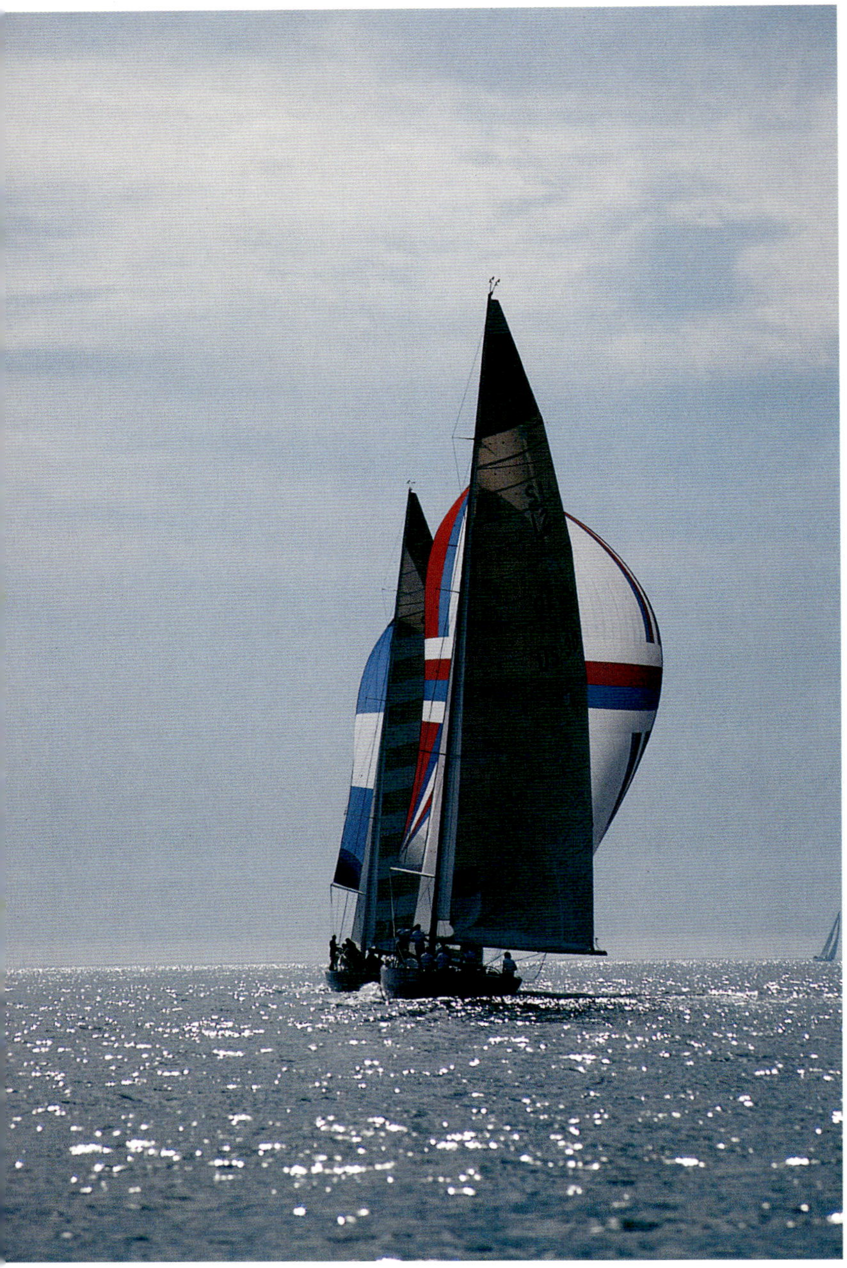

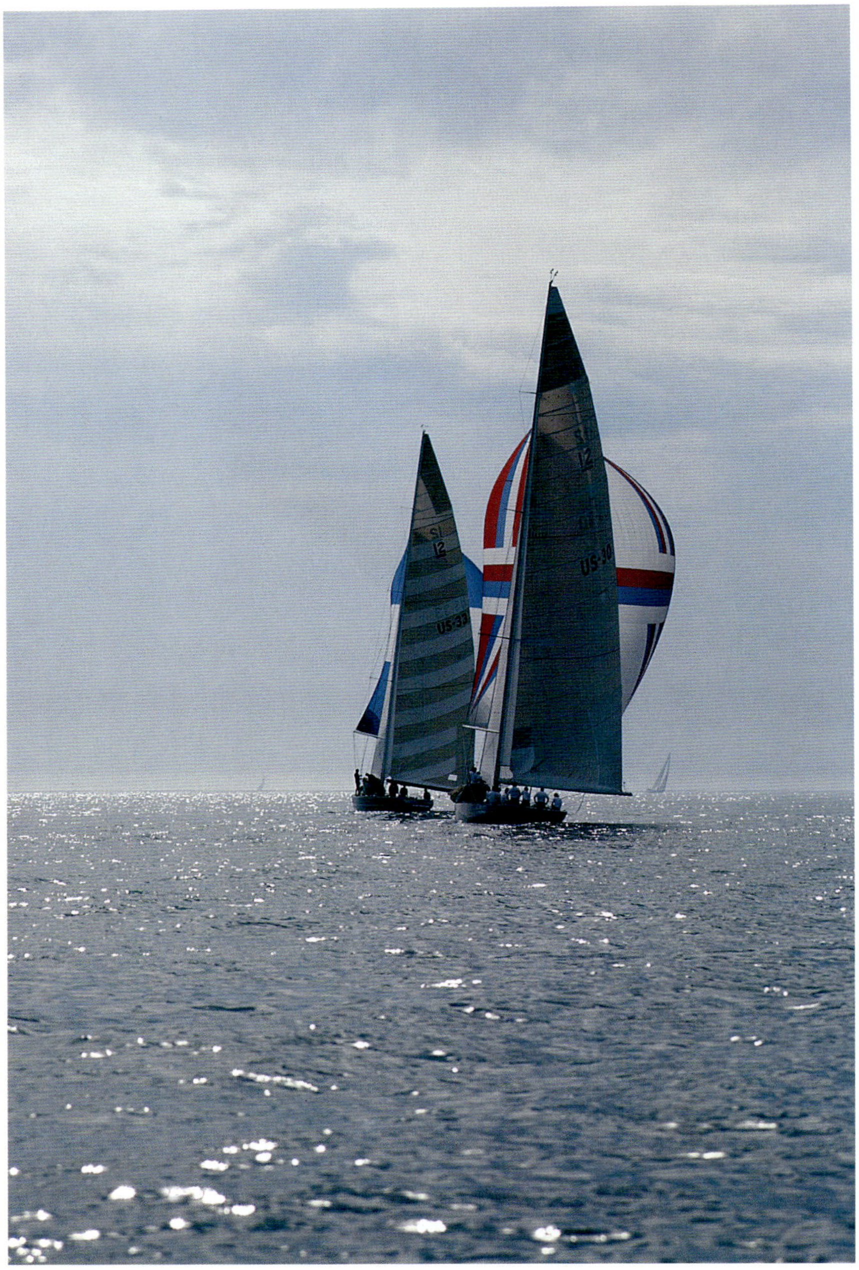

High Overcast

I was aware that the high overcast was an interesting foil to the sparkle on the water, and I framed the photograph so sky was more dominant.

Focal Point

Then I felt I should balance the area of water and sky, and perhaps the image of the yachts would be stronger if it was firmly at the focal point. Then I let my mind run free.

Gutter Line

I went to a horizontal format and the yachts were at what I then saw as the focal center of the image. That, however, would bring them too close to the center line, or gutter, if the image were run across a double page in a book or magazine. I have always been horrified when an editor placed an image so that the inner margins of a double-page spread compressed the image and destroyed its composition.

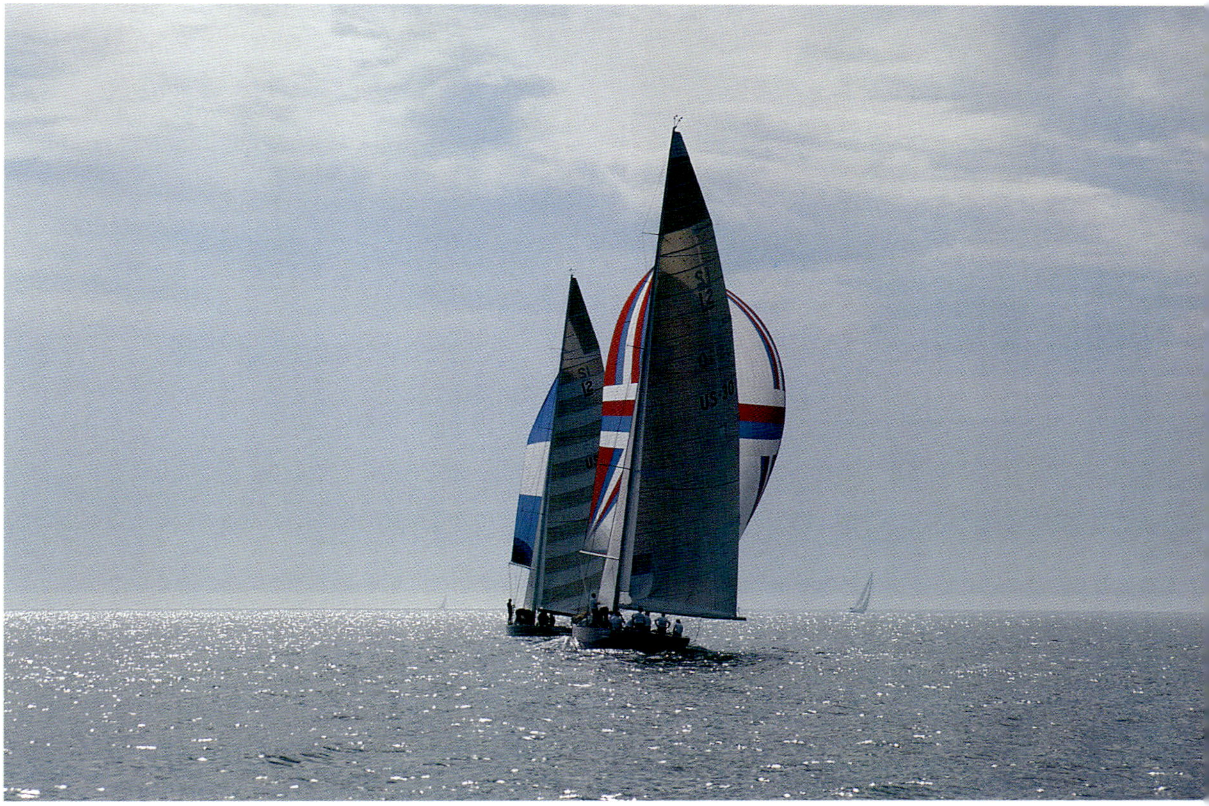

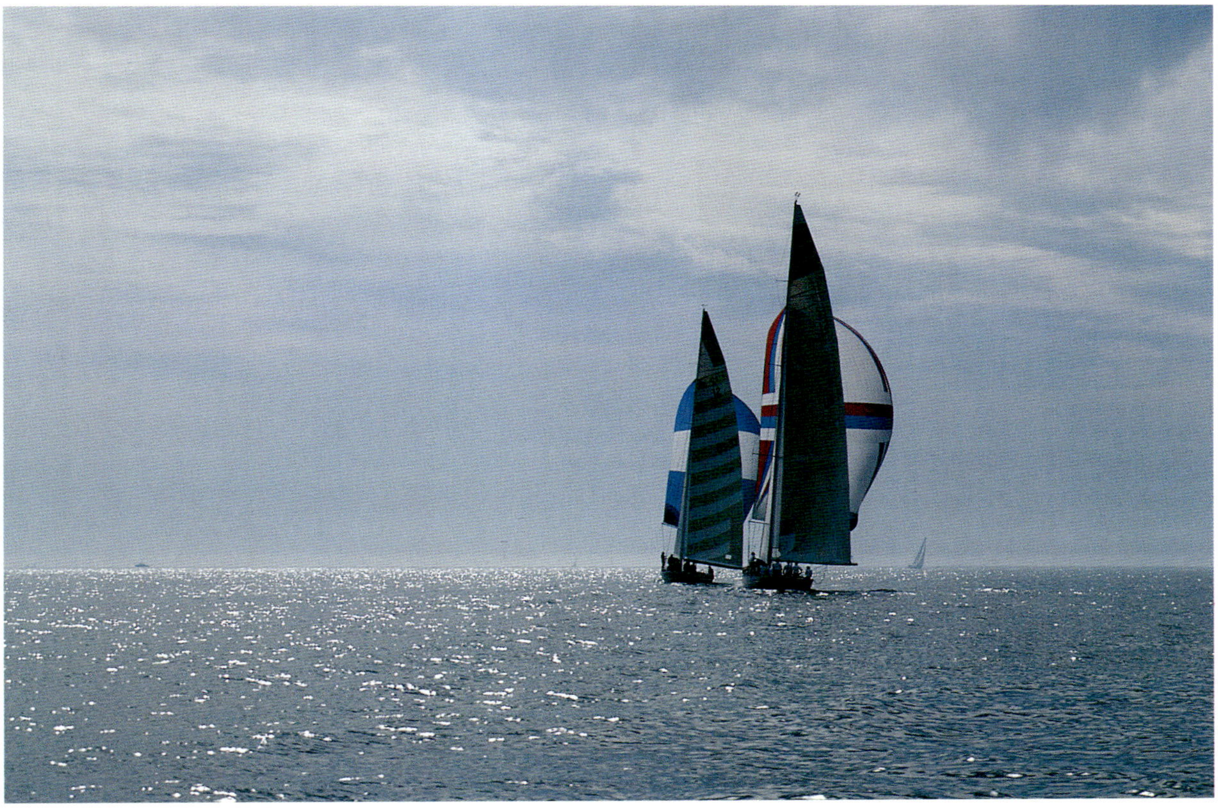

Off Center

I moved the yachts off center a bit more and balanced them so they could be used across a spread without being pierced.

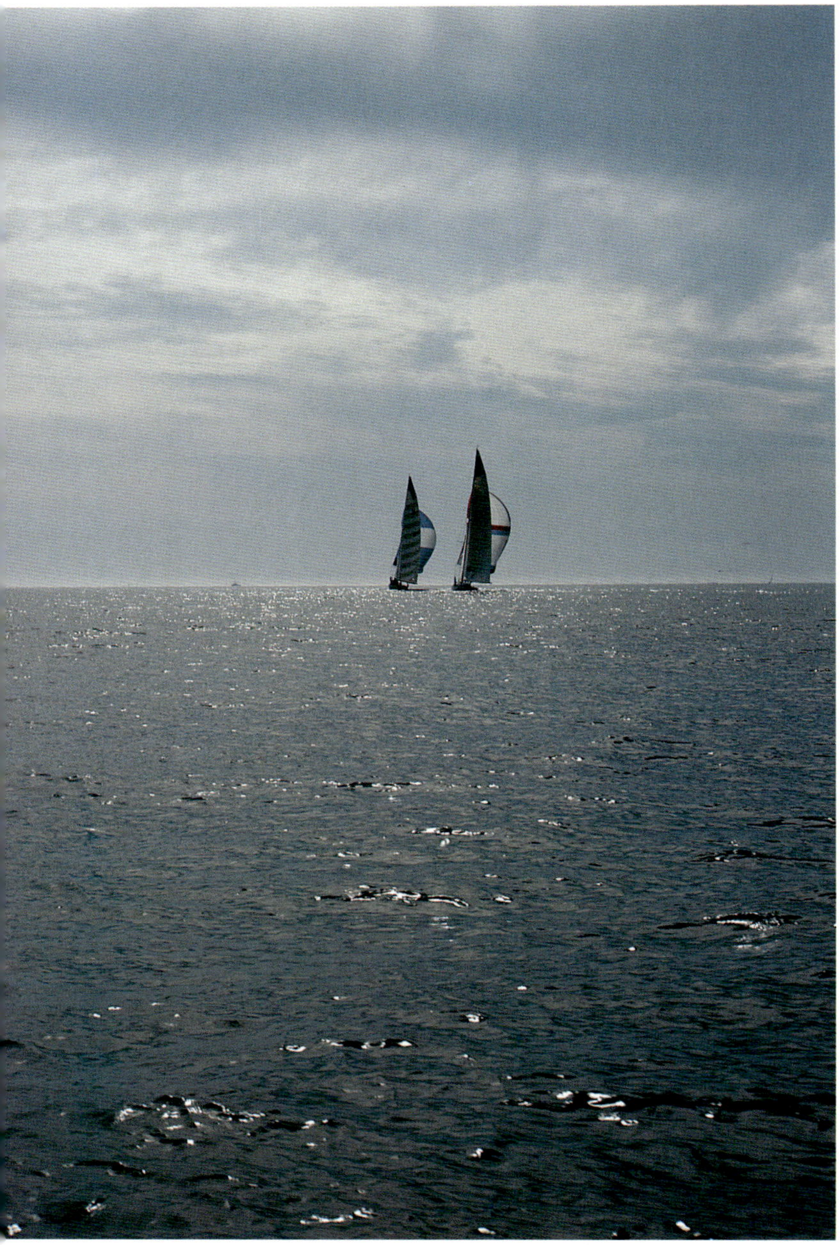

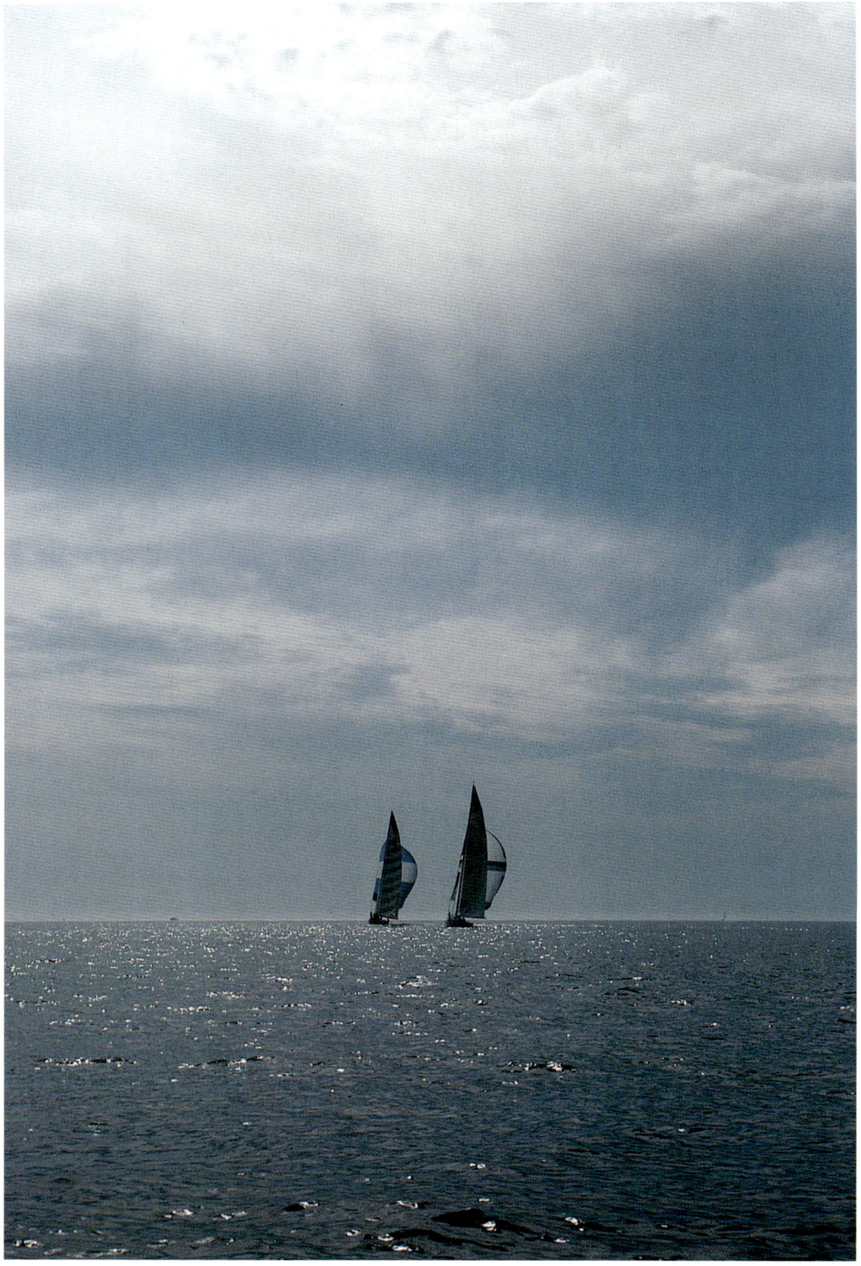

Dark Cloud

By this time, the yacht images were becoming small and I was thinking again of sky and water. I realized that a dark cloud mass that was overhead and out of the frame in the larger images was now drawn into the frame and had become the dominant sky feature. The message had moved from the yachts to the sky and water.

Sky and Water

In the often misguided notion that more is better, I added sky but realized the area of white cloud at the top of the image was too strong and carried the eye up and out of the image.

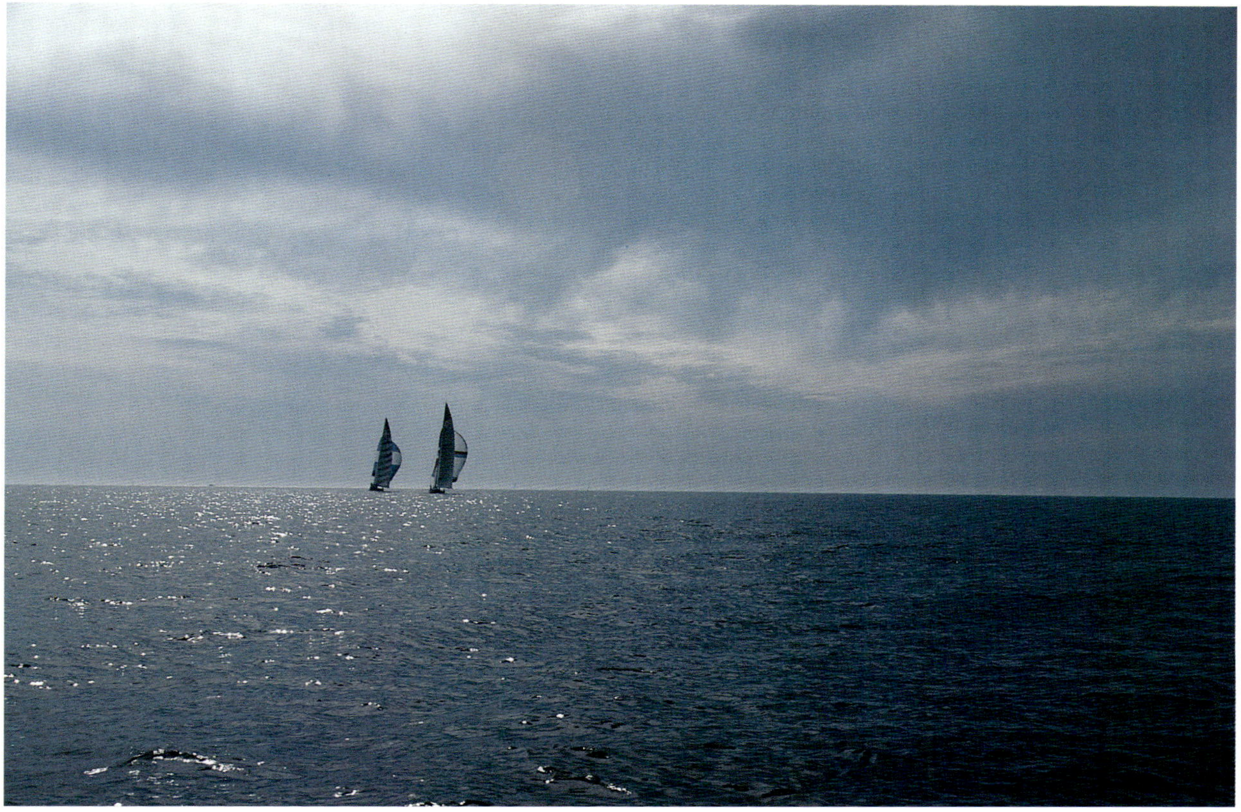

Balance

I went back to a horizontal format. Now the sharp line of contrast between the light and dark areas of the cloud at the top left carried the eye to the right into the strong, dark cloud mass and then down and back along the horizon line to the yachts. It was an image that satisfied me, so I moved on.

Reflections

A few moments later, I realized the sun's reflection playing on a wave close alongside, probably caused by the wake of our photo boat, had become the most powerful element of the composition, and I pointed the camera down to capture it. The sails were now in the sunshine, bringing a new element to the composition, but at this juncture some other action was calling.

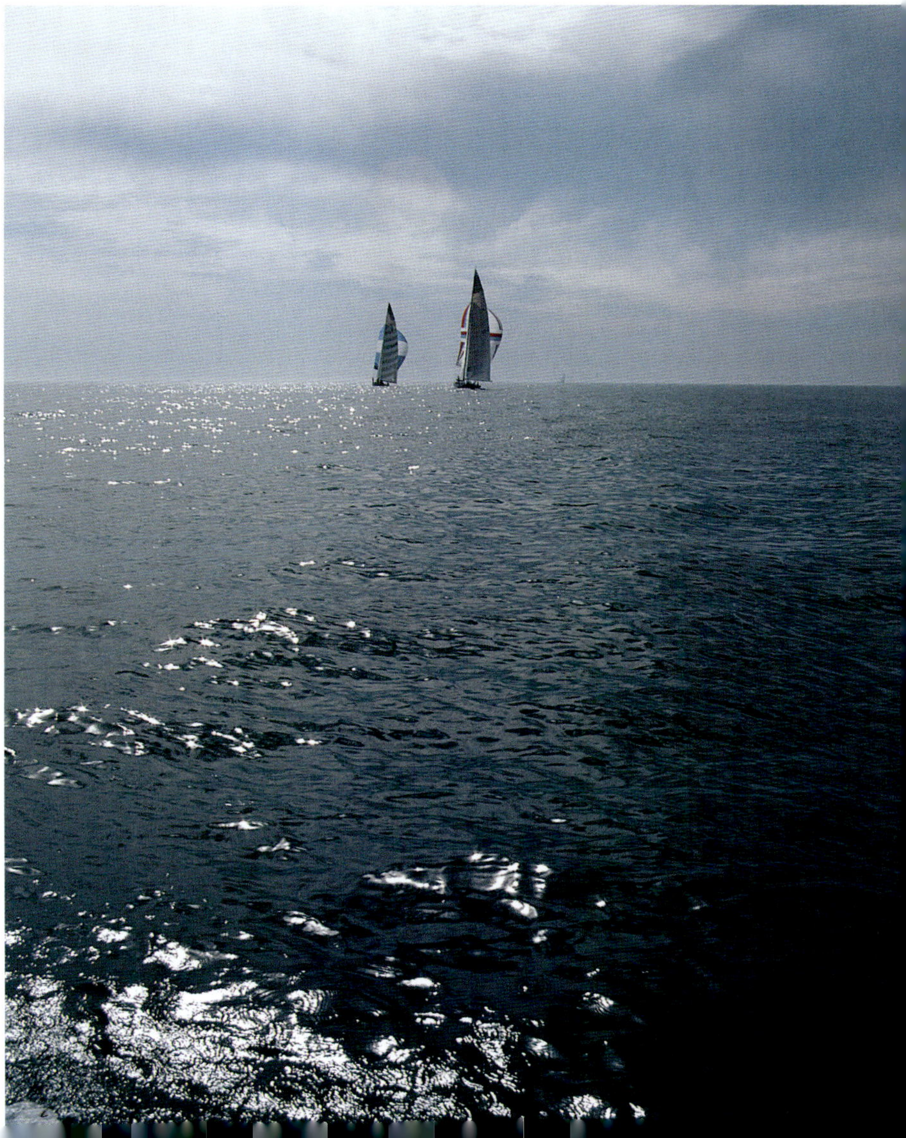

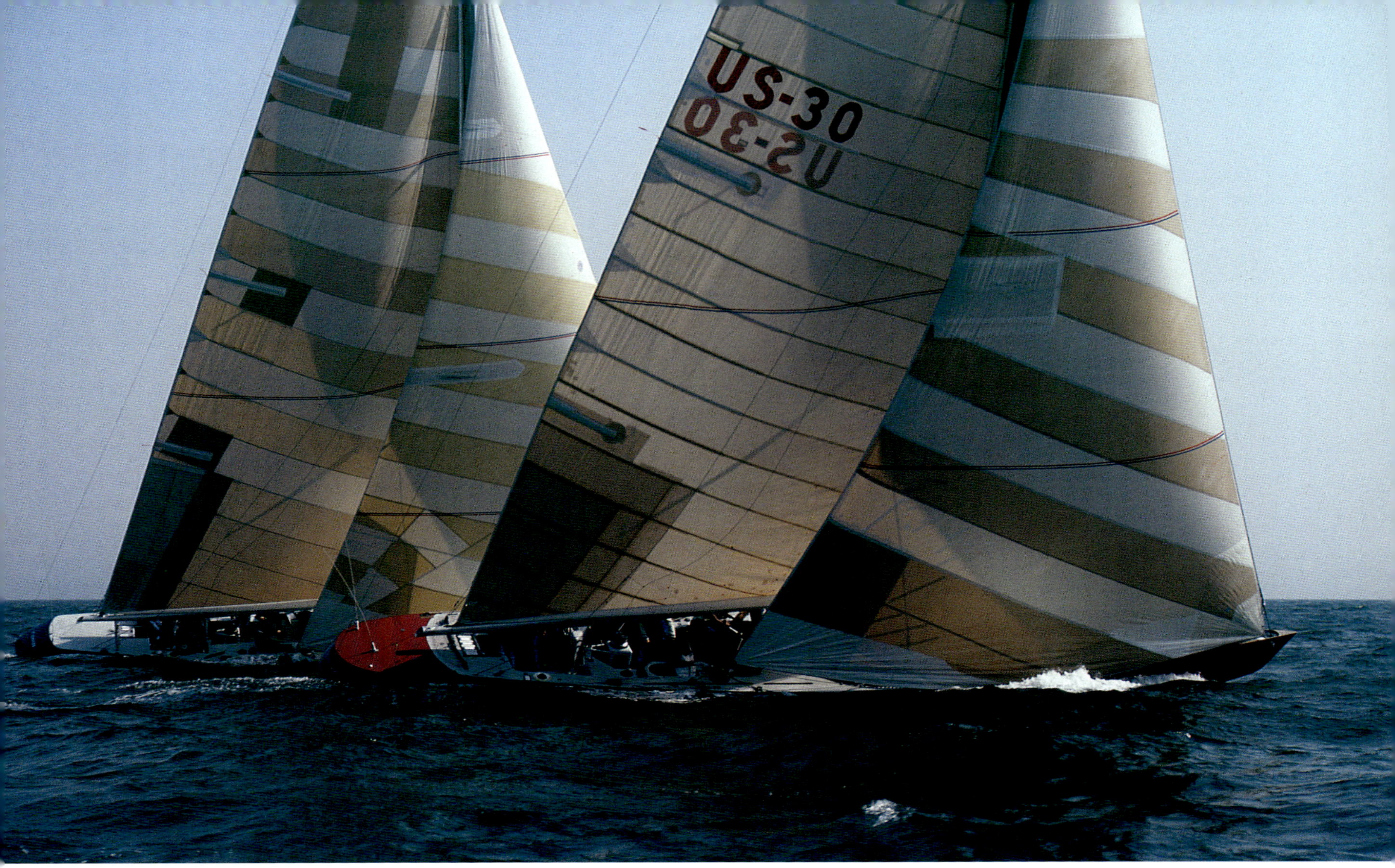
US-30

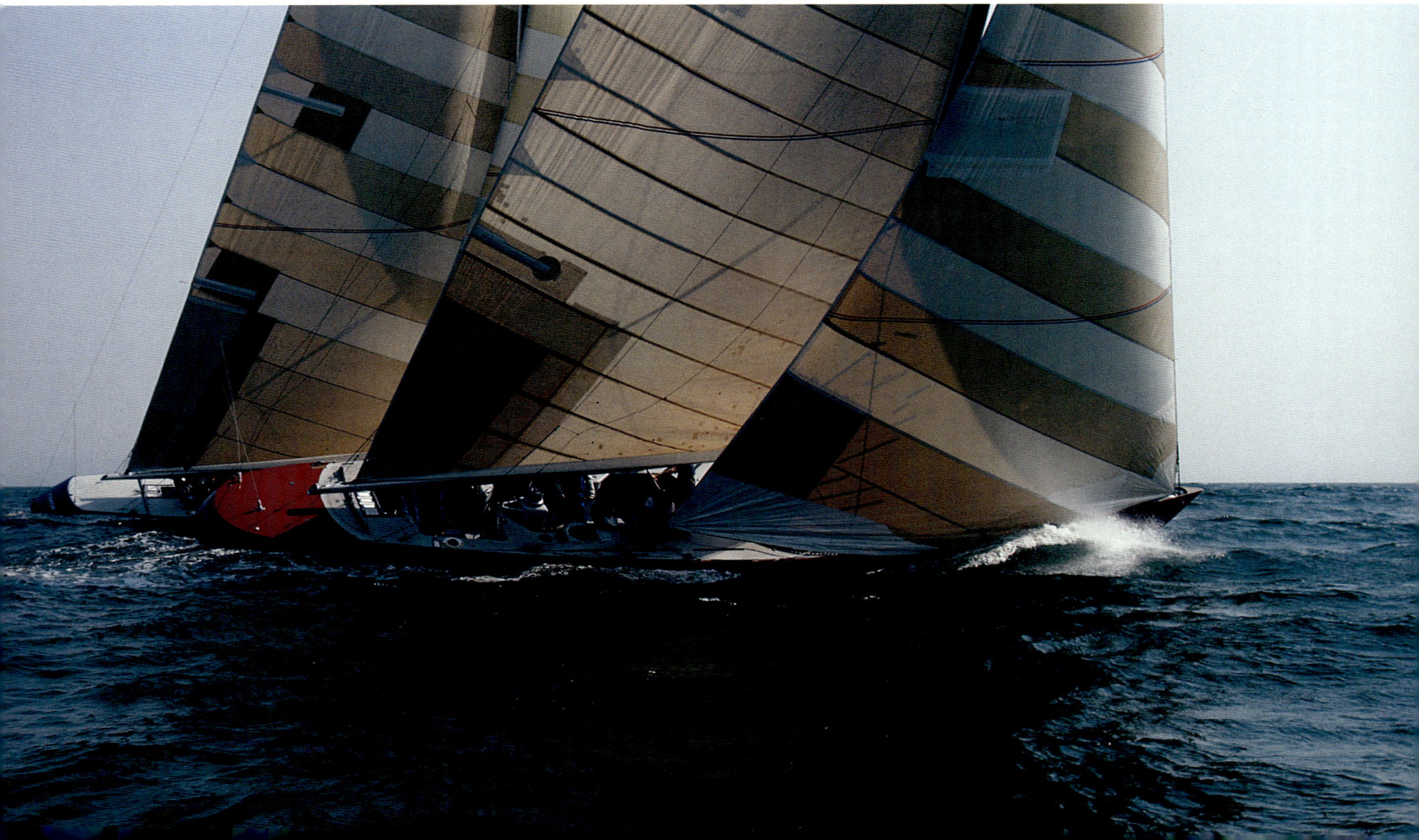

In 1983, the 12-meters carried their booms almost low enough to sweep the decks. The design may have enhanced sail performance, but it was unfortunate for the photographer. When the sails were trimmed and the yachts heeled on the wind, the low-cut mainsails obscured most of the action on deck, and very often the cockpit became a jumbled area without particular photographic interest. In the following sequence of 11 images, I worked with two cameras, and the images almost follow one another on the original film.

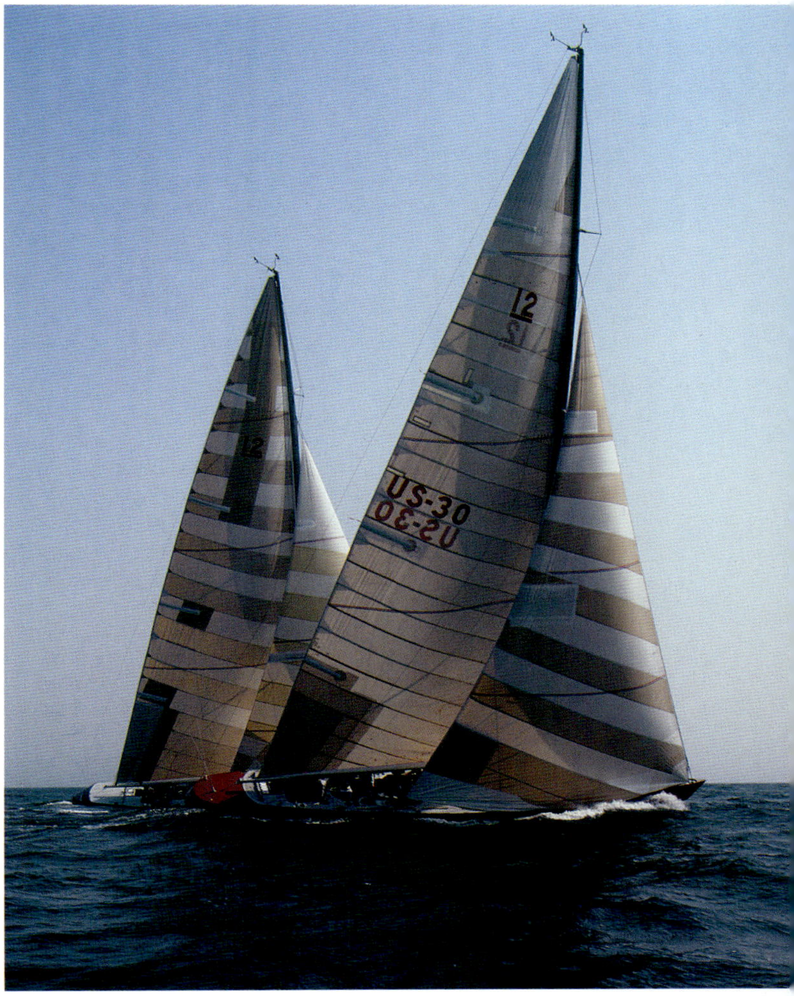

Low Booms

Opposite above, *Freedom* and *Liberty*, Dennis Conner's defender candidates, are trying out on the wind off Newport. We thought a lot about the sails when the defenders were on the wind in those days because the low-set booms and low-cut genoas almost sweeping the decks reduced the visual impact of cockpit action. *Liberty* in the foreground had been weaving in and out, either in response to shifting wind or in an effort to work the yacht forward. This weaving maneuver shows not only in the angle of the hull as it falls off in this photograph, but from the line of sunlight on the jib, starting just above the splash of white wake forward. The shadow line rises to the leech of the jib just above the first dark double line that stretches across the sail.

Line of Shadow

Liberty is now pointing higher, shown not only by its heading and the splash of white wake, but also by the line of shadow on the jib, which rises from the white water at the bow up to the leech again. This time the shadow is higher by more than a width and a half of sailcloth.

Seascape

When we move from the previous closeup to a view that encompasses all of the yachts and the sky and water around them, I feel a difference in the way the action in the image affects me. It may be a psychological overtone indicating we have moved into the classical format that I associate with a seascape. The character of the image changes from action to something else, and when I compose such a photograph I resonate to a different tuning fork within. Could it be that long after my father died, I still think of this image — seascape with yachts — as my father's? Sunlight falls on the sails at the optimum angle. I see a touch of sunlight along the luff of the genoa and mainsail; then just aft, a shadow line in the depth of the sails; and, finally, sunlight coming through each sail, showing the texture of the cloth. Countless possibilities abound for photographic images afloat, but somehow, in my mind, this one style still belongs to my father.

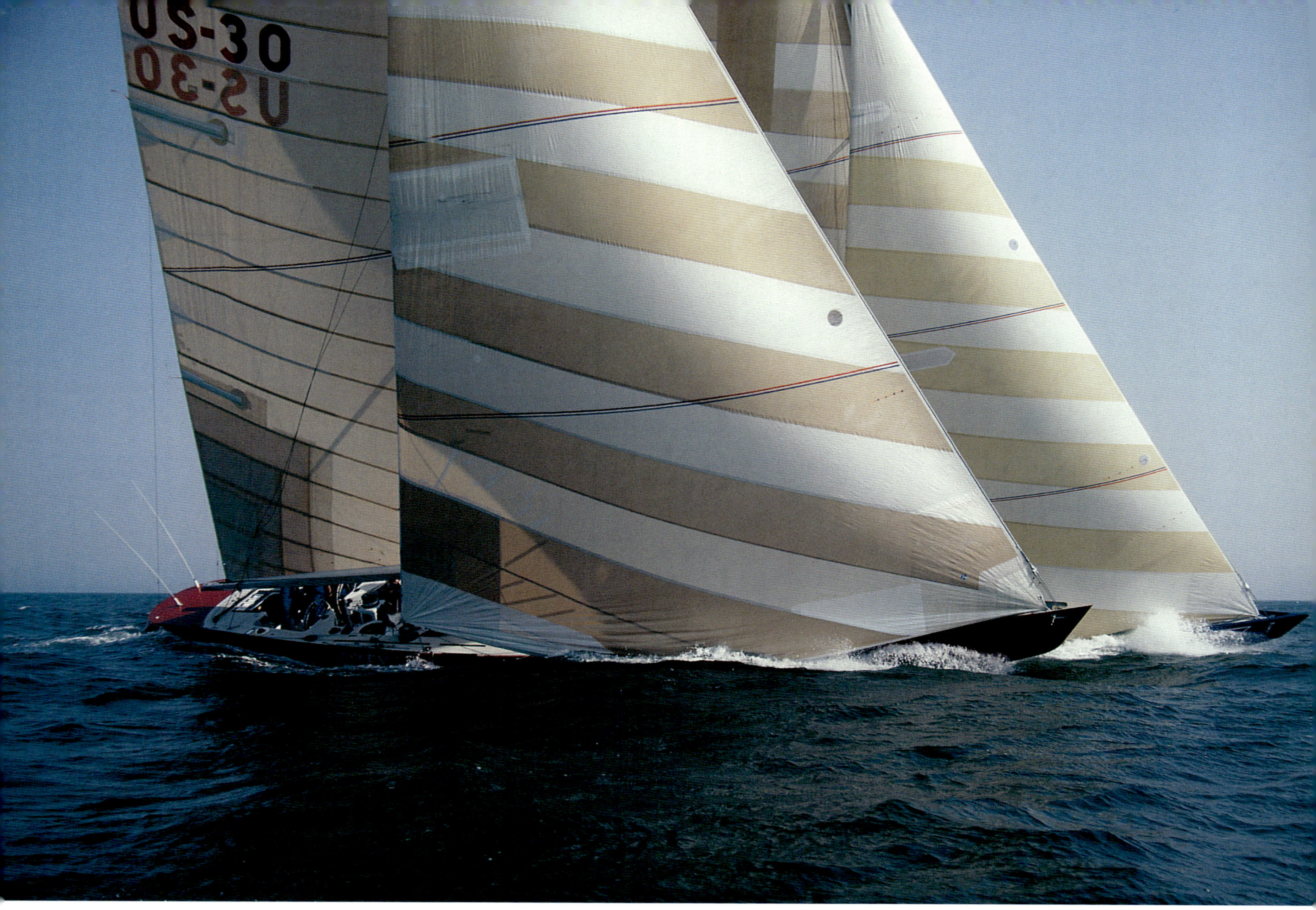

Designs in Sailcloth

In the 1983 America's Cup series, new designs in sailcloth were the fashion. Their properties as structural members were subtle, but their appearance was bold, perhaps brassy, to a taste honed on the gentle variations in cotton. *Liberty* and *Freedom* present the horizontal style of sailcloth in vogue in 1983. Formerly, the bows and bow waves would have been the key elements in this image, but now the sails fought for attention.

Geometry in Sails

In 1983, I was seventy years old and had spent a good part of those years afloat with a camera. Here was a new image with a new visual balance. The geometry of sailcloth suddenly was overwhelming. Before, I sought to find the texture of sailcloth in its subtlety, backlit; now the cloth itself dominated the stage.

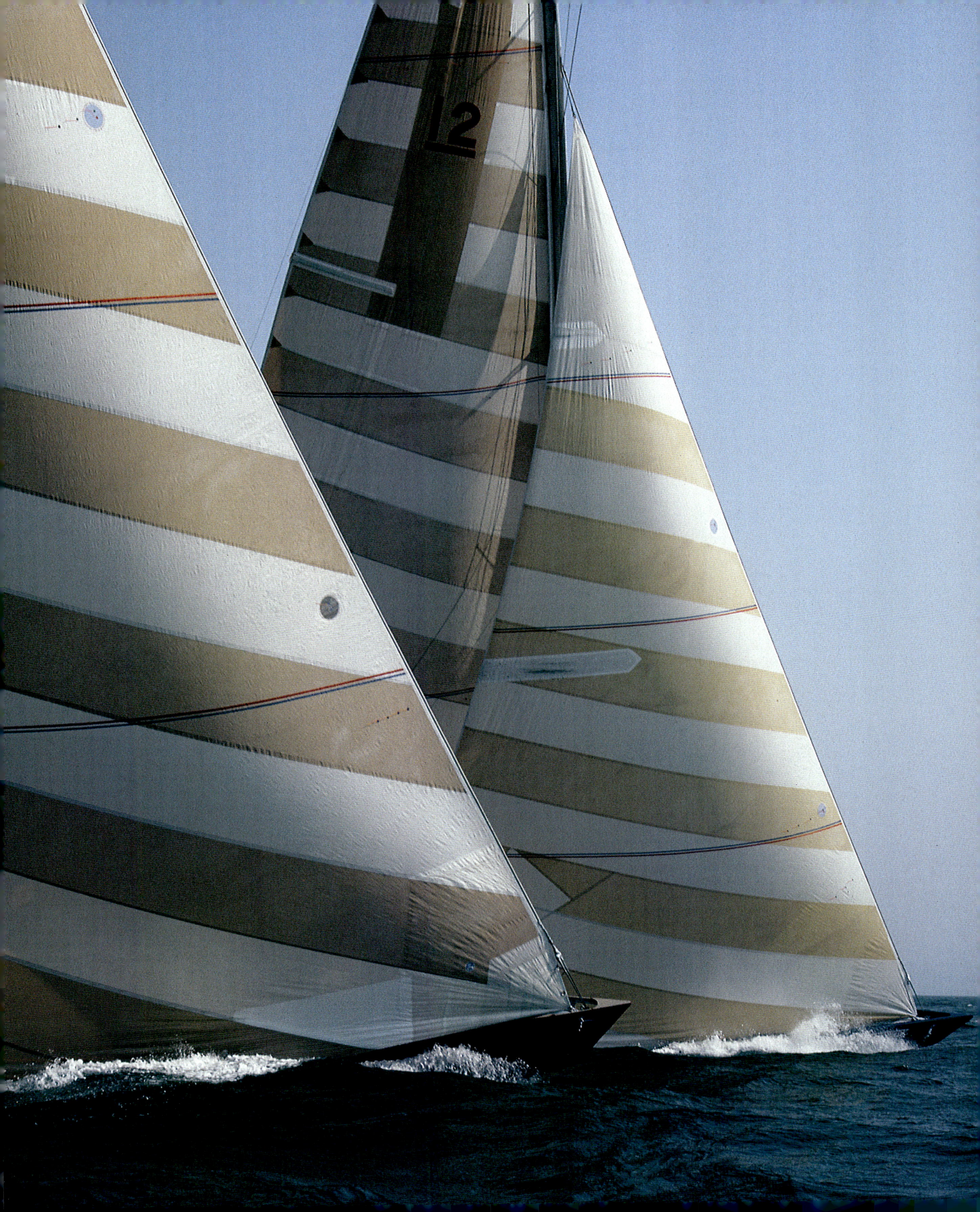
12

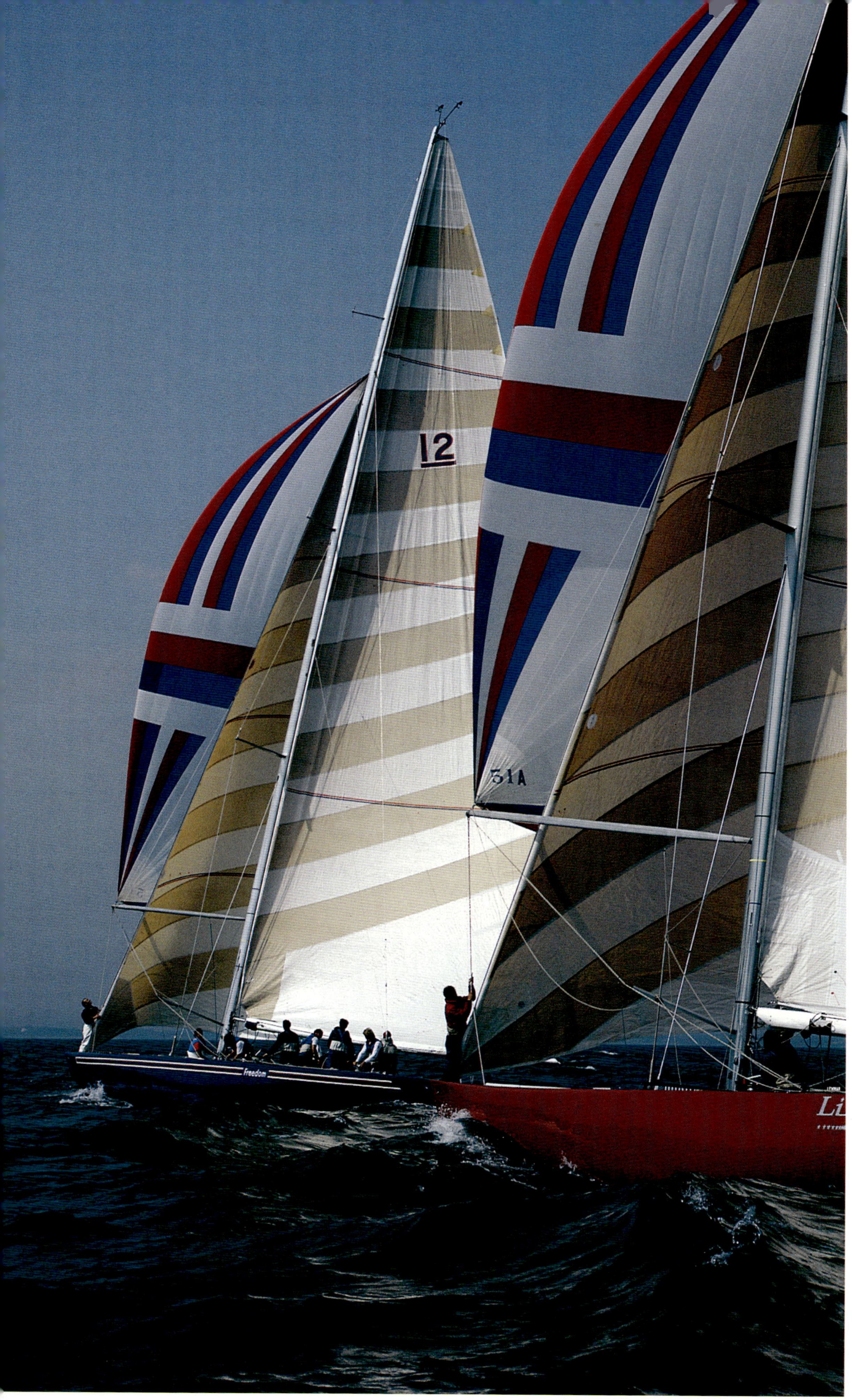

Colorful Cloth

The 12-meters *Freedom* and *Liberty* carry their colorful new array of synthetic sailcloth: red, white, and blue nylon spinnakers in taut curves, Kevlar and Mylar genoas and mainsails in golden stripes reaching boldly into a new era. The two yachts approach the leeward mark and, on the foredeck at the stem of each, the bowman is set to release the spinnaker.

Posture

Opposite above, when the 12s competed against each other, we had to be aware of the body language of the crew. The keenness found in an actual contest on the course was not always reflected in the experienced crew's posture, even when there was action in sail handling. As the spinnaker drops, most of the crew are standing and relaxed, apparently uninvolved.

Uninvolved

Opposite below, an instant later, in a more meaningful storytelling moment for the camera, tension shows in the skipper's body and in most of the crew; not, however, in the body of the man in blue and white standing nearest the stern. He is the non-working crew member, invited to sail aboard in recognition of financial, familial, or other support. He is there just for the ride and is obvious in the role. Note his uninvolved position in the previous image. Avoid him, my camera counseled.

In this series of three photographs, sunlight is reflected off the Mylar film in *Liberty*'s new sails and shows their form in a new light. For years, I had avoided photographing the sunlit side of a sail because it was usually just a dominant white blob. Now it had become a graphic source of design and performance information.

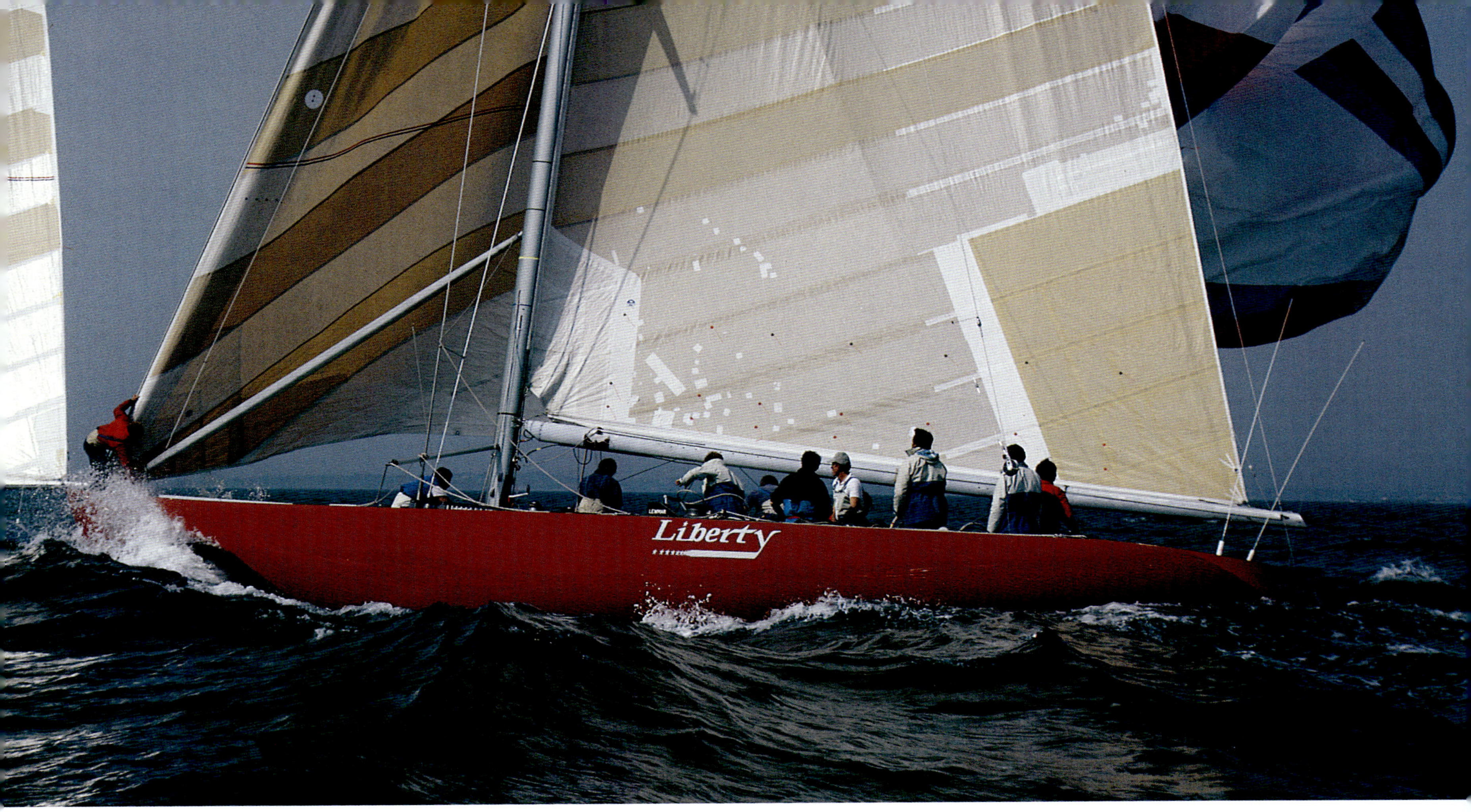
Liberty

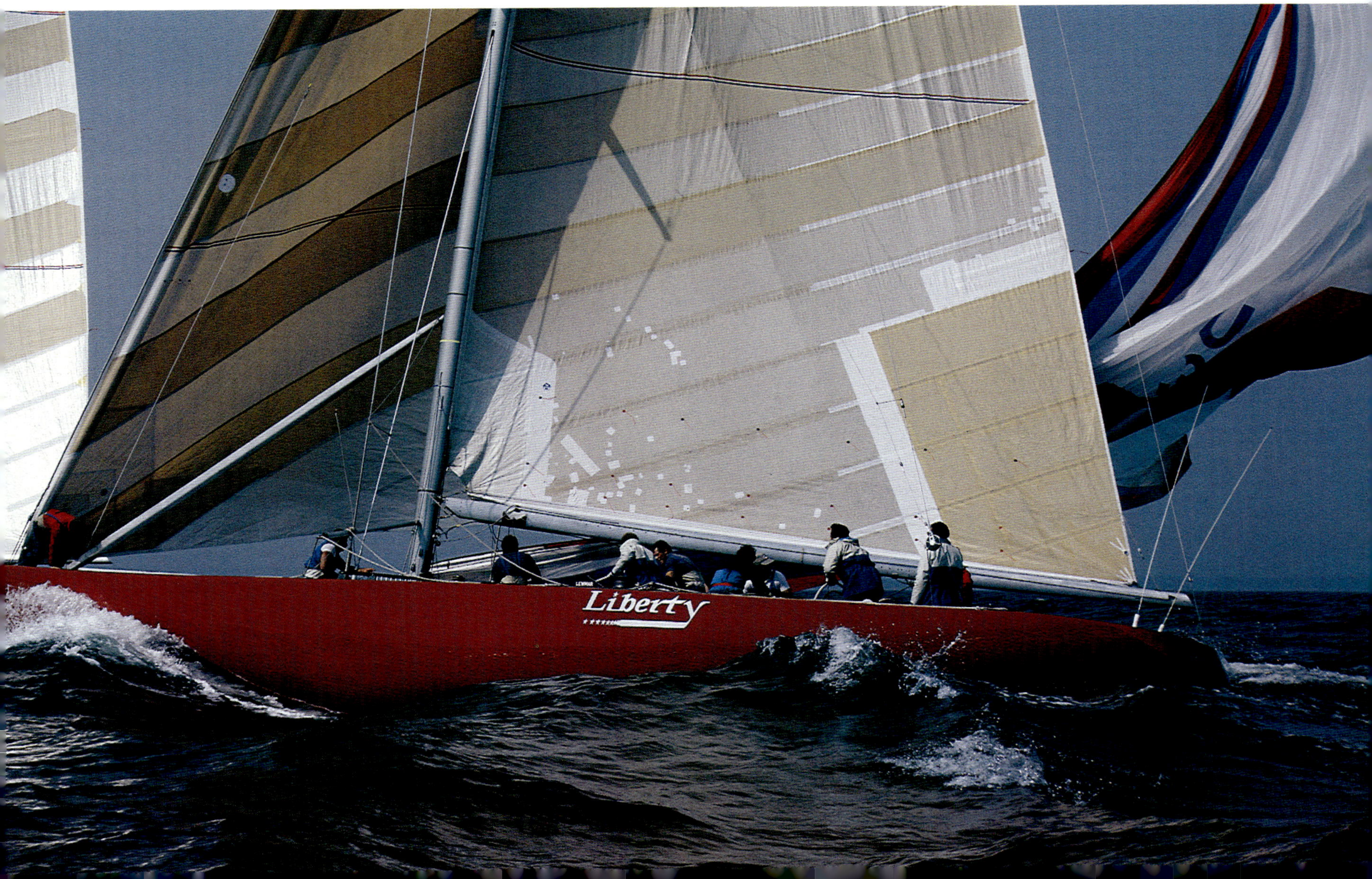
Liberty

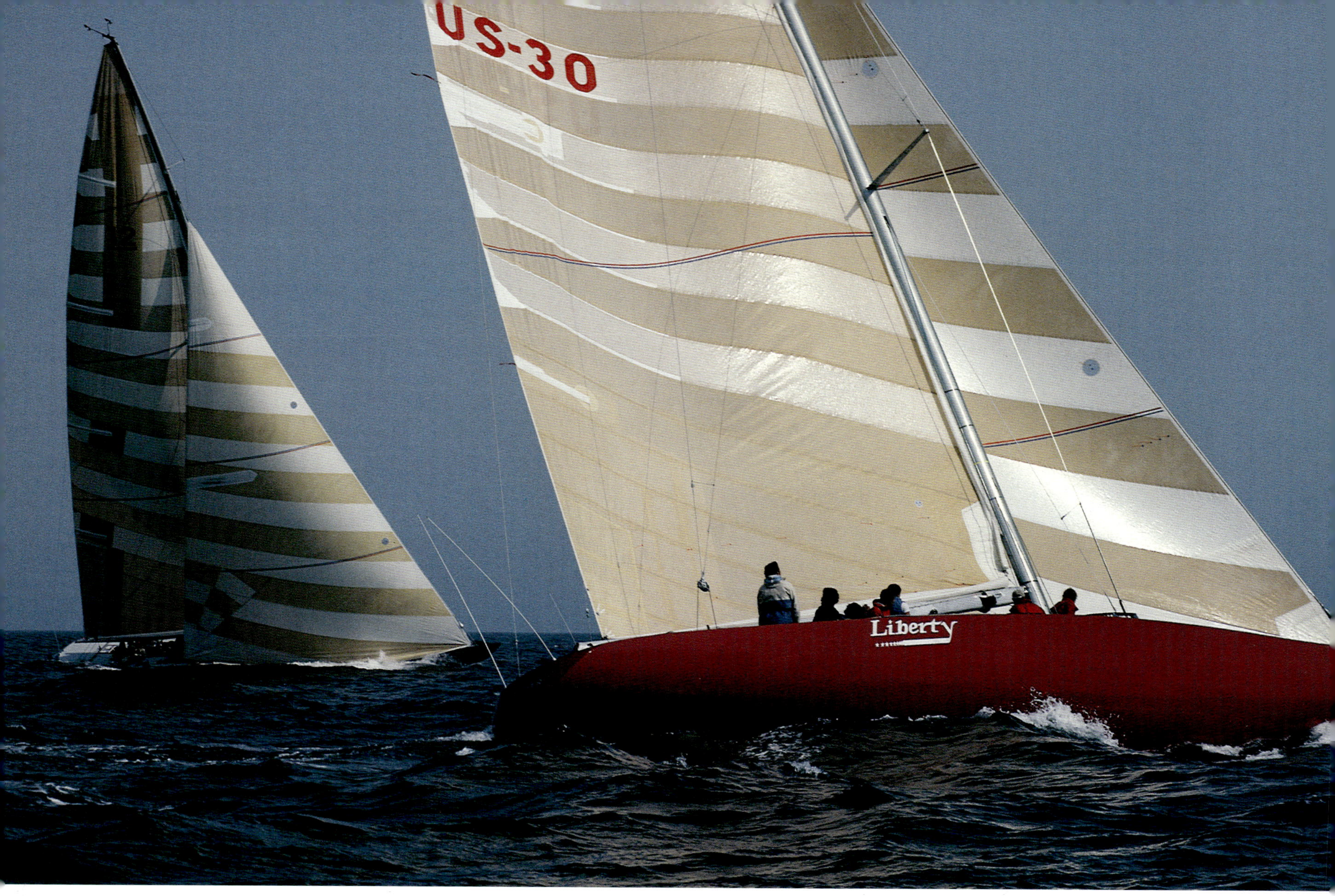

The seams of the new sailcloth clearly show with their curves how the sail is drawing. The cloth was designed to give strength and form to the sails, but in addition the sails gave a new dimension to the photographer.

Crossing Tacks

Freedom on port tack sails toward *Liberty* on starboard. The crossing-tacks situation always held the possibility of a dramatic photograph. A sense of danger spiced the crossing lines of hulls and masts.

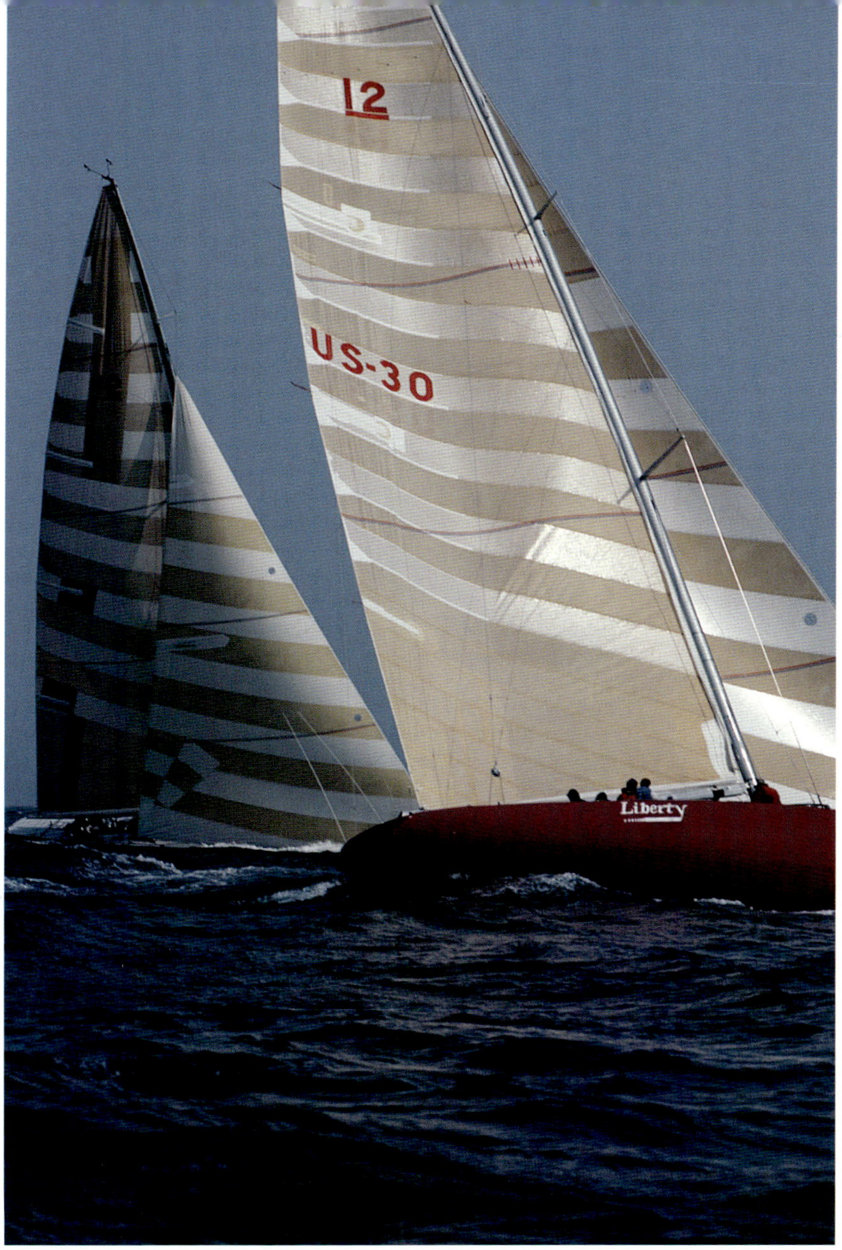

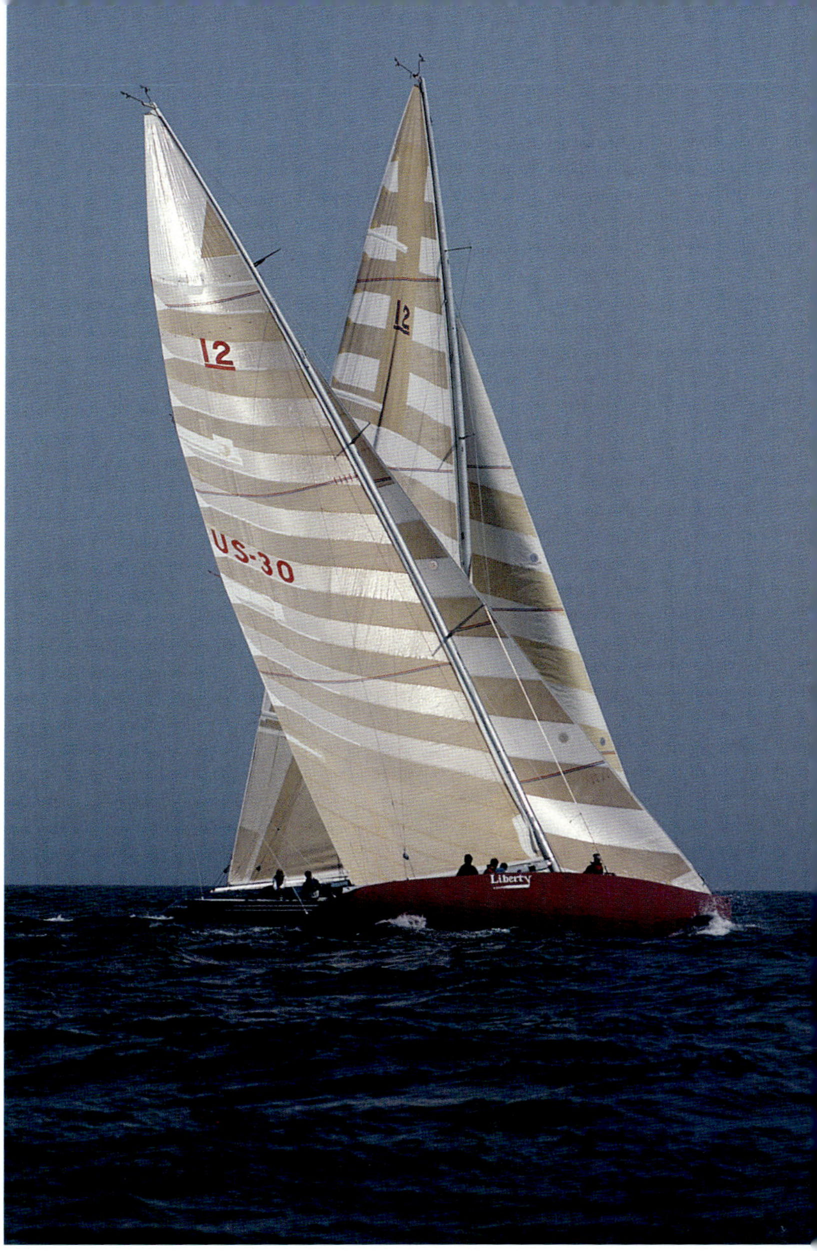

Collision Course

As *Freedom*, to the left, approaches the moment of crossing, we wonder if she can make it across *Liberty*'s bow. The luff noticeable in *Liberty*'s mainsail shows that skipper Dennis Conner is pointing very high, making *Freedom*'s crossing more questionable. The two yachts are on a collision course. After many long years covering these yachts, would it be surprising that the news photographer always present in me, though not intrusive, might on a rare occasion think: if they continue on course, there may be a dramatic collision photo and where should I be to get it?

Backwinded

At the last moment, *Freedom* tacks to get to leeward and ahead of *Liberty*. *Liberty* will be backwinded and forced to tack away. We are keeping the photo boat astern to be clear when she tacks.

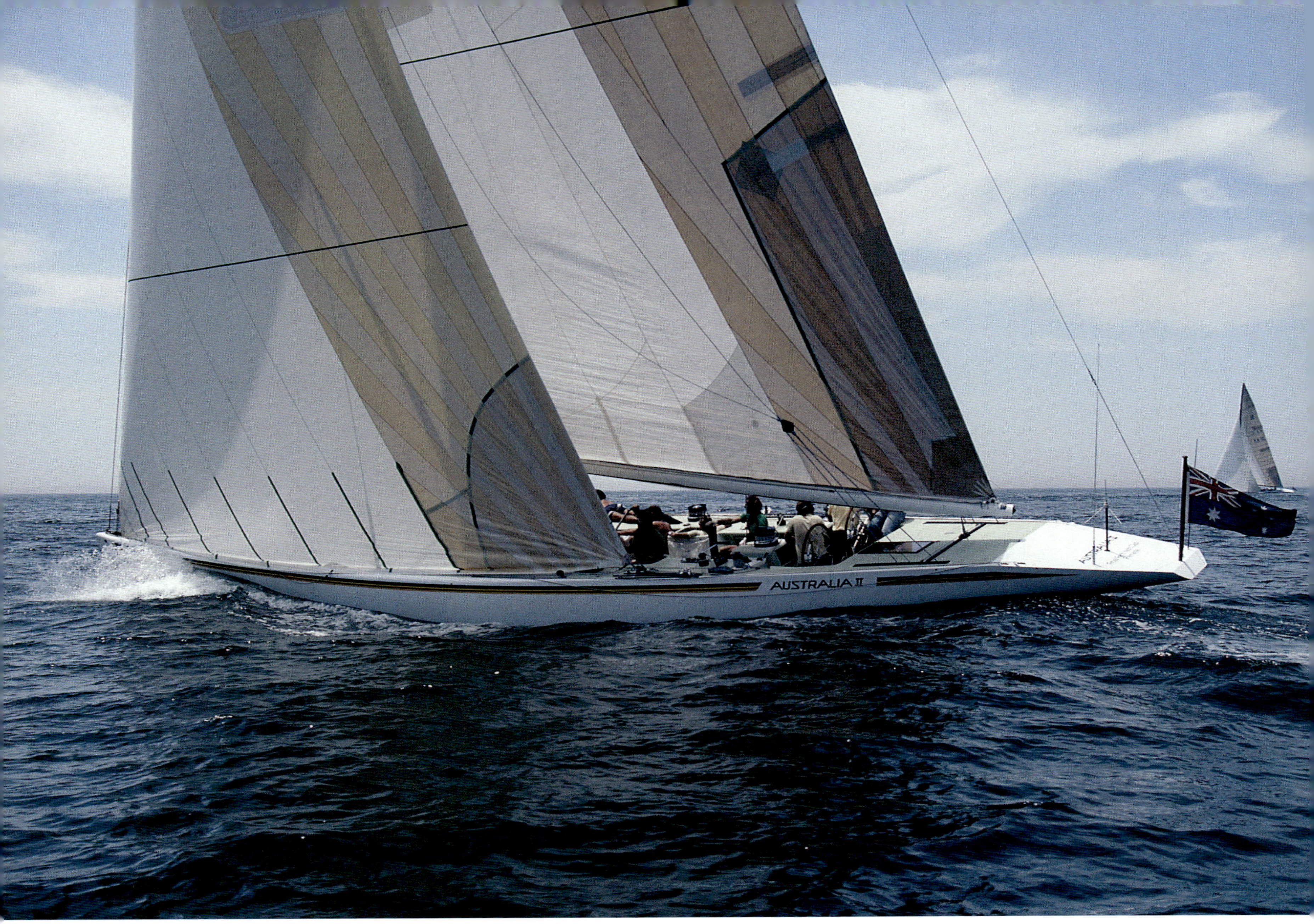

Bow Burying

The challenger in 1983 was *Australia II*, rumored to have fascinating innovations in her keel. More important for photography, her boom was higher off her deck than *Liberty*'s. As a consequence, when the boat was heeling, I could see the crew in action or, in this instance, standing by for action. One characteristic of *Australia II*'s behavior was the frequency with which her bow seemed to bury in the smallest wave, a stance that robbed the hull of its sense of power.

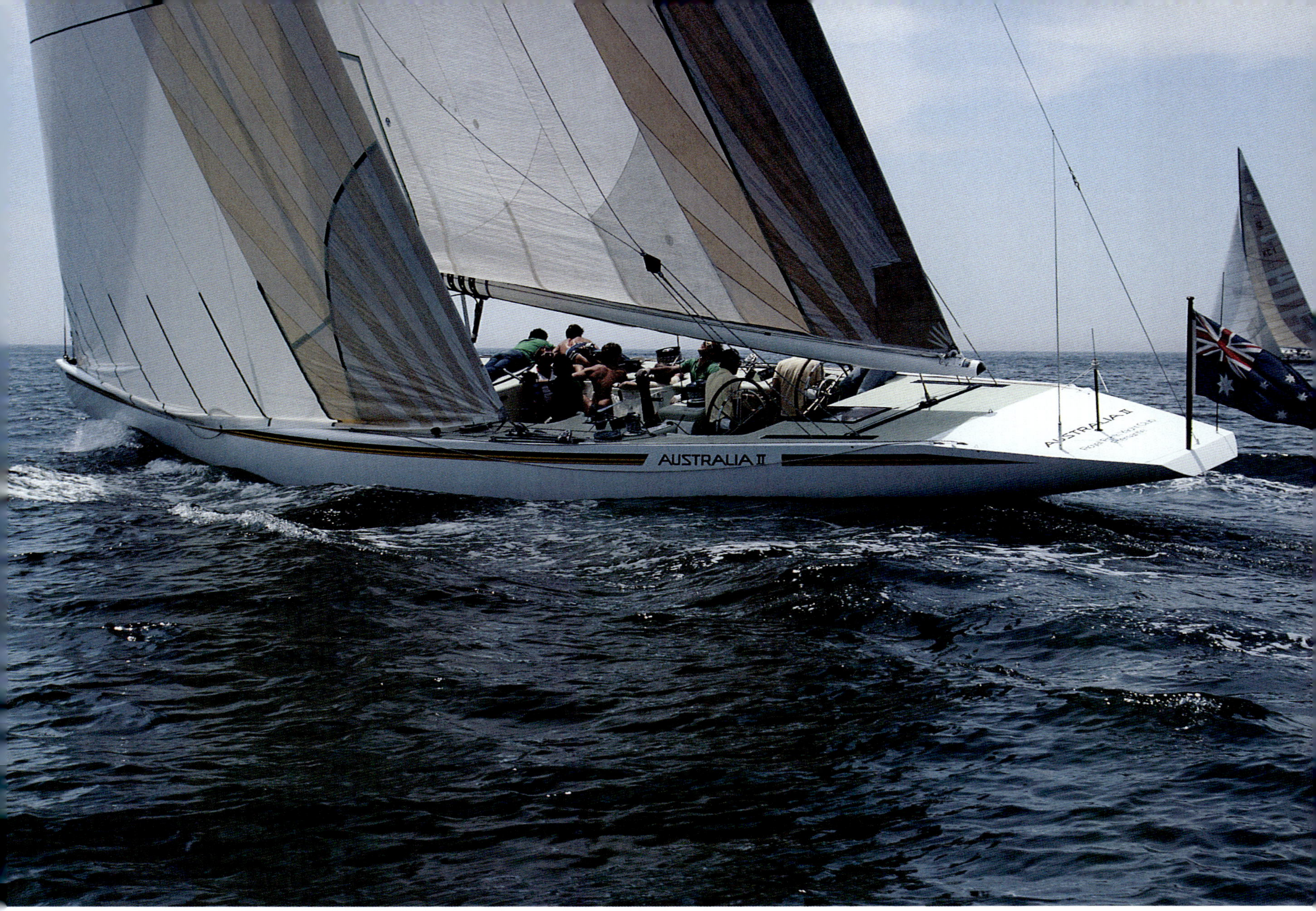

Bow Lifting

To photograph the hull of *Australia II* and provide it with the power latent in its lines, I had to show the bow lifting, with the long, low hull reaching out and aggressive in the water.

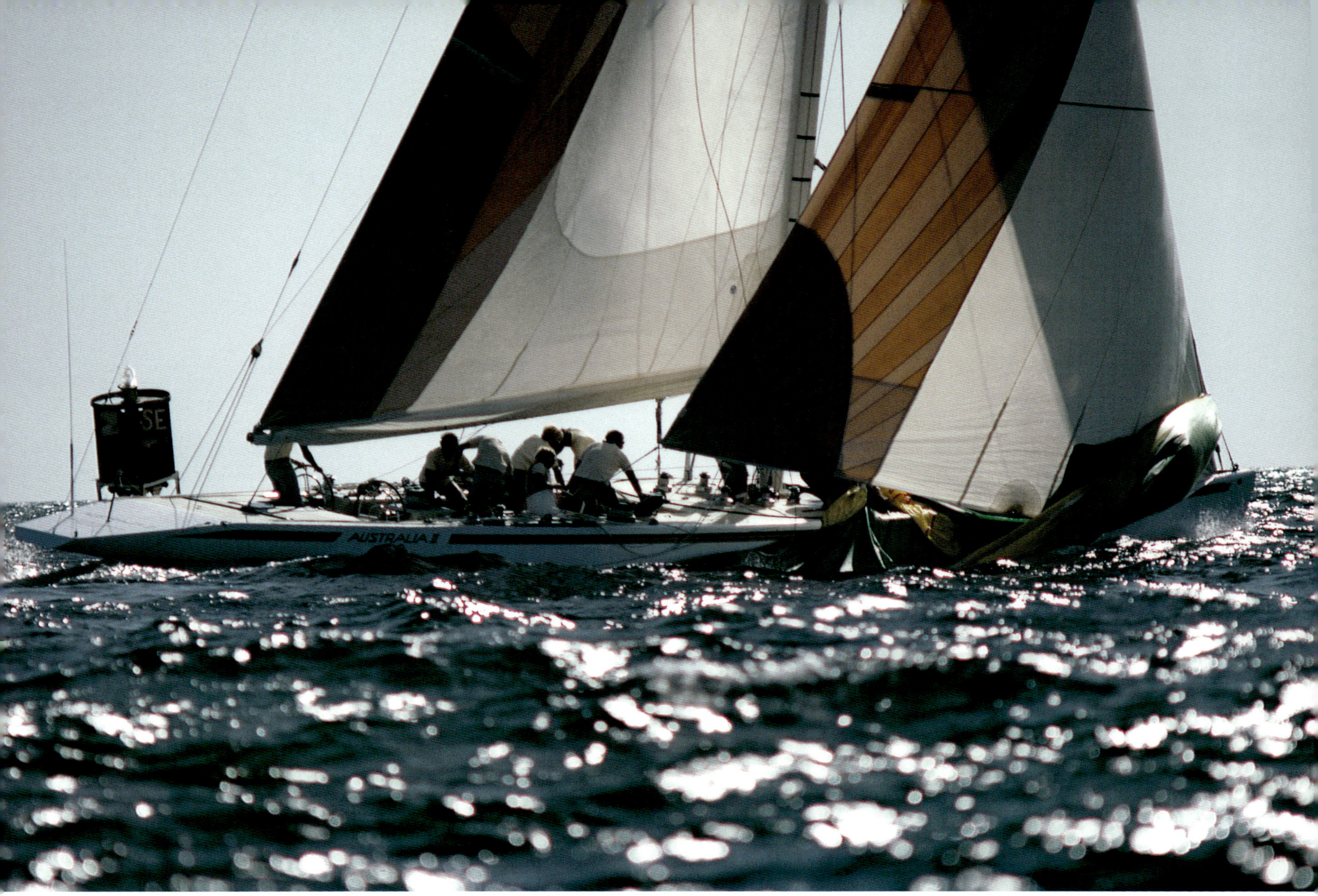

Tending Sheets

Australia II rounds the leeward buoy and, in the process of dousing her jib and trimming sail, the crew stands boldly above the line of the deck, working winches and tending sheets with arms and bodies extended upward. The bow of the yacht is also lifting, with the tip of the stem touching the horizon. This was a harbinger of the way hull forms were developing, with only as much above the water as absolutely necessary and weight kept low down in the keel.

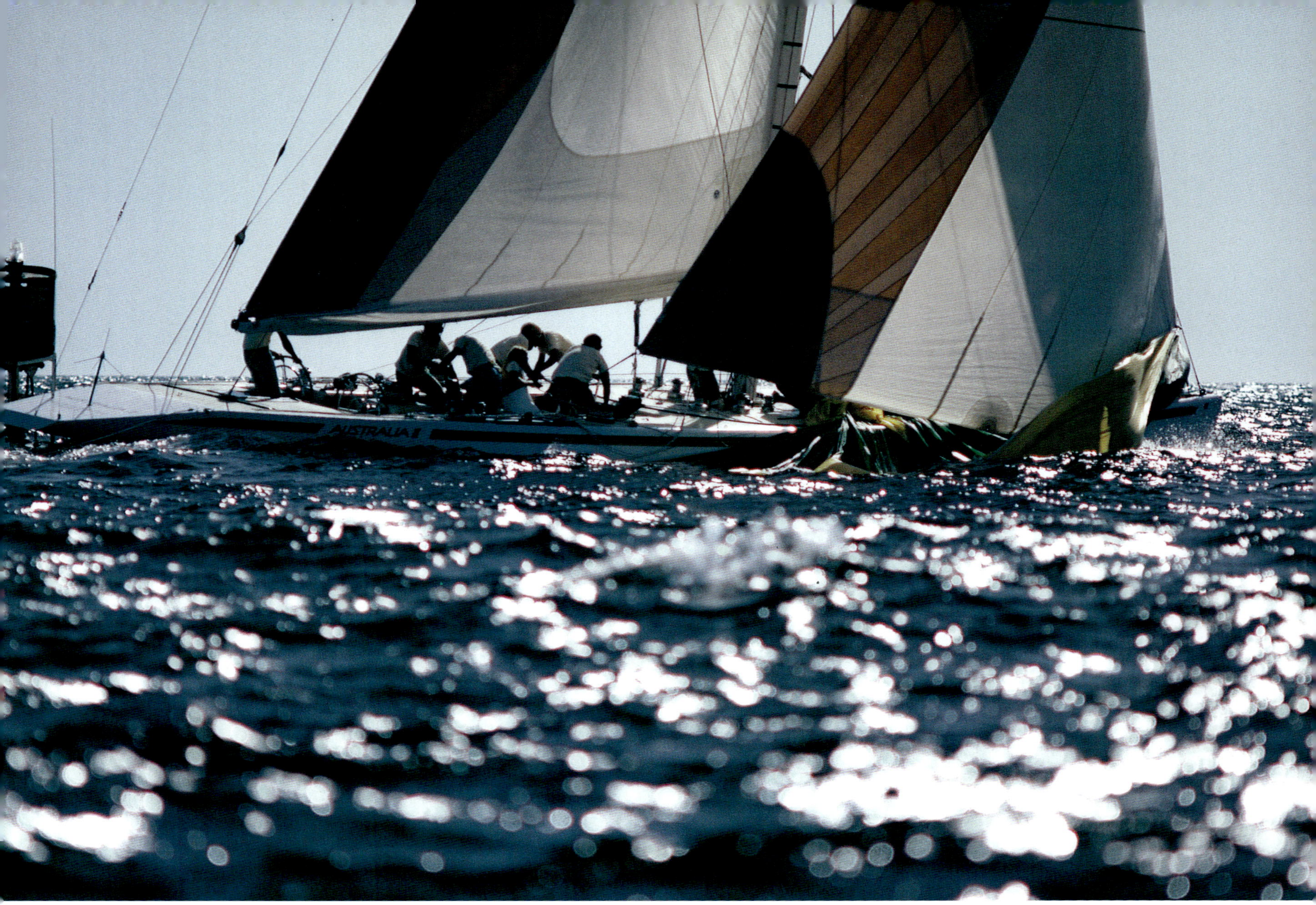

A Different Story

A short second later, the slightly different image tells me a different story. At first glance, the balance of sky, yacht, and water is more powerful. The waterline is higher, and the added mass of the foreground lends a significant power to the image. I thought of this as an improvement at first, but the large white area of reflected sunlight in the lower right corner diverts the eye too strongly and leads away from the storytelling action in the cockpit. Further, the crew's action, though perhaps more organized, has less thrust and power. The same is true of the lines of the hull. If I glanced at the two images, I would at first favor the second; after studying them, I would select the first and lay the second aside.

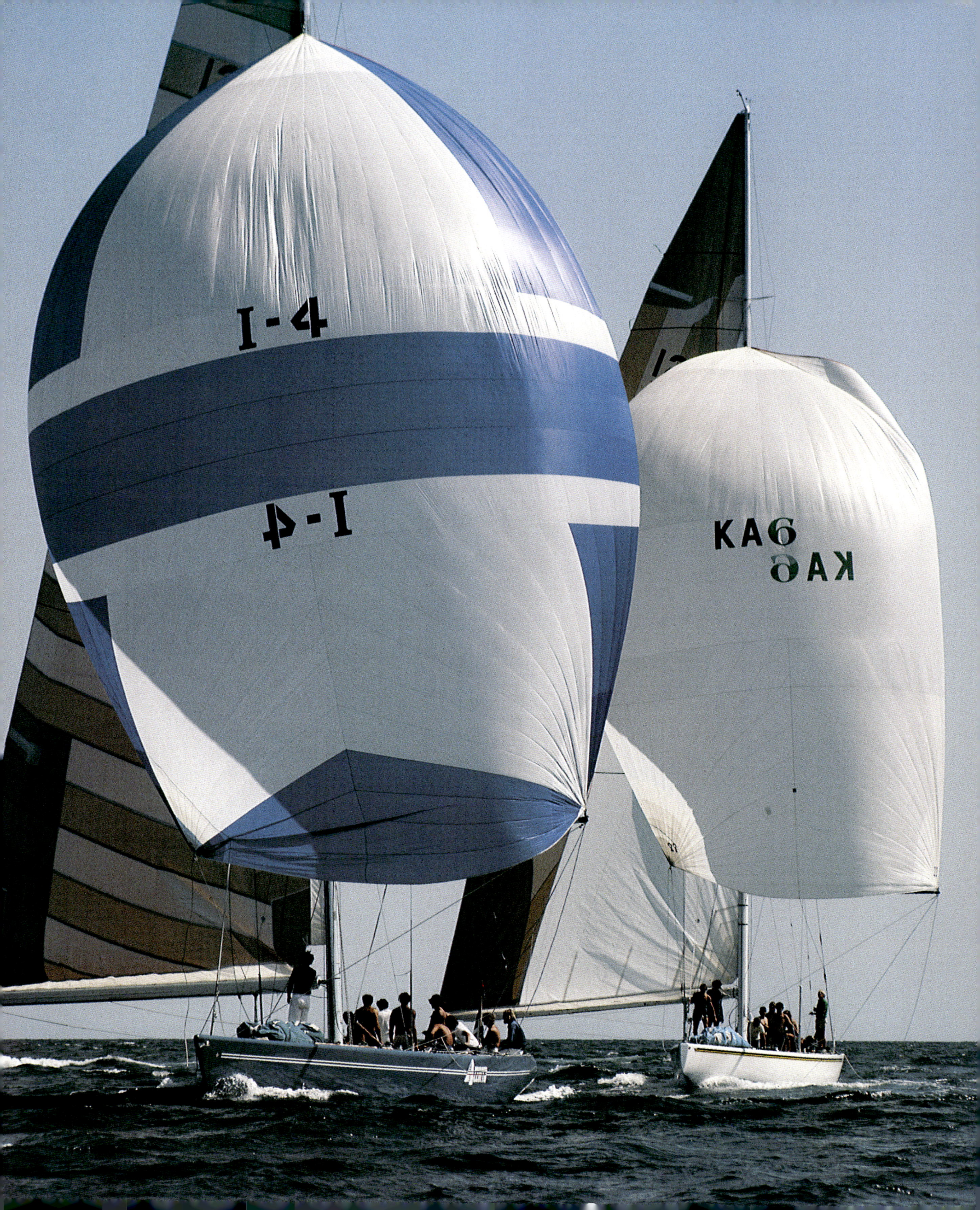
I-4
KA6

Trying Sails

Opposite, at the end of August 1983, I came across *Azzurra* and *Australia II*, sailing in toward Newport in a stately procession under spinnakers. I continued following them, and it wasn't until a sail change and a regrouping that I realized *Australia II* was trying sails, practicing the downwind overtaking and passing of *Azzurra*.

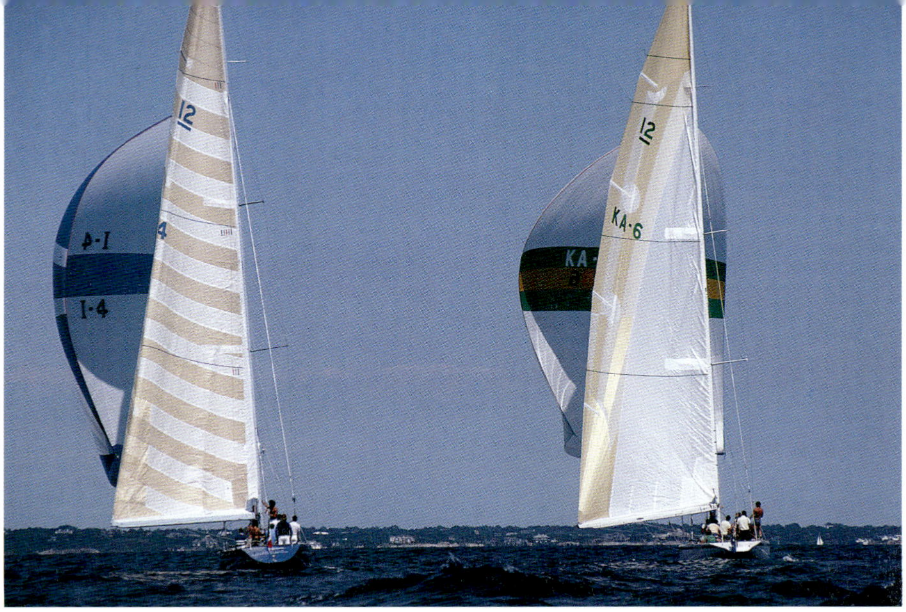

Australia II, on the right, is sailing higher than *Azzurra*.

The three photographs to the right show one of a series of maneuvers by *Australia II* to overtake and pass *Azzurra* on a downwind leg. Each time this sequence was repeated, *Australia II* came up to and passed *Azzurra*. It was a practice session that foretold *Australia II*'s critical seventh leg of her final America's Cup race against *Liberty*. On that crucial leg, Conner, ahead, split tacks and left *Australia II* with a long, clear, unchallenged run for the mark. To what extent her practice against *Azzurra* in the previous days contributed to her new-found speed we may never know, but *Australia II* sailed fast enough to round the mark ahead of *Liberty* with a clear beat to the finish line and victory. These three images that show *Australia II* practicing against *Azzurra* send a prescient message.

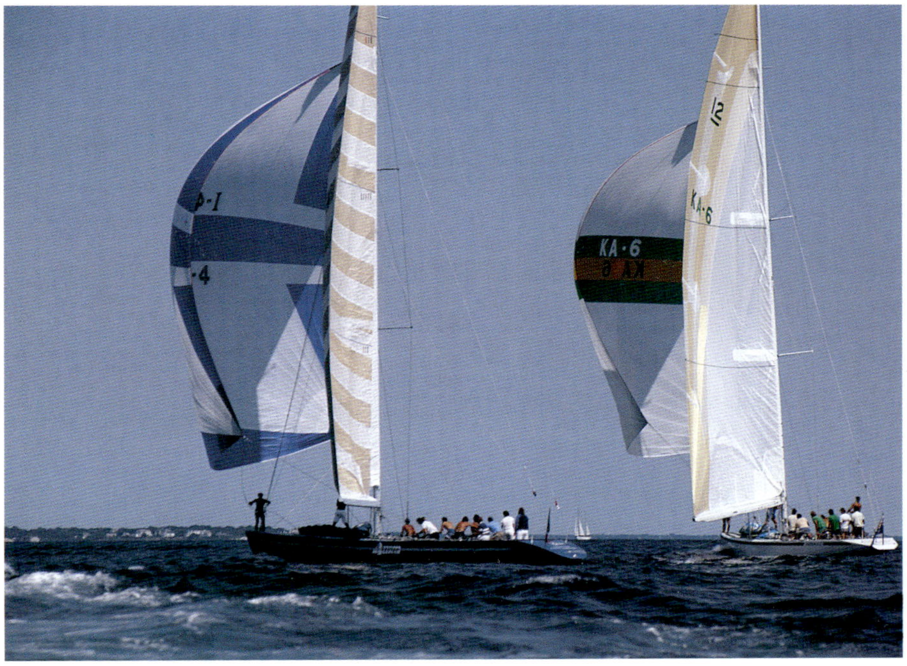

Now *Australia II* prepares to jibe.

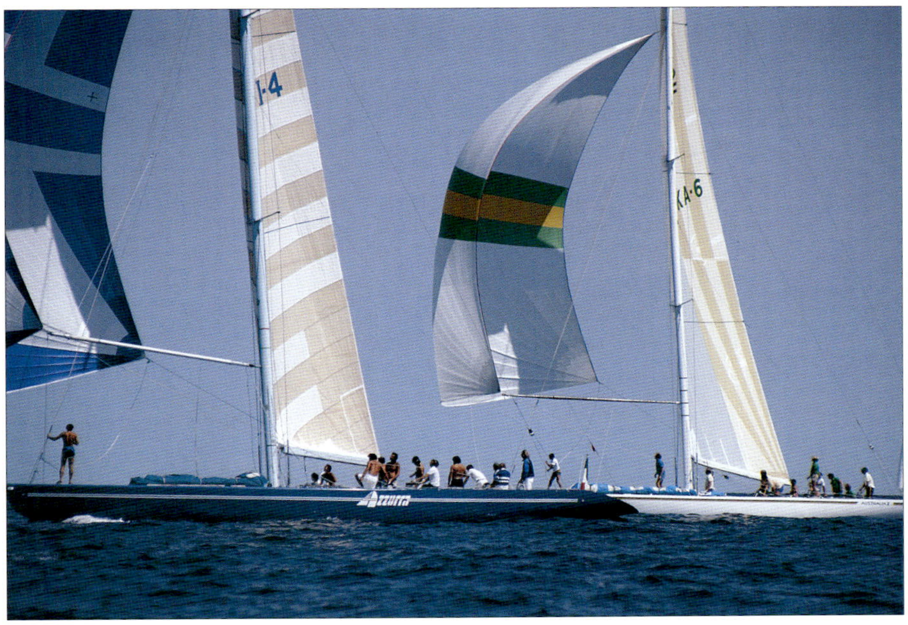

Both vessels have jibed and *Australia II* is overlapping.

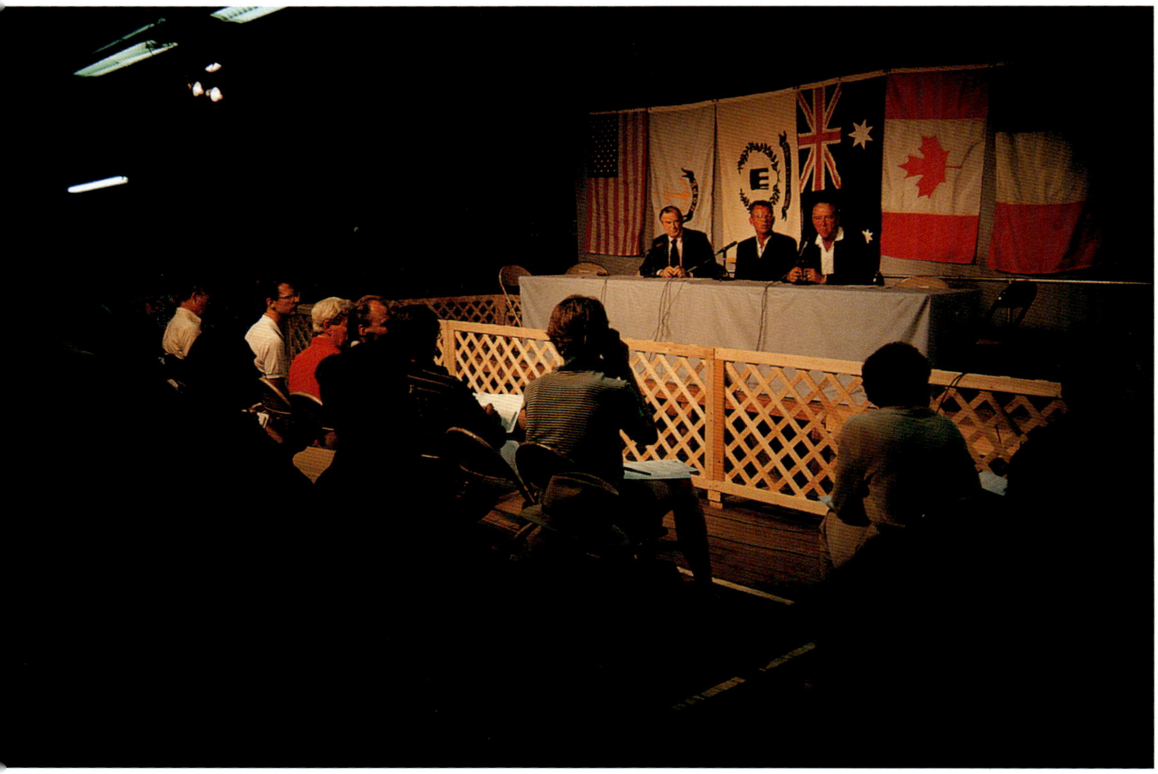

Post-Race Conference

Not all contests between the 1983 America's Cup challengers and defenders were fought on the racecourse. As the season progressed, at nightly post-race conferences, members of the press asked questions, heard charges, and saw sparks fly.

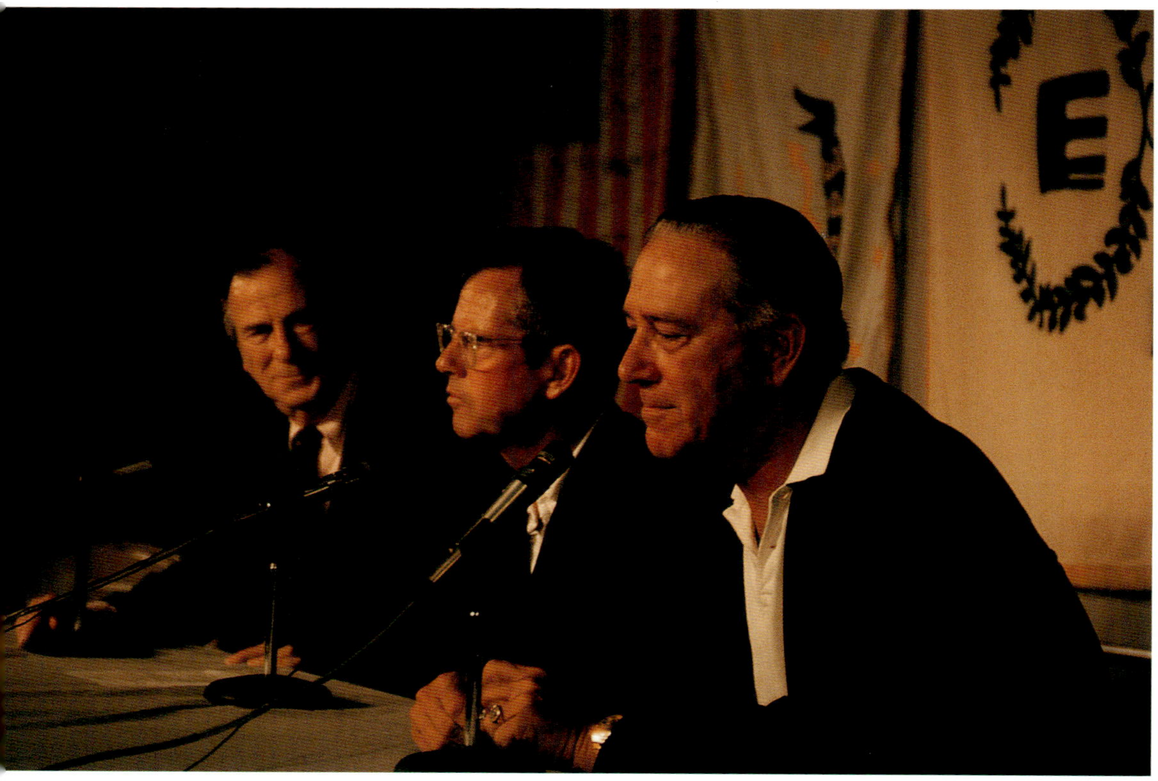

Tension

A sense of the tension enveloping the men on the podium shows in this session. Leonard Panaggio, the moderator, is on the left. Commodore Stone, in the center, and Commodore McCullough, both of the New York Yacht Club, face a particularly probing question. The New York Yacht Club was at a delicate moment in the season. It was generally known that *Australia II* had a new and different configuration in its keel, and questions arose about the legality of this innovation. Here, as they field provocative questions from the press, the New York Yacht Club representatives reveal tension, as well as partly hidden frustration and hostility.

Body Language

Tension is also shown here in the posture of Alan Bond, owner of *Australia II*, and Warren Jones, the syndicate spokesman: note their hands, their lips, their eyes, and the thrust of their heads. A year previously, at a press conference during the Clipper Cup races in Hawaii, Bond had made a very thorough and thoughtful analysis of the state of design development in the 12-meter class. He said the American sailors were so experienced that the only way a challenger could ever win the Cup was with some innovative design feature providing an advantage in speed or maneuverability. Now, a year later, his yacht apparently had such a design feature, and questions were raised about where the new design and technology had been born and developed. The rules governing the America's Cup races required that design originate in the challenging country.

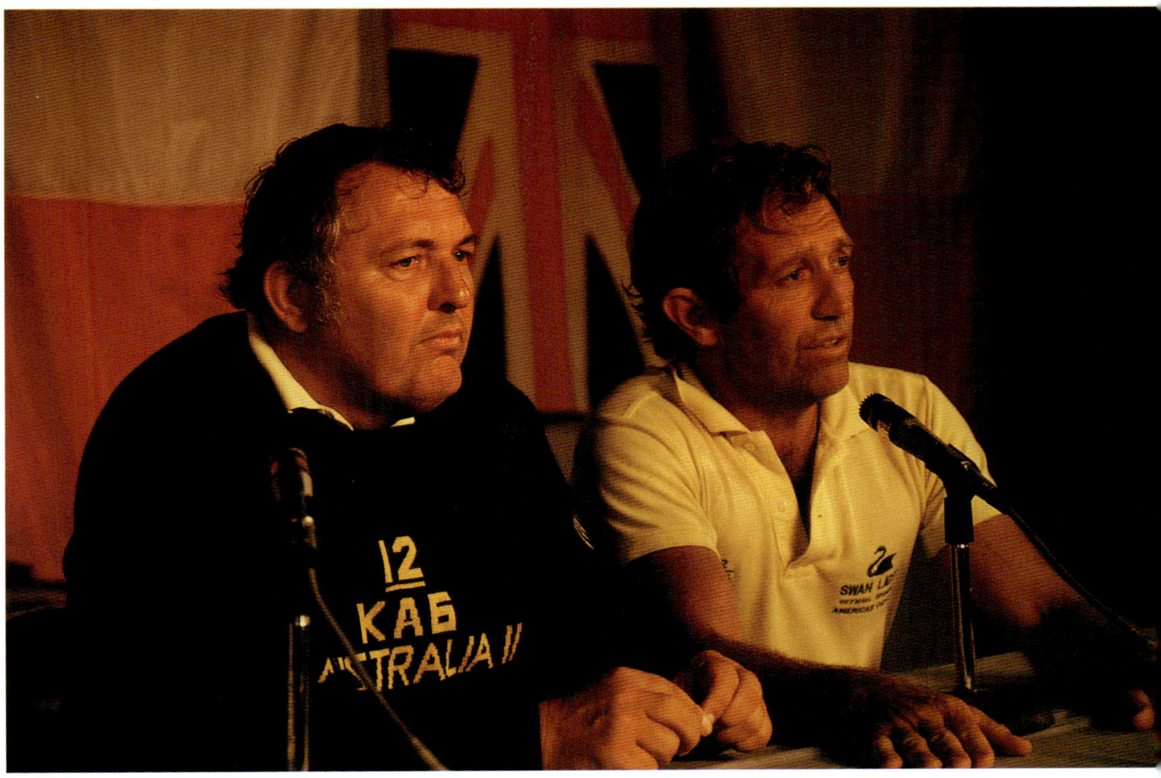

Explaining

Mr. Bond was quite willing to let the smooth-talking Warren Jones guide *Australia II* through the sea of controversy.

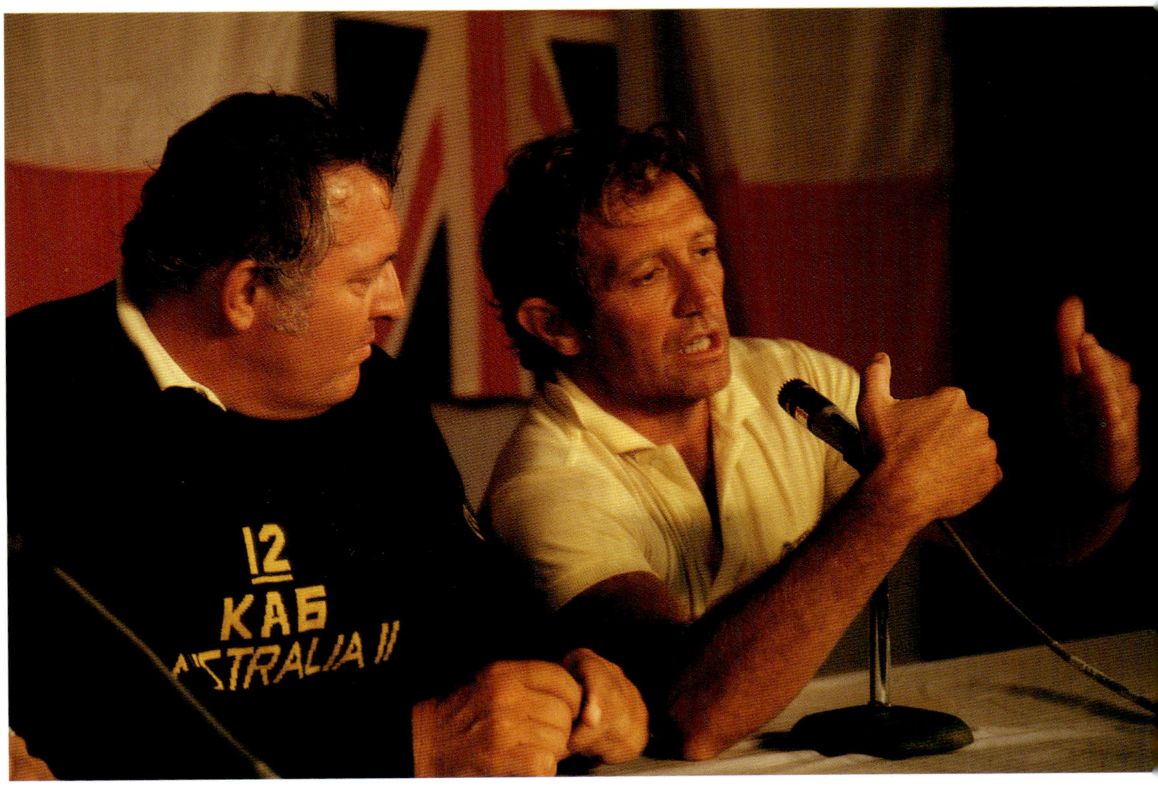

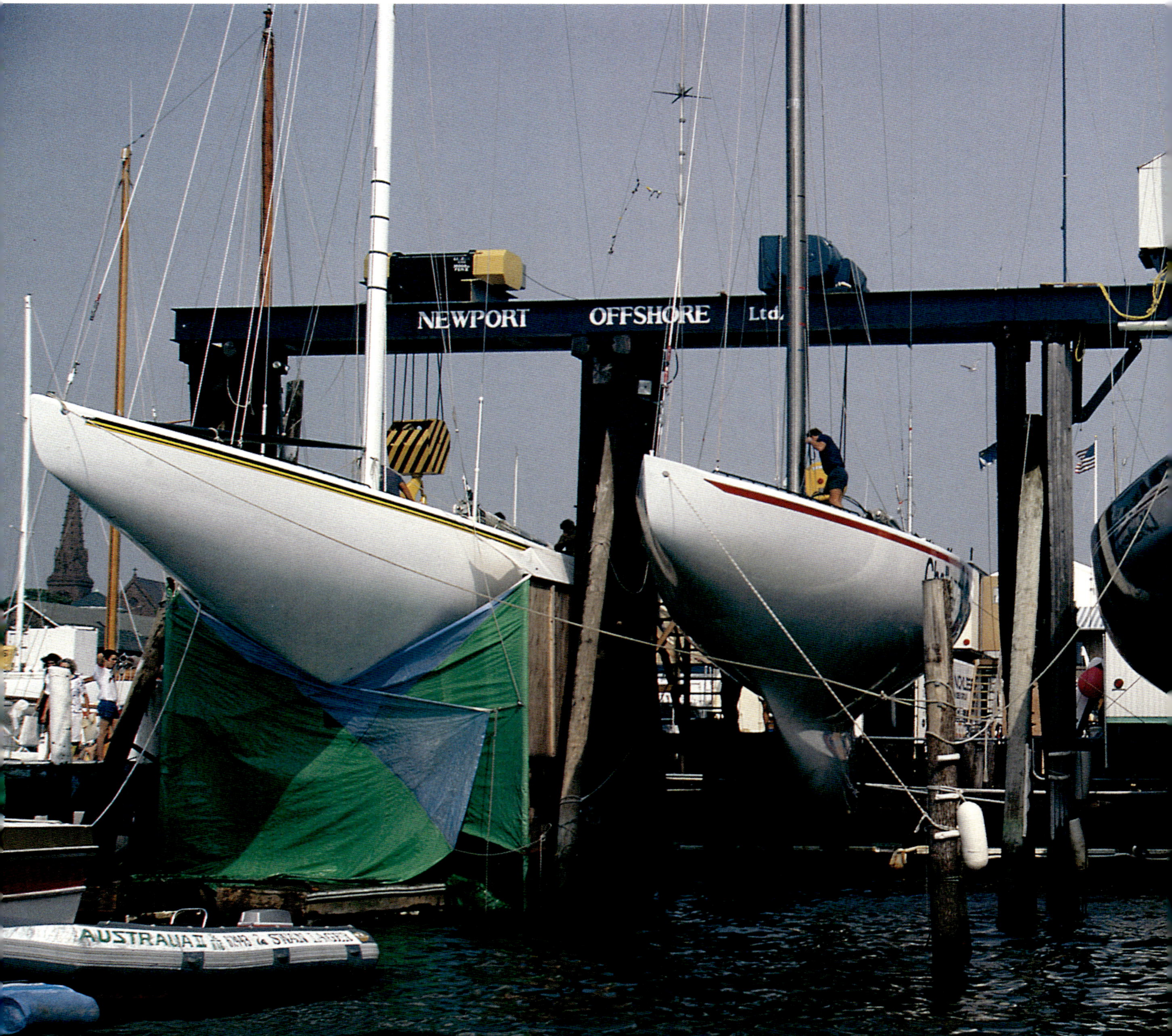
NEWPORT OFFSHORE Ltd.
AUSTRALIA II

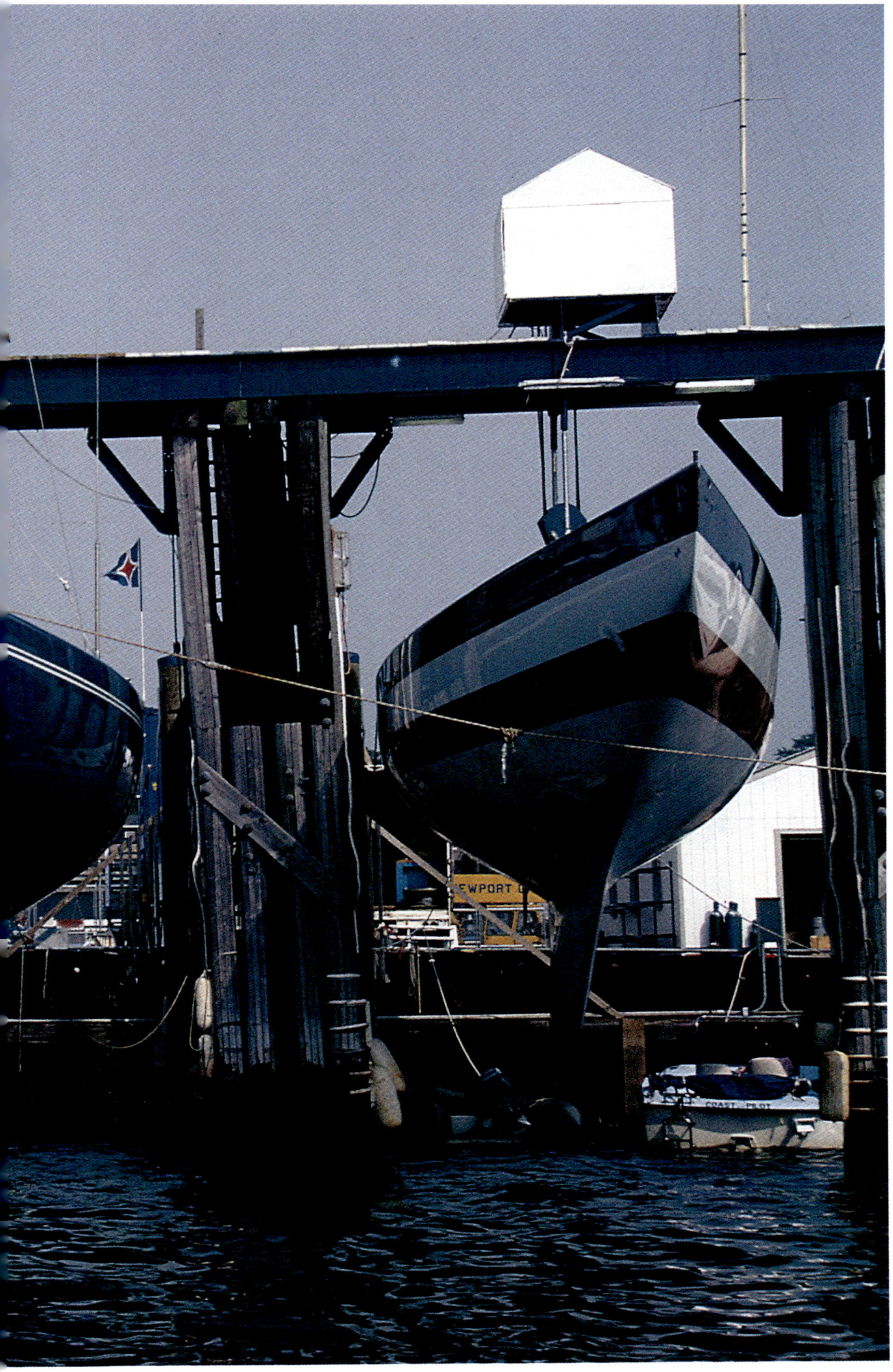

Modesty Skirt

The source of the legal turmoil involved the design of *Australia II*'s keel, which was shielded from public view by curtains dubbed "modesty skirts." In the shipyard at Newport Offshore, four challengers — *Australia II, Challenge 12, Azzurra,* and *France* — rest in their slings. Only *Australia II* shows any sense of secrecy: her underbody is shrouded, not to be revealed until after the final race. The green tarpaulin was a small sign, but it pointed to a new and volatile era of bickering and legal maneuvering in the America's Cup story. The shroud was also a sign that the 12-meter class itself would be moving out of the America's Cup. New Zealander Michael Fay would be the instrument of change.

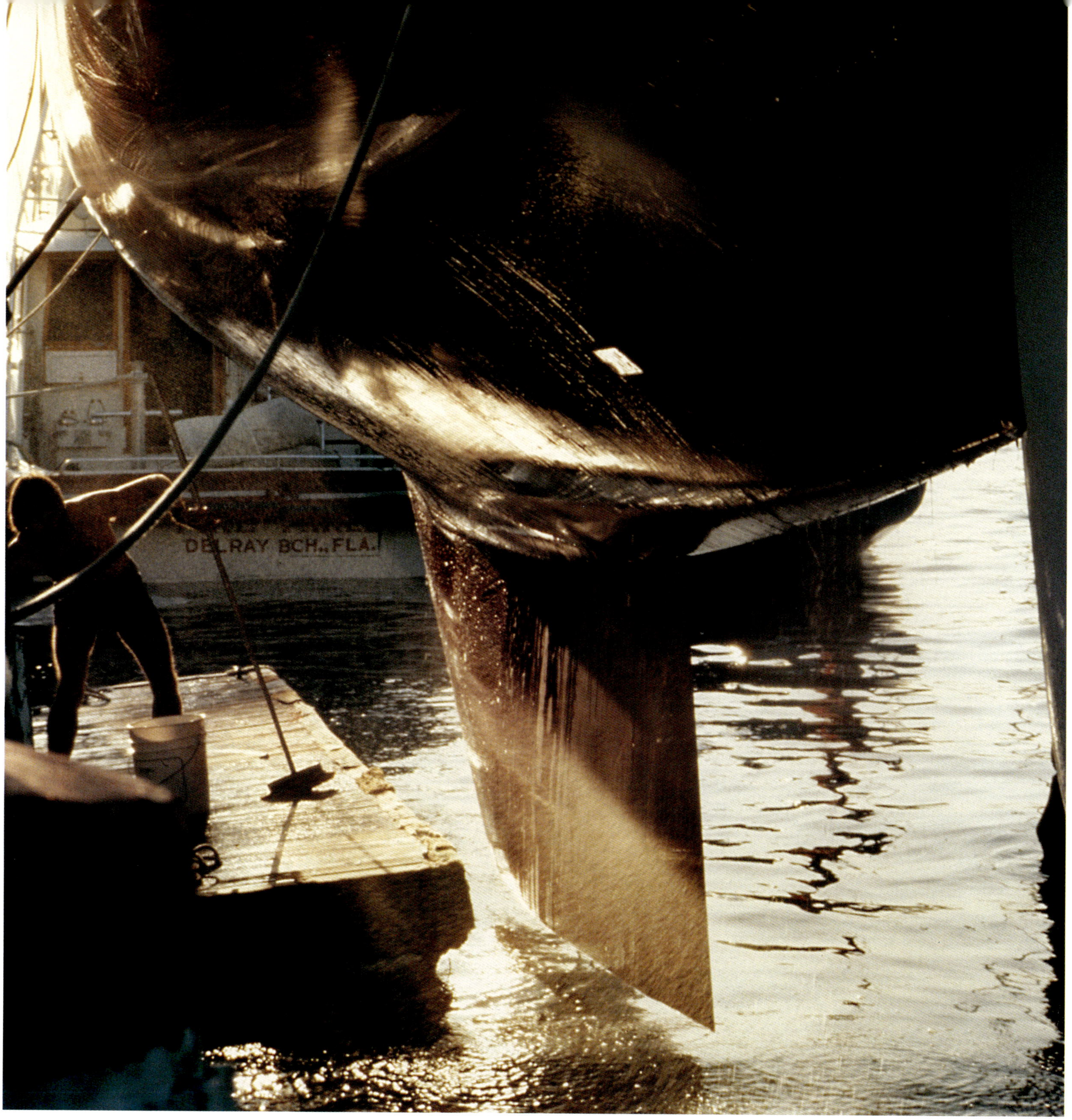

Classic Keel

After each sail, the 12s were washed down. The America's Cup defender *Liberty* is getting her usual scrubbing and her keel, in its classic form, is clearly shown. Its lines are clean and its edges are sharp.

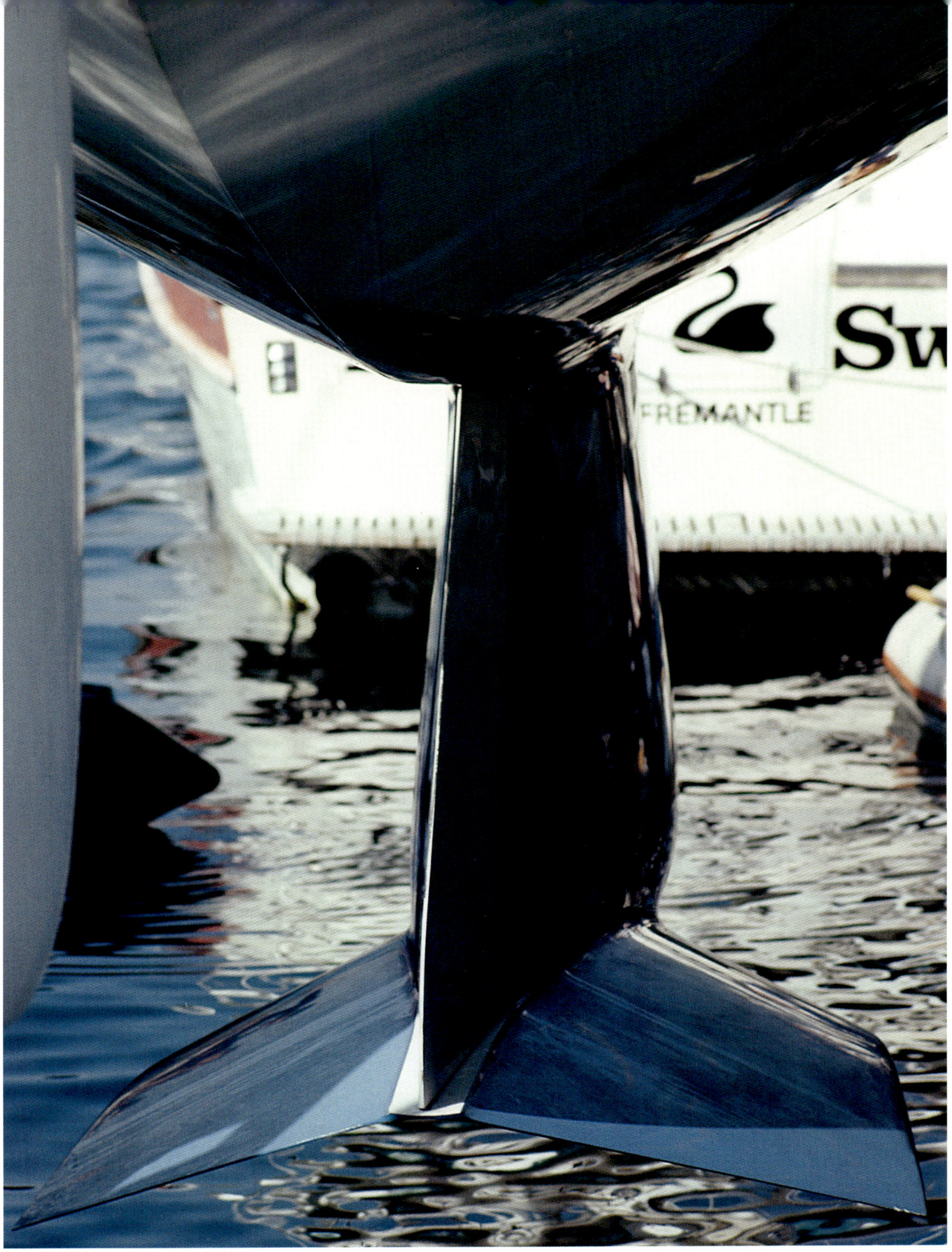

Winged Keel

When the keel of *Australia II*, the challenger, was finally unveiled, it was a wonder to behold. No longer was it a traditional, straight 12-meter keel like the others: it now had become a stubby winged creature. It was shorter fore and aft at the top next to the hull and long on the bottom. Heavy lead winglets were added that cut down on the tip vortex of the long keel bottom, but when the boat heeled, these winglets increased the effective draft of the keel. They were substantial and innovative appendages. Whether the new keel won the Cup for Australia or merely provided the dominant psychological edge in the racing, it was a huge success.

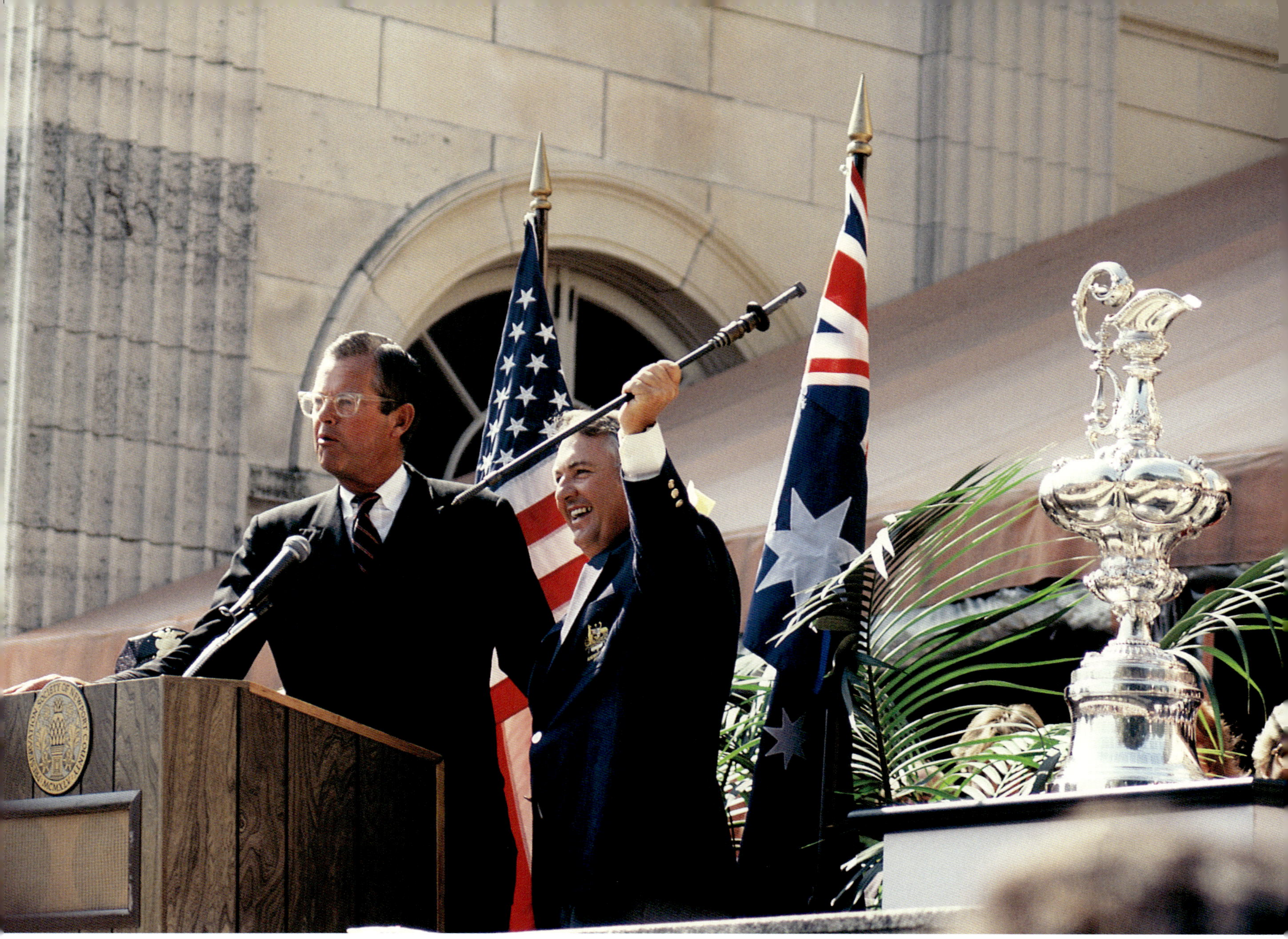

The Cup Unbolted

The America's Cup was handed over to Alan Bond and his victorious crew the day after *Australia II*'s upset victory over *Liberty*. Despite the controversy and sense of loss felt by the New York Yacht Club, Commodore Stone eloquently and graciously conducted the ceremony of Cup transfer. For many years, the Cup, a silver ewer with no bottom, had been mounted on a table at the New York Yacht Club and held securely in place by a long bolt. Alan Bond not only received the Cup, but the bolt that had held it captive all these years, which he brandished with almost as much joy as he had the Cup.

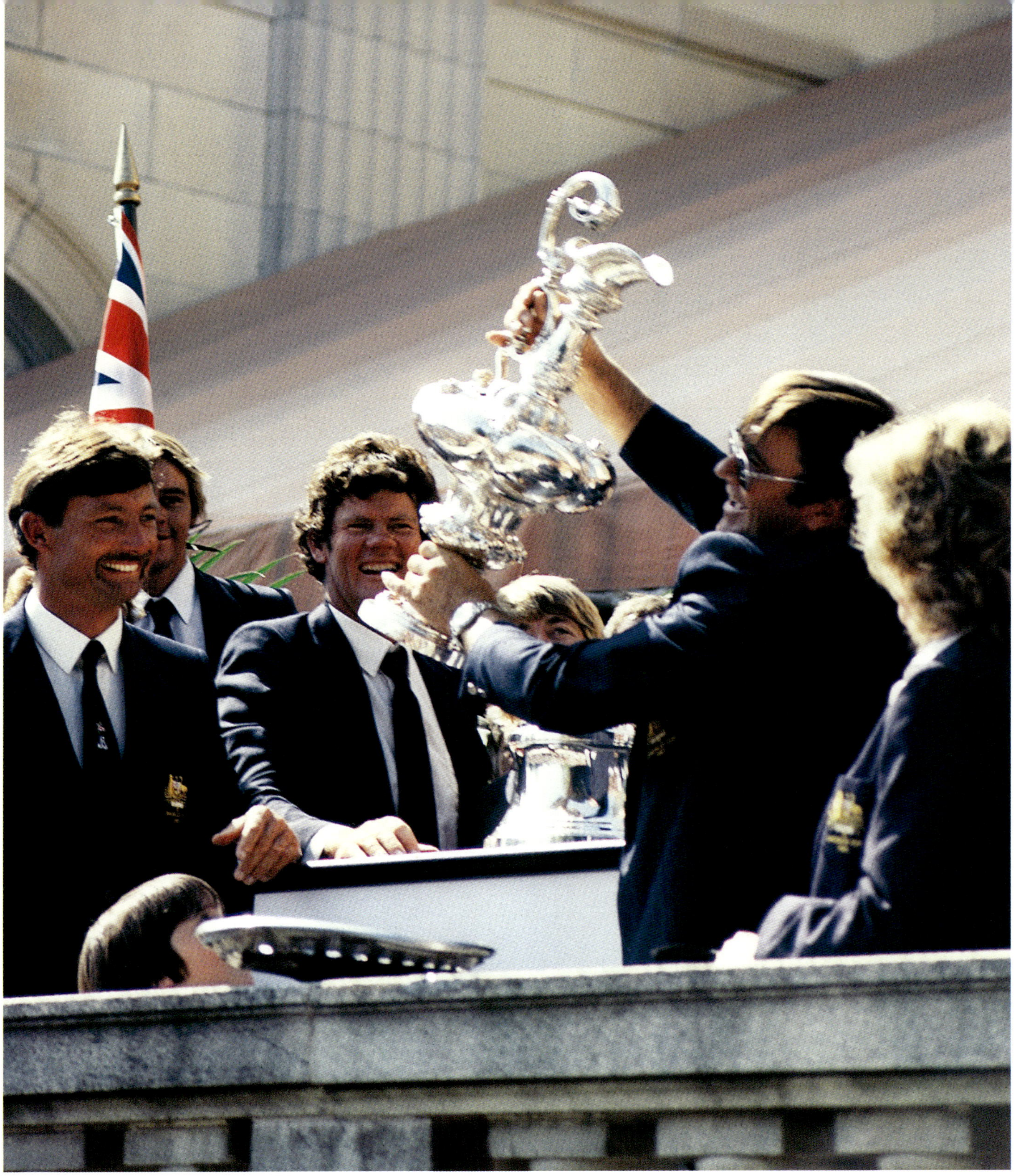

Lifting the Cup

John Bertrand, skipper of *Australia II,* and John Longley share the sentiments of designer Ben Lexcen, who literally and joyously is lifting the America's Cup.

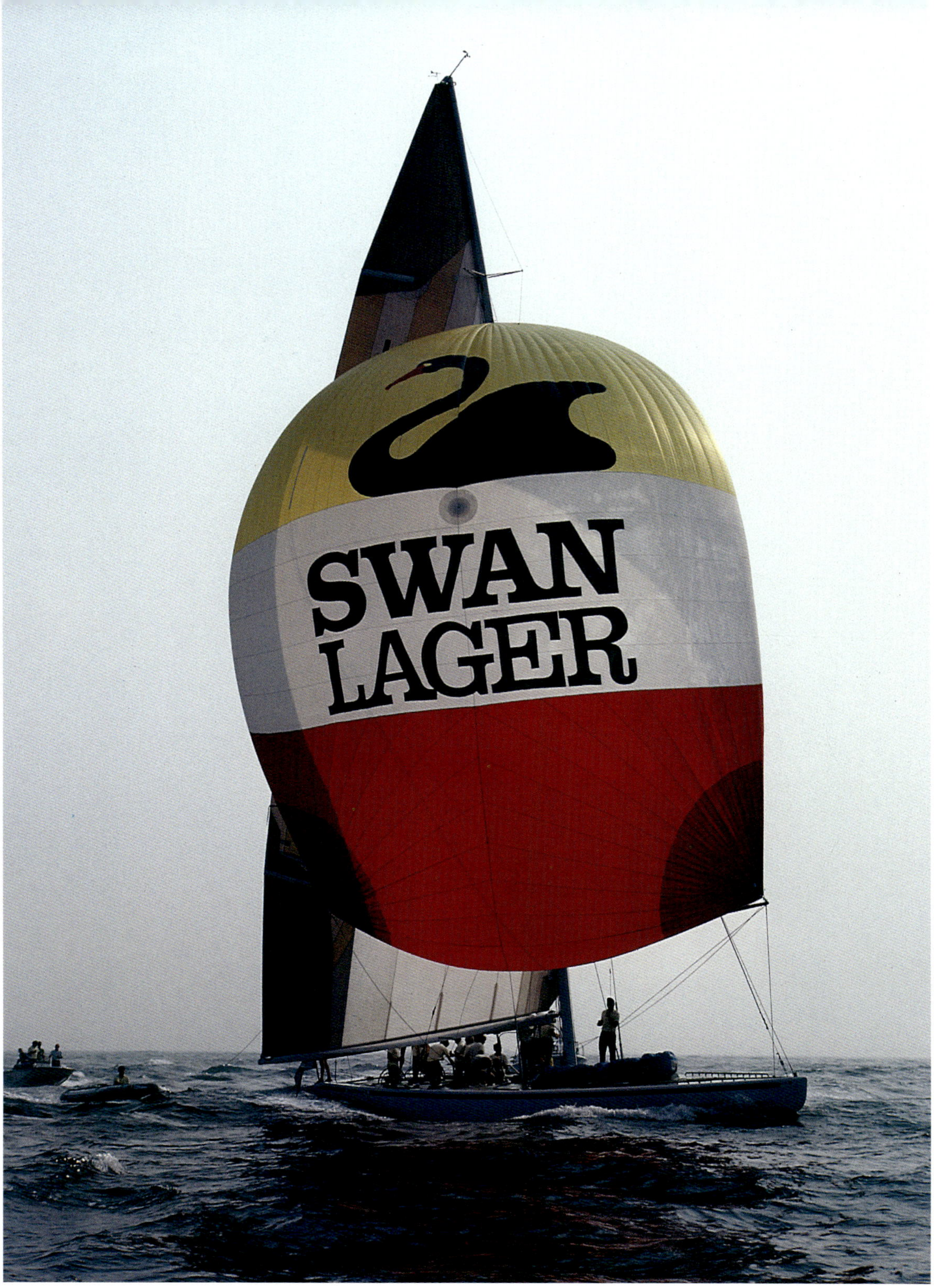

FORERUNNER

As *Australia II* sailed into port after winning the America's Cup, she hoisted a spinnaker bearing the name and insignia of Swan Lager, a beer made by a company in which Alan Bond had a financial interest. The logo was observed at the time with some amusement, but it was the forerunner of a trend that placed commercial logos on the sides and sails of most of the contestants. For me, this jarring visual intrusion was to totally alter the photographic story of America's Cup racing.

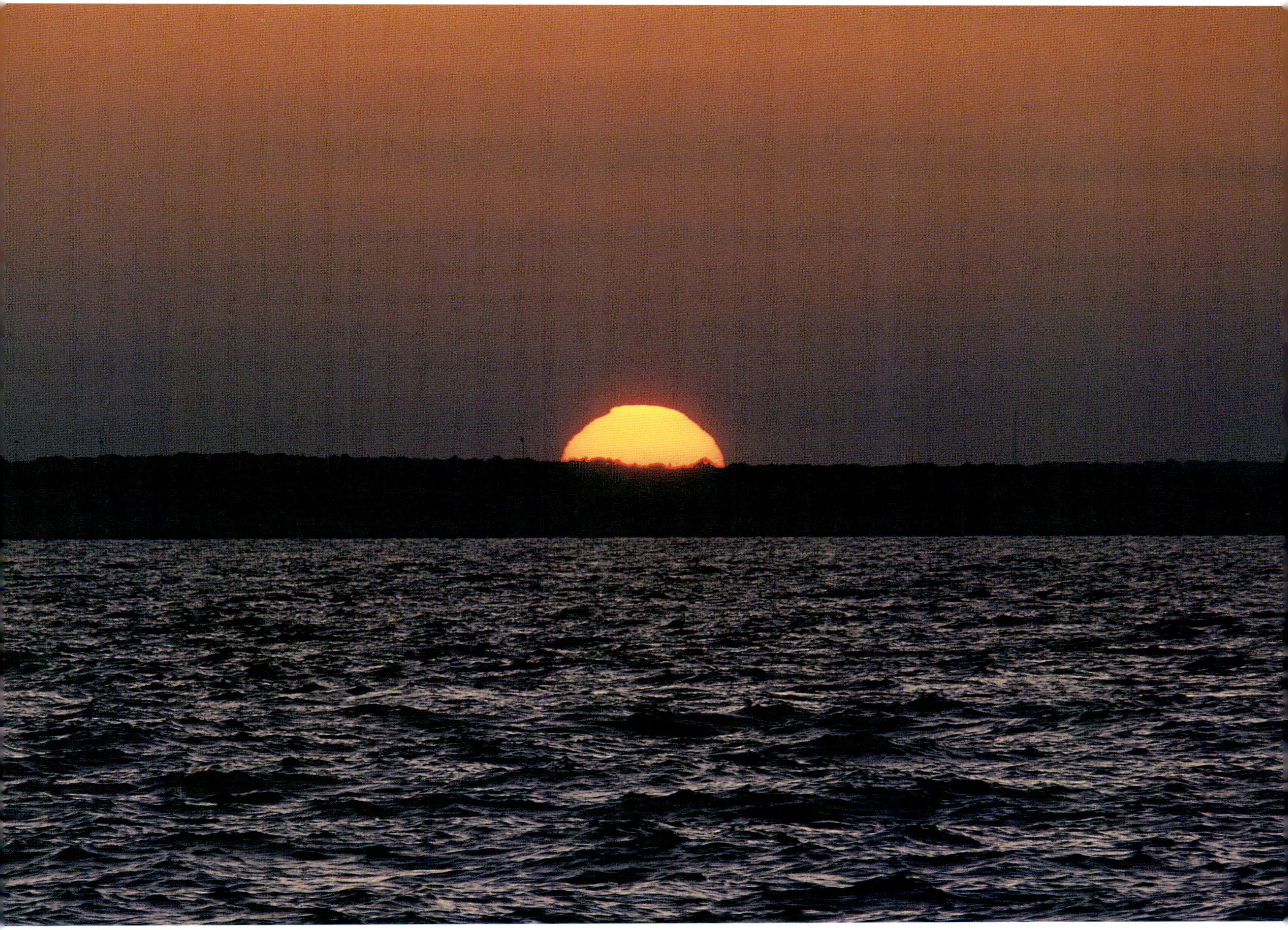

The Setting Sun

As we returned to port late in the day the Cup was lost, the sun set behind the Rhode Island shore. It was a beautiful sunset and, in retrospect, disturbingly symbolic of the end of America's Cup yachts unsullied by advertising.

Cloud Cover

In reviewing the photographs in this section — made off Newport — and those in the previous section — made off Australia — I notice that the sky is predominantly blue and that very seldom are clouds in evidence. Not many racing days featured clouds. We had a few, however, and to pay homage to them, I include this image of *Australia II* and *Victory*, on one of the very special days when Mother Nature graced the sky with a lively pattern of cloud cover to give form and mass as background to the sunwashed sails and sea. Cloud cover adds its element of beauty to the image, but the changing areas of shadow and light that fall on the subject cause a variety of problems; they can alter the emphasis of every area on which they fall, not always to my liking. Their moving patterns are the photographer's palette, but the wind controls them, and I must wait and take advantage as they evolve. Some beautiful days could hold extended periods of waiting for the sunlight to work its magic on my subject.

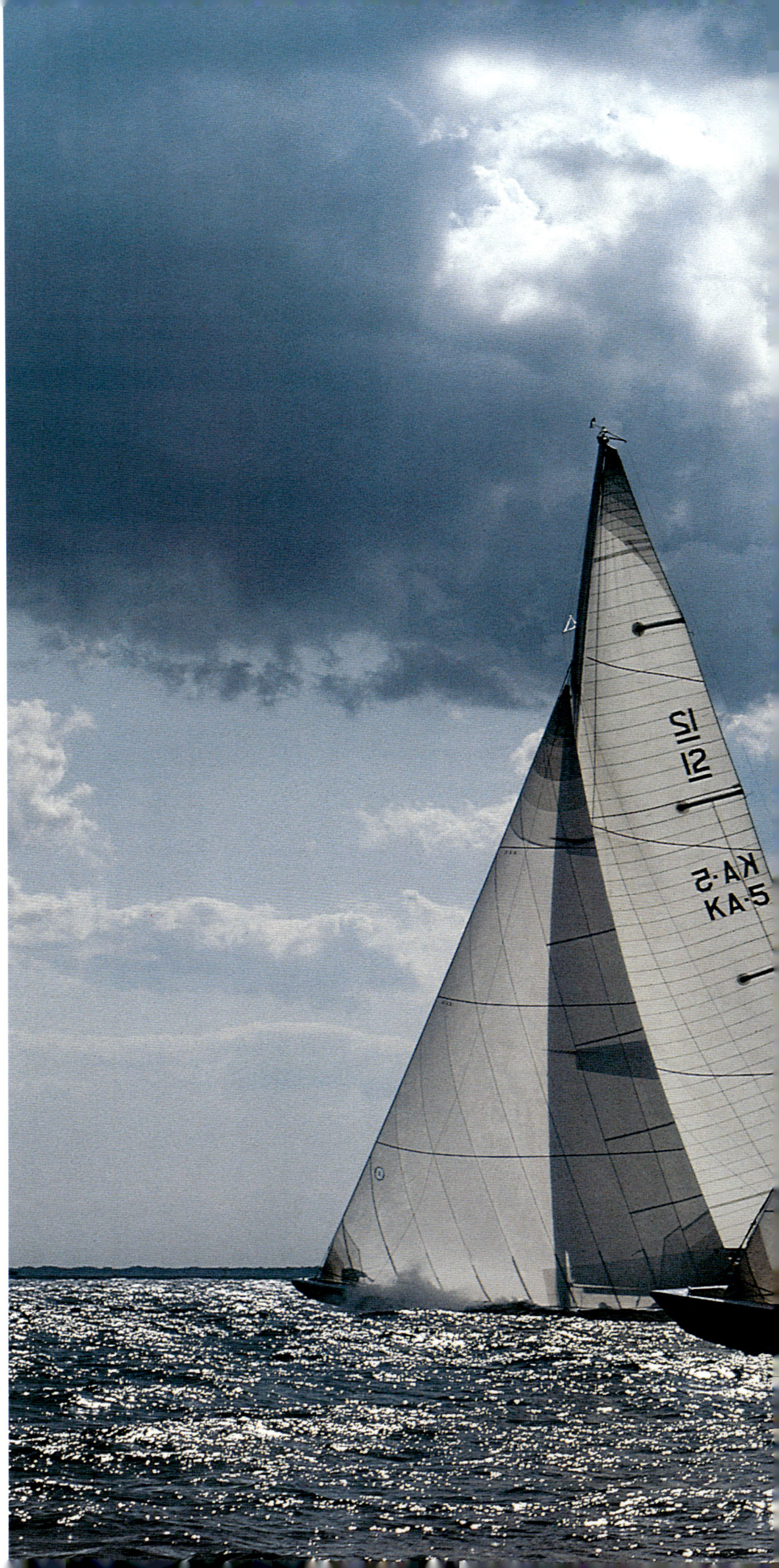

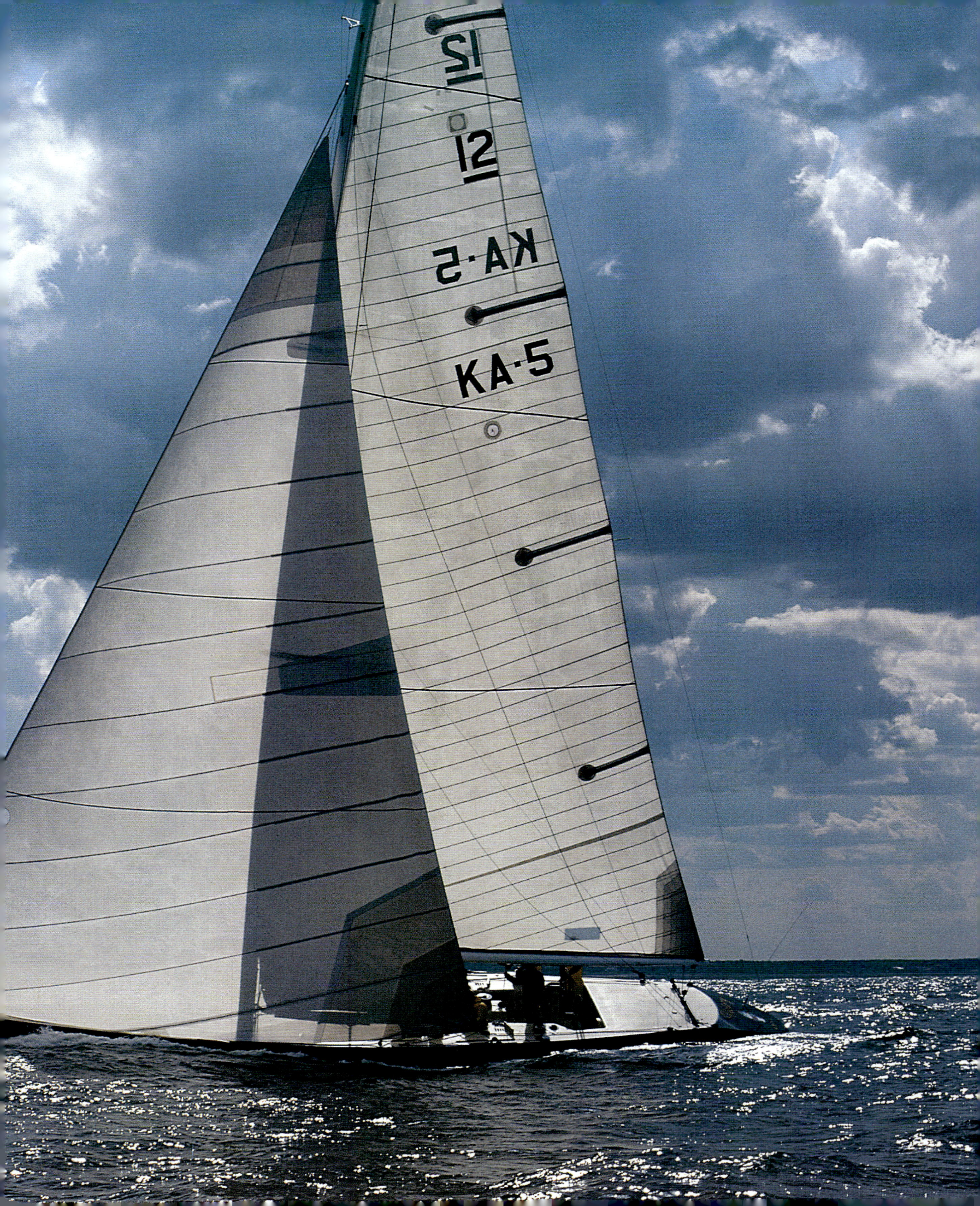
12
KA-5

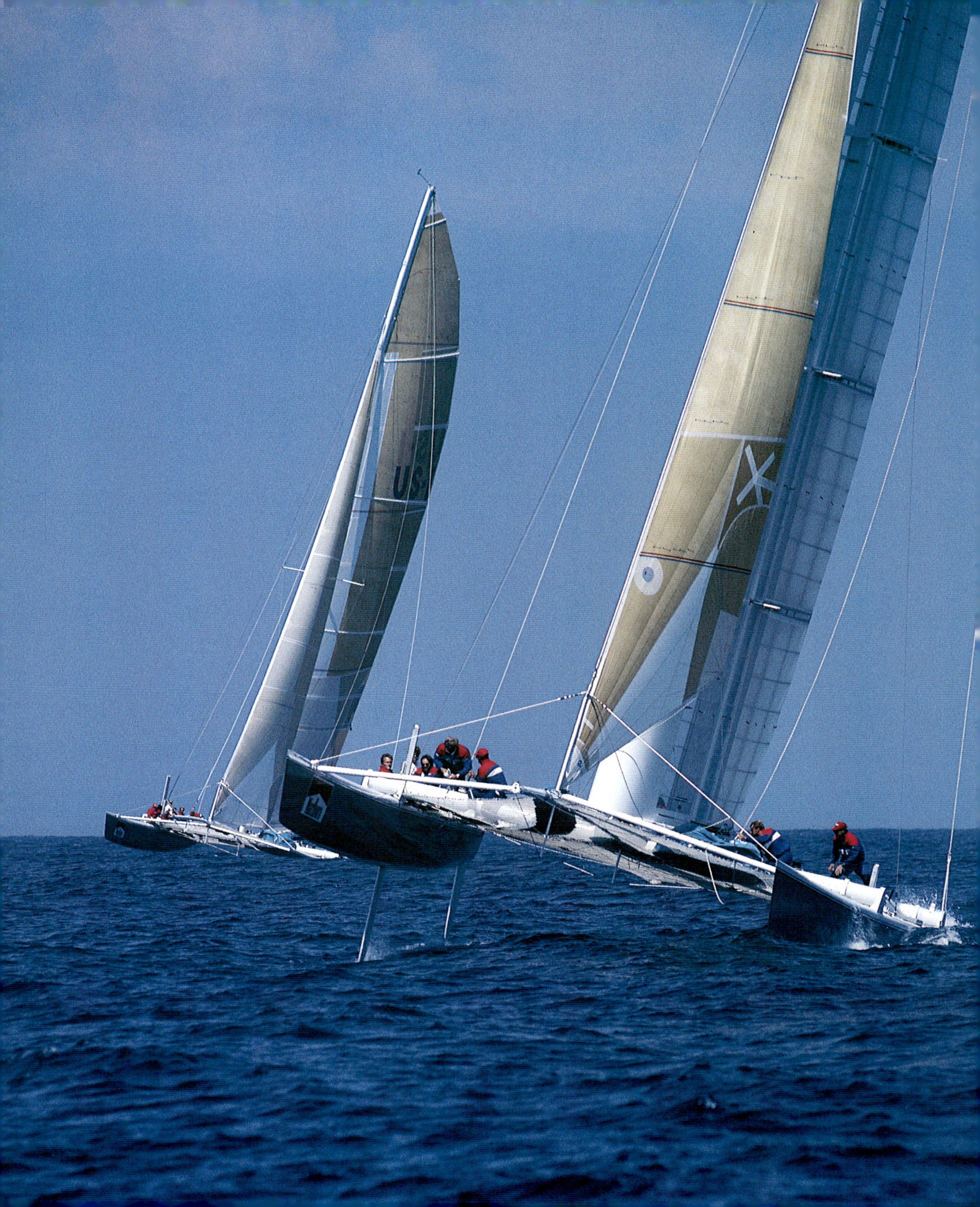

Controversy and Change

The catamaran was a light-footed beauty, but a questionable America's Cup defender

My friend, John Rousmaniere, the eminent yachting historian and writer, summed up the background to the 1988 America's Cup series as follows: "In 1987, Dennis Conner, representing the San Diego Yacht Club, won the America's Cup in Australia. Now the cup's defender, the club made the mistake of not following the New York Yacht Club's precedent of immediately accepting a challenge from another country and negotiating the conditions for the next match. As months passed and no conditions were forthcoming from San Diego, a lawyer for Michael Fay of New Zealand studied the cup's rules (in a document called the Deed of Gift) and concluded that the cup defender was actually obliged to accept any challenge. So Fay challenged with a 120-foot keel boat that, though almost twice the size of a 12-meter, qualified under the Deed. After a New York court ruled Fay's renegade challenge legal, San Diego decided to defend in a catamaran that was obviously faster than the keel boat. This led to the greatest mismatch in sailing history."

Fay's monohull, *New Zealand*, resembled the 1903 cup defender, *Reliance*, more than it did a 12-meter. It had little wings extending from its deck to support the weight of the crew, and the long, narrow, deep keel had a torpedo-like bulb at the bottom. If the old yacht *Reliance* had gone through a normal evolution during the intervening years, it might have looked similar to Fay's new challenger.

Lumbering?

I have always agreed with the saying that the camera does not lie, yet the image to the right blithely implies a pair of untruths. This photograph was made shortly after the start of the first of two races for the America's Cup in 1988. In the foreground is Dennis Conner's catamaran, *Stars & Stripes*, and beyond it is Michael Fay's challenger, *New Zealand*. The big monohull seems to be lumbering along, when actually it sailed the course at a faster clip than the giant J-boats of the 1930s. *Stars & Stripes* is sailing on both hulls, a ridiculous confounding of the function of a catamaran, but it made the catamaran move slowly enough to give the false impression that there was a real contest between the two boats.

One can get an idea of the size of Fay's vessel after close examination reveals that seated along the side of *New Zealand*, on her small deck wing, are 18 of the crew, dwarfed by the huge rig.

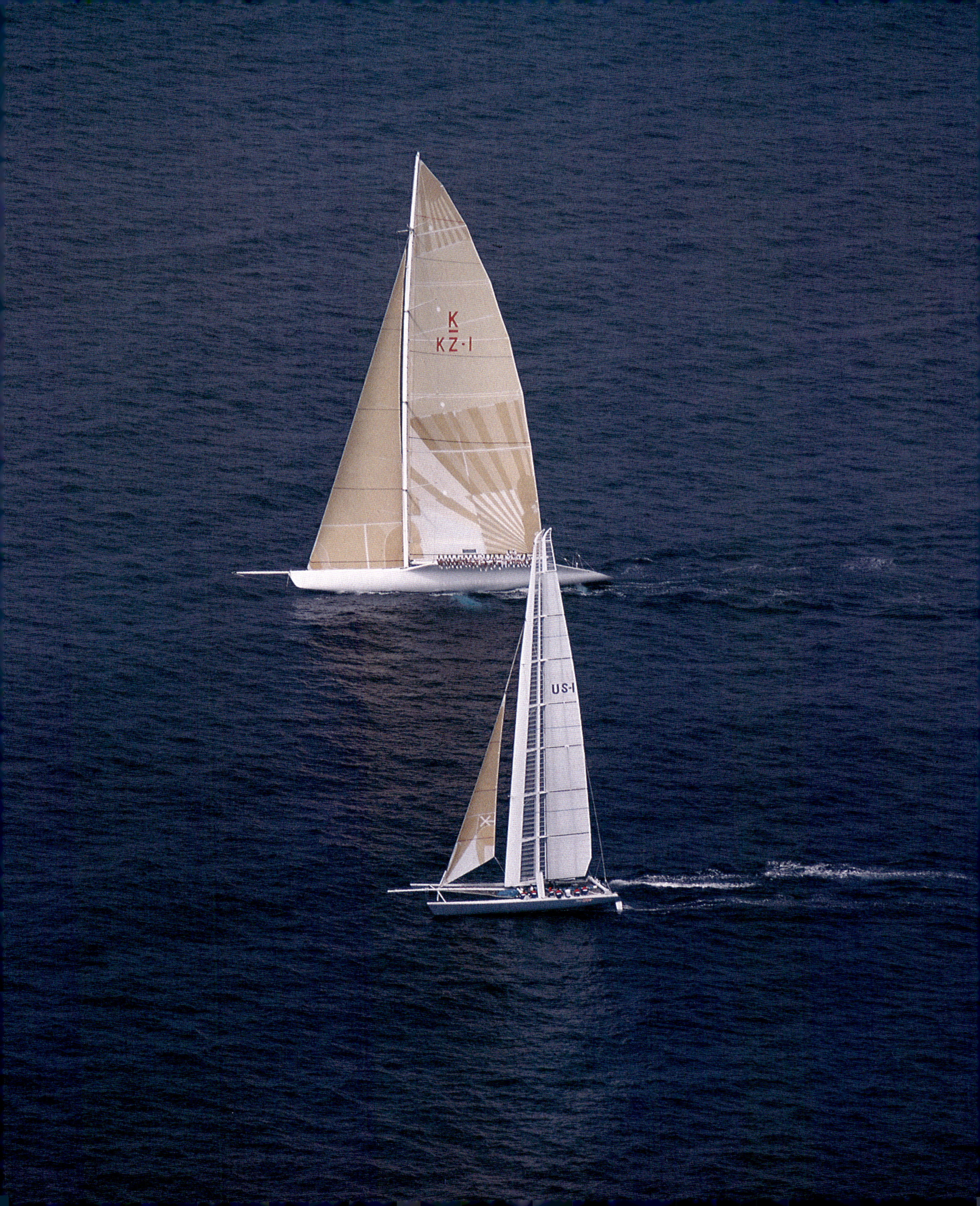
K
KZ·1
US-1

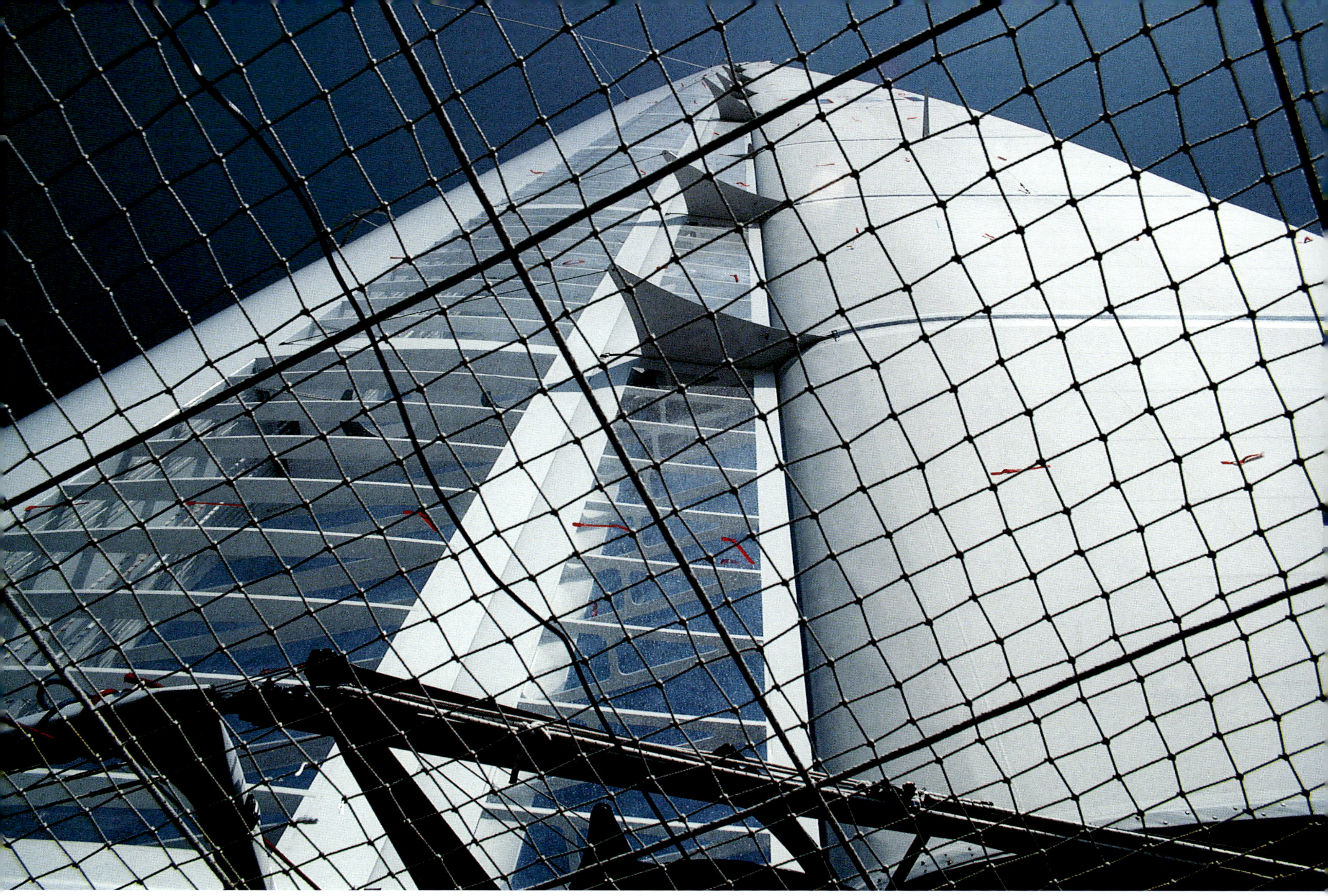

Wind Foil

Viewed close up, the catamaran's rigid sail might be described as a mechanized, articulated, wind-foil airplane wing. It seemed too complicated to any longer be called a sail in a traditional sense.

High Speed Wonder

Opposite above, actually, Conner's new craft was not just a fast catamaran, it was a remarkable design and building achievement. The rigid sail could be angled to the wind for ultimate aerodynamic proficiency. In effect, *Stars & Stripes* was a 6,000-pound, high-speed wonder afloat.

Exultation

Opposite below, at times Dennis sailed his cat around the harbor at well over 20 knots and lifted the windward hull high in what seemed a burst of exultation in the monster he gamboled with. This was the joy of sailing a catamaran. Compare it to the insipid posture he affected as he sailed alongside the challenger *New Zealand* in the actual race — in my opinion an attempt to make the world believe the farce really was a race.

Out of the acrimony and lawsuits engendered by this event, the new International America's Cup Class of yacht was born.

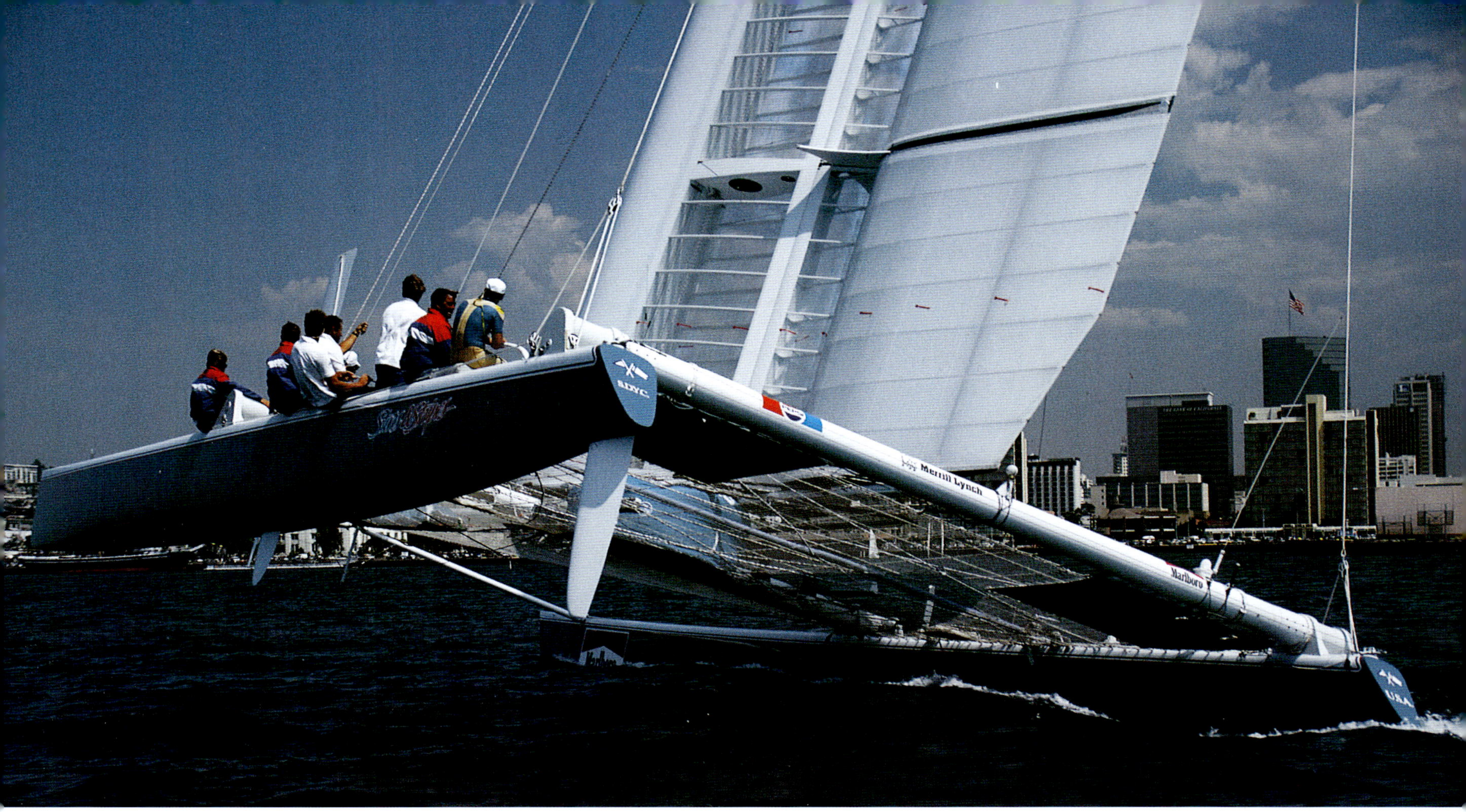
S.D.Y.C.
Merrill Lynch
Marlboro
U.S.A.

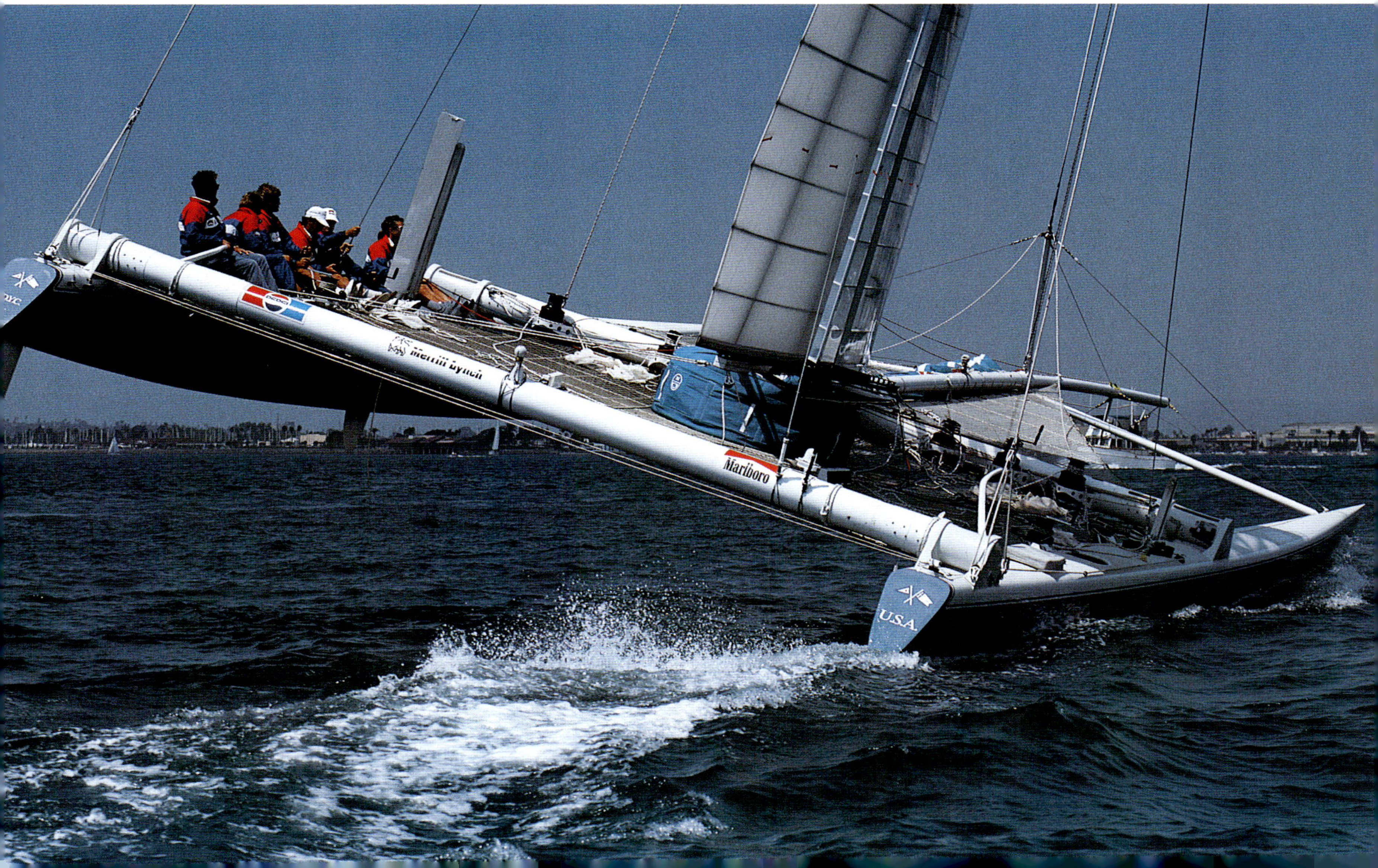
Merrill Lynch
Marlboro
U.S.A.

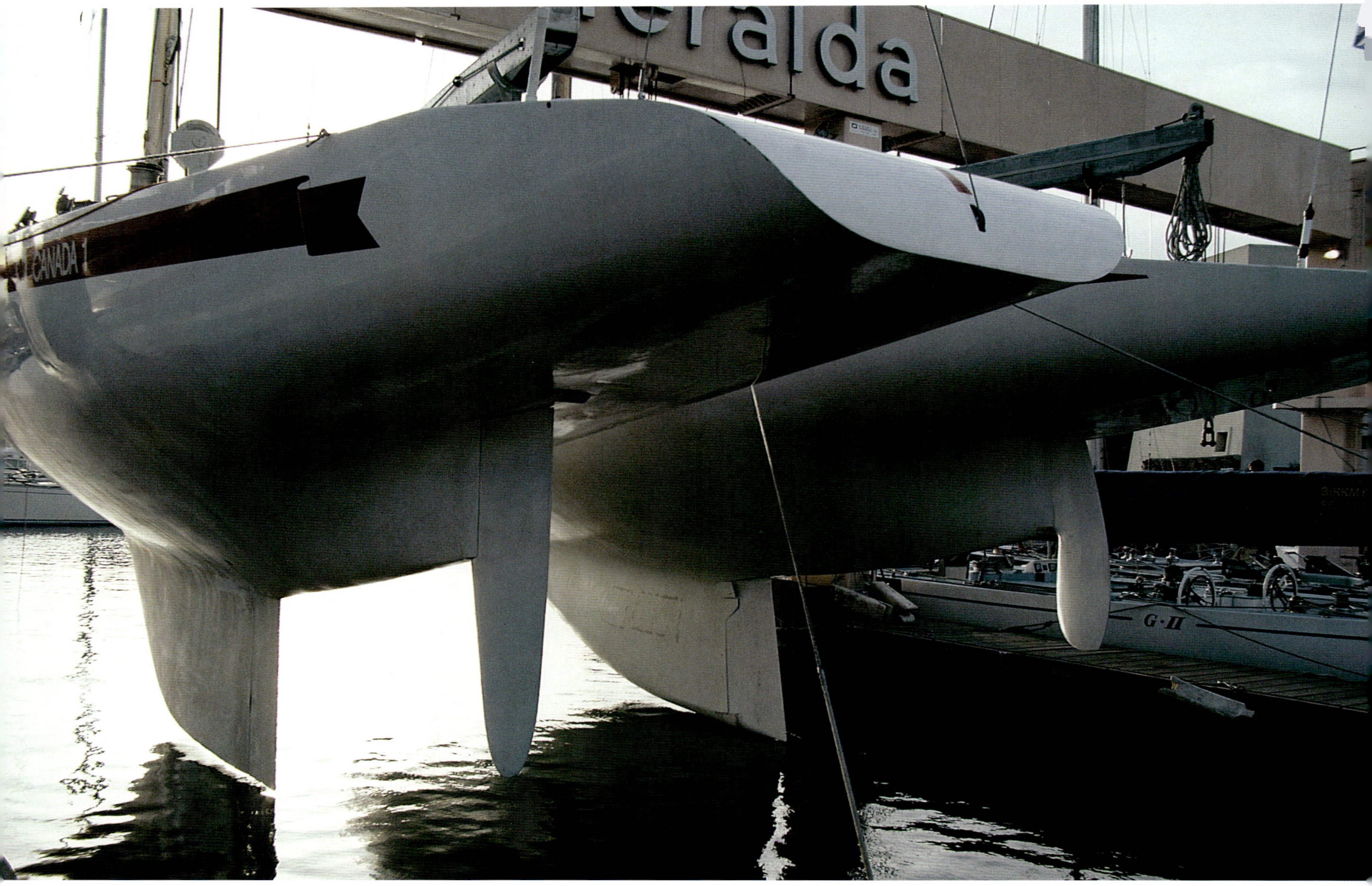

Gentle Curve

The underbodies of these 12-meters hauled out in Porto Cervo, Sardinia, in 1984 were a graceful poem in clean lines and gentle curves and a pictorial tribute to America's Cup yachts of the past.

The 12-meter yachts in the 1980s were undergoing design changes in their hulls and innovative changes in their keel structures. The wings on the keel of *Australia II*, America's Cup winner in 1983, were to dominate design thought on the keels of all the America's Cup yachts that followed. The unadorned lean fin was gone, and design moved to a smooth, canoe-shaped hull with fin attachments on a blade-shaped keel.

Changing Hull Lines

In 1987, the 12-meter *America II* represented the New York Yacht Club at Fremantle. The lines of the underwater hull show the changes that were occurring in the transition from the classic, deep-bodied form of a few years previously to the scow type that was to emerge when the new class of yachts followed the 12-meters. The keel and its torpedo-type appendage on *America II* are hung amidships, with the rudder a separate structure aft.

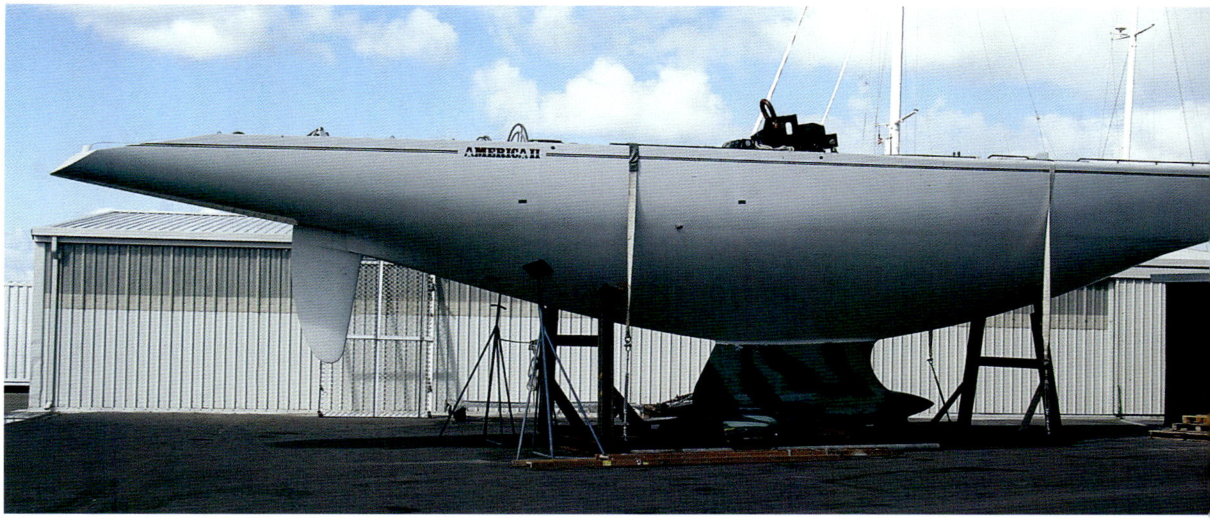

Forward Towards The Past

In 1988, Michael Fay built his big monohull, *New Zealand*. It featured wings extending from the deck to support the weight of the crew and a deep, narrow keel with a torpedo-shaped bulb at the bottom.

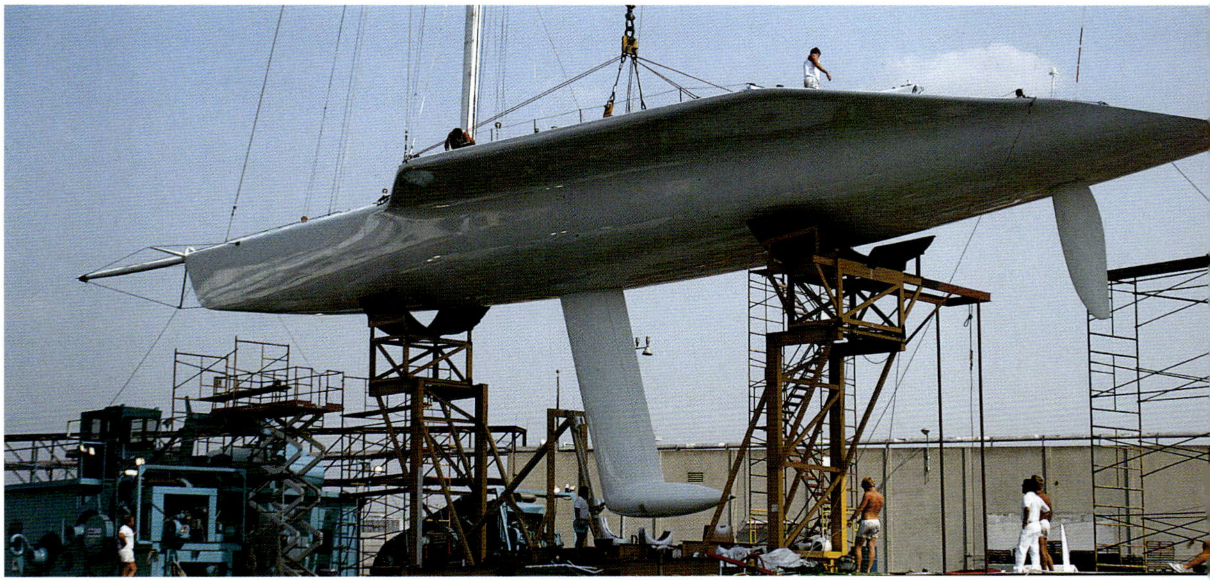

Modified Scow Type

Il Moro Di Venezia was one of the new America's Cup class that followed Fay's megayacht. In outline, the hull bears a strong resemblance to Fay's 1988 challenger. *Il Moro*, too, is a modified scow-type and, like its predecessor, resembles the 1903 defender *Reliance* much more than it does the 12-meters of a few years earlier. When ashore, it had a camouflage structure for both the keel and rudder configurations to provide cover from prying eyes.

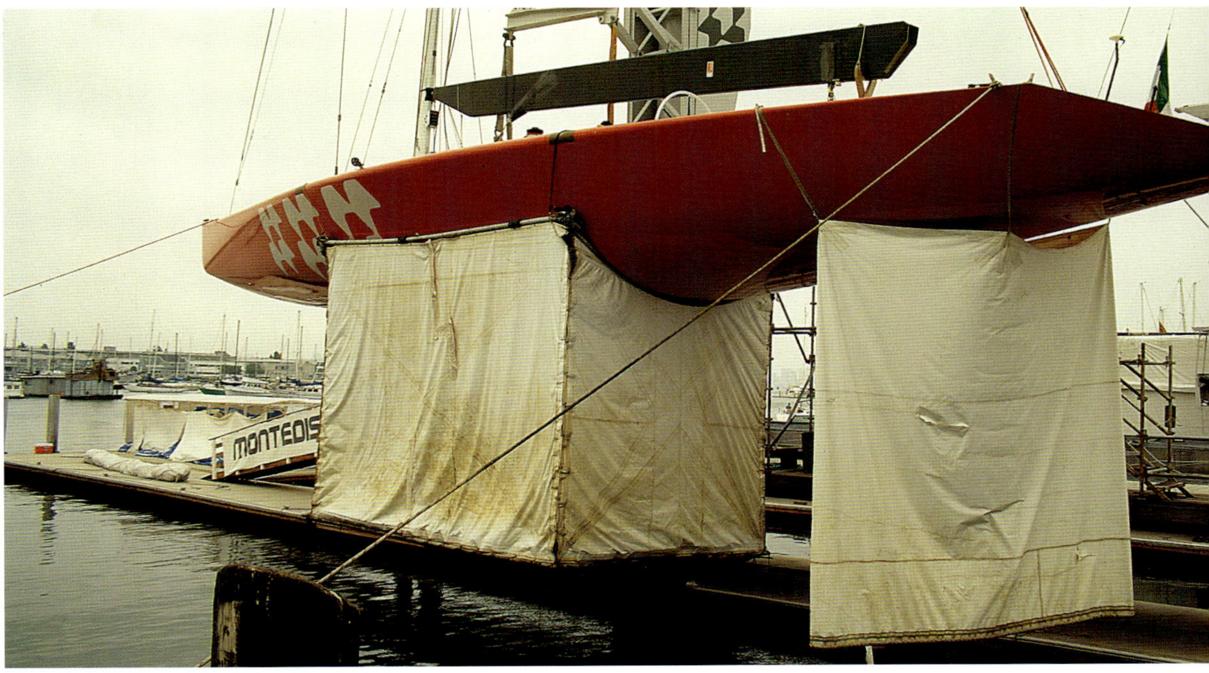

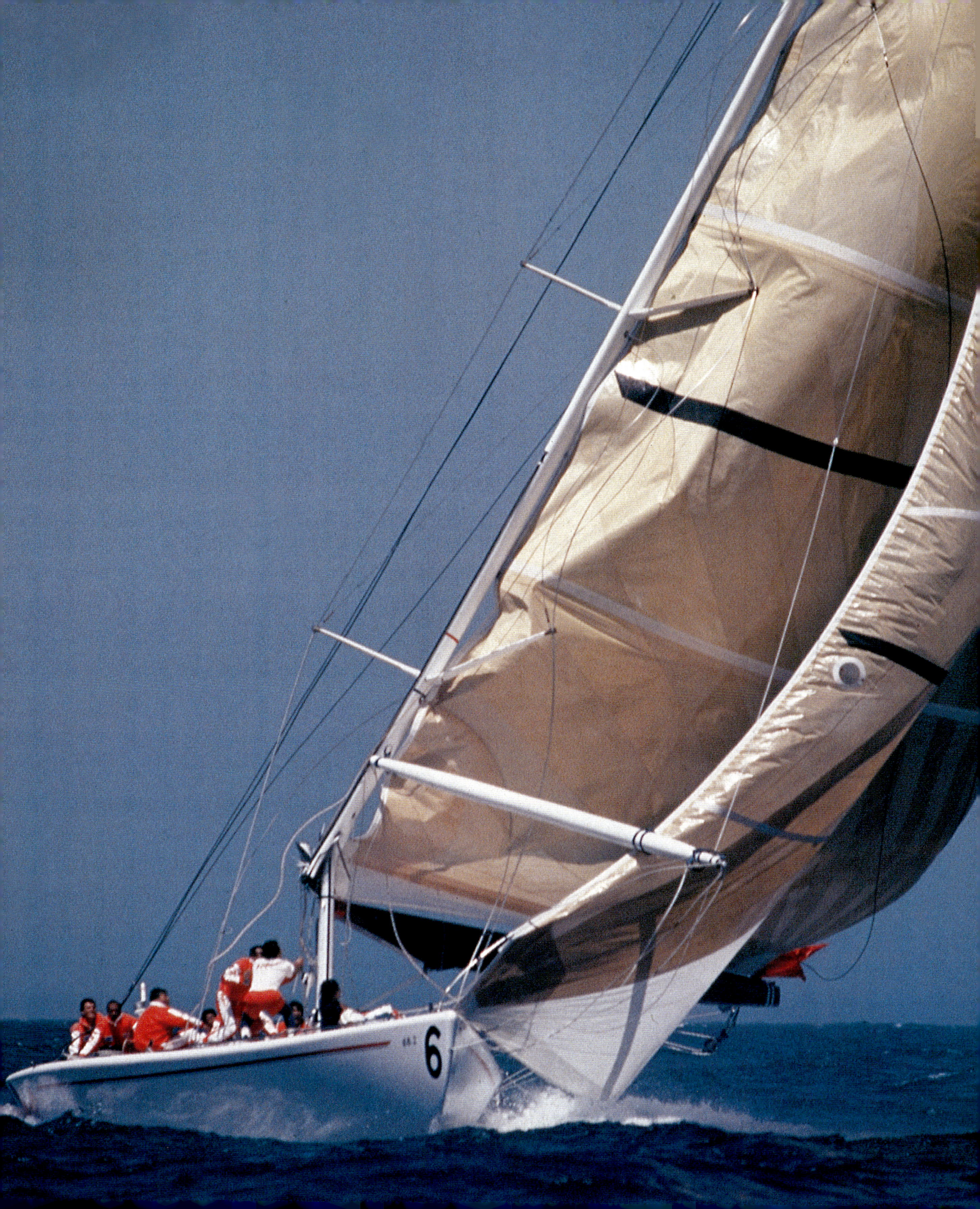
6

SAN DIEGO

A new Cup class with a rapid learning curve

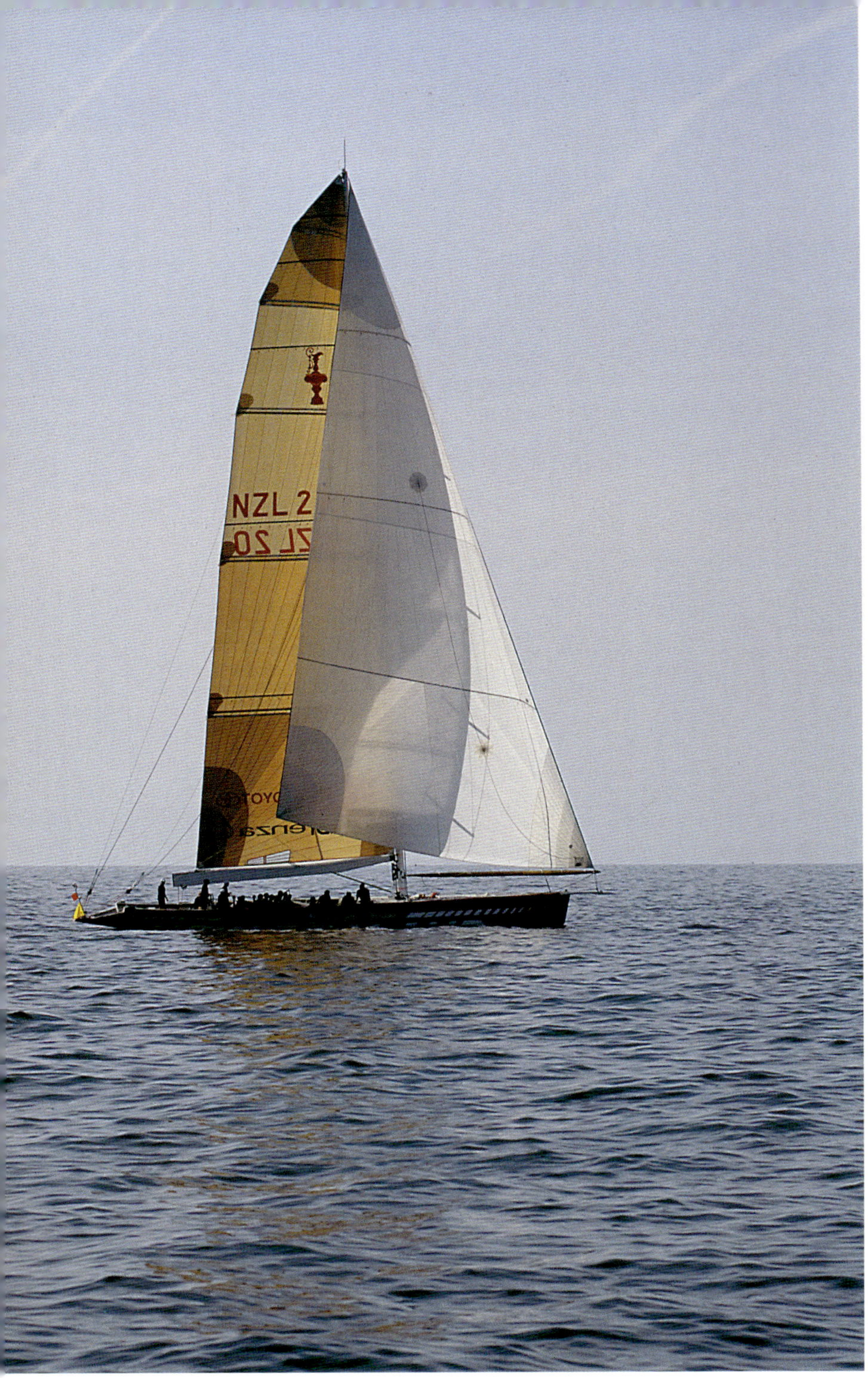

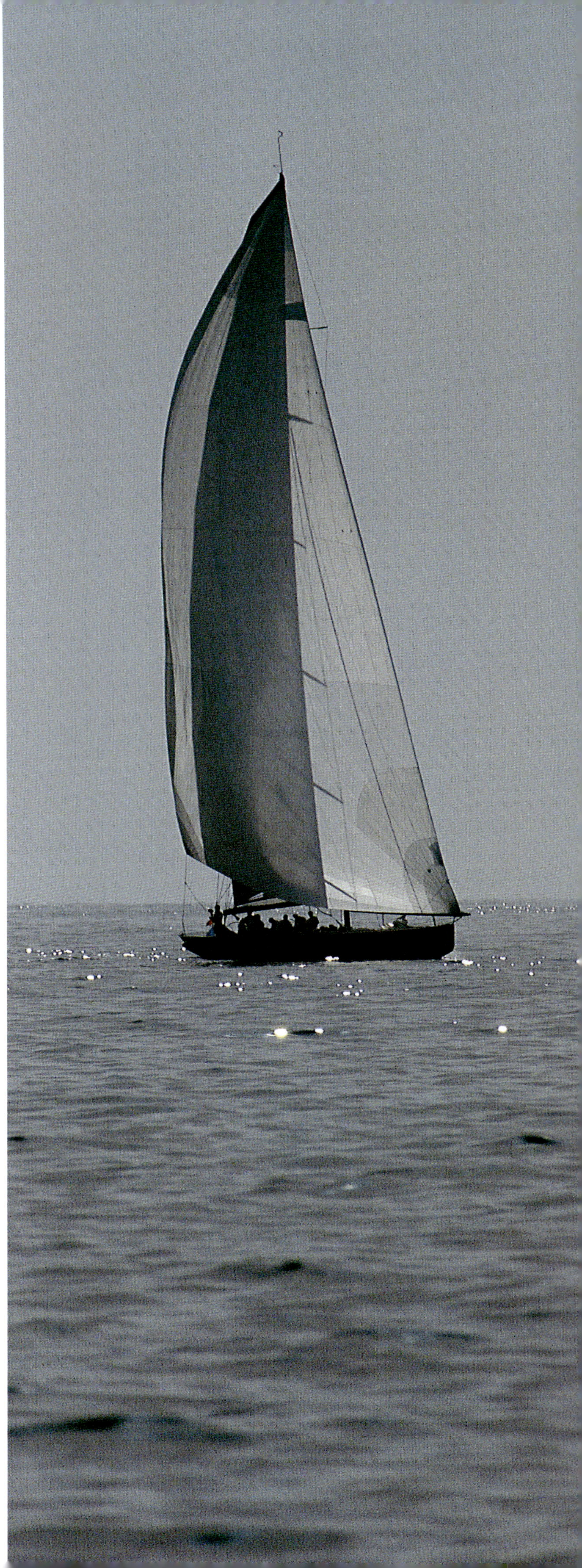

The first meeting of the new America's Cup class established after the 1988 series was in the IACC World Championships that took place off San Diego in 1991. In the first race, the wind piped up to 20 knots and wreaked havoc with the class. The design went back to the drawing boards, and a stronger, improved version of the new hull form and rig came to the 1992 America's Cup series off San Diego. Throughout the races that year, the wind was kind.

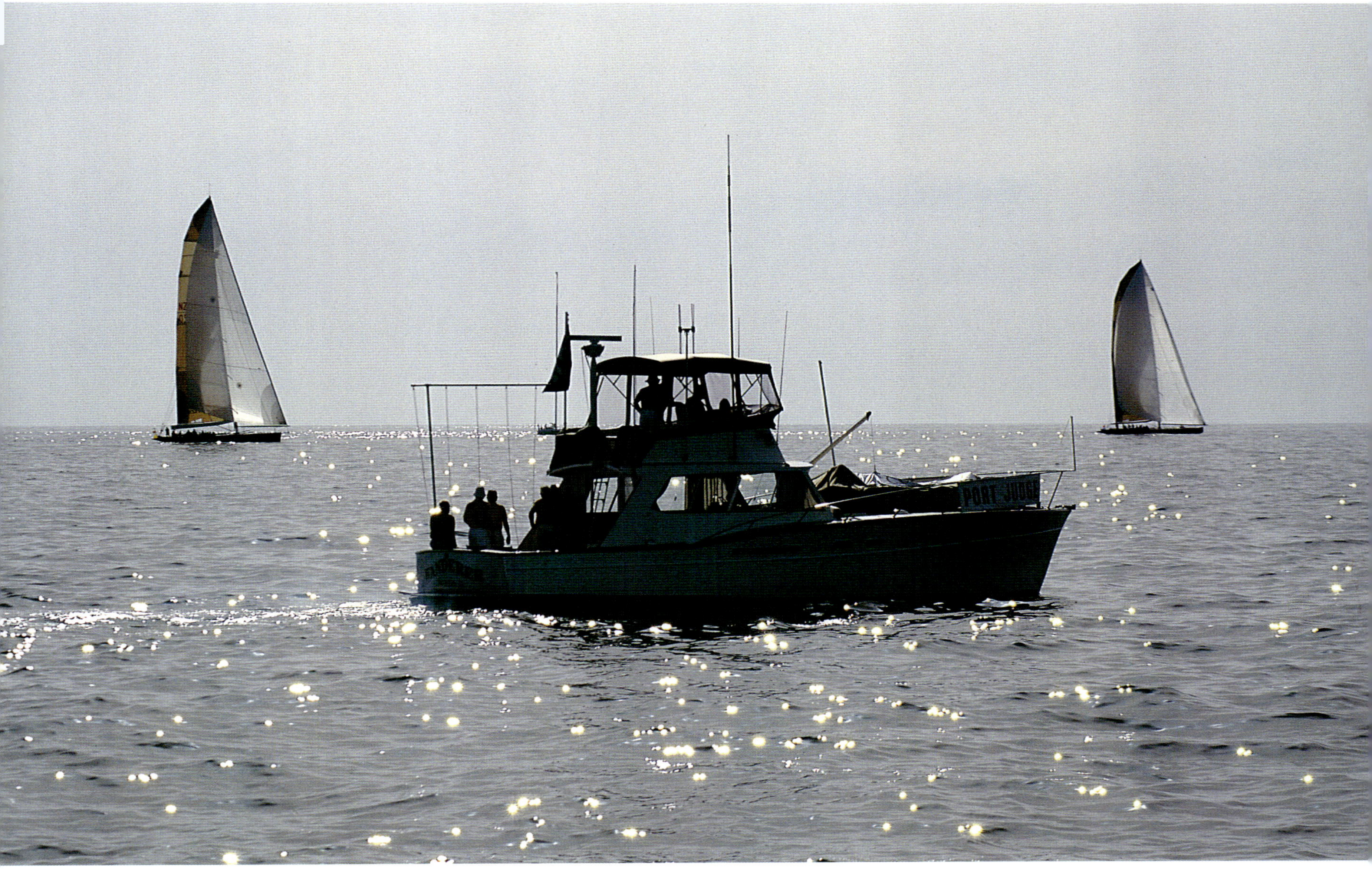

Pacific

Far left, on many days of trial racing in 1992, the Pacific Ocean was aptly named. Often, the surface of the sea was marked by no wind patterns, but the tall rigs of the America's Cup yachts reached high enough in the sky to snag every vagrant wisp of breeze, so they maintained steerageway even when there seemed to be no wind to move them. *New Zealand* moves gently, with her wake trailing lightly astern and her sails filled. Though no evident wind pattern ruffles the surface of the sea, in my mind's eye a flow of air moves overhead with sufficient strength to keep the tall sails filled.

Sparkles

Near left, when sparkles of light on the water revealed the slightest breeze, the yachts trimmed and moved to take every advantage.

New Wind

Above, some days the patterns of light would reveal more than an errant wisp of wind. Here the pattern hints at the possibility of new winds emerging. The Race Committee, which set the marks, was as interested in the emerging winds as the contestants themselves.

HEADSTAY

The new class had very tall, narrow rigs, but the sails were not triangular, for at the peak the mainsail curved in to the mast. The fullness at the peak added a few more square feet to the sail, but the curve produced a new dimension. The line of sight, rather than soaring up to a sharp angle at the masthead, instead curved in to meet the mast, and the sense of rig height was diminished. One way to emphasize the height of these new rigs was to photograph the yacht from forward. The rig then reached toward the sky in a narrow, ascending spire. The Swedish and Spanish yachts in this image accentuate mast height, particularly when the tall rigs are compared to the tiny figures of the crews below on their narrow craft.

When I cross ahead of a sailing yacht, I observe the tautness of the headstay, for when it sags off from the straight line of the mast, the curve in the ascending headstay introduces a strong new element to the composition. The yacht on the left has a headstay that actually falls off very slightly. However, it seems to establish the single thought of a tall, straight line reaching high aloft. This is because the ascending line really is the straight mast itself, not the headstay or luff of the genoa.

The mast of the yacht on the right reaches tall and straight aloft, but the slightly sagging line drawn by the headstay introduces a new note, a technical bit of information that changes the meaning of the image. It moves from a purely aesthetic composition to one that reveals information about the rigging. I believe that whatever its aesthetic component, an image is richer if it also provides information and — where yachts are involved — a key to performance. Beyond the yachts, a heavy bank of clouds hangs low to the water, while a thin veil rides high in the sky. It was a day of soft light and filled shadows.

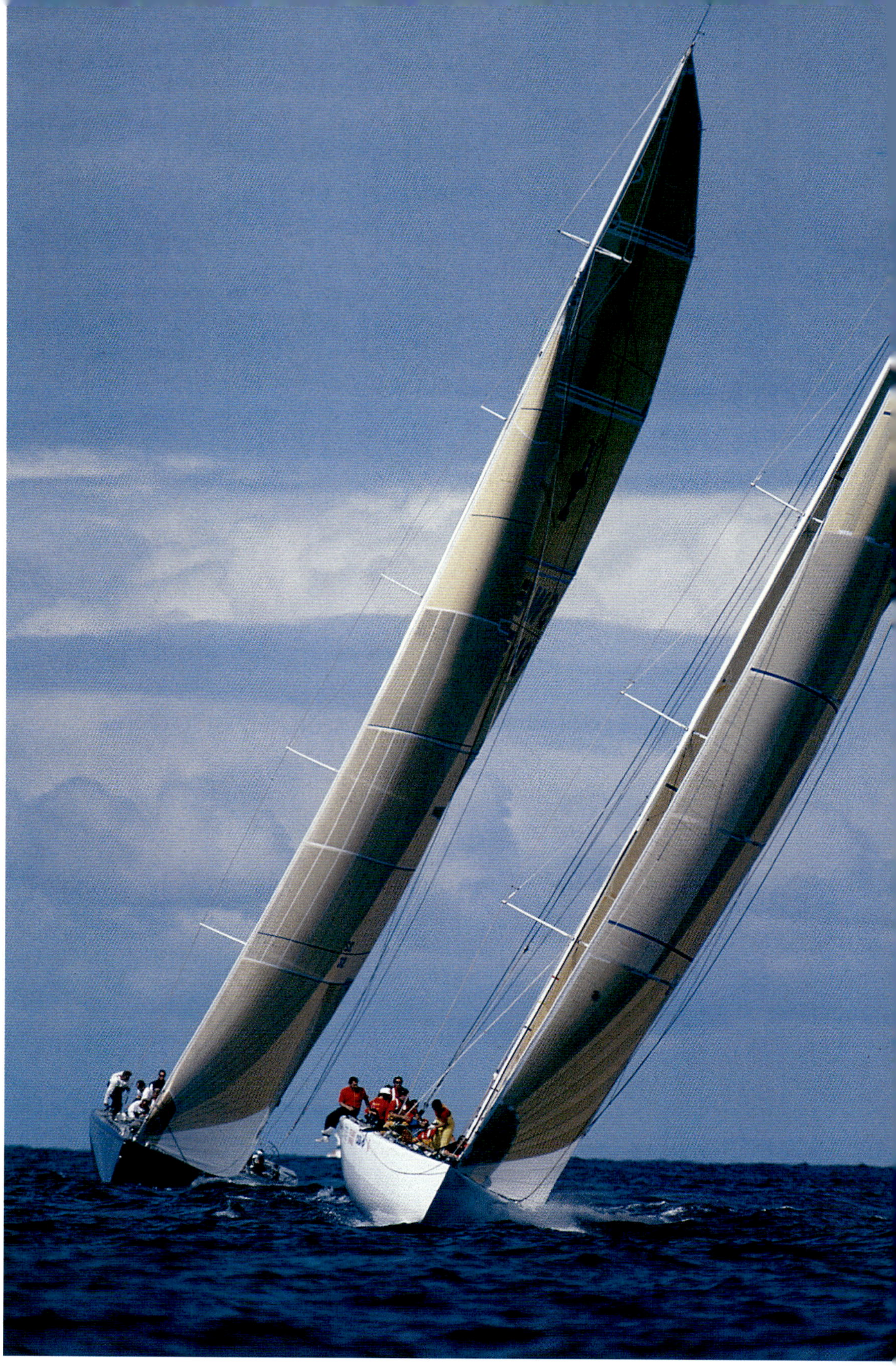

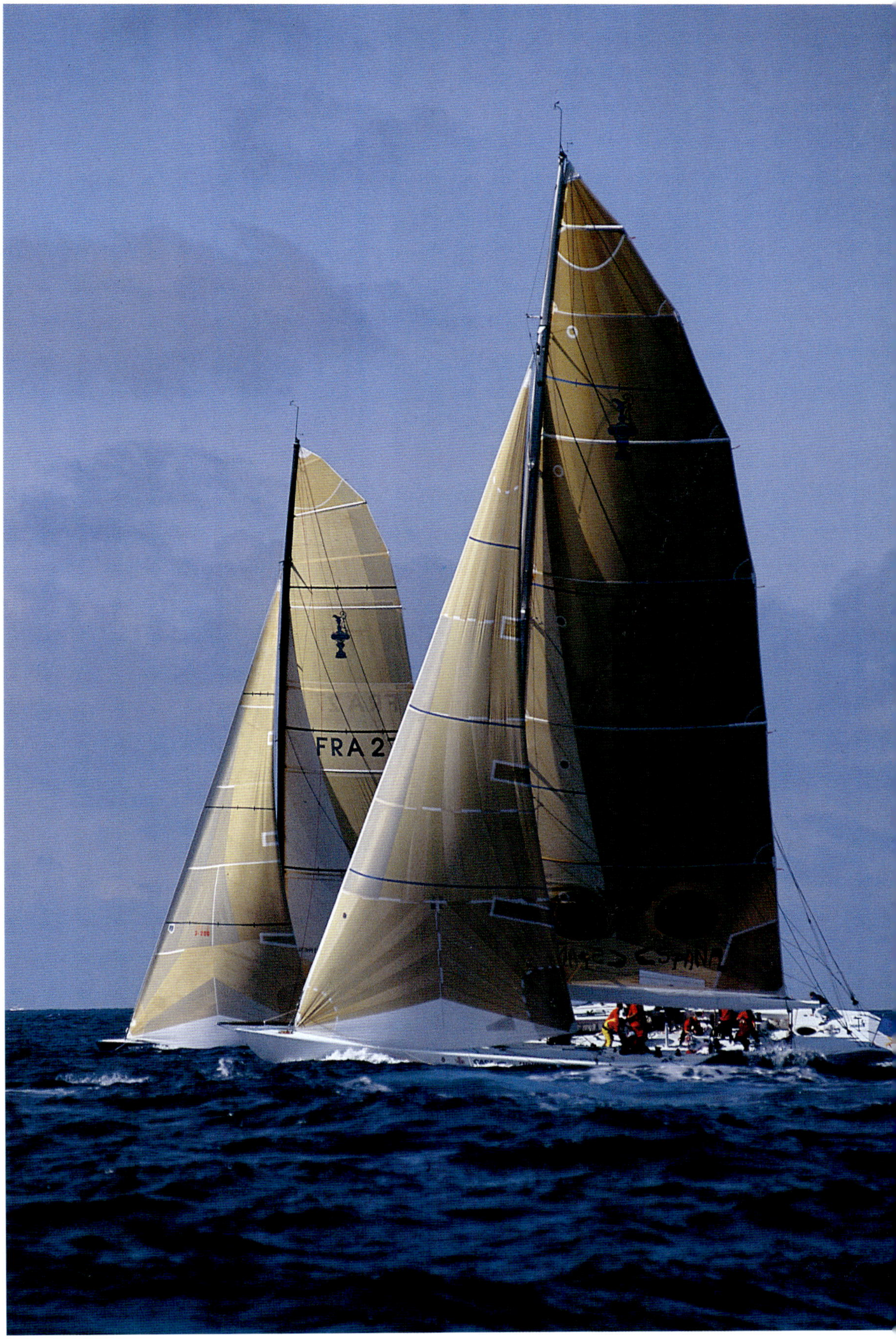

Sharp Relief

On a day of unusual clarity, with sharp sunshine and strong contrasting shadow, *France* and *Spain* are on the first windward leg shortly after the start. The breeze has piped up and the sun is above the yachts, so the crew on deck is washed in sunlight while bright sunlight and deep shadow sharply mold the sails. The crispness of the day sets line and color in unusually sharp relief, which lends a three-dimensional quality. The thought of a photographic image being three-dimensional is never really in my mind, but I always think of a photograph as having depth. I have no idea when and how, long ago, the concept of image depth fixed in my mind, but it includes subject, lens, photographic film, paper, and chemistry. For as long as I can remember, each has made its own contribution to the character of an image.

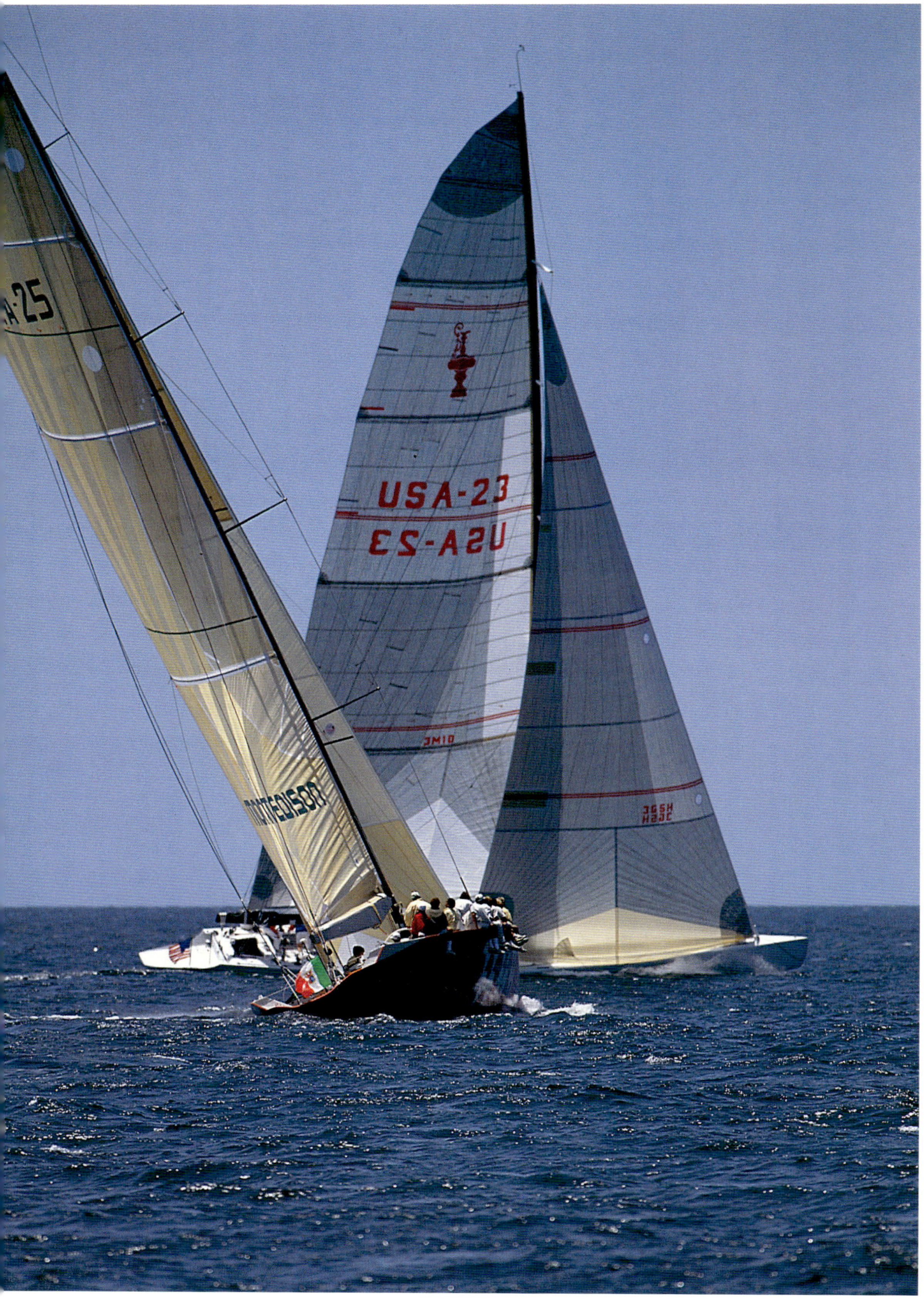

SUNLIGHT

Il Moro Di Venezia and A^3 in the America's Cup race of 1992 are crossing tacks. The effect of sunlight shining directly on a sail or coming through a sail is seen in their mainsails just above the boom. Every wrinkle on *Il Moro*'s mainsail is clearly marked in harsh lines, etched there by the sun. Whatever similar little pattern there might be in A^3's sail is softened. Just when to shoot, as the yachts move through the pattern of their crossing, is determined for me by the power of the crossing lines of their hulls and rigging. At this moment, the tense figures of *Il Moro*'s crew seated on the windward rail are intersected by the dark leech line of A^3's genoa. That point is also the apex of the line formed by *Il Moro*'s headstay and is strengthened by the line of her mast reaching down to the deck. The center of the crossed lines is the massed figures of *Il Moro*'s crew. The angle of *Il Moro*'s hull toward A^3 gives some promise of contact between the vessels and so heightens the implied tension. Our photo boat is moving to the right along with A^3, so the image of *Il Moro* is rapidly sweeping across my camera viewfinder. In my mind, one little voice prompts me not to shoot too soon, while another urges me not to wait too long. I depend on the third little voice, which urgently prompts "NOW" at just the right instant of the crossing.

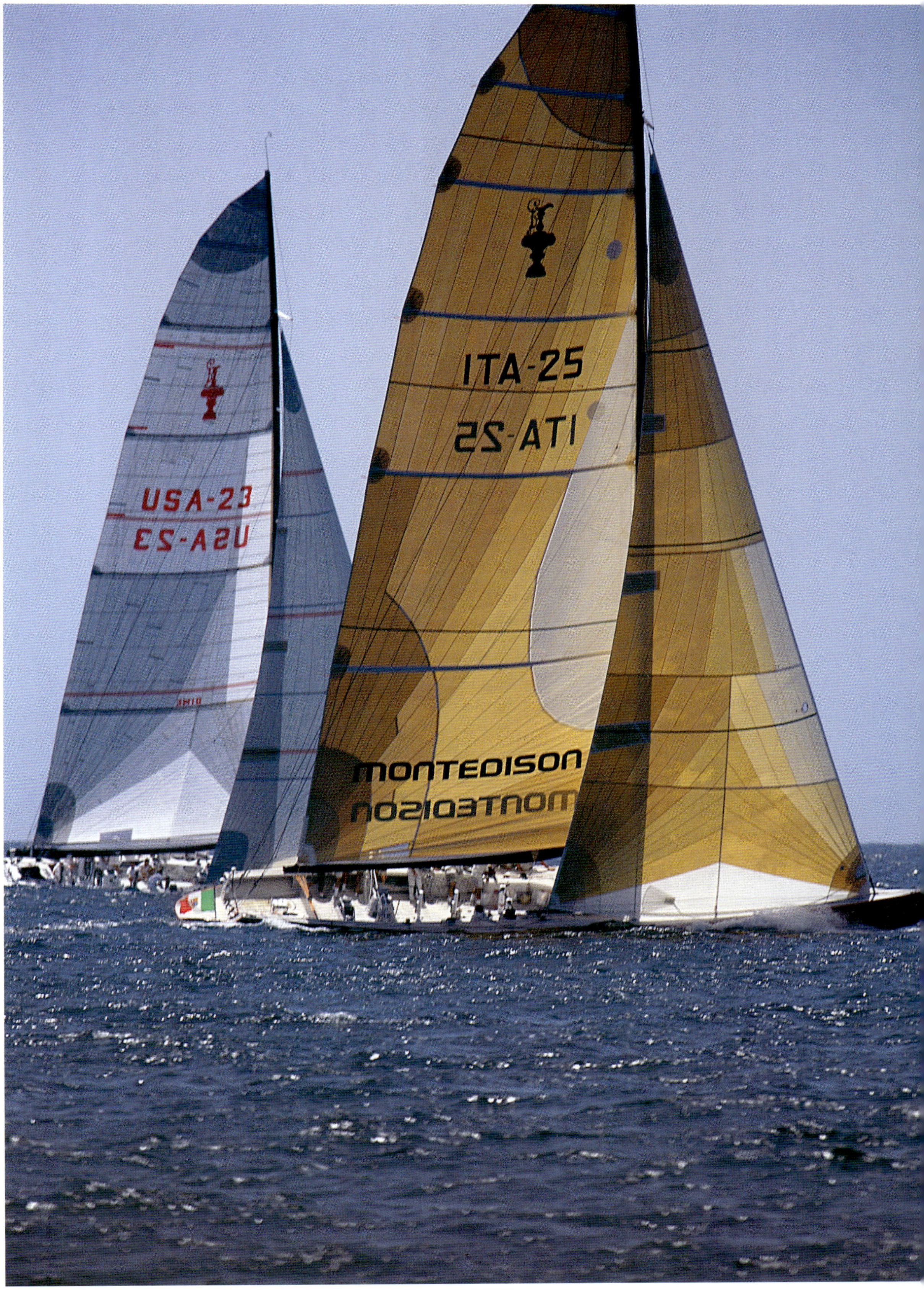

A New Palette

A^3 and *Il Moro* have the same high backlighting coming through their sails and bathing their decks. The intricate pattern of the fabric of their sails is clearly shown. The golden sails of *Il Moro* are a laminate of Kevlar and Mylar, and the white cloth at the bottom is made of Mylar and Dacron. The gray-blue cloth A^3 is using is called Cuben fiber, after the cube in A^3, and is a combination of Spectra film reinforced with Kevlar fiber. The new geometry of sailmaking is painted with a new palette. Enhancing the liveliness and color of the yachts, the surface of the water sparkles with reflected light. To shoot against the light, when the sun is high and so perfectly matched to the course of the yachts, is the best of all possible worlds for the midday photographer. Some photographers avoid the harsh midday sunlight, but this is not possible, and often not desirable, when racing is in progress.

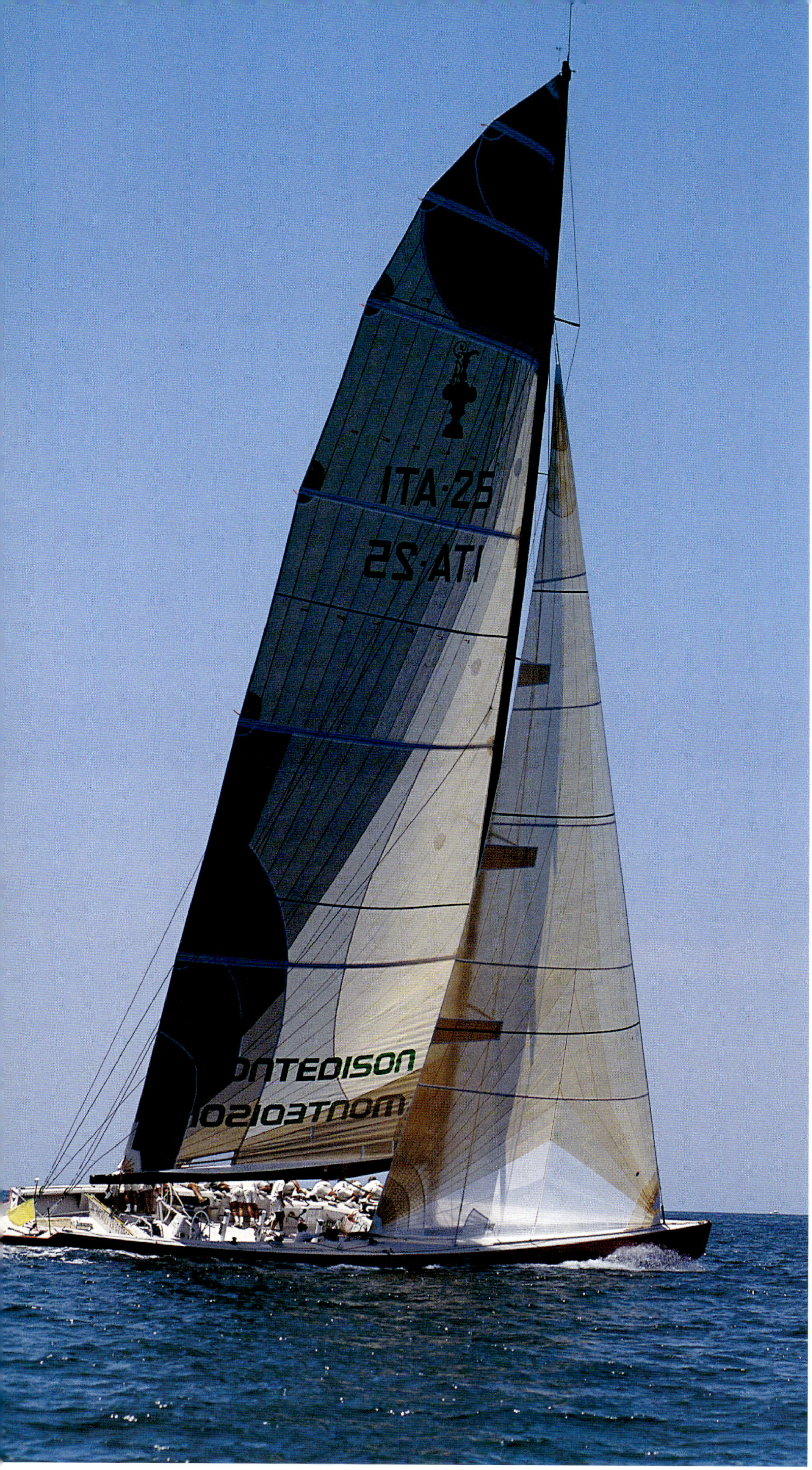

Illusion

Camera distance and focal length of the lens both affect the apparent height of the mast and rig when photographing these America's Cup yachts. This image captures a moment when both elements combine to give *Il Moro Di Venezia* all the height and dignity of her rig. In addition, to contribute to the illusion of size, the small individual figures of the crew can be seen lined up along the windward rail under the boom. The foredeck length out to the rail is visible through the transparent panels at the foot of the genoa, extending the long line of the windward rail. In another pattern of lines, see how clearly the vertical rising seams of the sailcloth in both the main and genoa carry the eye upwards. In all, we have an unusual harmony of line that sings of size.

START

New Zealand and *France* are at the starting line as the gun goes off. To the left, the judges' boat flies the signal flags that mark the compass direction of the first leg. The triangular yellow starting-line buoy is just under *New Zealand*, and the committee boat at the other side of the line appears between the two yachts. The contestants had separated a minute before when *France* had gone on port tack toward the committee-boat side of the line. For me, this start photo told its own story, but my interest by now was tuned to the spot where the two yachts would meet when they both tacked and approached each other a short way up the course. Which of the skippers had chosen the correct side of the starting line? On which side would the wind direction or strength be most favorable? My concern was that our photo chase boat be in the right spot for a meaningful crossing-tacks photo that would show a gain made by one skipper's choice of the better side of the starting line.

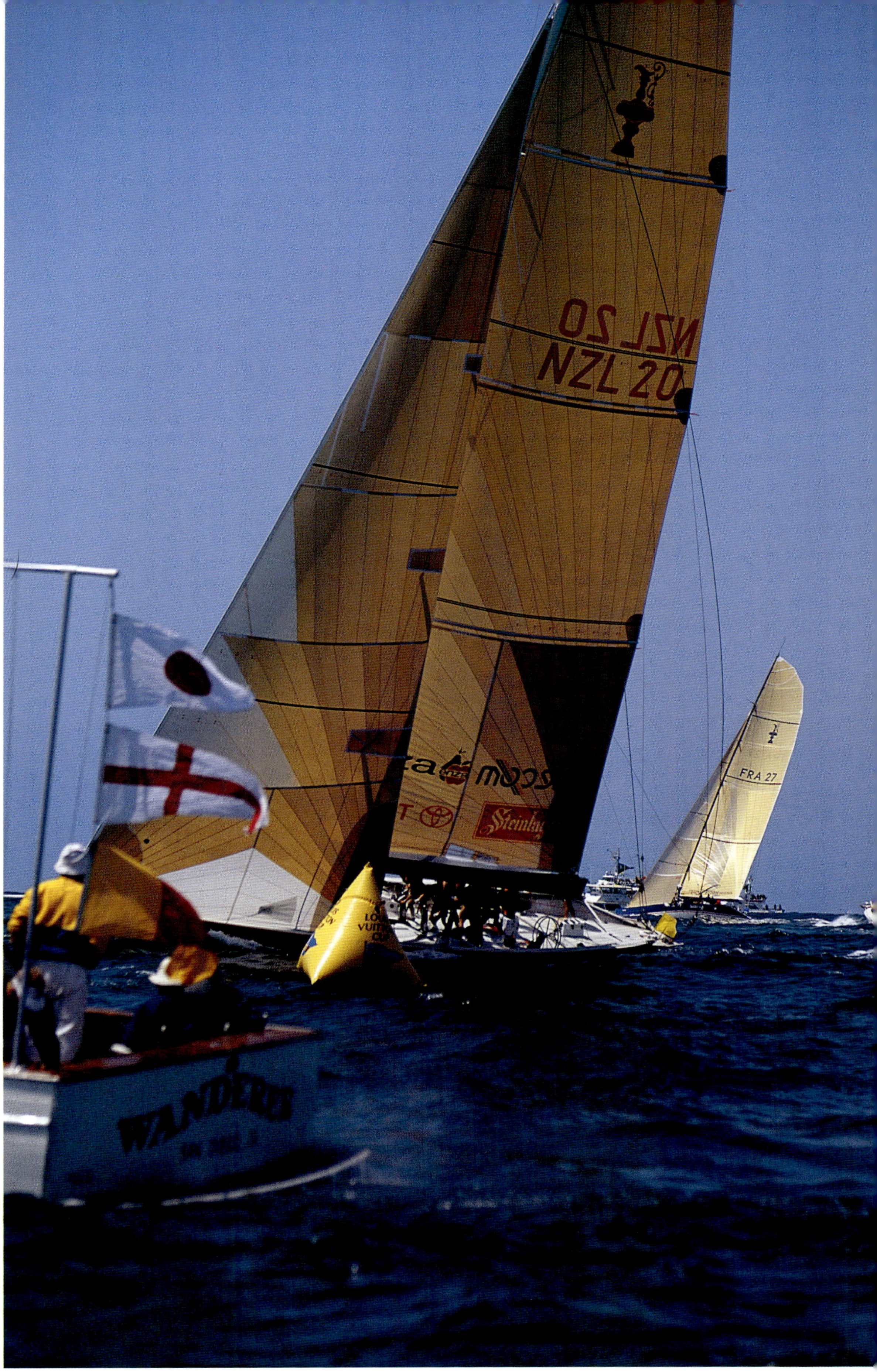

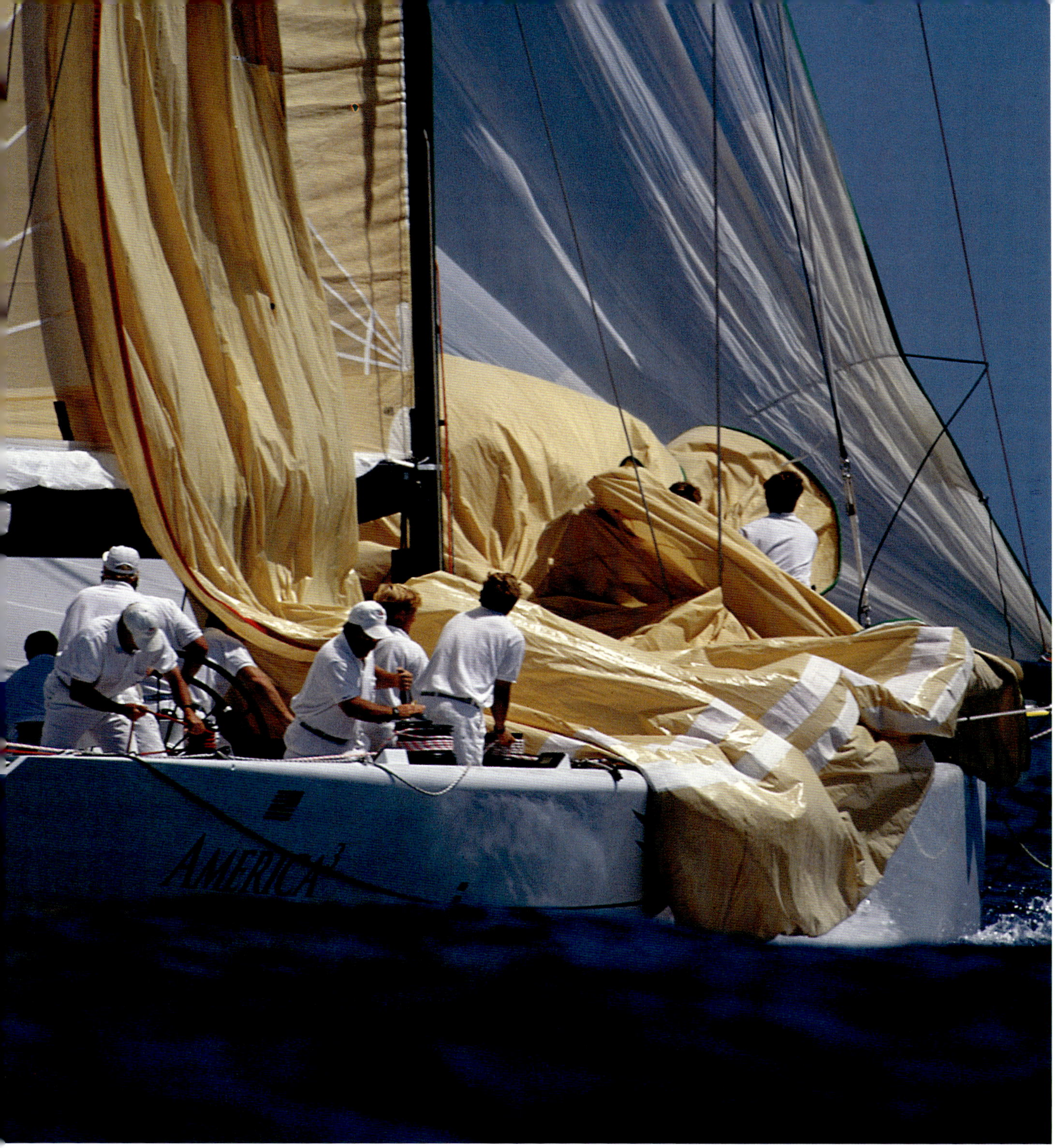

Falling Sails

After the 1992 races, the fifth and reaching leg of the America's Cup course was eliminated. In the image above, the confusion of falling sails covering the deck and the action of the men underneath show a typical moment in the mark-rounding from the fifth to the sixth leg of that course. I was sorry to see the leg eliminated, for it was an instigator of photographic opportunities. This moment, just after the rounding, suggests that some of the crew of A^3 would not be unhappy with the new and simpler windward-leeward course.

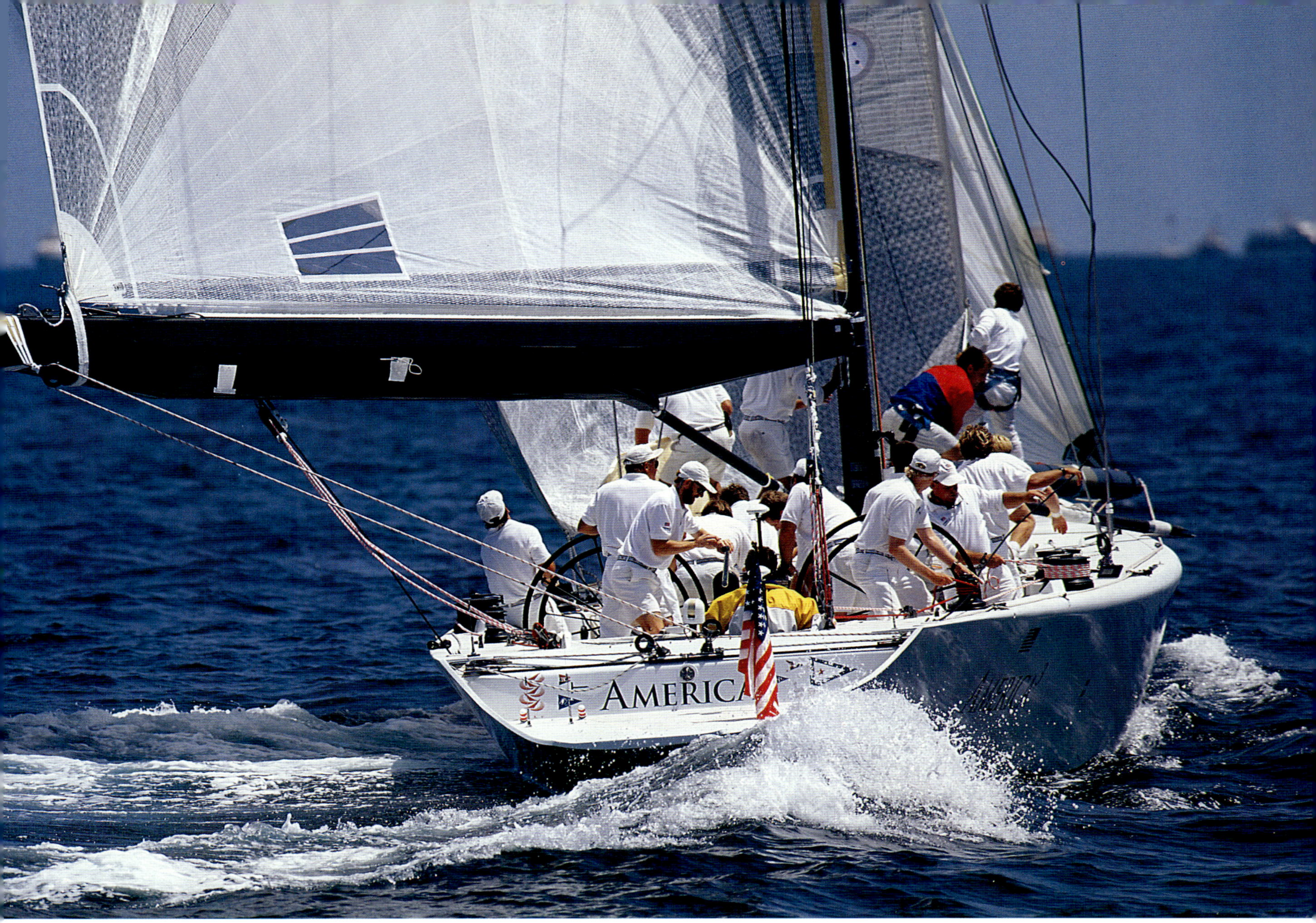

ROUNDING

A^3 is rounding a windward mark, the gennaker is set, the jib is being dropped, and the bow is turning to leeward. Two things interest me here: first, the deck is fairly clear of sail at a key moment of sail change and trim; and second, the action and individual interest of each crew member is evident. Astern, the pattern of wake and the motion in the water indicate the turning course of the yacht as it rounds the mark. They also show the heaping action of the wave pattern as water is being thrust out and to starboard of the yacht's track. It was not so much wave and foam themselves that interested me as what secret they were revealing about water displaced by the advancing and turning hull. There is more to an image than appears on the surface, and photographs can lead the mind beneath the obvious.

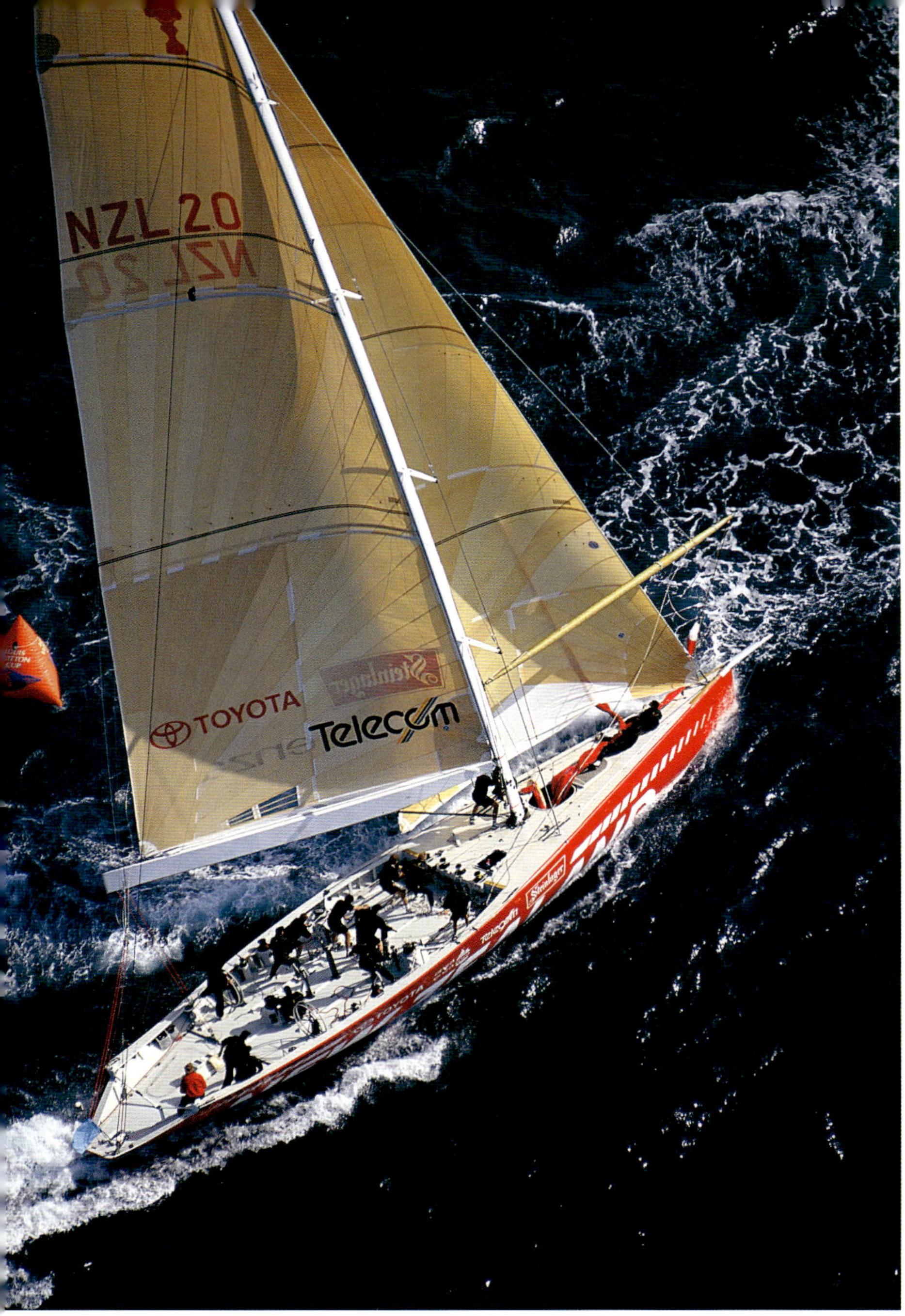

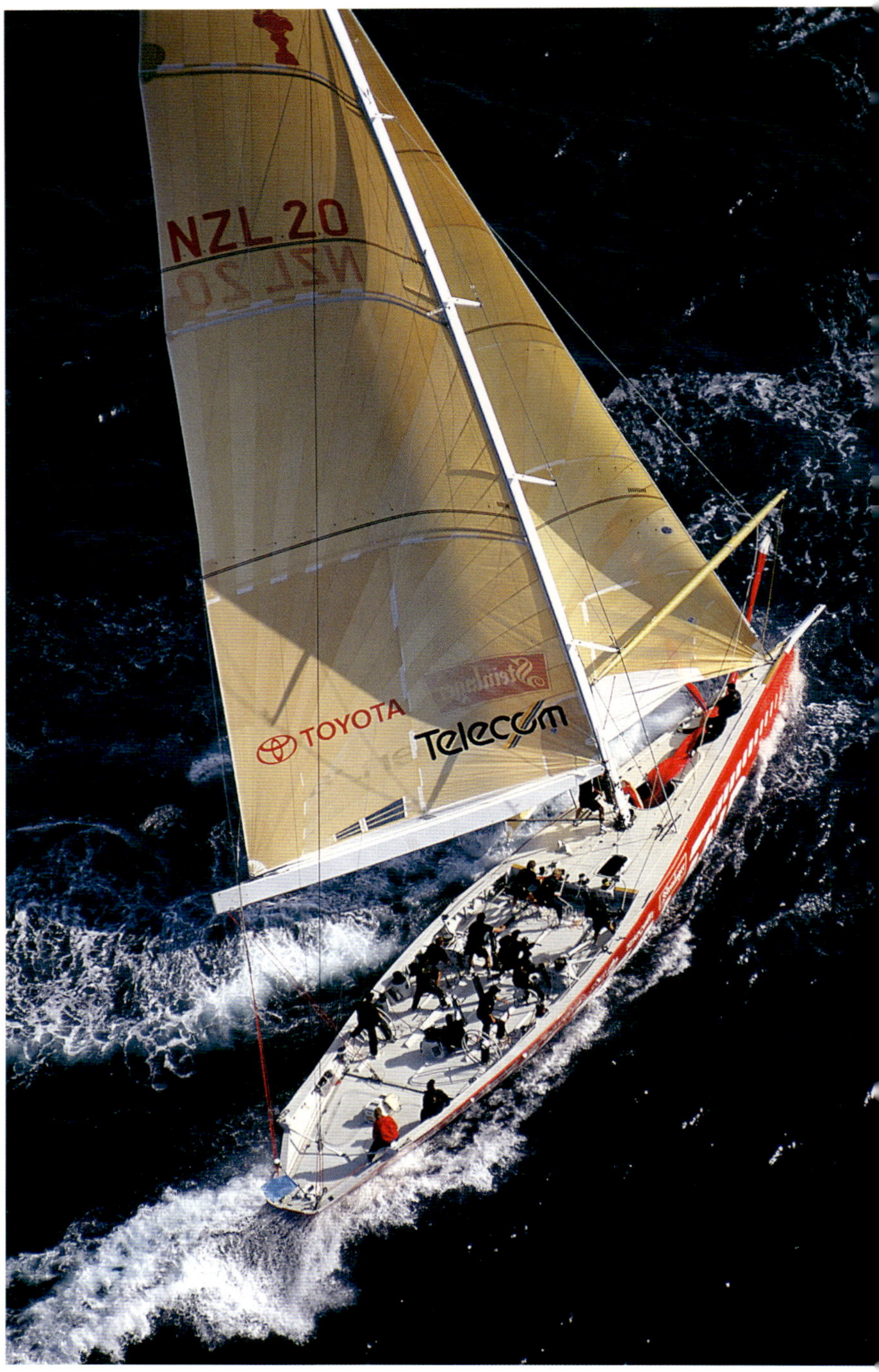

Hard Over

New Zealand with her rudder hard over is rounding the windward buoy, her bow swinging to port and to leeward. When the rudder is put over to turn sharply, the hull pivots around the turn and the stern swings into a longer radius than the bow. The white water of the wake and along the side of the hull shows this advancing, pivoting, turning motion. As *New Zealand* passes the red buoy well into her turn, there is a gush of water at the transom, and the white wake is pushed out along the side at the cockpit.

Boiling

Farther into the turn, the white water at the transom is really boiling and has moved forward along the side.

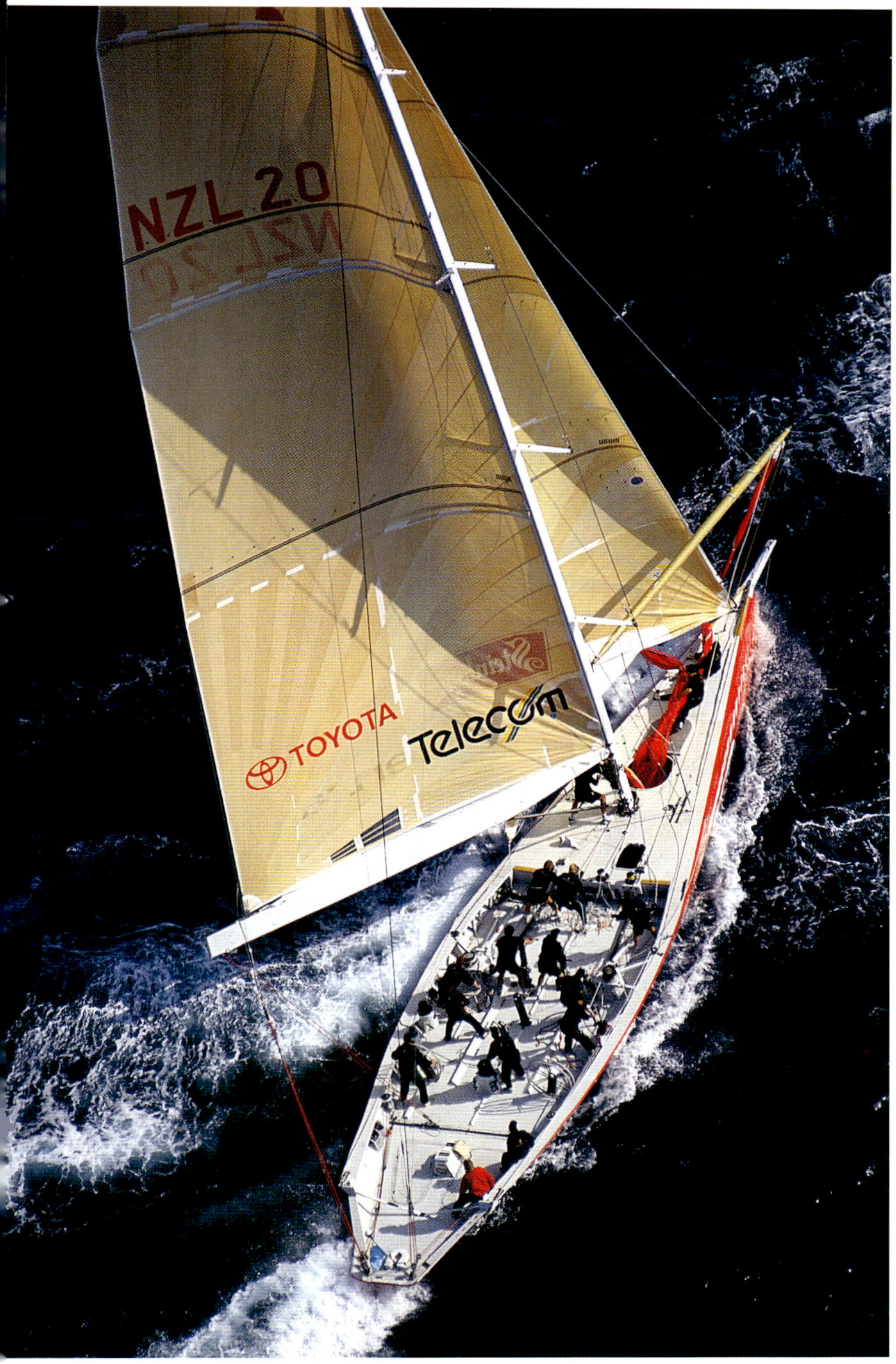

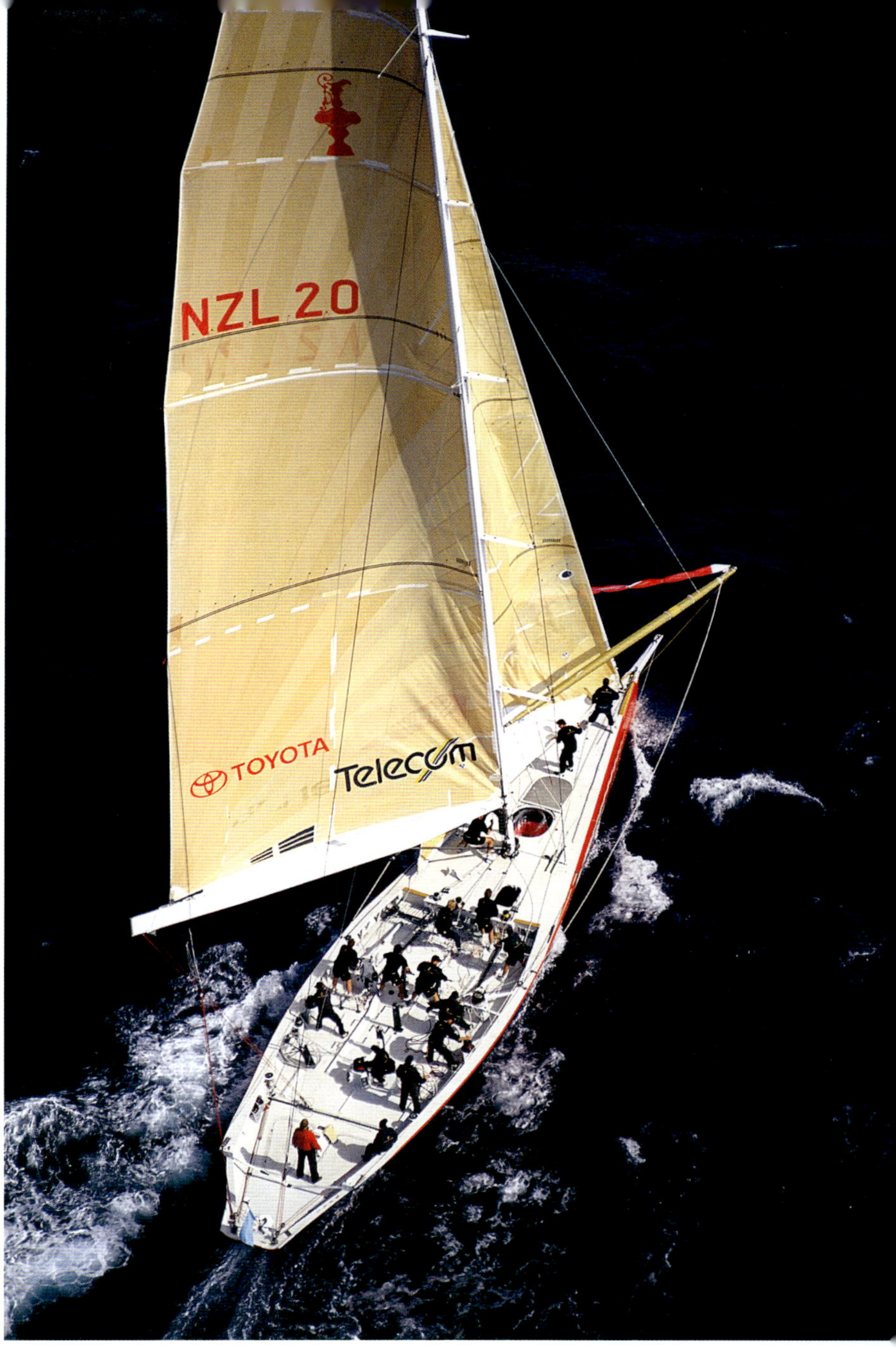

New Course

The turn is complete, the rudder is amidships, and the white trail of wake is almost gone. *New Zealand* is headed on her new course.

The pivoting motion of the stern in the turn is clearly shown in this sequence of photographs. Usually I would choose one of such a series to submit with a selection to a magazine. Here I would have been in conflict between the second image, with the most action, and the first, which more obviously tells the story of a mark-rounding (the mark is shown on the left). There is another aspect of the story written by the white pattern of wake in the water ahead of *New Zealand* as she rounds the buoy. *New Zealand* is rounding the mark just astern of *Il Moro*, which was her ultimate fate at the end of this series.

Easing

The skipper has begun to ease the tiller. The wake at the stern is less violent, but white water shows all along the windward side. To leeward, the white line of wake reaches outward in a straight line.

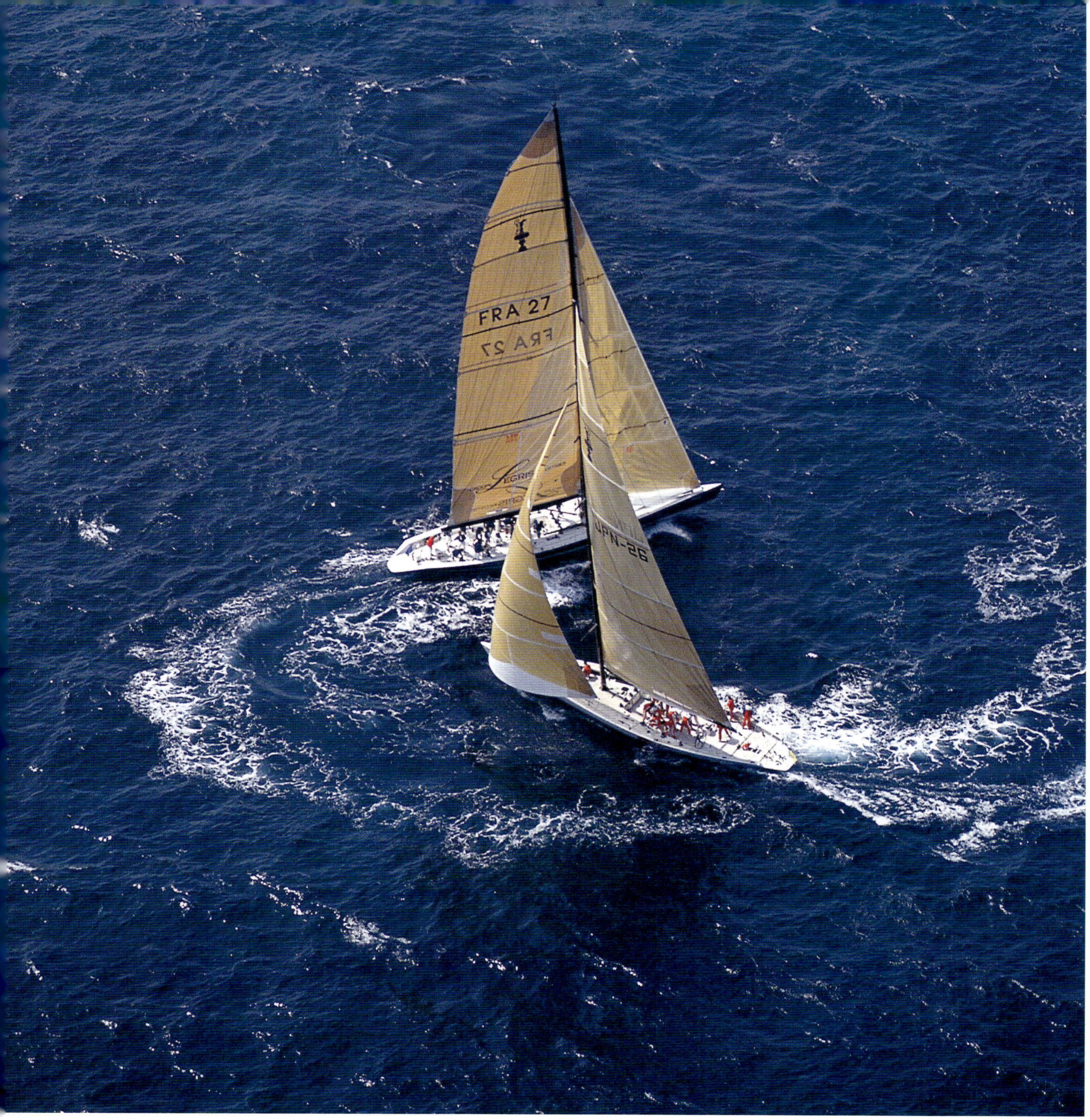

Circling

Here the yachts are turning to windward in pre-start maneuvering. The turning pattern of the wake of *Nippon* in the foreground is different from that of *New Zealand* in the previous photograph. On the inside of the turn one can see the white circles in the wake spreading out astern and, on the outside of the turn, the stronger single white line of an advancing wave. Behind *Nippon*, *France*'s main and jib are luffing. The direction her hull is headed and the slight surface pattern of the wind waves indicate that the wind is coming from the right. Stronger, deeper waves are forming a pattern from top to bottom of the entire image. Lively activity in the circular motion of the yachts maneuvering before the start holds my attention. Each part of the image reveals something and leads on to thoughts of what is still unseen.

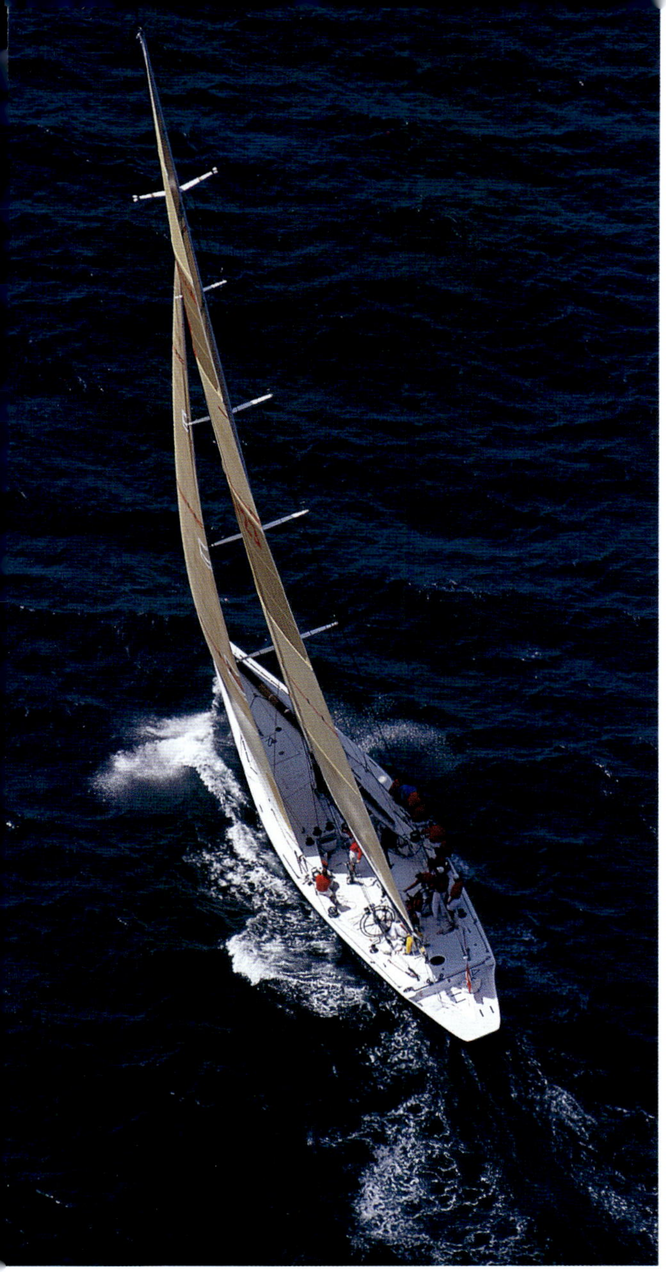

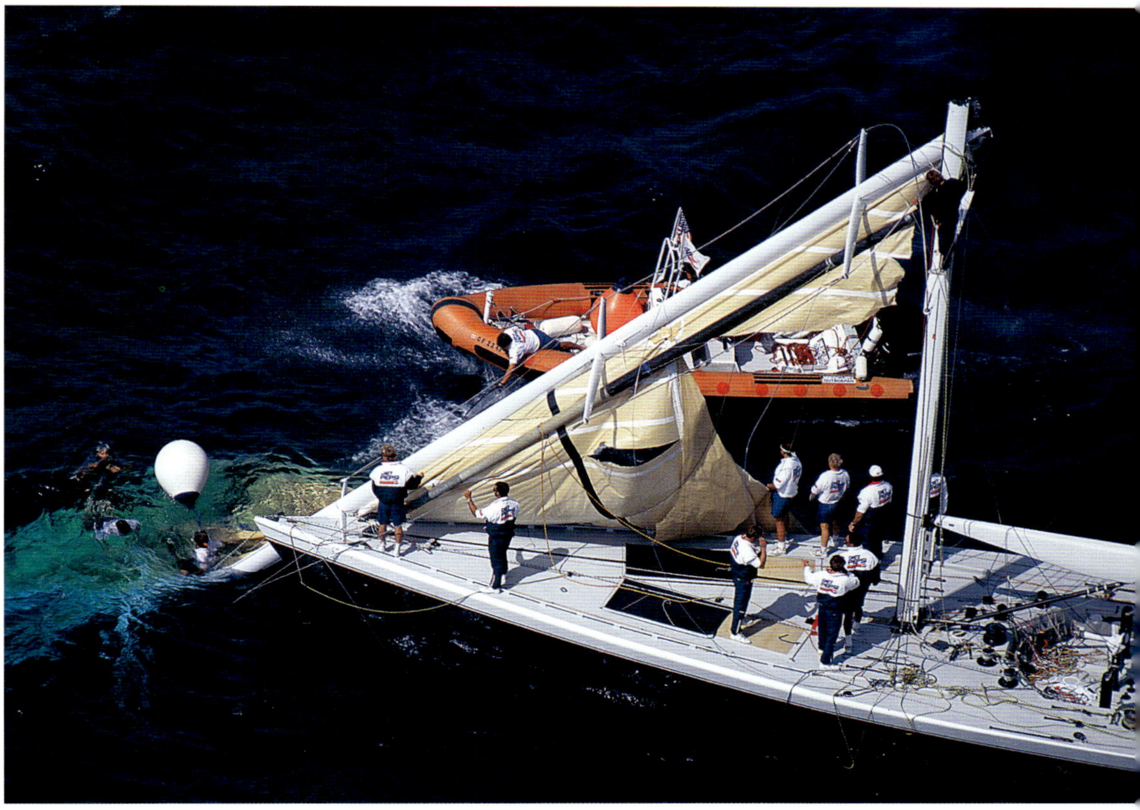

Rod Rigging?

Whether seen from the surface of the water or from a viewpoint high above, the height of the rig of these America's Cup yachts and the seeming fragility of their masts were always impresssive. As I made this image I was thinking that the spreaders were clearly shown, but there was no reflection off the rod rigging and it had disappeared from view. The mast seemed to be standing on its own. At this time, masts had a high rate of breakage, and I knew they had trouble standing, even with all their shrouds in place. I did not really need any illusions to make me wonder about the future of each tall mast.

Mast?

At about the time the previous image was made, *Stars & Stripes*, sailing out of my sight, lost her mast. The pilots of the photo helicopters kept in touch with each other and, the moment the mast fell, word went out to all the other photographers flying the course. By the time we arrived, *Stars & Stripes*'s mast had been buoyed and the operation to retrieve the sail was underway. The uneven cross section of the break in the mast is shown clearly. The broken section is still hanging, sustained by the internal rigging of the mast and shreds of torn sail.

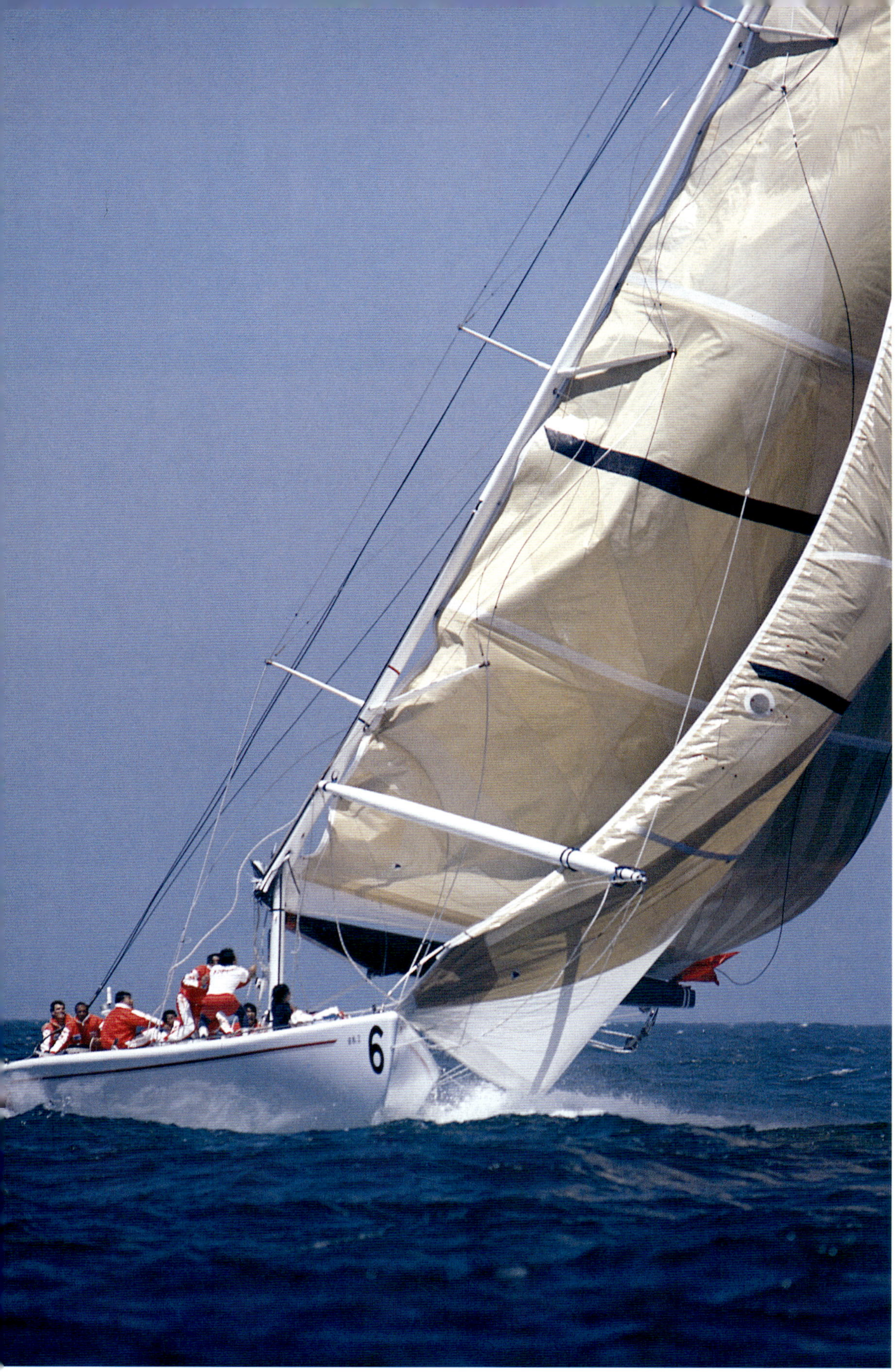

Falling

I have been on the course many times when masts have broken just out of camera range, but at a lucky camera instant in the 1991 International America's Cup Class World Championships, as *Nippon* rounded the windward mark with her spinnaker pole already set, I heard the sharp report of a mast snapping. My camera lens was a 300 mm with manual focus, as I had not yet moved into the autofocus era. However, I had previously focused on the buoy, which at this instant was just ahead of *Nippon*'s bow, and though my head was turned away from the mark, when I heard the crack I swung around, moving the camera to my eye so that an instant after the mast started to move I had aimed the camera and made the first exposure. The spinnaker pole is leaning against the headstay, which is already curved in its collapse. The break in the mast is clearly shown, with a section outside the boom splitting. At the foot of the mast, the bowman is seated on the deck. Two crewmen, their hands still on the halyard, look up at the looming threat of the broken boom end pointing at their heads. The rest of the crew look forward at the new events evolving, their hands still occupied with their previous tasks. Above them, along the length of the mast, the sail, with its tension released, is folding in its track.

Falling II

The outboard end of the spinnaker pole is now in the water. Though the foredeck man's hands still work with sail, his head is raised and his eyes must be on the descending path of the spinnaker pole. One of the two men at the mast has lunged aft, the other, with his hands still on the halyard, is falling away, while the silvery, knife-like shrouds gleam in a wicked, curving arc beyond him. The cockpit crew's attention is riveted on the break in the mast, which now has split, revealing its innards. The falling section is balanced precariously on the edge of the stump, still upright below.

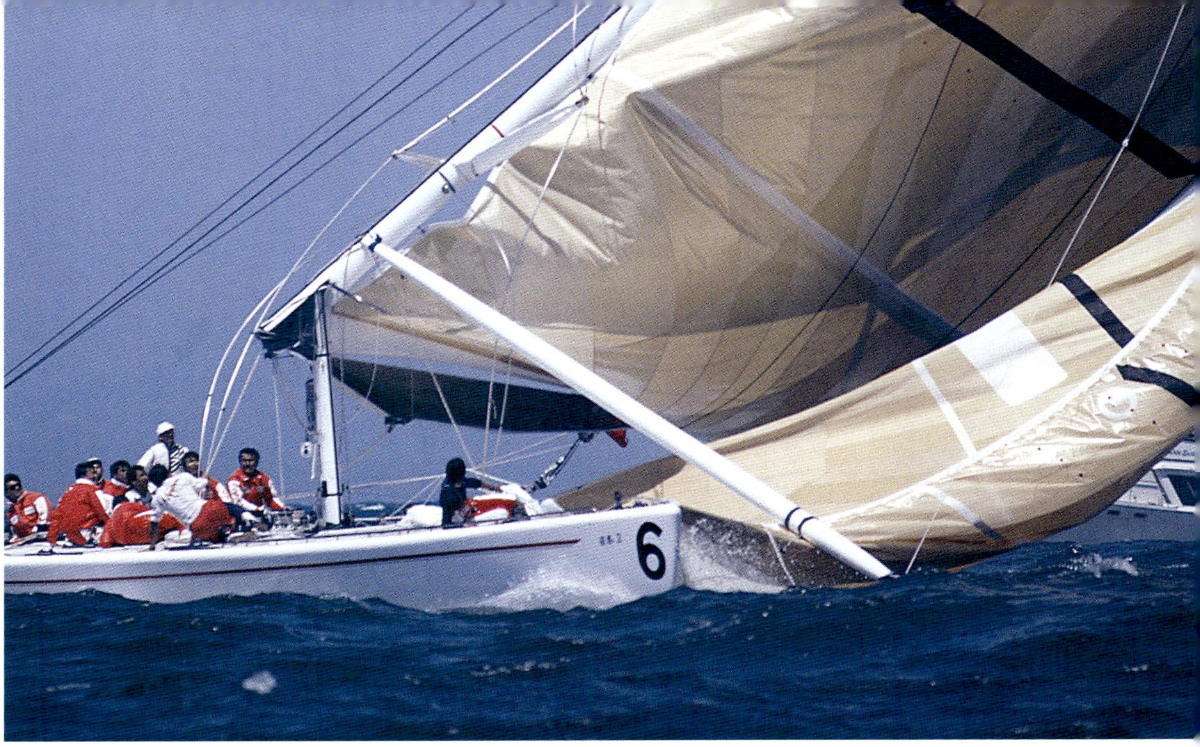

Falling III

I became aware that, to establish location, I had to show the orange mark, which was just disappearing under the jib. The spinnaker pole has been dragged aft by its movement through the water, and its path, now guided by the edge of the deck, is clear of the foredeck man. The falling mast appears to be clear of the stump that was previously the pivot point. It now seems to be held by the end of the boom and perhaps the rigging internal to the mast.

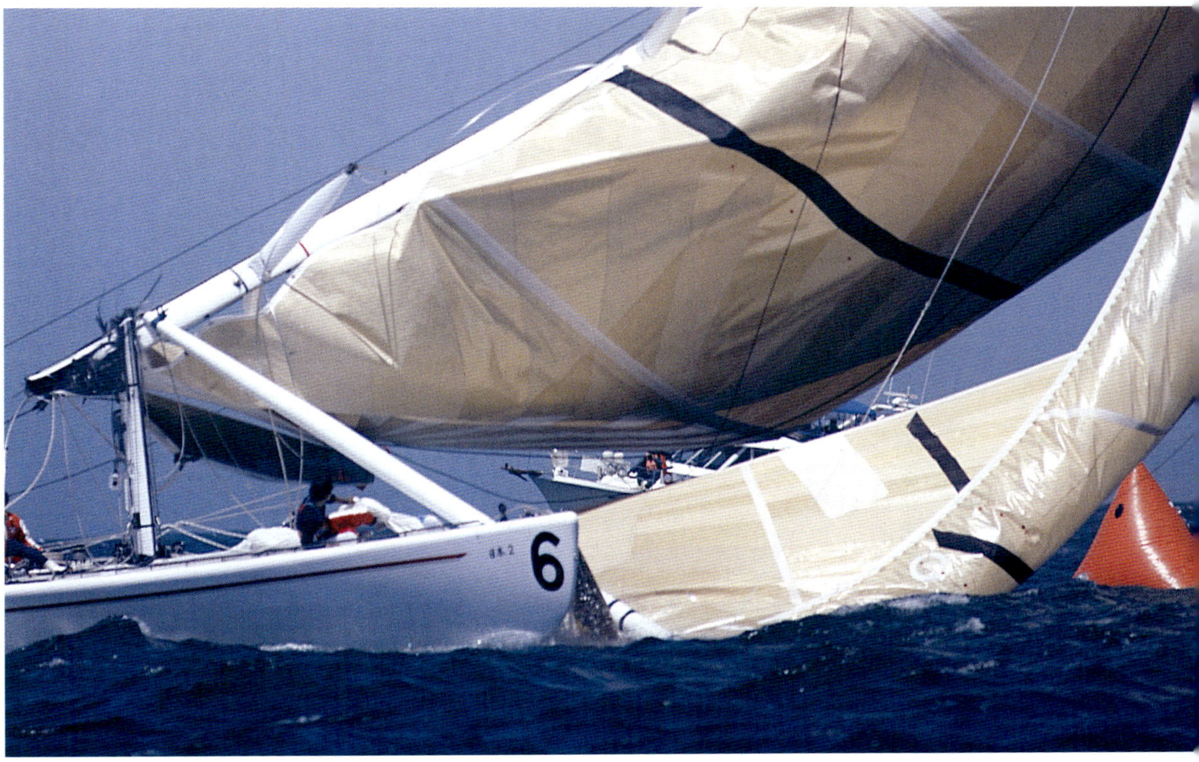

Falling IV

Through the sequence, *Nippon*'s bow wave has been evident, indicating that, though the boom and part of the jib are dragging in the water, *Nippon* has been carrying her way, powered on by the momentum inherent in twenty-odd tons of lead keel. The bowman is relieved because the boom is sliding past him, but the crew at the forward end of the cockpit have eyes only for the broken mast end, which fortunately continued to pivot in place.

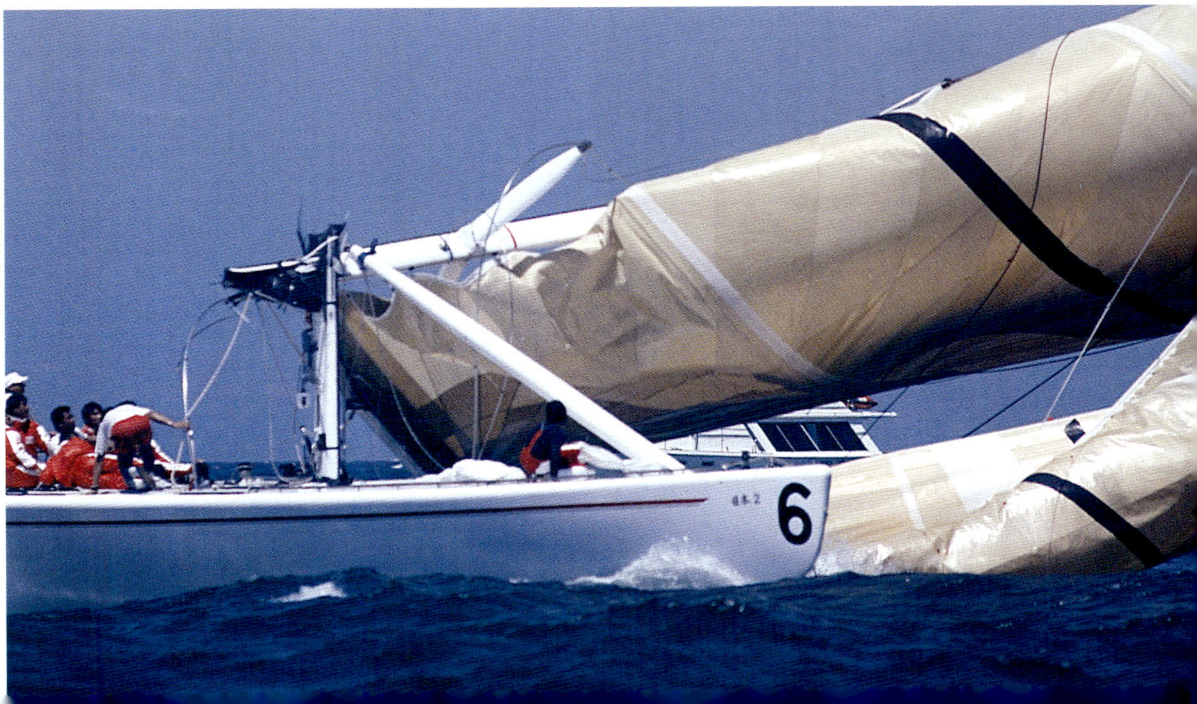

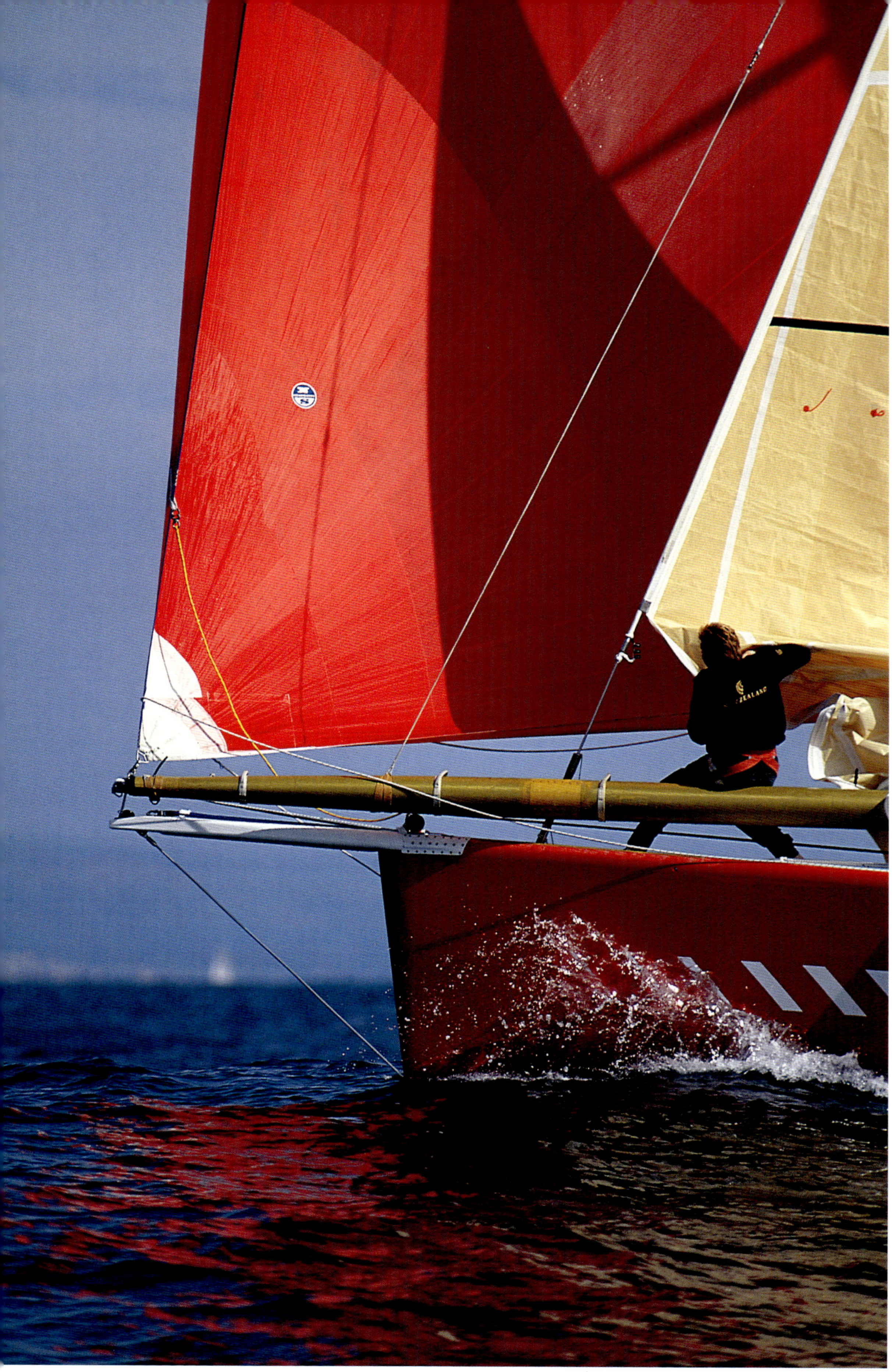

SHEET ANGLE?

The 1992 America's Cup contest was marked by considerable controversy among challengers off the course, much of which involved the little bowsprit installed on *New Zealand* and the angle of the sheet lead between the end of the bowsprit and the spinnaker pole. In this photograph, made on March 31, the sheet angle leading from the spinnaker pole to the end of the bowsprit seems to be angled slightly forward. Notice that the splash of spray near the bow seems to be moving forward and up, an unusual angle.

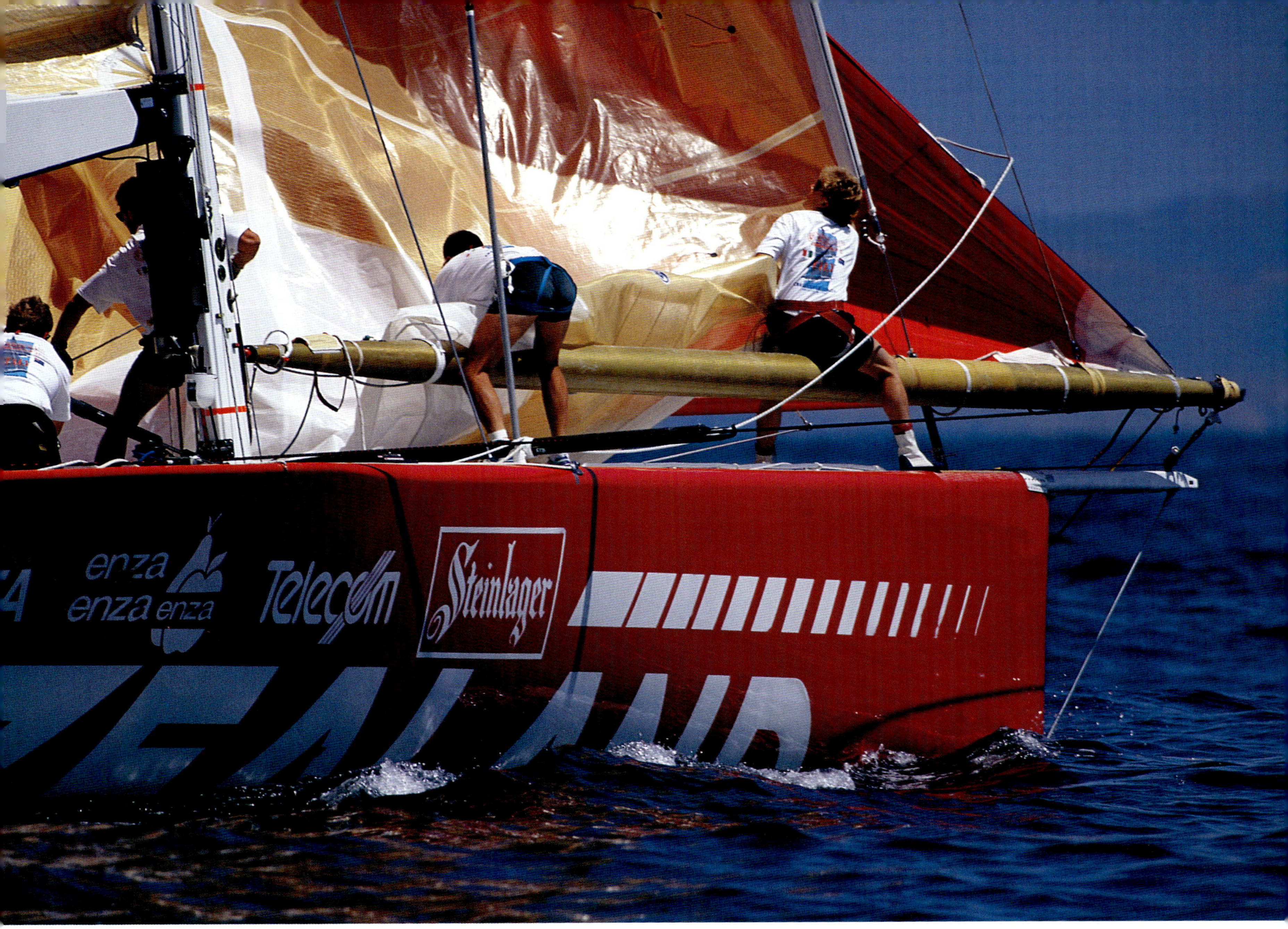

Sheet Angle Aft?

On April 28, after a heated Protest Committee meeting, the bowsprit on *New Zealand* seems a little shorter, and the angle of the sheet leading from the spinnaker pole to the block on the bowsprit seems to lead aft.

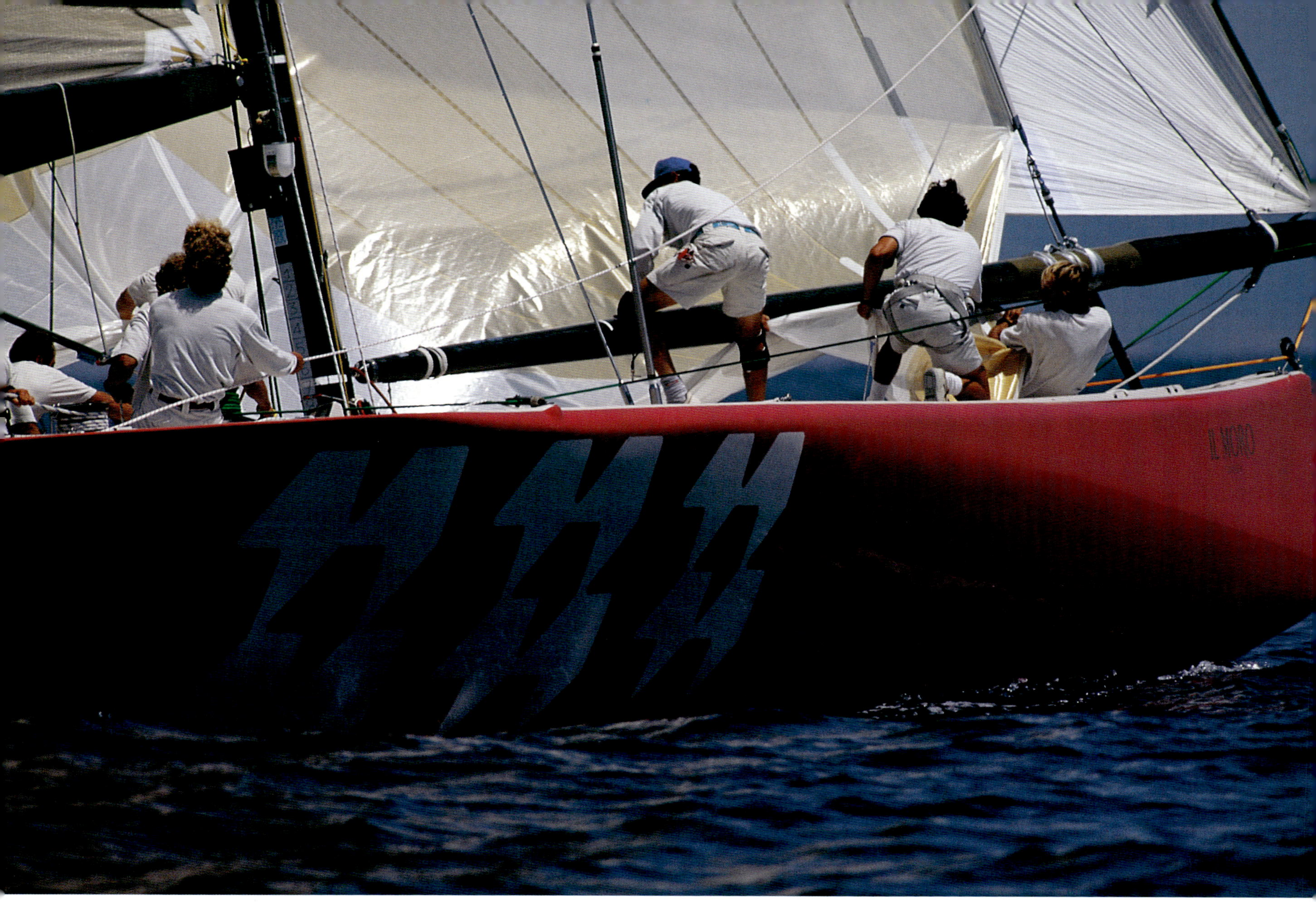

Sheet Angle Aft

Il Moro Di Venezia carried no bowsprit and the angle of the sheet leading to the block on the stem clearly leads aft. Hours of controversy, initiated and continued by Paul Cayard of *Il Moro,* ensued over the actual angle of the sheet lead to *New Zealand*'s bowsprit.

Pointing I

The controversy escalated to acrimonious accusations by the Italians against the New Zealanders. At a press conference, Paul Cayard, skipper of *Il Moro,* vehemently advanced his arguments against *New Zealand*'s sheet lead angle. He pointed to a drawing of the bowsprit to illustrate the contested design of the lead.

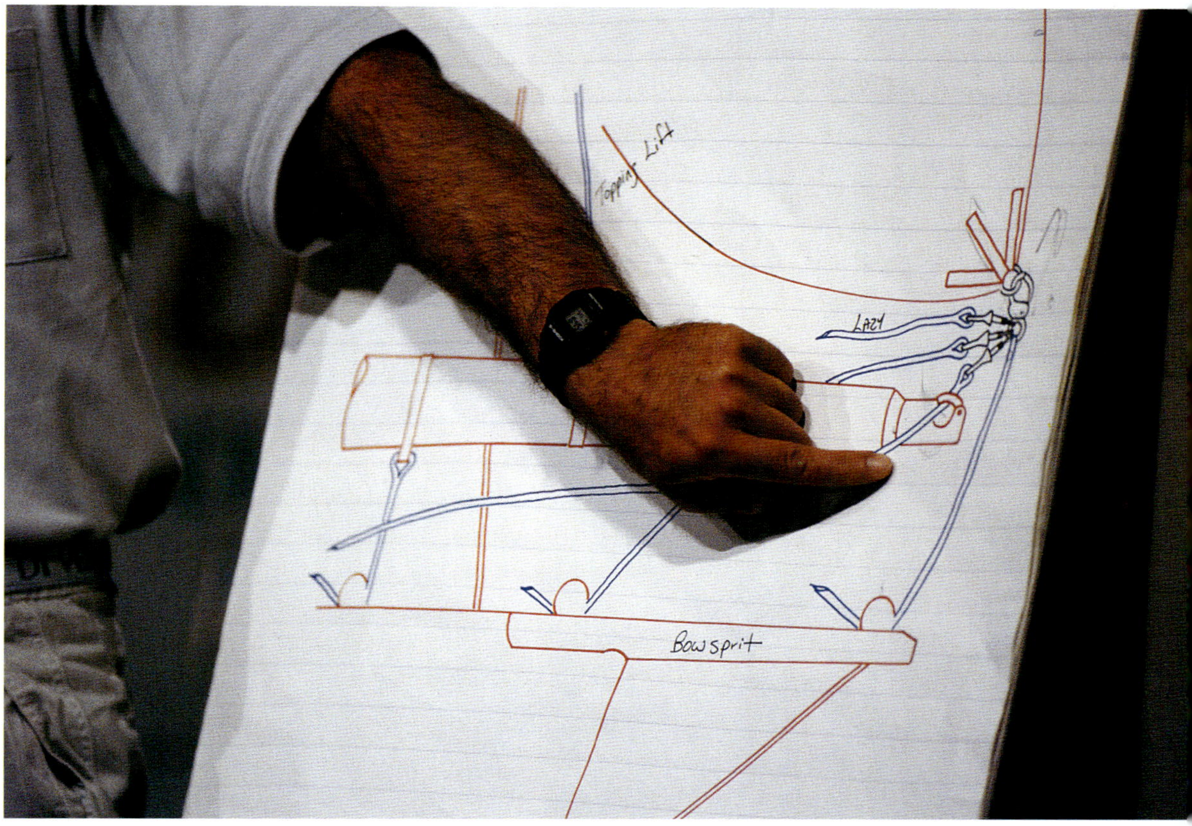

Pointing II

Bruce Farr, designer and spokesman for *New Zealand,* used the same drawing to illustrate his concept of the legal nature of *New Zealand*'s sheet lead. I found varied aspects of the argument to be trifling, but the vitriol introduced into the argument by Paul Cayard brought a new note to an otherwise sporting contest. To me, it was belaboring a technicality, a form of legal harassment. The sheet lead had seemed to have no noticeable effect on *New Zealand*'s performance, but following the sad legal maneuvers in the hearing room, *New Zealand* lost its edge out on the racecourse. Cayard and *Il Moro* came from behind to win that series and become the official challenger. On a lighter note, the only difference clearly visible to me in the evidence of the two antagonists was that Paul Cayard used one heavy finger of his left hand to make his points on the chart, while Bruce Farr used two fingers of his left hand to outline his different opinion. Their method of pointing to the chart seemed at the time more interesting than their argument.

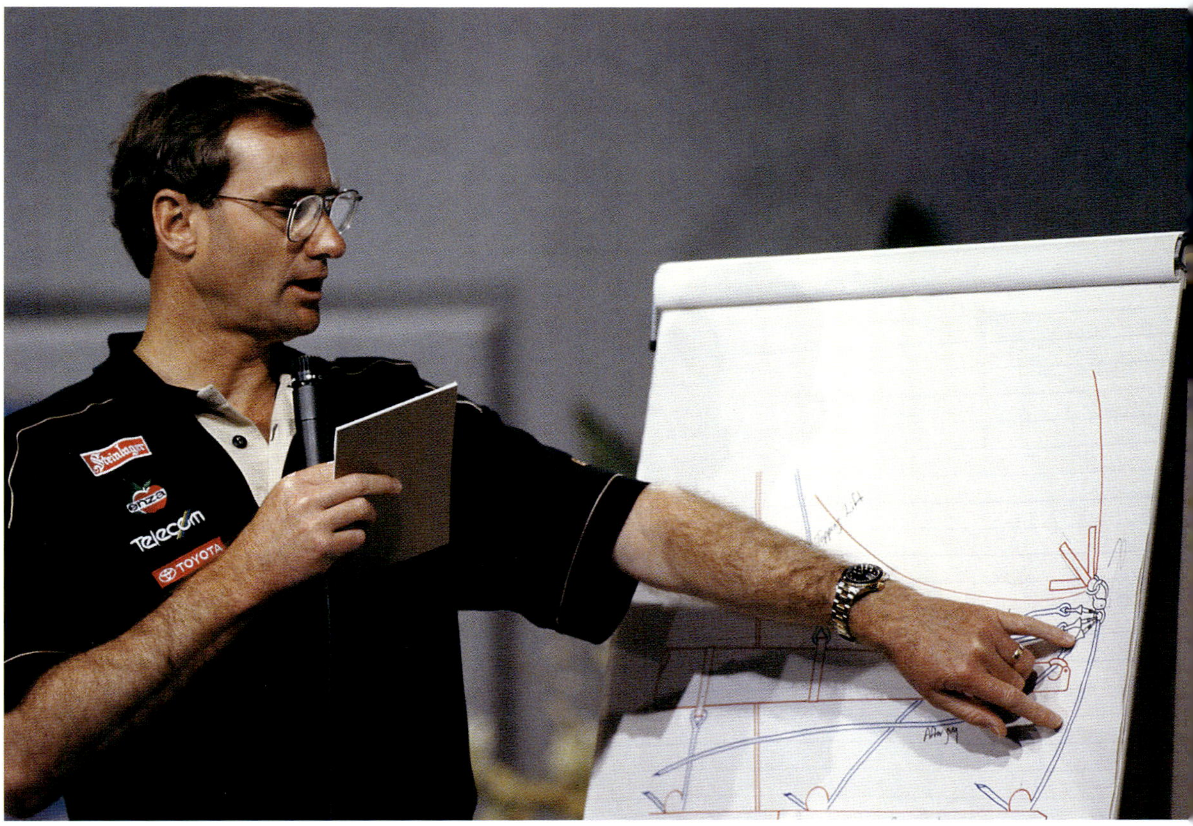

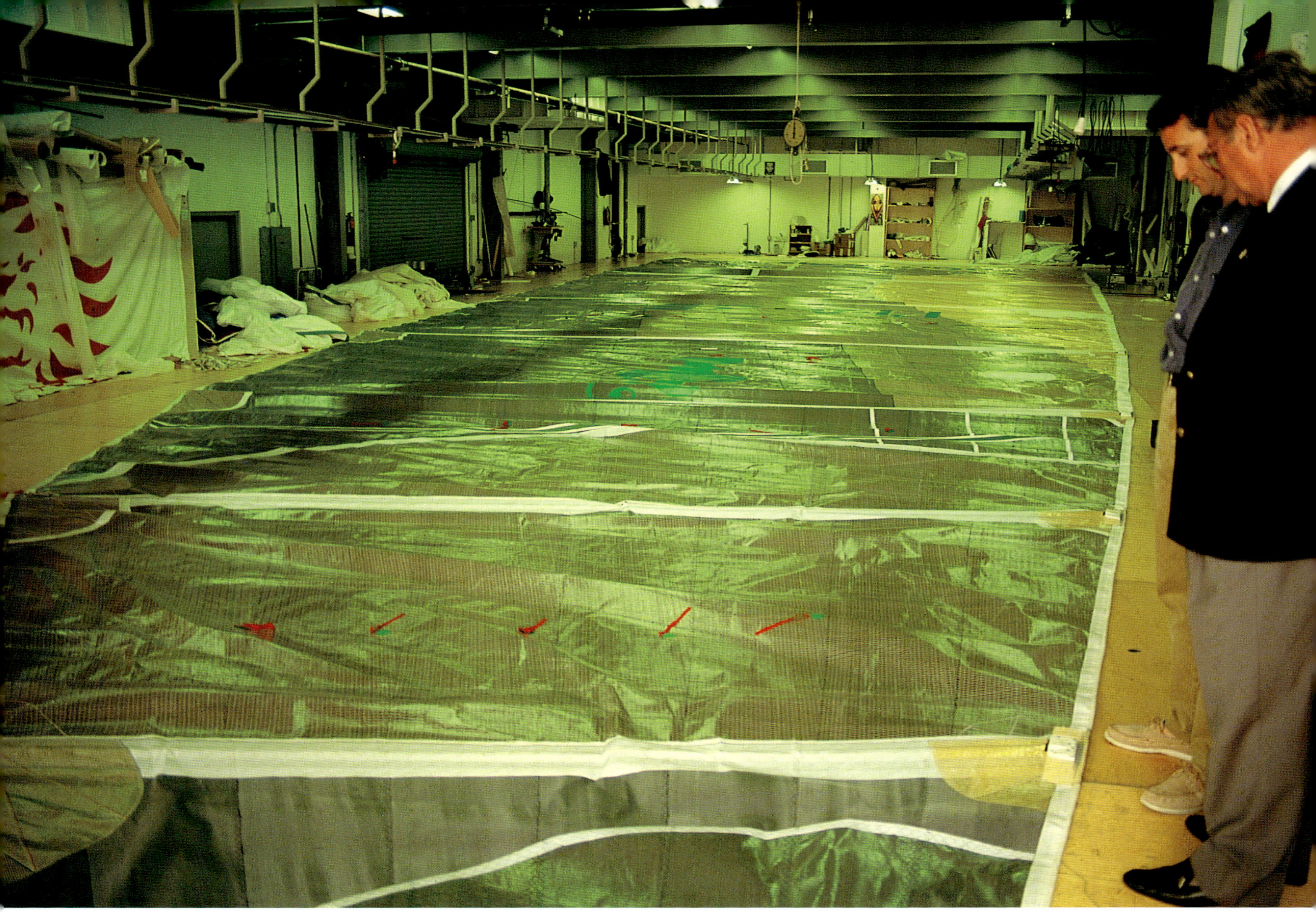

Glued

The mainsail stretched out on the floor of *Il Moro*'s sail loft made a wonderful contrast to the sail lofts of Ratsey & Lapthorn, where in 1930 many of the mainsails for the J-boats were cut and sewn. The floor of the old loft held a score or more of workers, plying their needles through the canvas sailcloth. This sail is glued and bonded together, stitches are scarce as hen's teeth, and the scores of sewers are long gone. The photographic challenge was in getting reflected light to emphasize the construction of the new synthetic surface of the cloth.

Crystal

Set and drawing, the synthetic cloth had a fascination of its own, more closely identified with crystal and metallic elements than canvas, but its surface was strangely forbidding. It did not ask to be felt between the thumb and fingers the way the old sailcloth was evaluated. It was a long step away from the personal contact a yachtsman had with sails of yore.

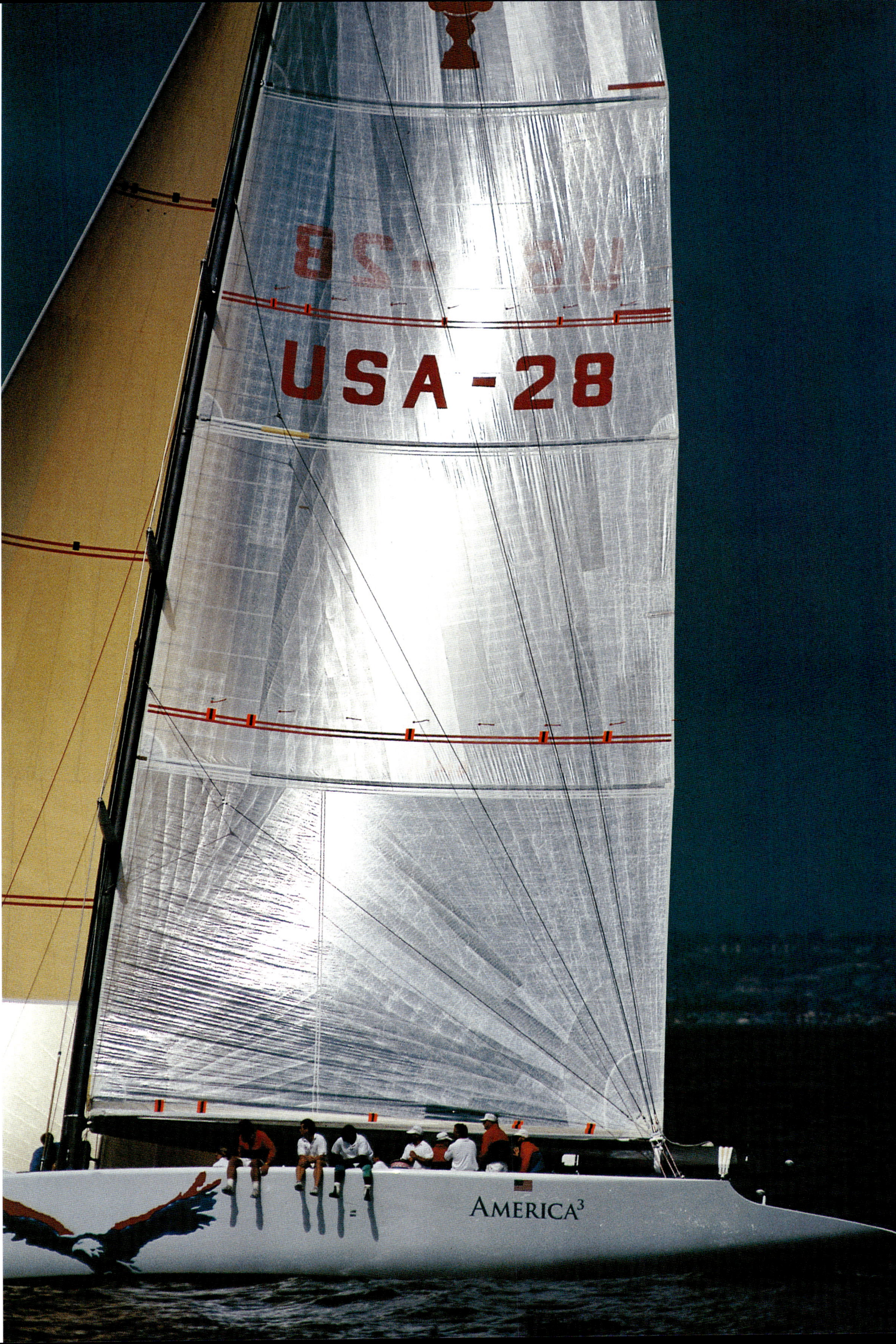
USA-28
AMERICA^3

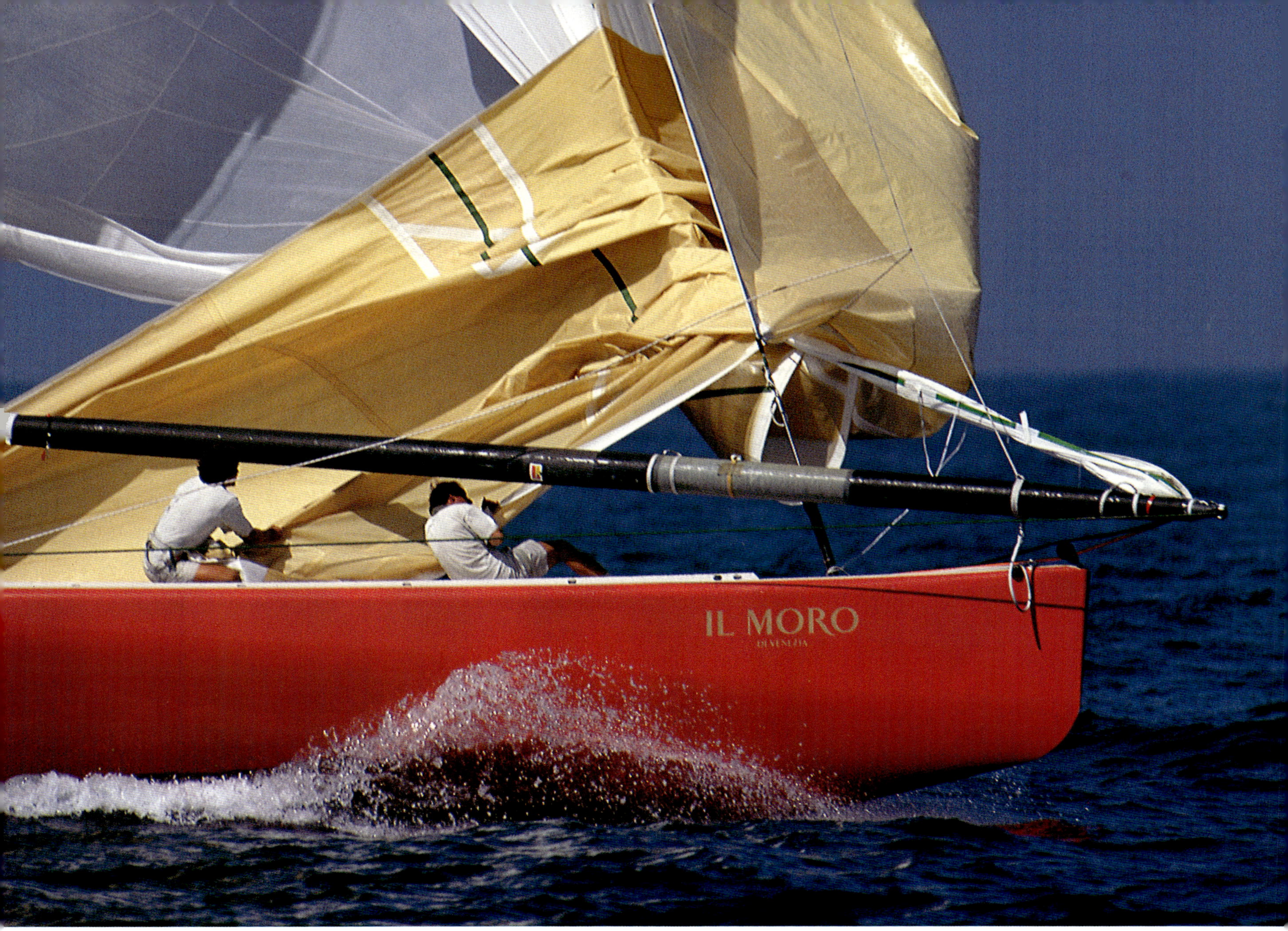

Combat

Whatever their surface or texture, at some moments the huge sails were a playing field of personal and valiant combat for the foredeck crew afloat. Some convoluted configurations of sailcloth seemed to set up obstacles mere humans on the foredeck would never overcome.

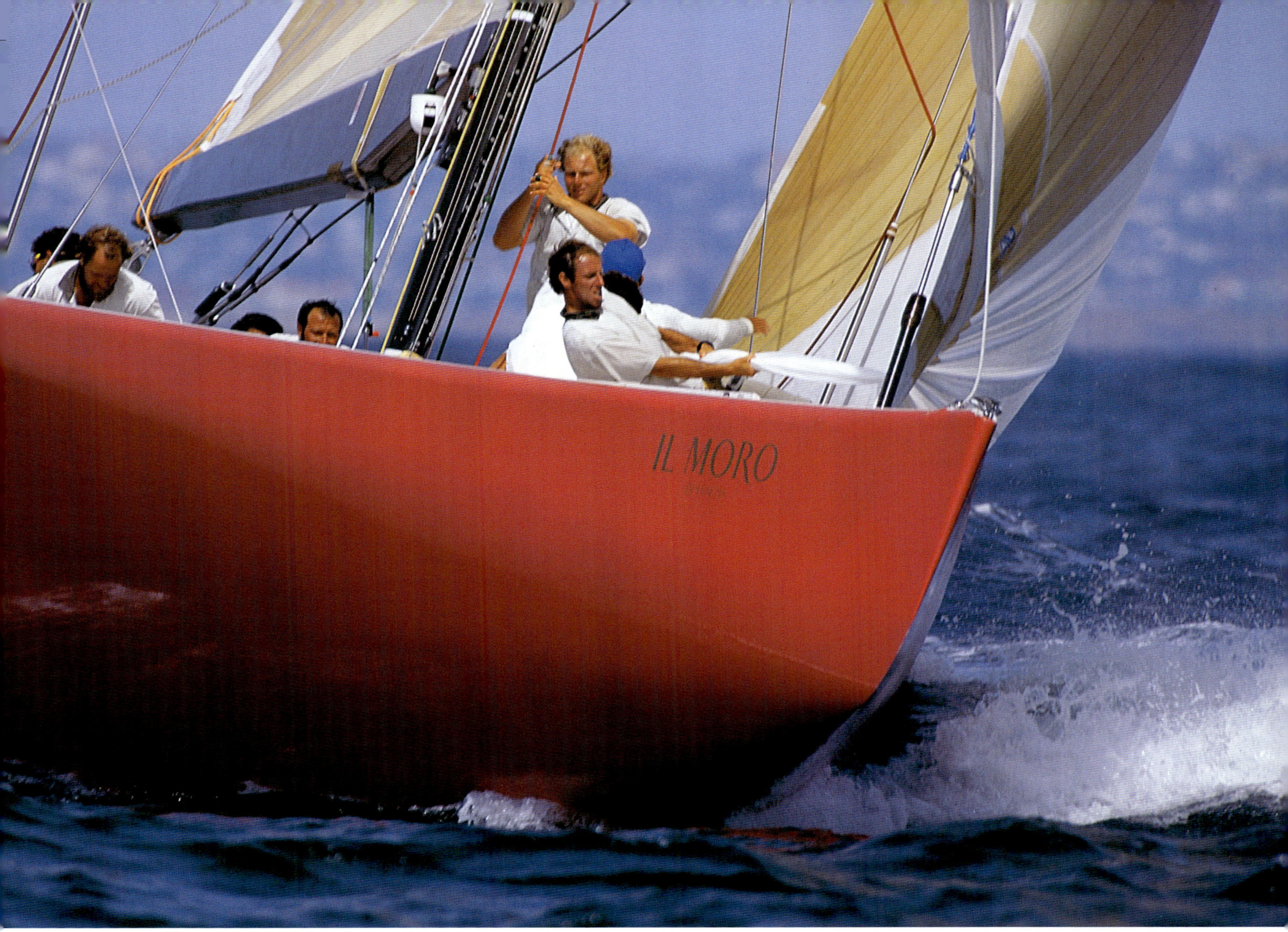

Control

At other times, though the crewmen seemed under pressure, they controlled and tended their sails with masterful technique.

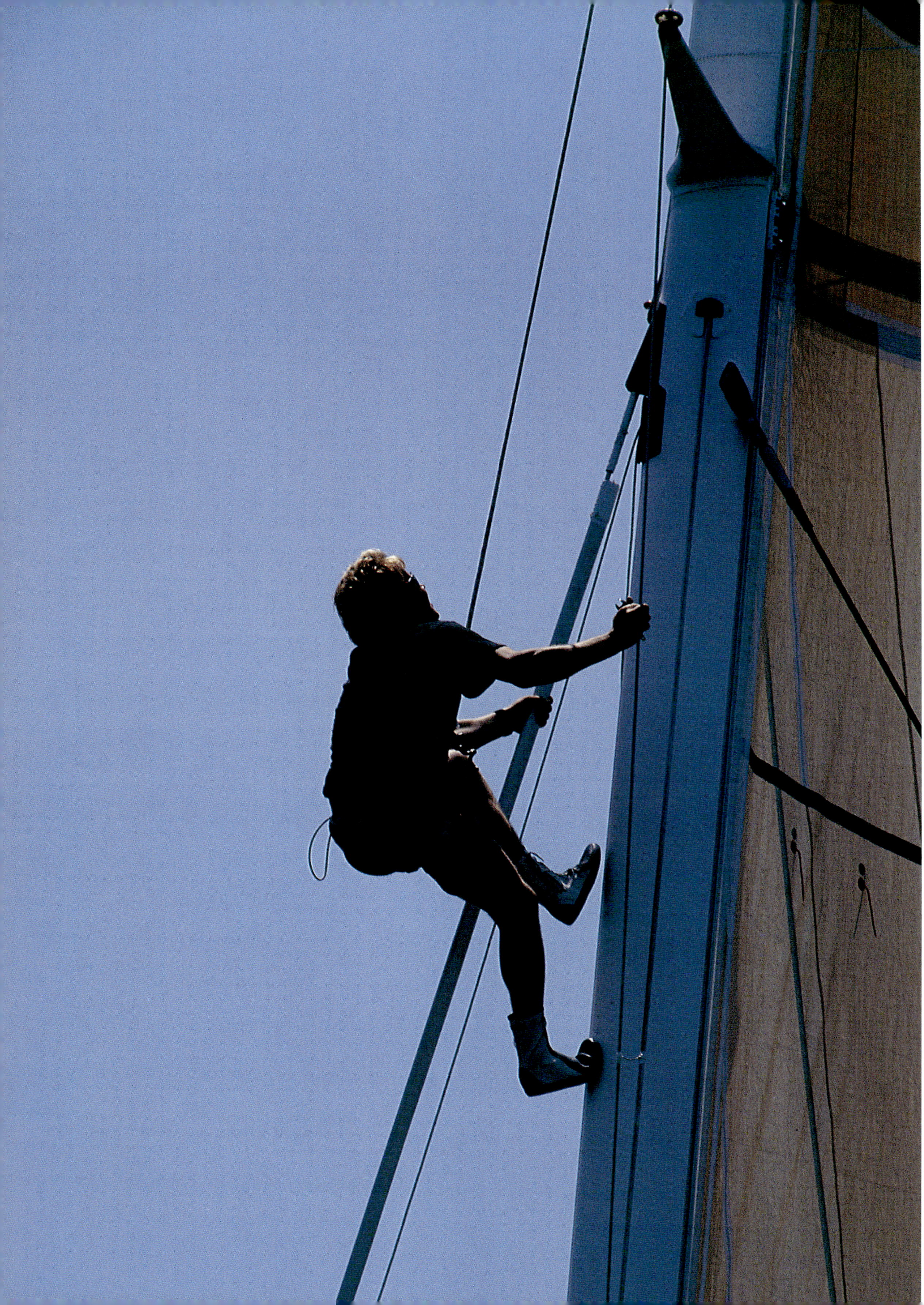

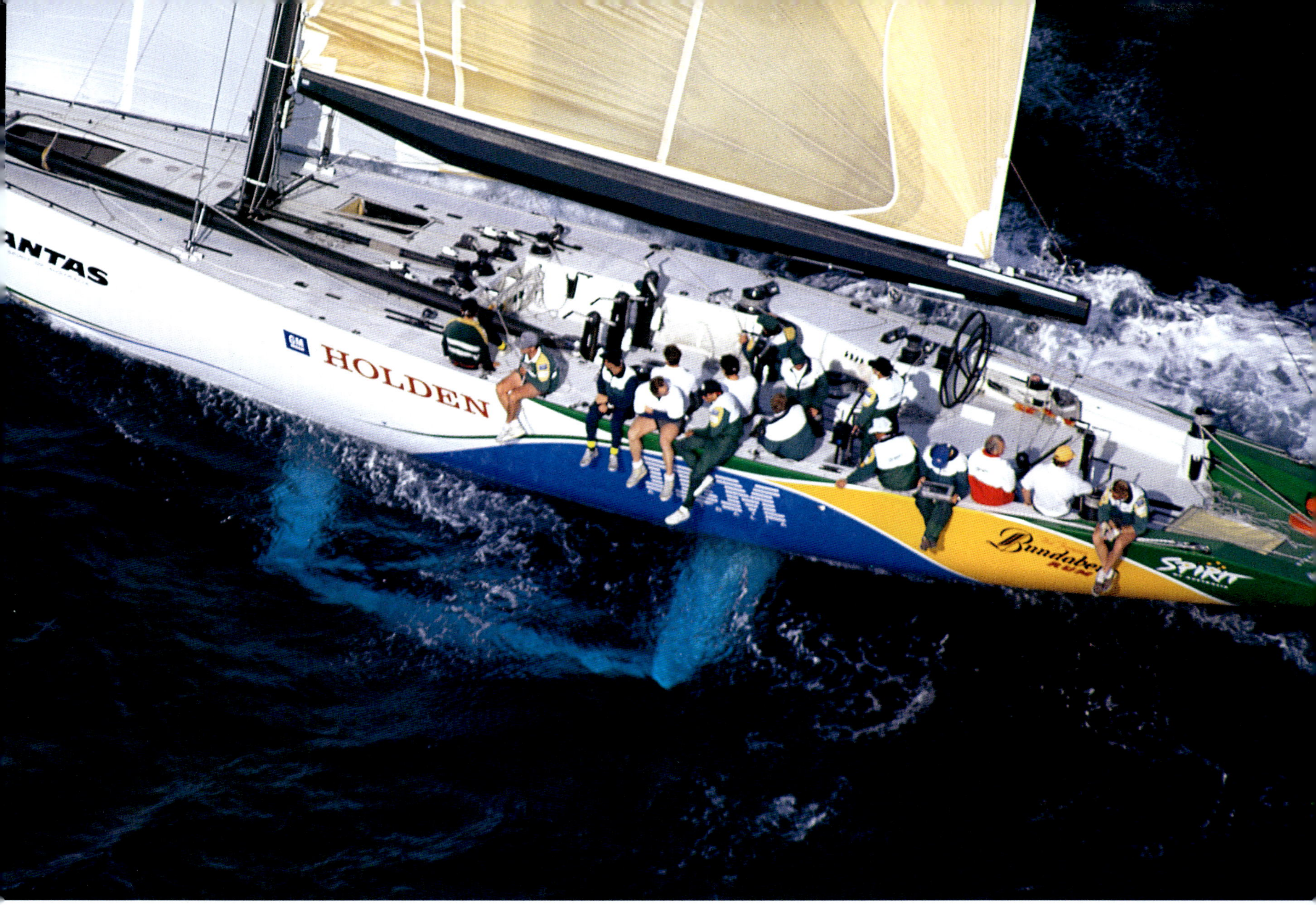

Going Aloft

One had to be reminded that however forbidding or mechanical the rigging appeared, it often still had to be tended by a man going aloft in the old-fashioned bosun's chair.

Keel Innovation

Experimentation in keel configuration brought some extreme examples of innovation. Some keels were camouflaged to prevent observation, but others, like this carried under *The Spirit of Australia*, were painted so that their form was visible from the air. Getting these engineering innovations to perform to their design optimum was a problem difficult of solution for the design engineers, but leaving them without camouflage was a boon to the photographer.

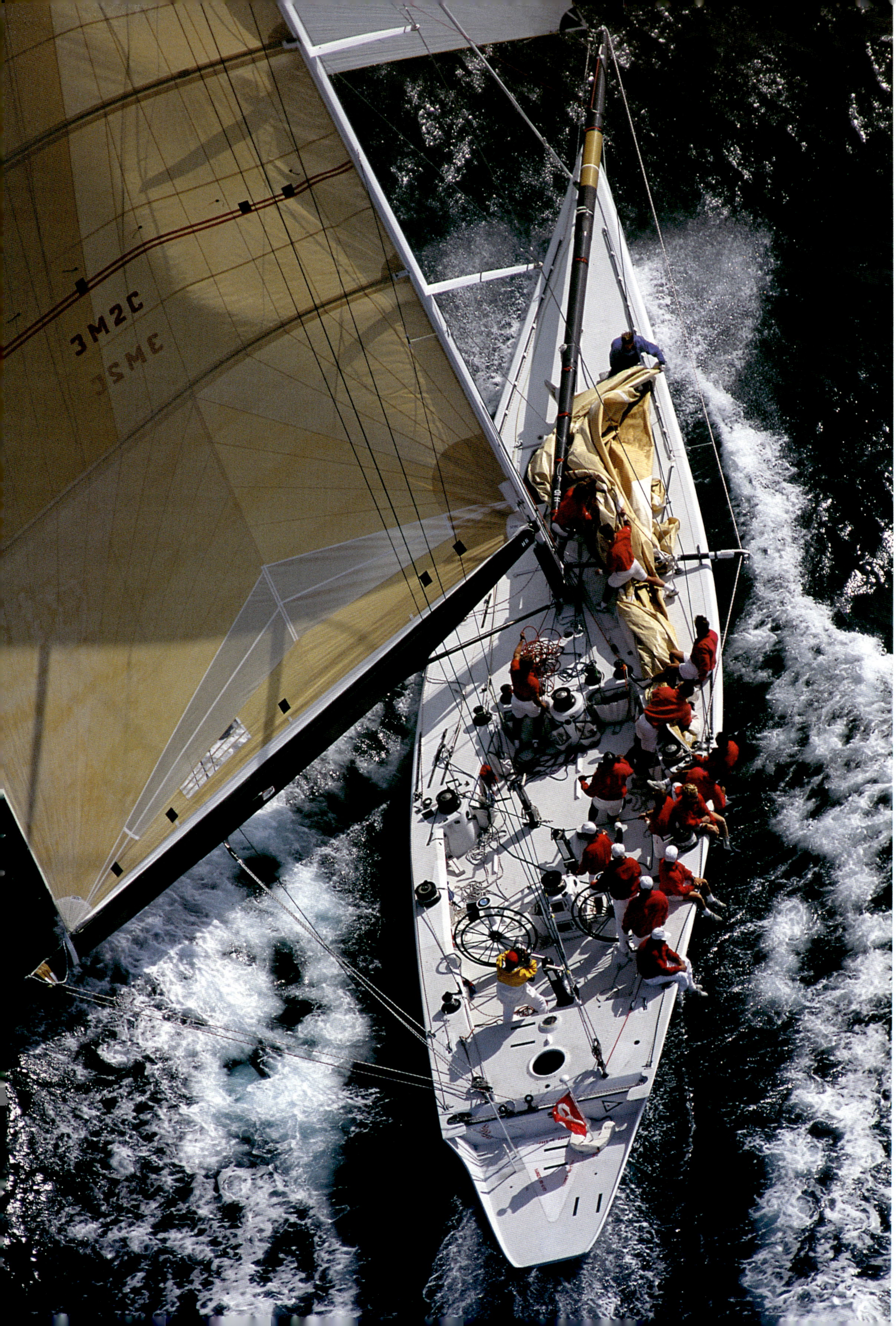

Ease

Opposite, when sails were trimmed and drawing nicely, the crew had moments when they exuded the ease and joy found on a gentle afternoon sail in local waters.

Power and Beauty

There were other times, when these magnificent yachts spread their tall rigs to the skies, that the crew looked woefully puny. The power of the massive rigs so delicately held by the pencil-thin spars seemed overwhelming, but that was the original design concept: a great yacht that a talented, expertly trained crew could drive to its design limits. They were vessels capable of sparkling performance and endowed with great beauty. I was very sad to see their beauty later trivialized by advertising logos. By 1992, the interest and joy I found in every moment spent at sea with America's Cup racing craft were severely tried by the advertising logos appearing on their hulls and and sails. The logos not only diminished the integrity of the craft, they unsettled and compromised me. I felt used by the advertisers, abused by their advertising, and sad that the skippers and crews of the yachts were so branded. I spent most of my photographic time afloat on the course that year trying to shoot around the logos, trying to hide or ignore them, but it became increasingly difficult. In 1995, although I twice made plans to fly to San Diego for the America's Cup trials and races, I cancelled out both times rather than face another year of what had become a dispiriting struggle.

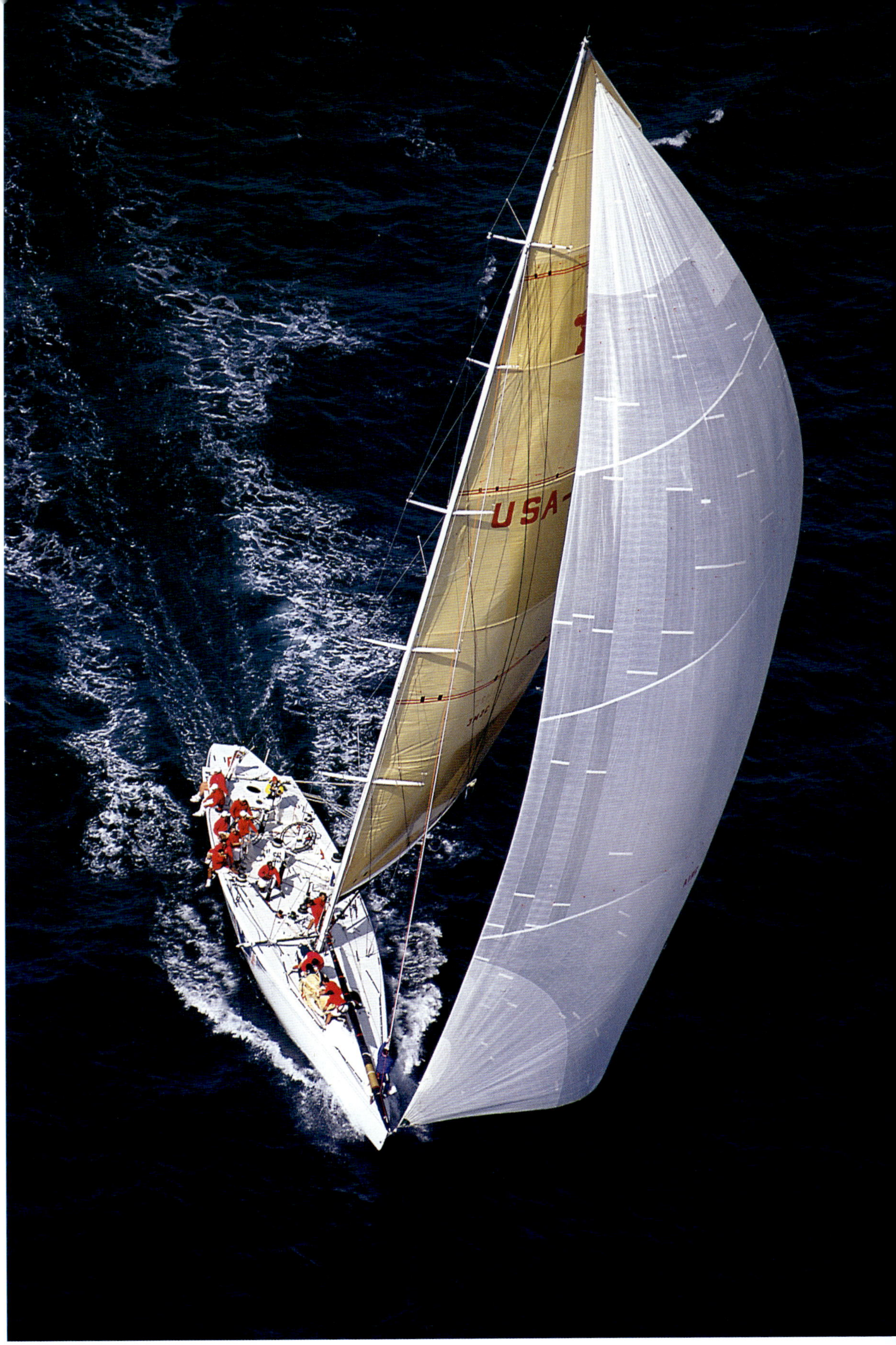

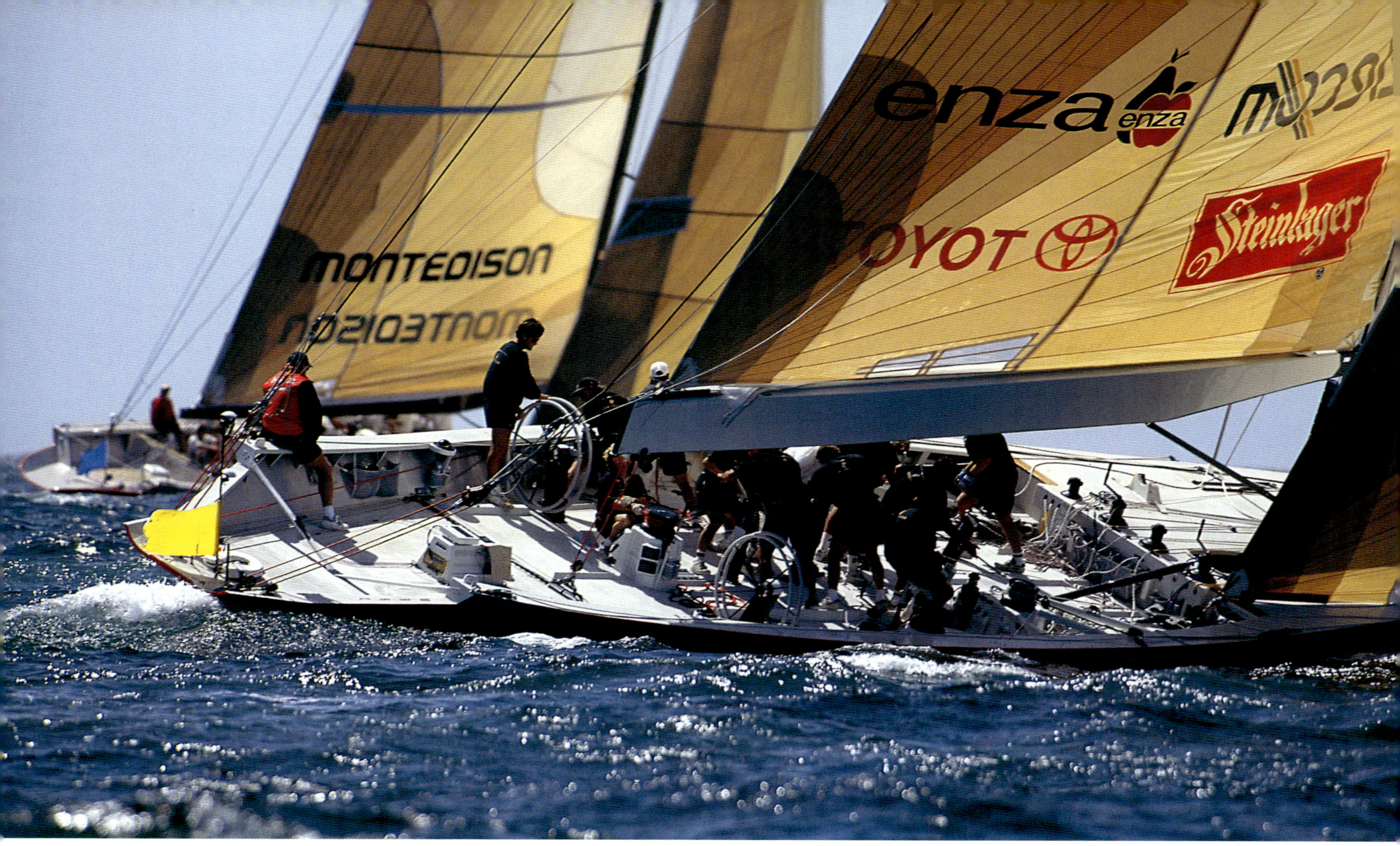
MONTEDISON
enza
Steinlager

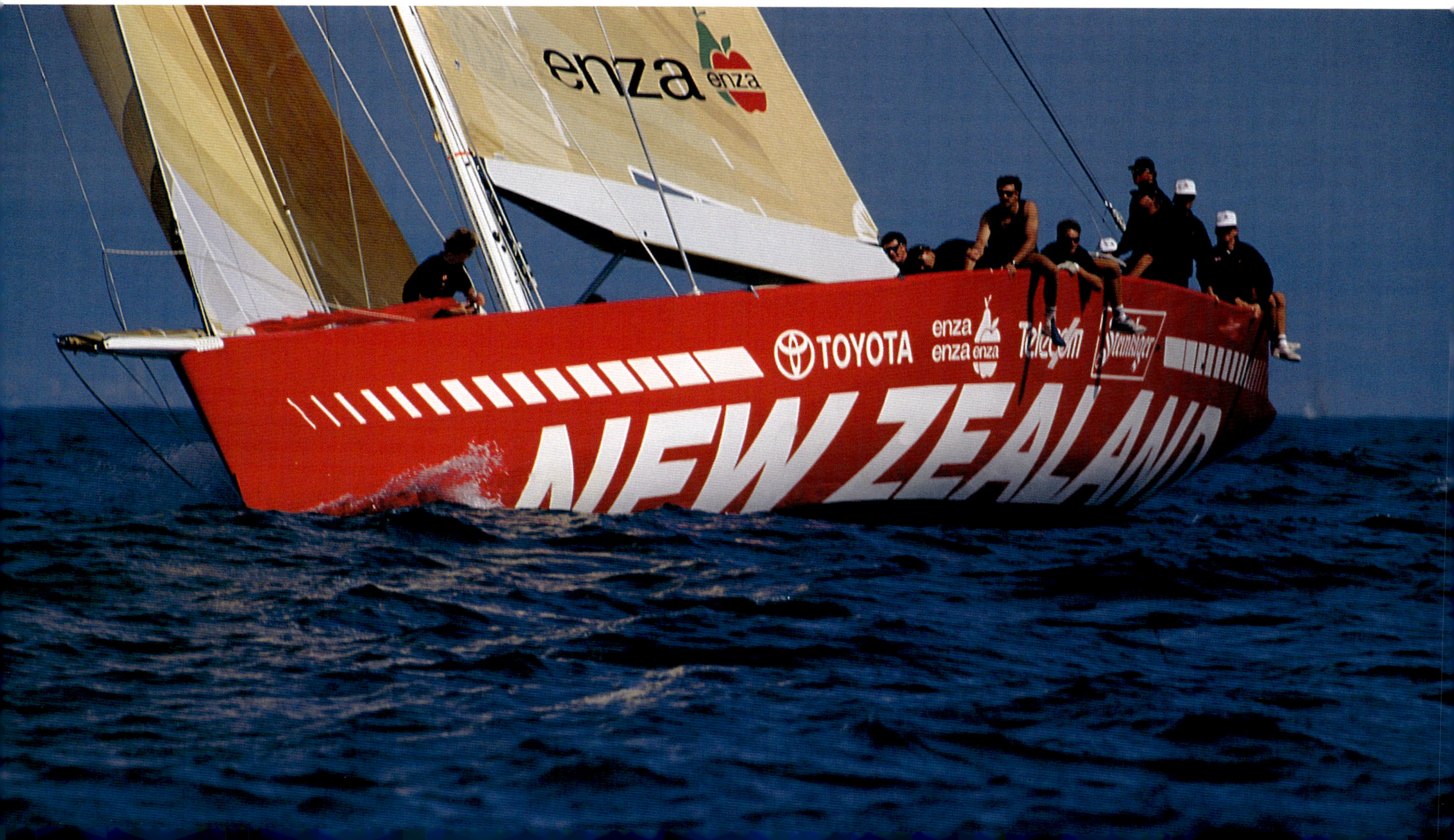
enza
TOYOTA
NEW ZEALAND

Distraction

Opposite above, in one of their 1992 trial races, *Il Moro Di Venezia* to weather and *New Zealand* in the foreground are hard on the wind on port tack. *Il Moro* is pointing higher, but *New Zealand*'s crew is straining at the winches. The observer aboard each vessel is sitting along the weather rail aft of the helmsman. *New Zealand*'s helmsman stands clear against the distant sail. The sun is overhead, the sails are backlit, and the water sparkles. I should be most happy with the composition, but the advertising on the sails distracts and disturbs me. How can man take a thing of such beauty and so disfigure it?

Billboard

Opposite below, *New Zealand* is again on the port tack. Seen from windward, its hull rises out of the water, blatantly wearing all of its advertising. This is now not really a yacht, but a form of billboard, which compromises both man-made and natural beauty.

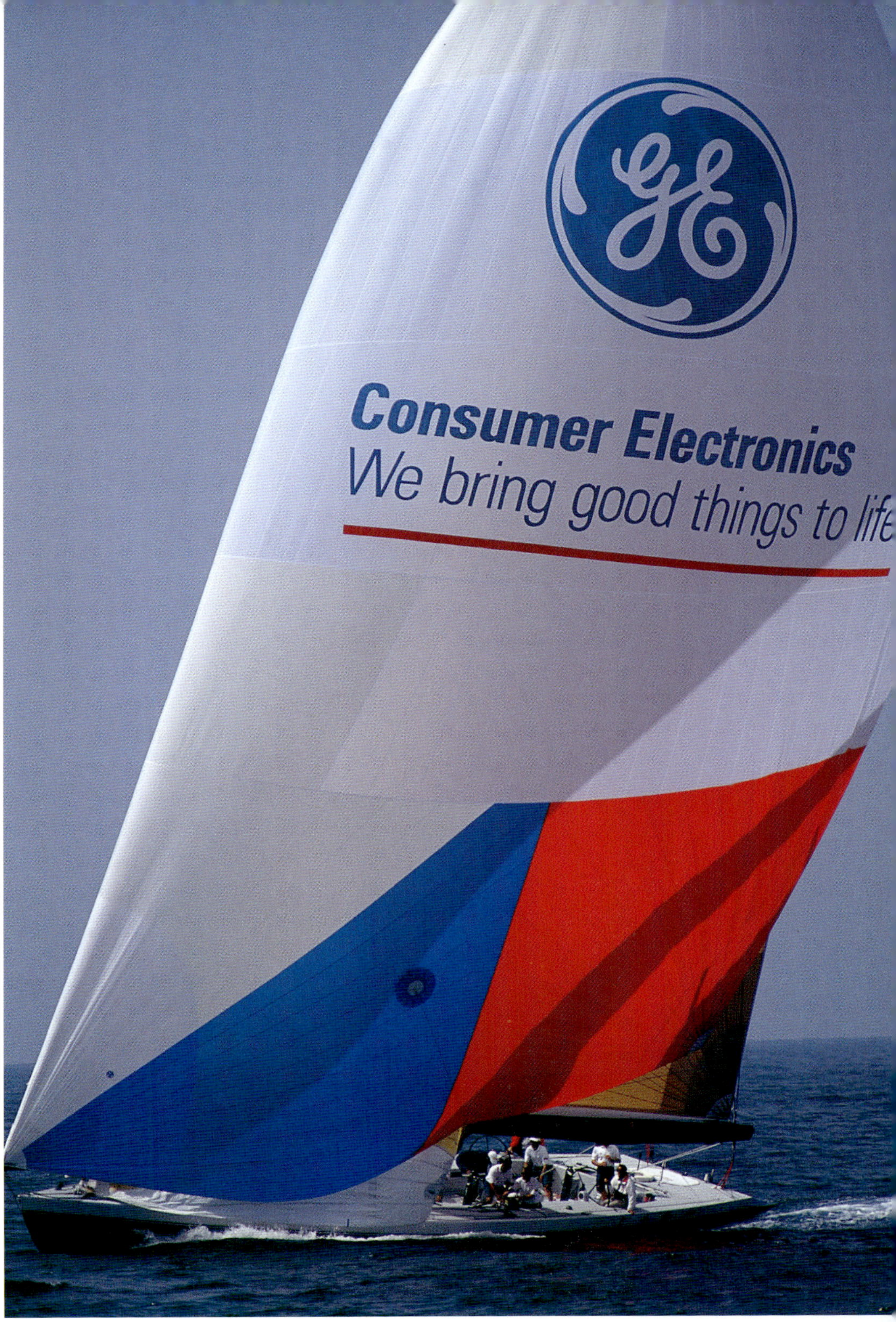

Power or Pollution

From Alan Bond's first spinnaker logo in 1983 to Dennis Conner's spinnaker billboard in 1992, we have traveled the road from clever to crass. Some may think I find this kind of advertising deplorable because I am old, but I still find sweet joy in living. Advertising has a place as information, not pollution.

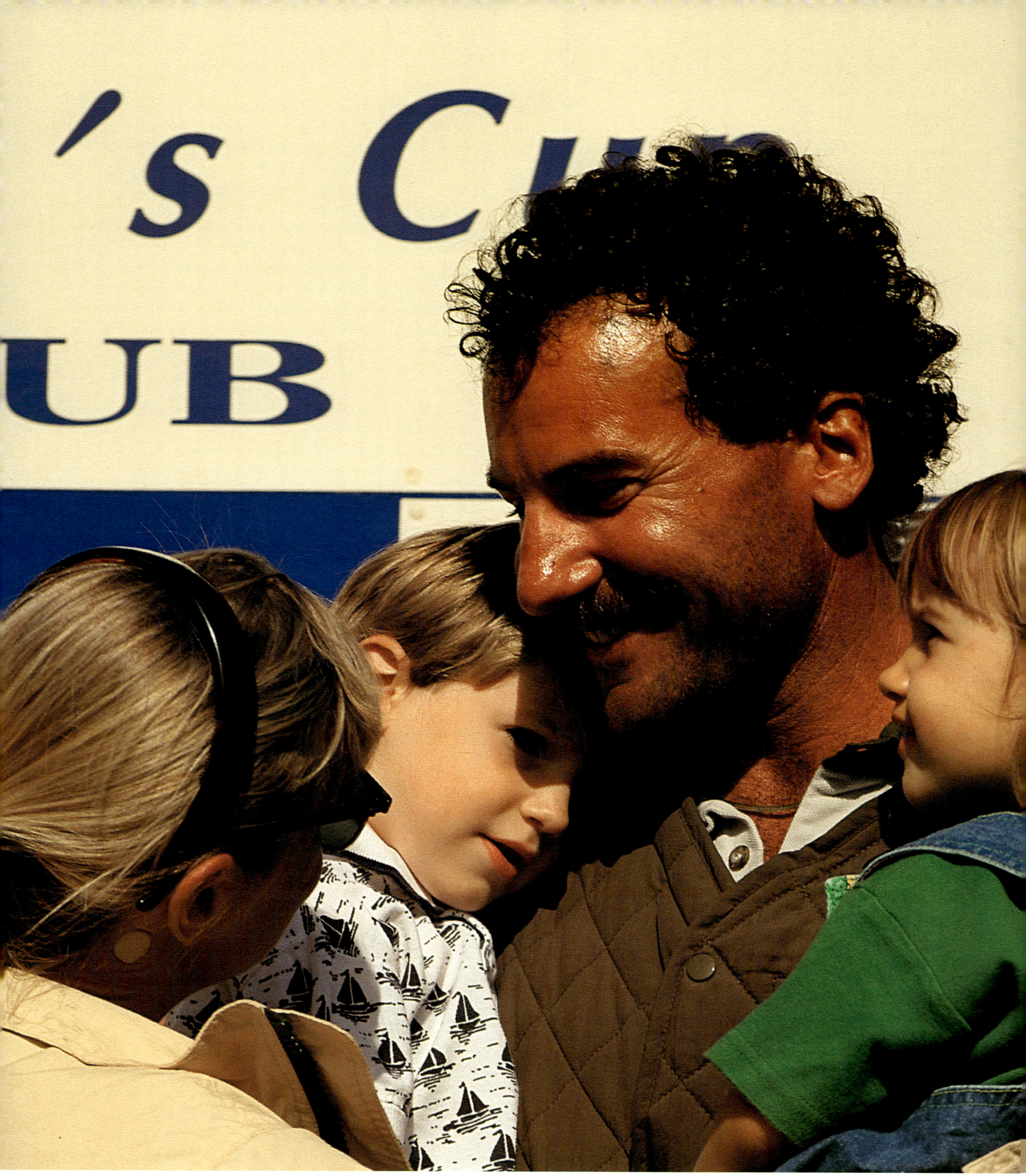

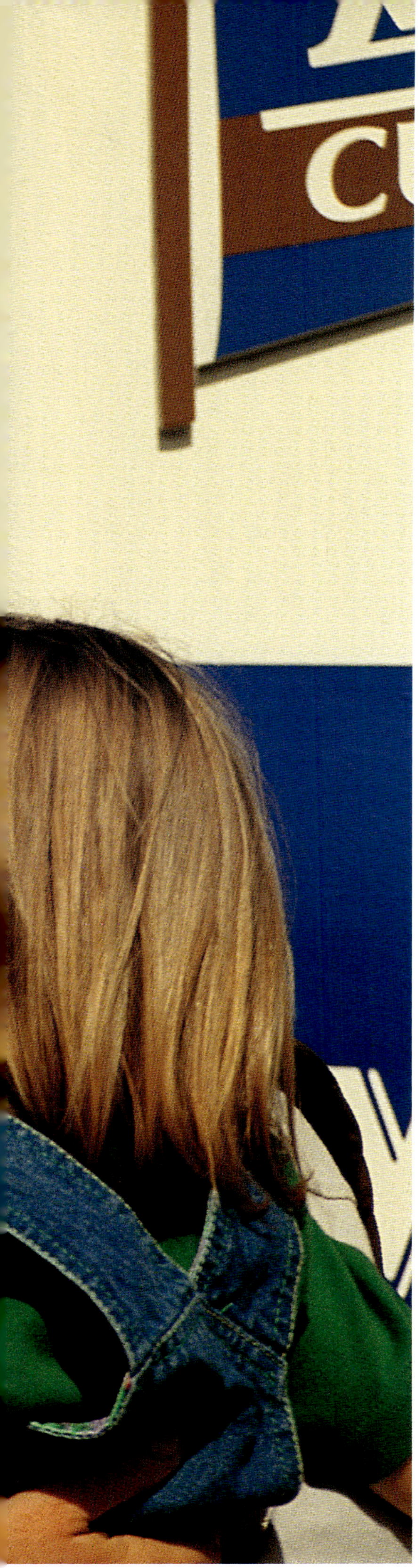

Expressions

There's always a story under the surface

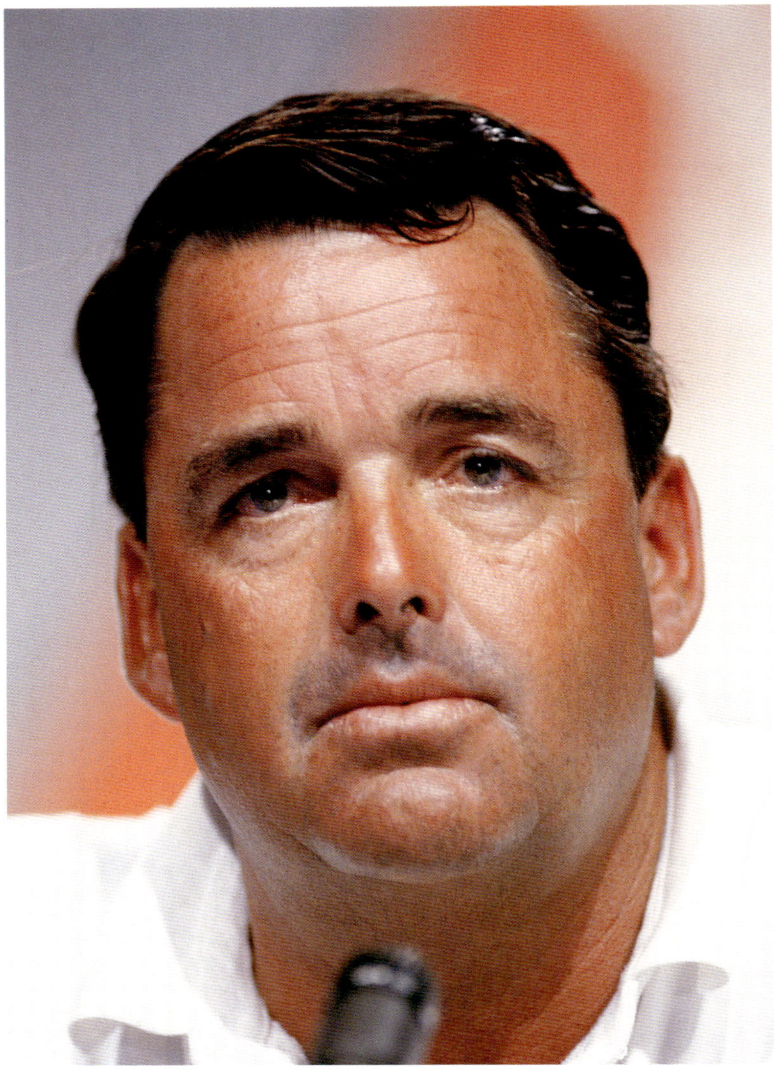

Dennis Conner is a champion skipper, a legend to many. He raises capital for his sailing projects on a massive scale, he is a gripping and persuasive lecturer and he is becoming an artist of renown — yet his has involvement in the 1988 America's Cup controversy prompted criticism of his judgment and sportsmanship. In 1992, he was skipper of *Stars & Stripes*. In this photograph, Dennis holds the controlled, though somewhat removed, demeanor he brought to the press conferences.

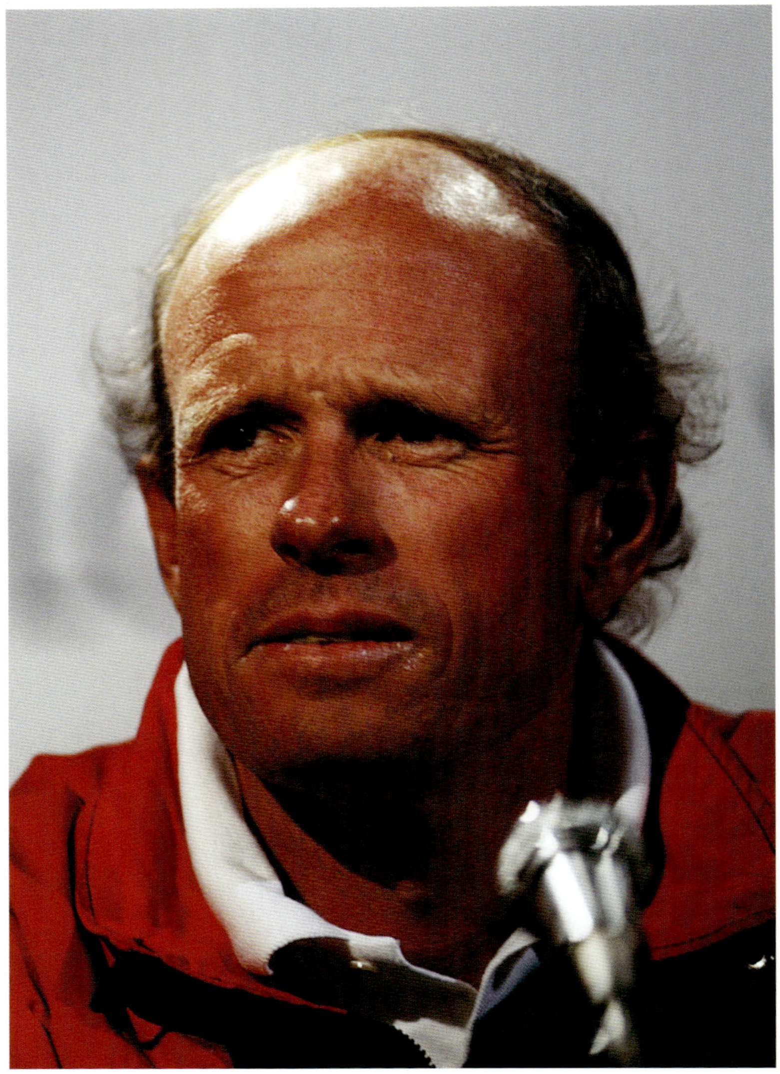

Tom Whidden, executive sailmaker, was tactician with Dennis Conner in the years spanned by the photographs in this book. Both talented sailors, they made a wonderful team, for Whidden was as solid and reliable as Conner was mercurial. In addition to his skills with sails and sailing, Whidden was usually approachable and ready with a thoughtful concise answer to questions, whether about tactics in the day's racing or about sail design, construction, use, and development.

As the yachts have become more and more complicated racing machines, so too have the men racing them become more complex. Just as I have tried to understand the yachts, I have tried to understand the crews who sailed them. A photograph afloat is an image captured in an instant, and — to be successful — it must reflect more than one surface aspect of the complicated whole. Most of the following portraits were made at press conferences during the America's Cup trials and races in the spring of 1992.

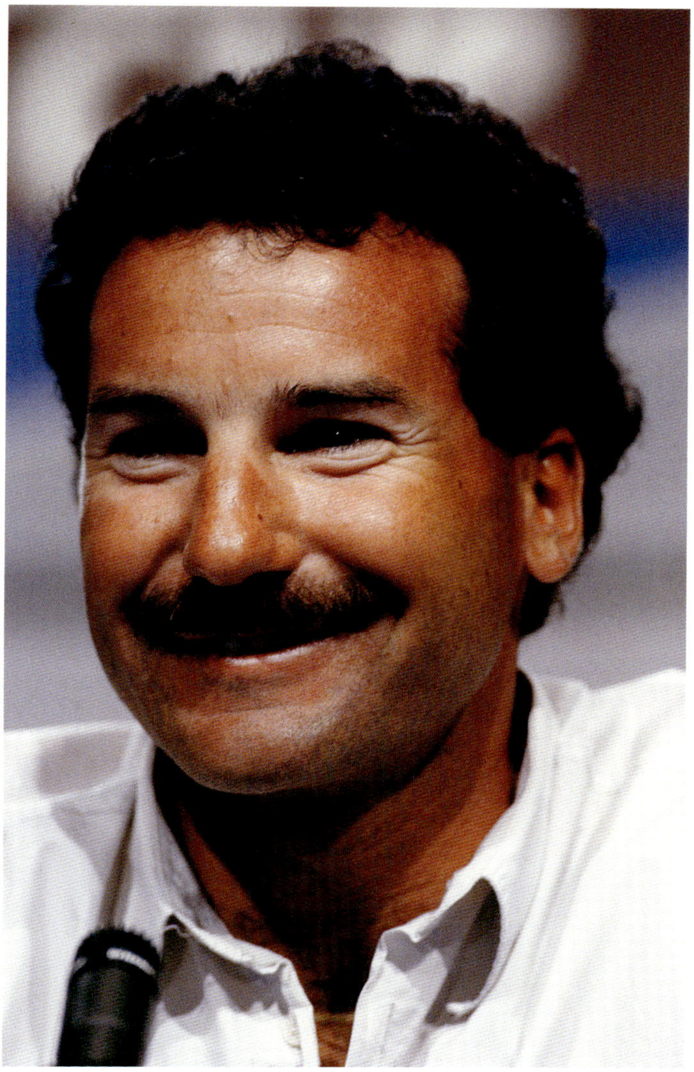

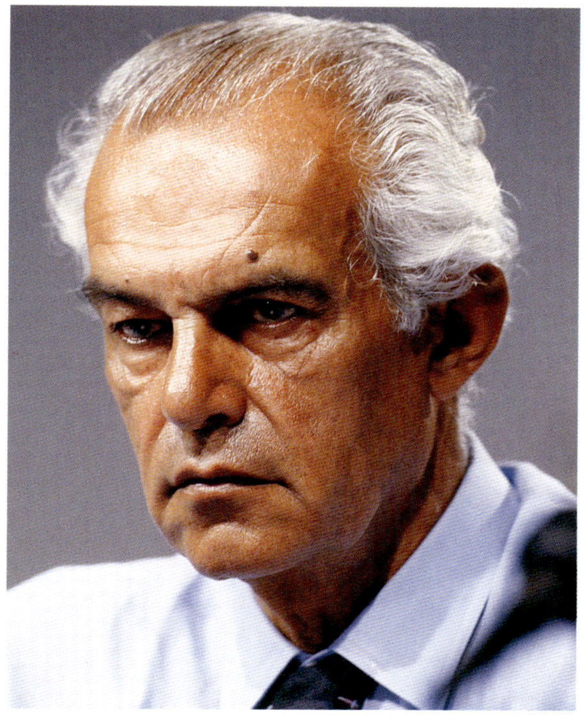

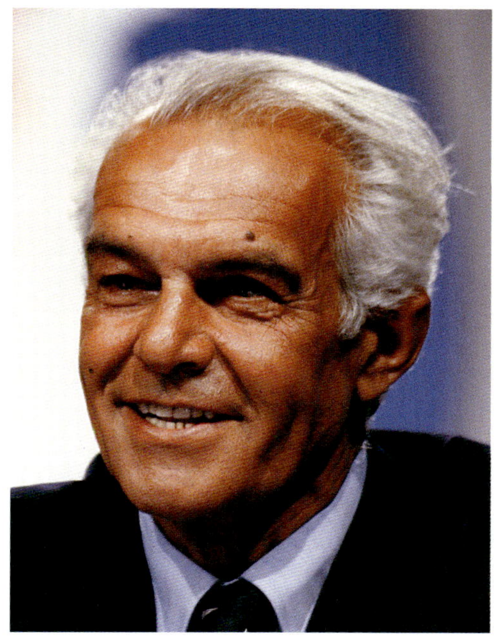

Paul Cayard is a world-class sailor, often a rival to Dennis on the course and sometimes a teammate. In the 1992 series, he skippered the Italian challenger *Il Moro Di Venezia* against the defender *A3*. In the course of the elimination series, Paul spearheaded serious legal challenges against *New Zealand* and, for many weeks maintained a fiercely combative aura. At press conferences, he usually conveyed a strong, serious, and purposeful image. I tried to photograph him with a different visage than he usually projected, one with the good humor I recalled.

Raul Gardini was the Italian multimillionaire industrialist who in 1992 backed his country's America's Cup challenge. He exuded tremendous personal power, a magnet that drew the Italian press in swarms about him. At the 1990 christening of his contender, *Il Moro Di Venezia,* in Venice, he staged a million-dollar spectacle that illuminated the basin of St. Mark's in a re-creation of the magnificent imagery of its past. At the moment of the photograph above, Gardini was following the argument Paul Cayard was making against *New Zealand*'s rig. The inner tension reflected in his face was more than a reaction to the argument in progress, for the huge empire he had built was threatening to collapse.

Gardini closely followed the racing in San Diego and seemed to enjoy it intensely. His smile, however, did not always reach into his deep-set, haunted eyes. His subsequent suicide shocked the financial and sailing worlds.

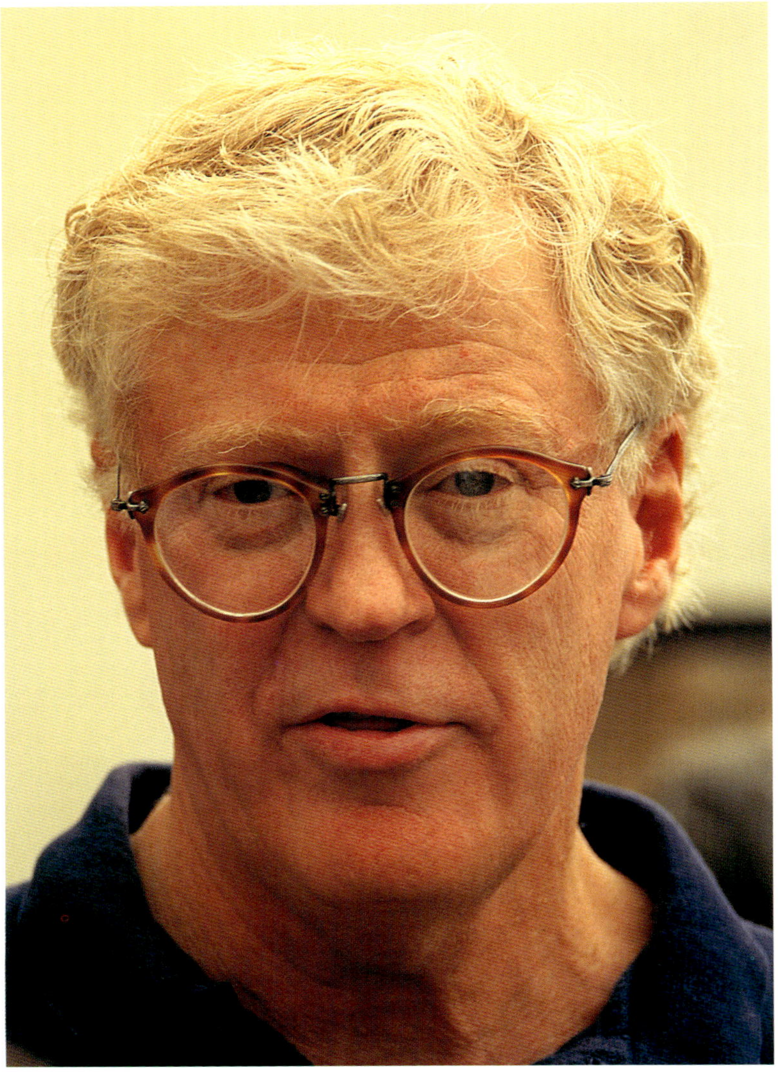

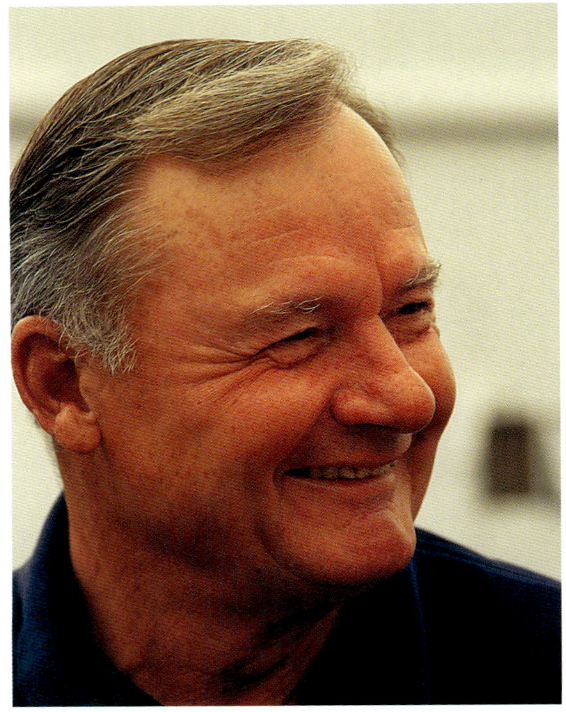

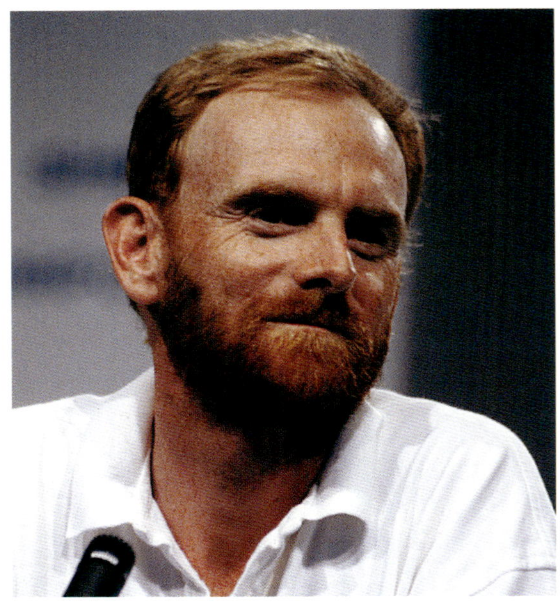

Bill Koch, the unconventional multimillionaire and MIT engineer who financed the A^3 defense, ran it with a most individual style. His decisions directed all aspects of the syndicate, and the many millions of dollars he spent in research and development enhanced the high degree of his technological organization and ultimately won the Cup. Koch's concept was to approach the challenge scientifically. He wanted no stars on the boat or in the syndicate, and the human units were to be interchangeable, as much as practical. It was a theory with some humanitarian limits, but it worked for the 1992 defense.

Buddy Melges, co-skipper with Bill Koch of A^3, was a man of broad experience afloat. He brought to the afterguard of A^3 both competence at the helm and a positive philosophy, leavened with a wonderful sense of humor and appreciation for the sport. He lent a very human face to an organization that was run by Bill Koch's book of rules.

David Dellenbaugh, the youthful tactician aboard A^3, spent his first few weeks seated at the press conference table with his head bent down, apparently in contemplation of the day's activities. It presented an unfortunate angle to the photographer. After one session, I approached him and suggested that he was projecting an unhappy image, and that it would be a kindness if he lifted his head higher and perhaps even smiled on occasion. He obliged with an easy demeanor at future press meetings.

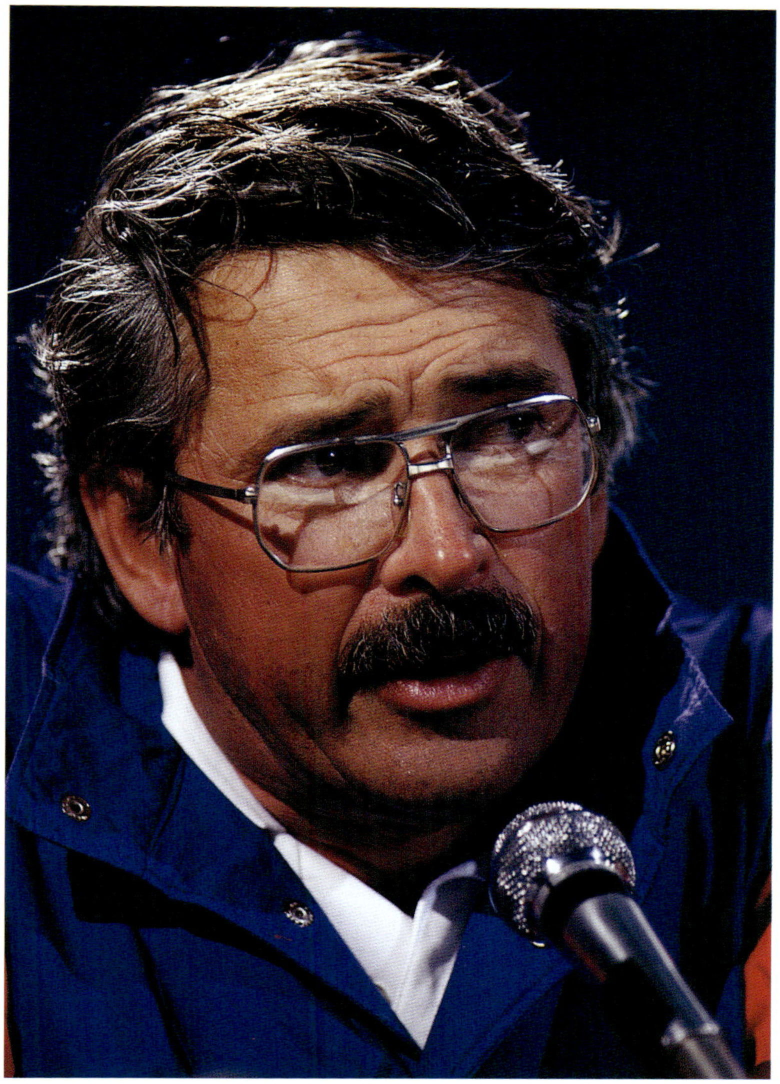

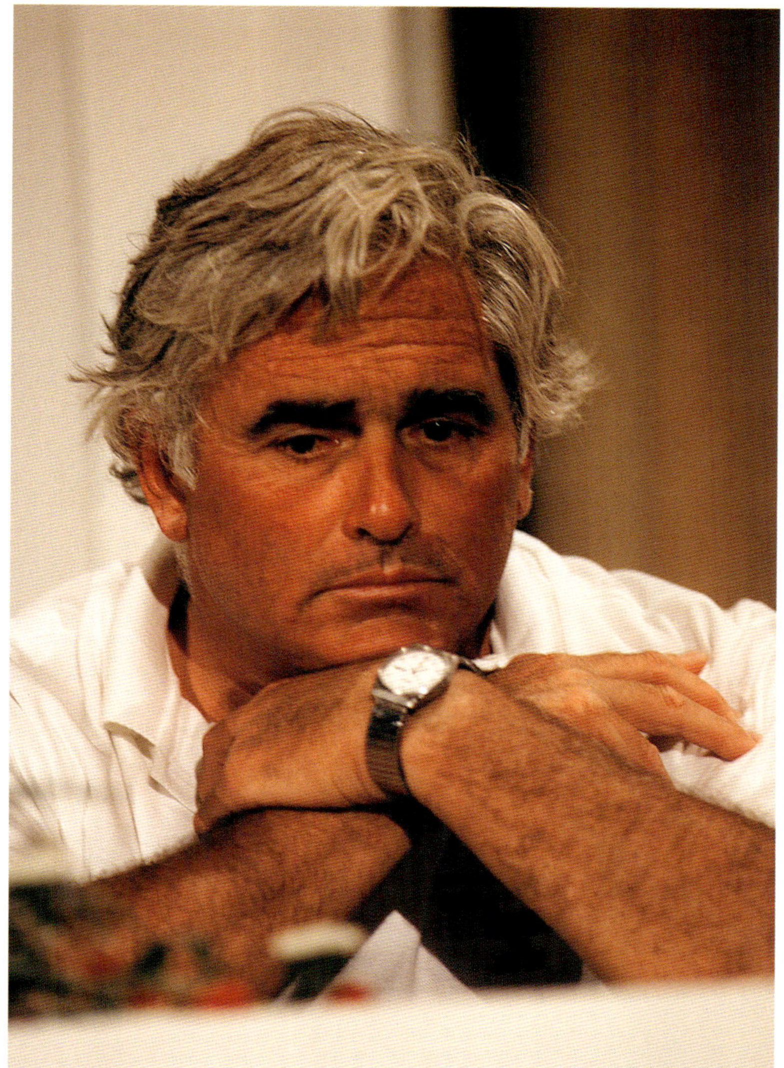

John Marshall, active in the cockpit of America's Cup yachts since 1984, was mainsheet trimmer on Dennis Conner's *Stars & Stripes* as well as a dominant figure in the ill-matched 1988 catamaran defense against Michael Fay's megayacht challenge. It surprised some in the press corps that the experienced Conner team did not anticipate the hostility the catamaran would engender. Their realization of the mounting resentment became evident in fleeting moments of haunted, bewildered expressions.

Tom Blackaller was an expert sailor, whether racing scows or the America's Cup class. In the 1986 racing off Fremantle, Western Australia, he skippered *USA*, the America's Cup entry from the St. Francis Yacht Club of San Francisco. *USA*'s innovative design seemed to have unusual speed potential, but it required an inordinate amount of delicate tuning. The usually irrepressible and cheerful Blackaller had moments when his accumulating frustration and fatigue were evident.

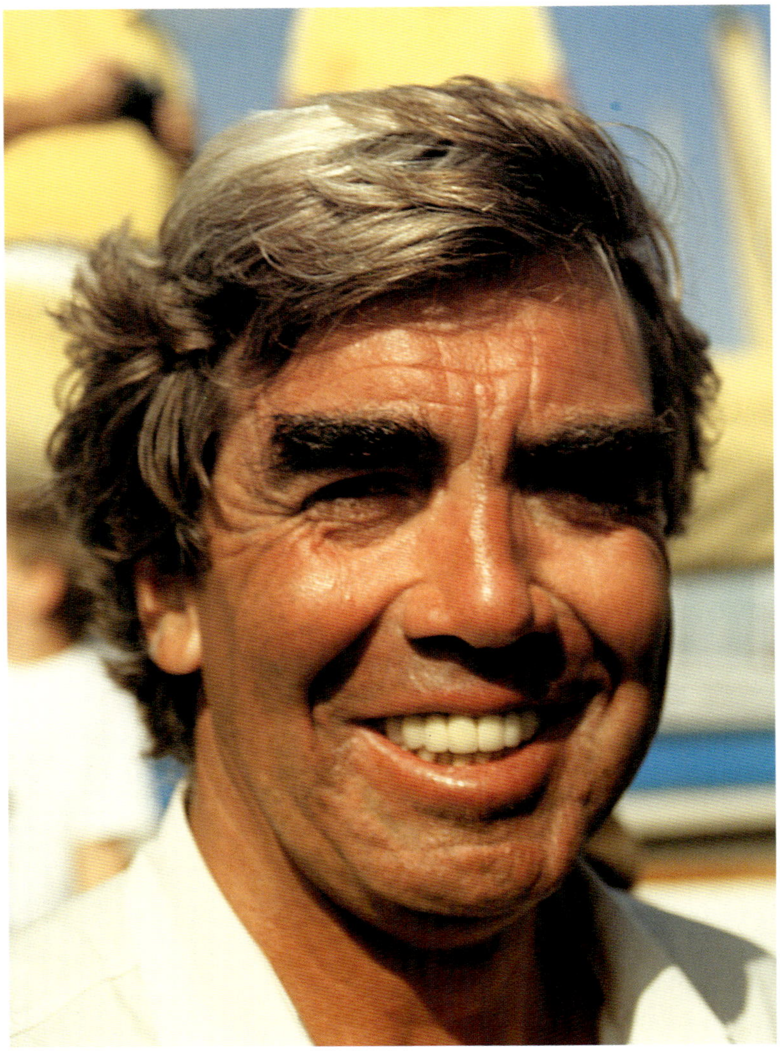

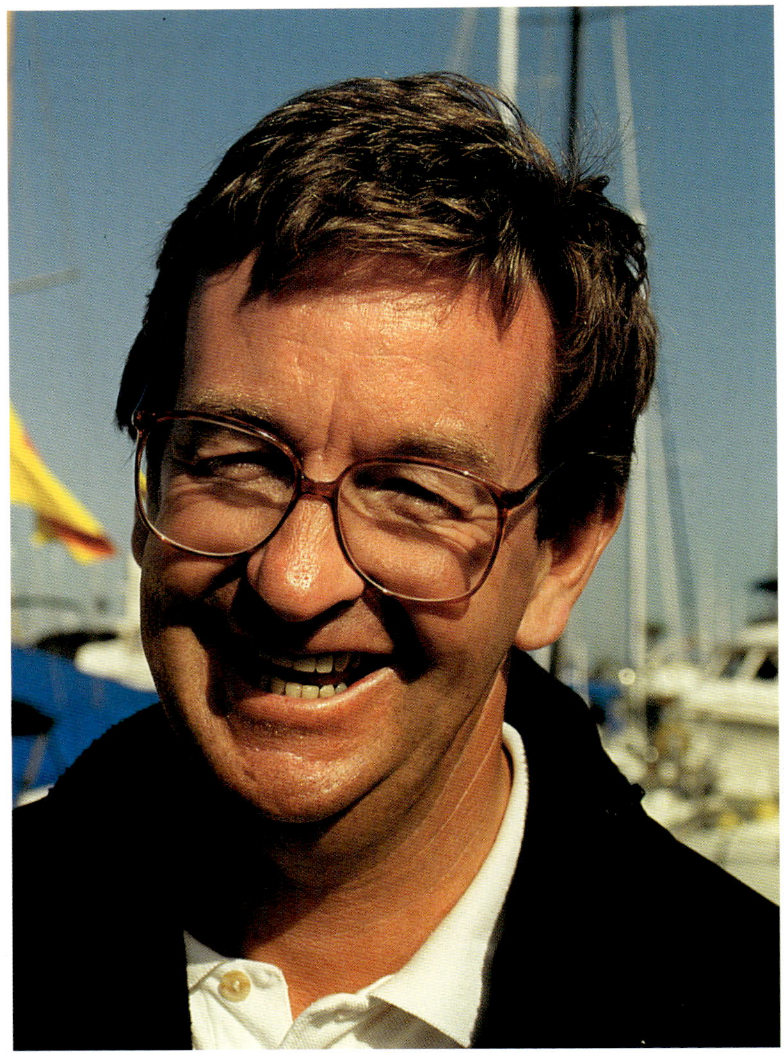

International yacht designer German Frers apprenticed in the legendary firm of Sparkman and Stephens, so it was a special joy to him when his design, the Italian Cup challenger *Il Moro Di Venezia*, beat *New Zealand* in the elimination trials of 1992 and won the right to meet the American defender. His smile at the awards ceremony expressed not only joy, but a job well done.

Michael Fay appeared, unintentionally, to be achieving a reputation equal to Sir Thomas Lipton's as a gracious loser. In 1987 his 12-meter *New Zealand*, the first fiberglass America's Cup challenger, was defeated in a cliffhanger by Dennis Conner. In 1988 his megayacht went down to ignominious defeat by Dennis Conner's questionable catamaran. This photo was made in 1992, at the ceremony celebrating the victory of Paul Cayard's *Il Moro* over Fay's *New Zealand*. It was a most disappointing moment for Fay, but he smiled cheerfully. In the previous photograph, Frers was deeply happy that his design was going on to the finals; Fay had to be disappointed that his craft was not. Frers smiled in happiness; Fay smiled as well, but it must have hurt.

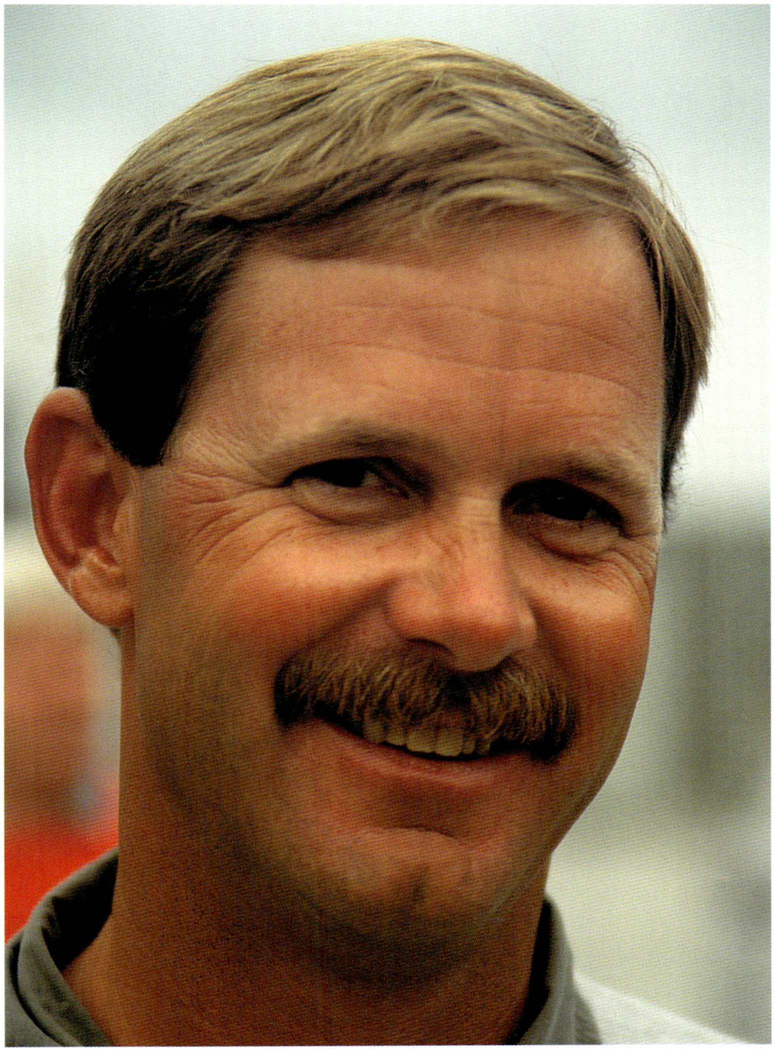

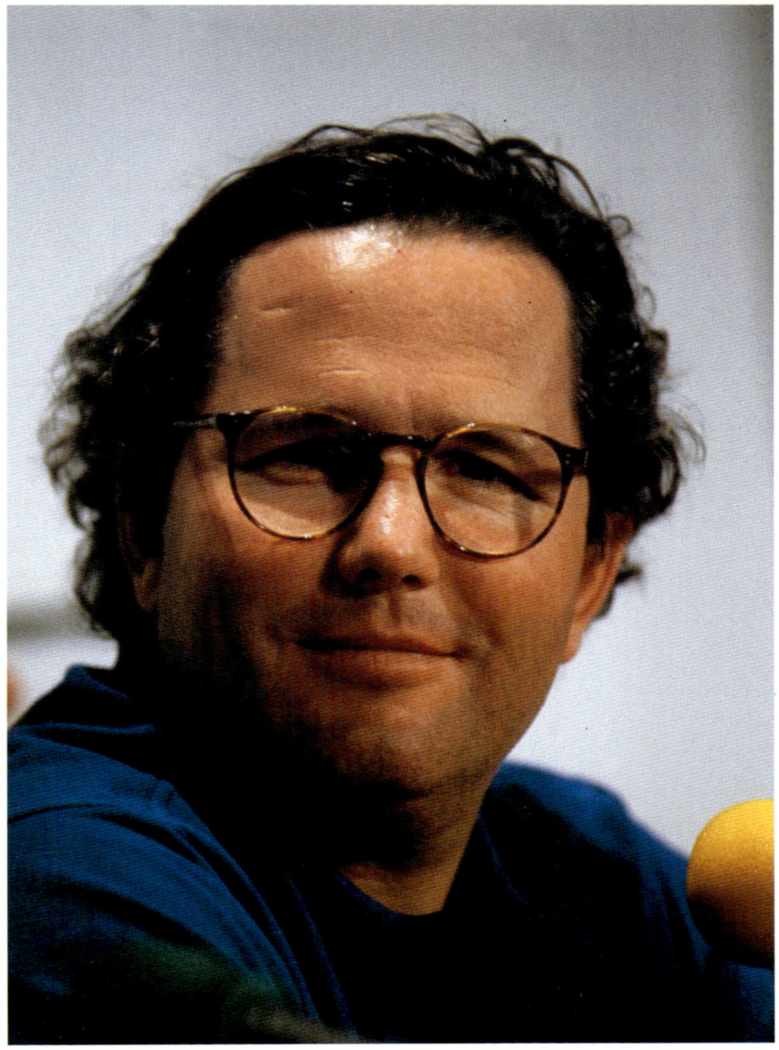

John Kolius has been a fierce competitor from his win in the Soling class in the 1976 Olympics to his America's Cup class experience. In addition to his achievements, Kolius has a most appealing personality and an engaging smile. His smile seems to have just enough of everything, including wit, joy, camaraderie, openness, and healthy good humor.

Bruno Troublé was skipper for Baron Bich's America's Cup effort in the 1970s and has stayed active in the America's Cup. Since 1986, he has been coordinator of the Louis Vuitton media organization that oversees the challenger rounds, culminating in the Louis Vuitton Cup, which determines the new challenger. The press center under his influence reflected gracious civility and Old World cachet, combined with real efficiency. His smile, too, portrayed a quality of charm and subtlety, melded with a pleasant reserve. It was a wonderful foil to the more open expression of John Kolius.

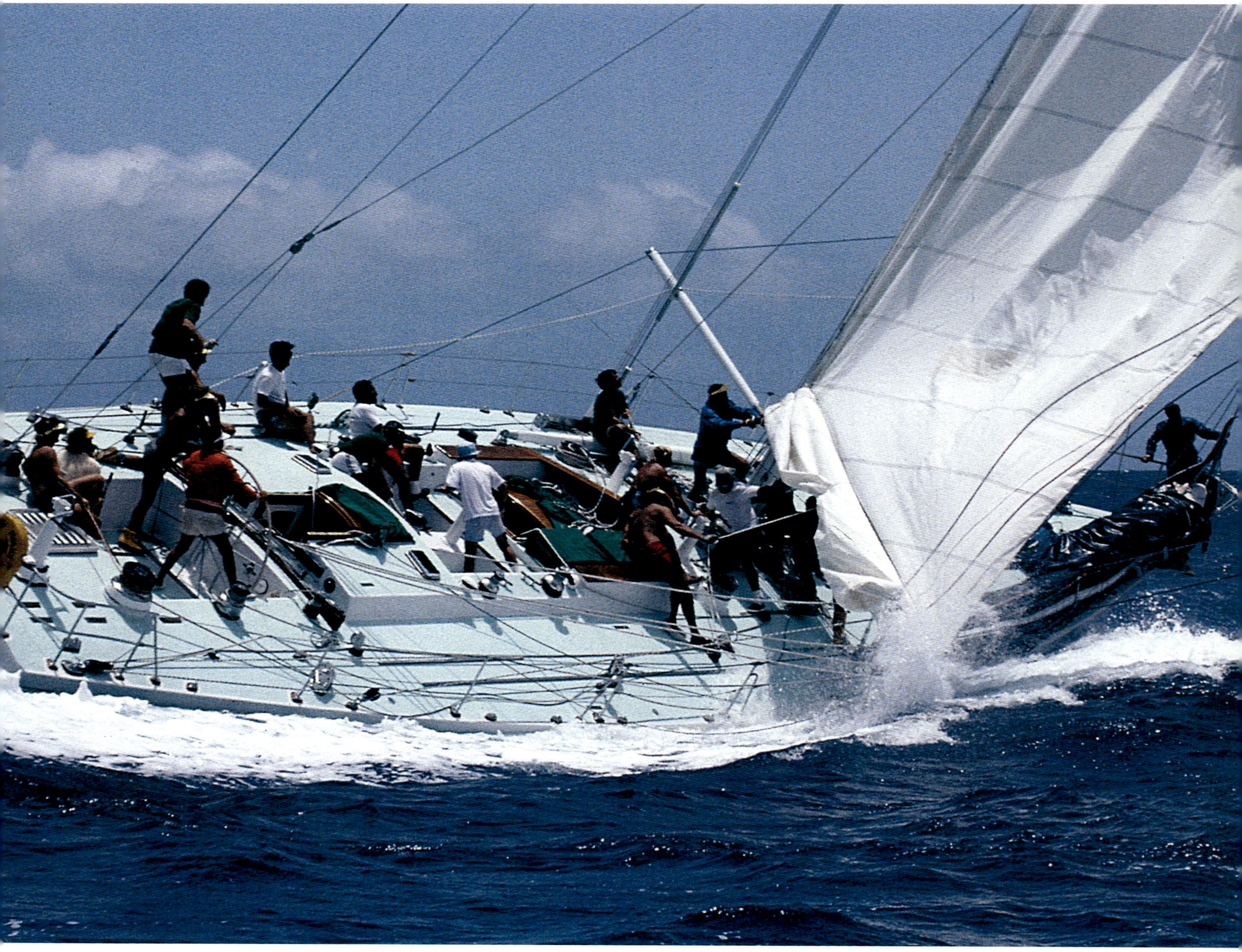

WINDWARD PASSAGE

Spirited sailing and sparkling imagery in Hawaiian waters

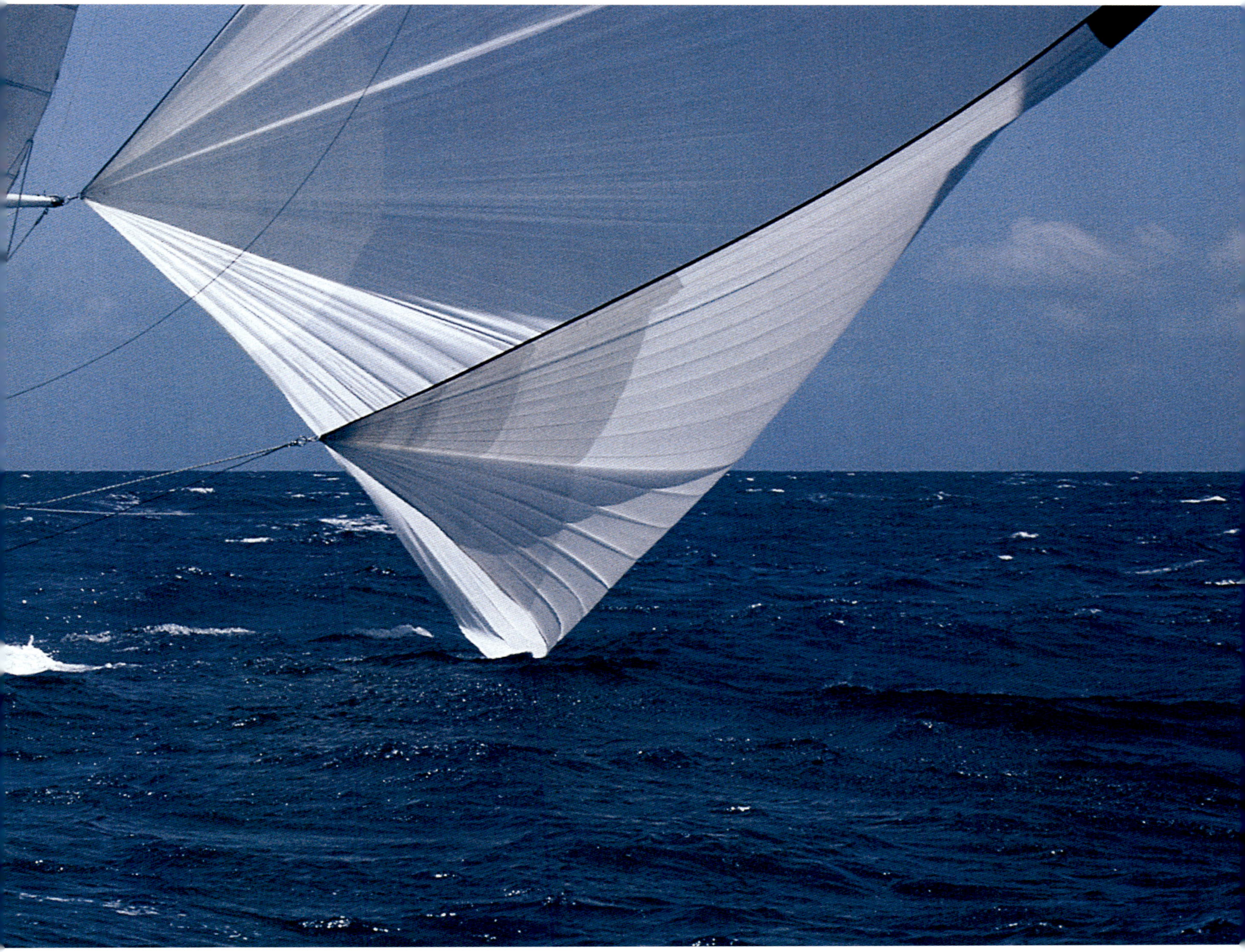

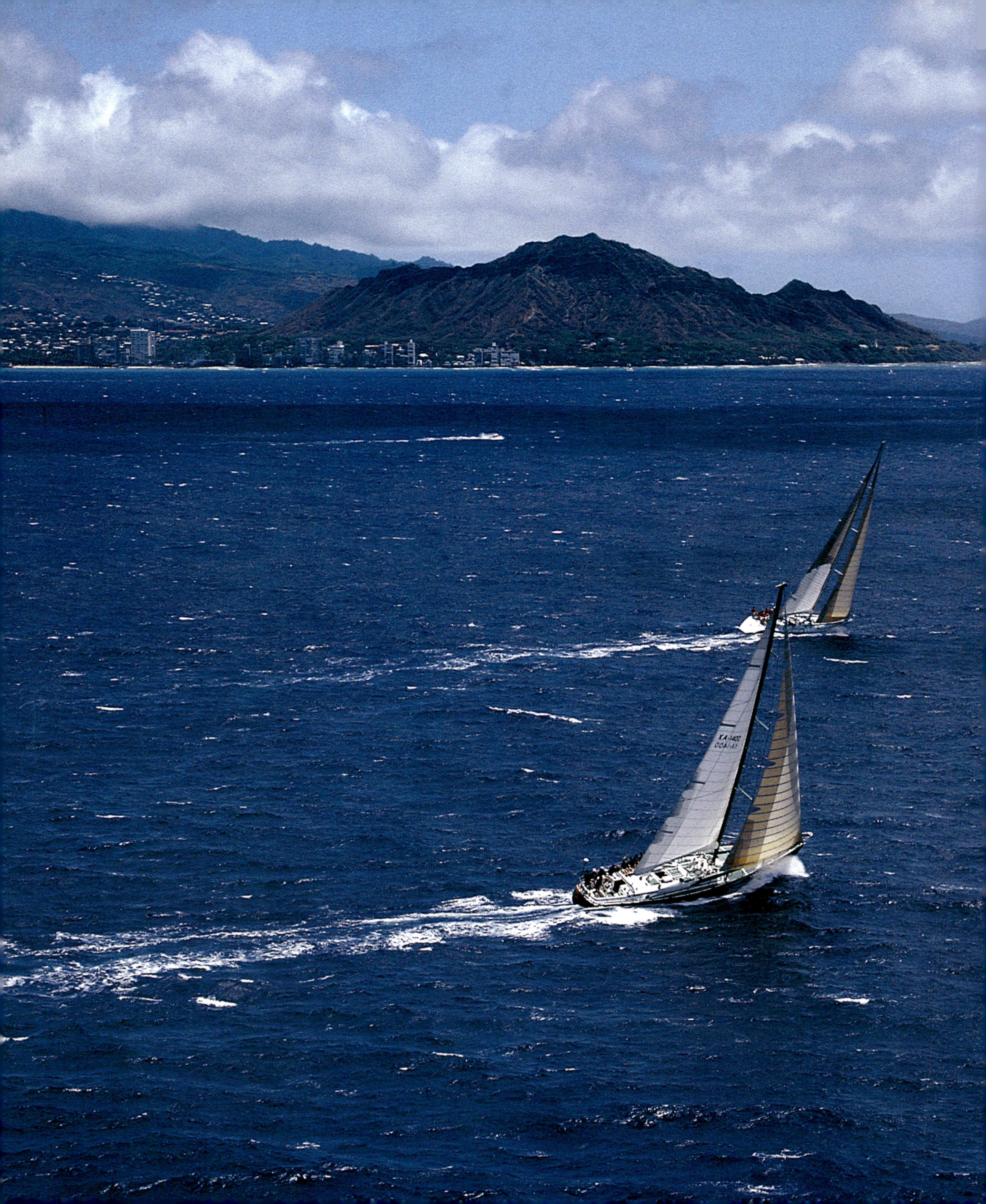

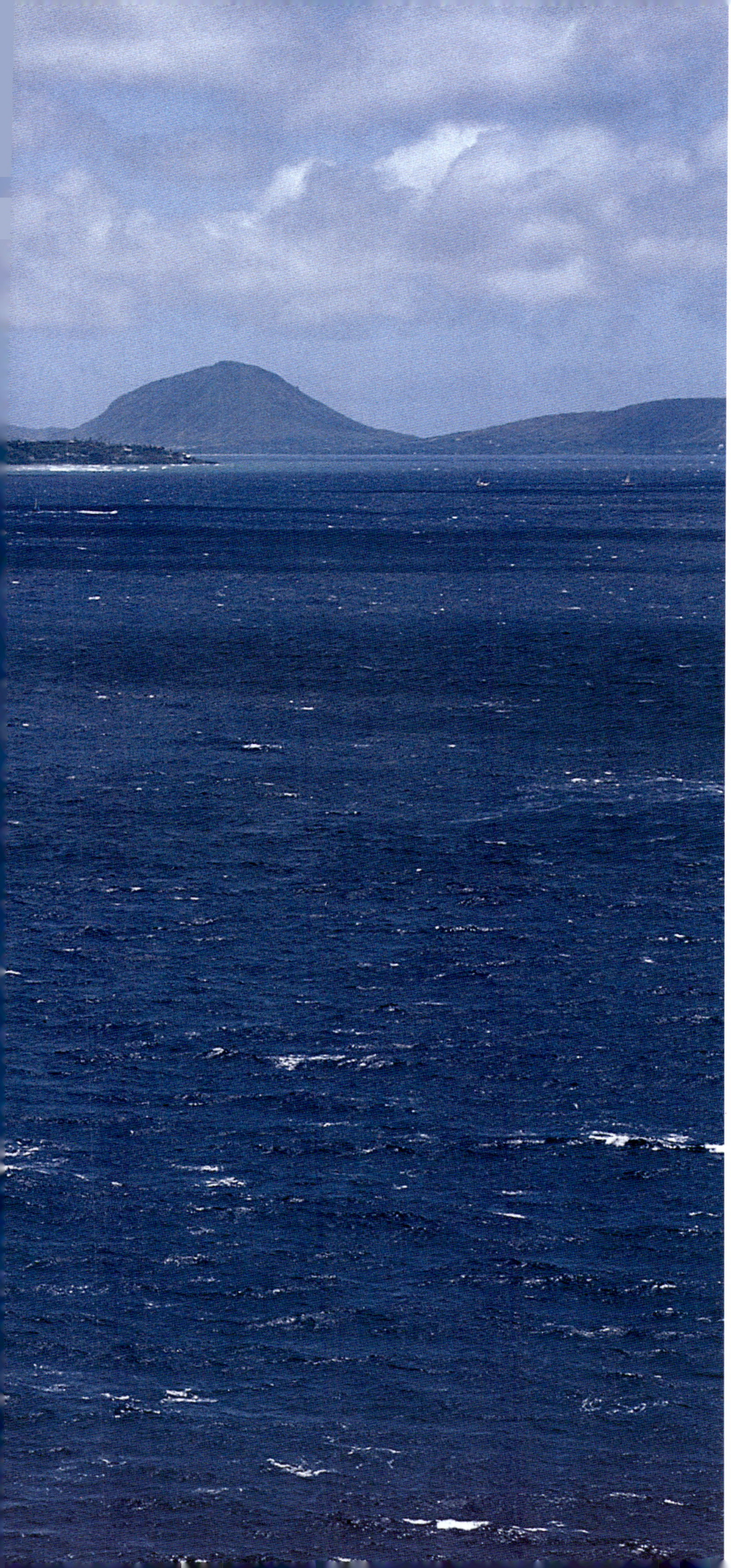

In 1982, I had the pleasure of photographing yachts racing in the most idyllic venue imaginable: the waters off the Hawaiian island of Oahu. There the brisk trade winds blow regularly, the sun usually shines, and the sea is interestingly varied — usually kindly, but with the potential for seagoing drama and good nautical theater. If the America's Cup ever comes back to the United States, this would be a wonderful course for the series. The Cup yachts would probably have to be more ruggedly designed and built for ths venue, but it would be a marine photographer's dream to see them racing there.

OAHU

Here we are looking toward the stretch between Diamond Head and Koko Head on the island of Oahu. The area of Waikiki Beach is to the left, and the city of Honolulu lies behind.

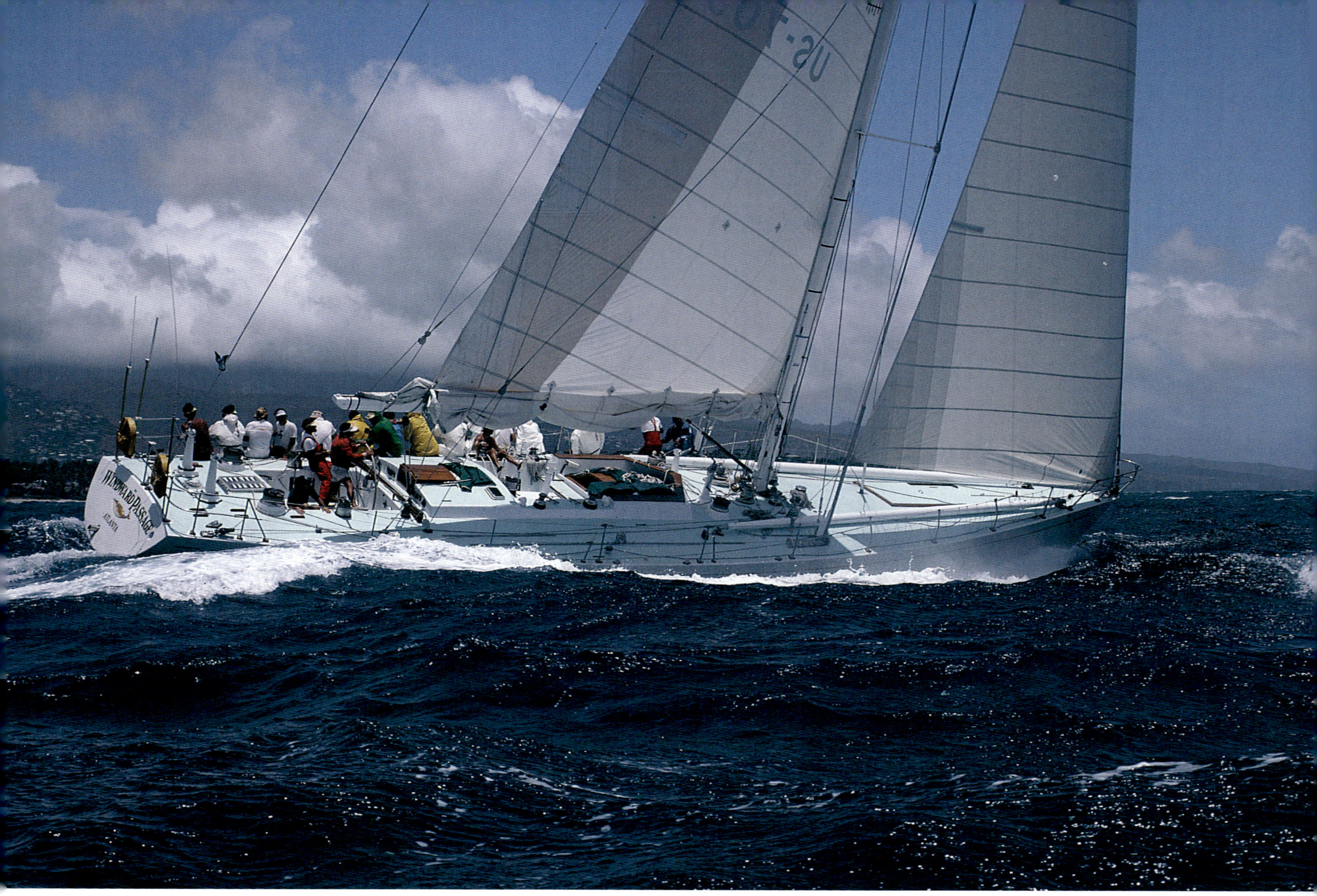

The following photographs of the yacht *Windward Passage* were made at the 1982 Clipper Cup Races off Oahu. As the sequence illustrates, an America's Cup series here would offer action-packed sailing to challenge both boats and sailors.

Meeting a Wave

With reefed mainsail and a short jib, *Windward Passage*, an early, more rugged variation of the present America's Cup class design, is ready to meet a wave on the windward leg of the Oahu course.

Flying Spray

Opposite above, *Passage* dips her bow into a sea and sends a solid splash of spray into the air.

Opposite, as she moves forward, spray flies high and away at the bow, and the wave curls aboard at the shrouds.

Opposite below, the flying spray at the bow falls back, the hull lifts, and the wave now amidships washes aboard along the leeward rail and passes astern. The crew sits snugly along the windward rail enjoying the scenery, and *Windward Passage* rides smoothly over the wave and prepares for the next.

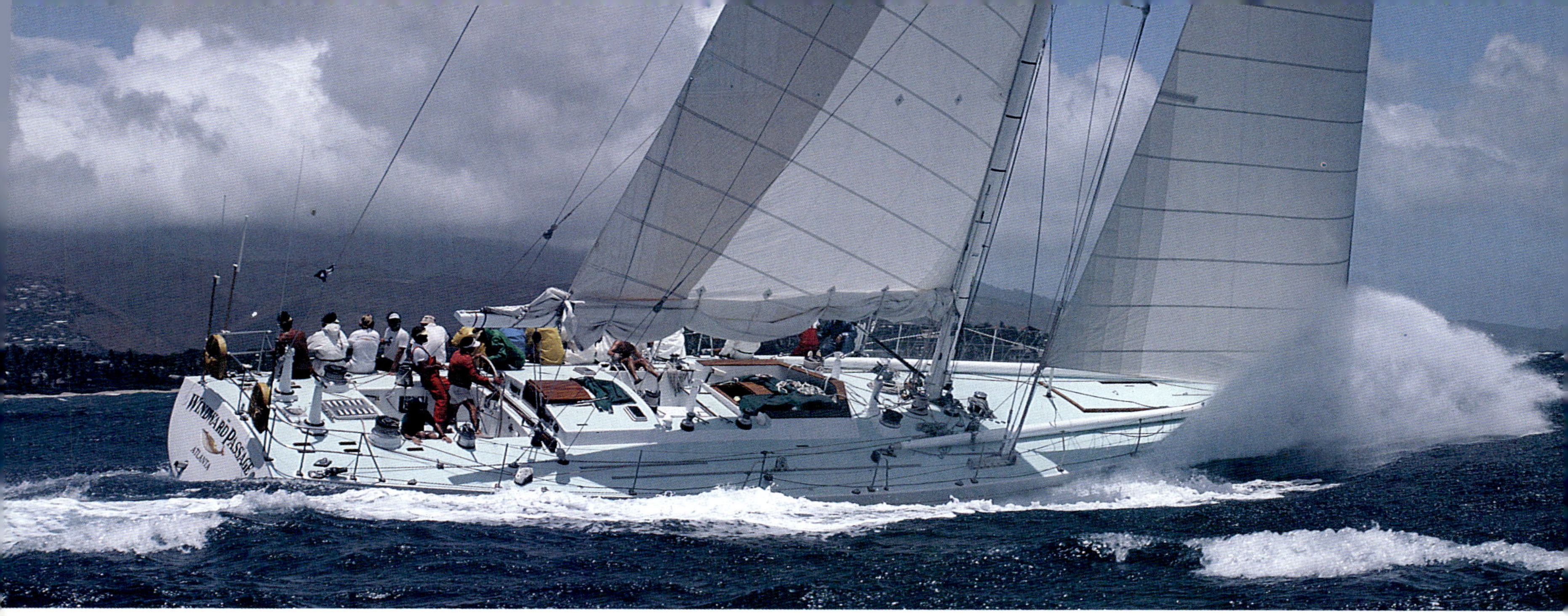
WINDWARD PASSAGE
ATLANTA

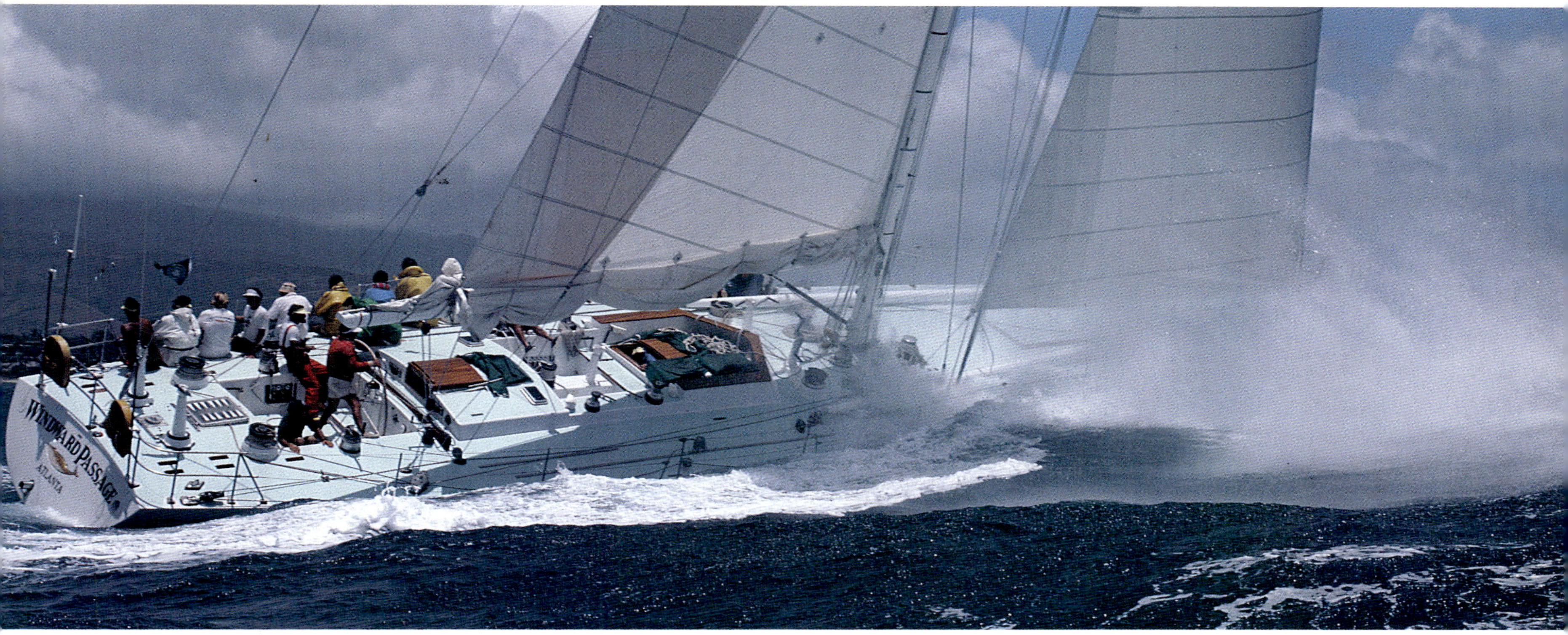
WINDWARD PASSAGE
ATLANTA

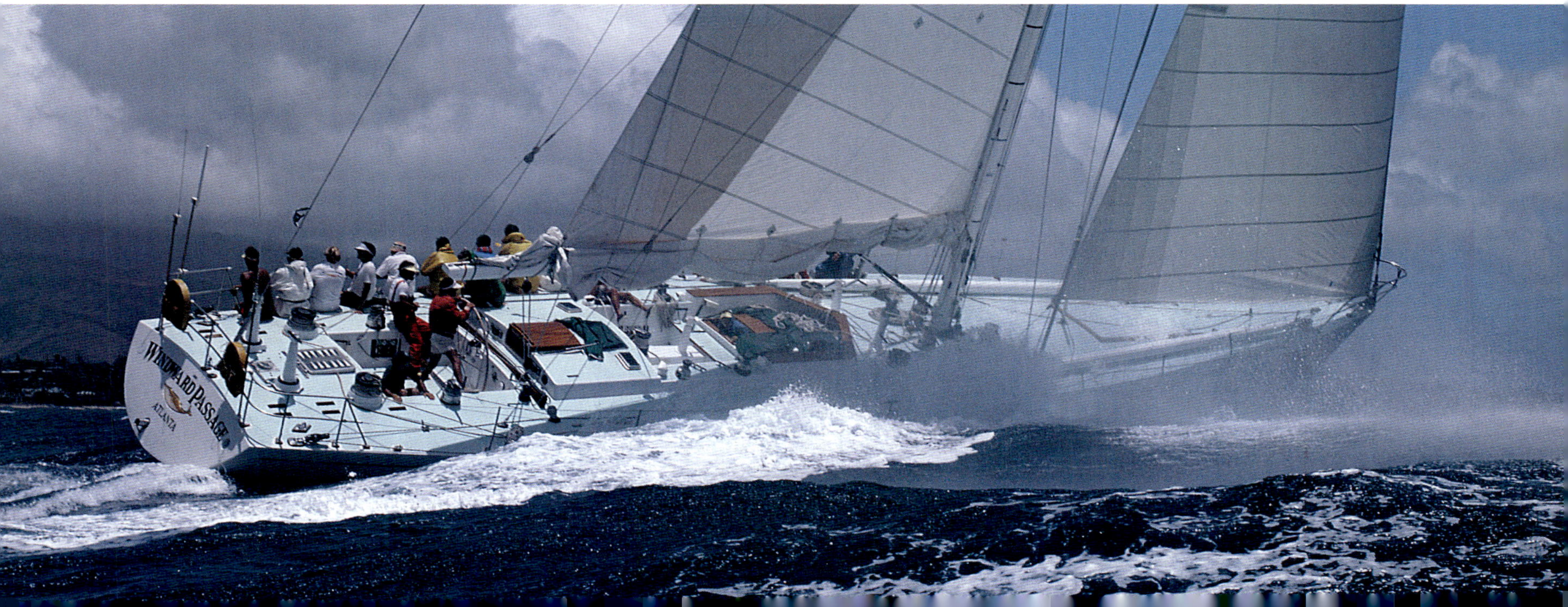
WINDWARD PASSAGE
ATLANTA

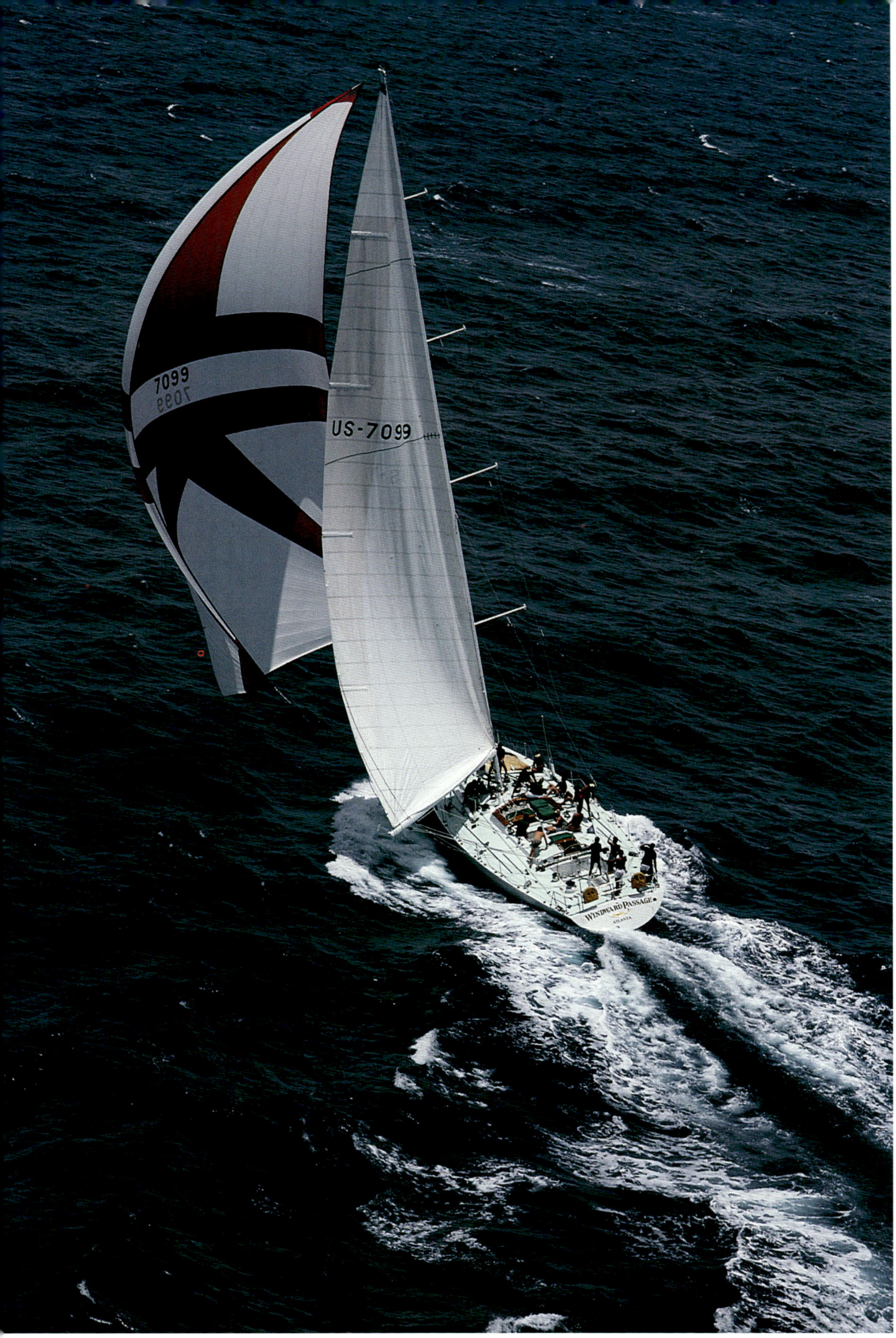

Reaching

Left, on the Oahu course, where yachts often approach hull speed, I could on occasion forget the beauty of their flight over the waves and concentrate on the flow of water underneath the graceful hulls. *Windward Passage* scurries along, reaching under a tugging spinnaker. The hull is almost on even keel, and the rooster tail emerging from under her transom catches my eye.

Double Rooster Tail

Opposite above, I am intrigued by a double stream of white foam emanating from astern of the rudder on *Windward Passage.* Is the rudder turned so that the passing stream of water is divided, creating the two lines of foam? Is the rudder angle necessary to hold the boat on course? The answers are probably yes. When a lot of sail is up and drawing on a windy reach, the boat wants to go toward the wind, so the helmsman is always pushing it down. Is that what the little rooster tails are showing?

Rooster Tail

Opposite below, a short while before, we had passed *Kialoa* and had noticed the very powerful line of white water streaming amidships in her wake. Perhaps it was the recollection of this image that made me wonder about the flow of water behind *Windward Passage.* In the same vein, I look at the two images of *Windward Passage* and *Kialoa* in almost the same racing trim and notice the difference in the white water along their leeward sides and the angle of the waves that rise toward the transom. Are the differences caused by surface wave action? I wonder what the towing tank would show about the flow of water beneath and across the underwater hulls.

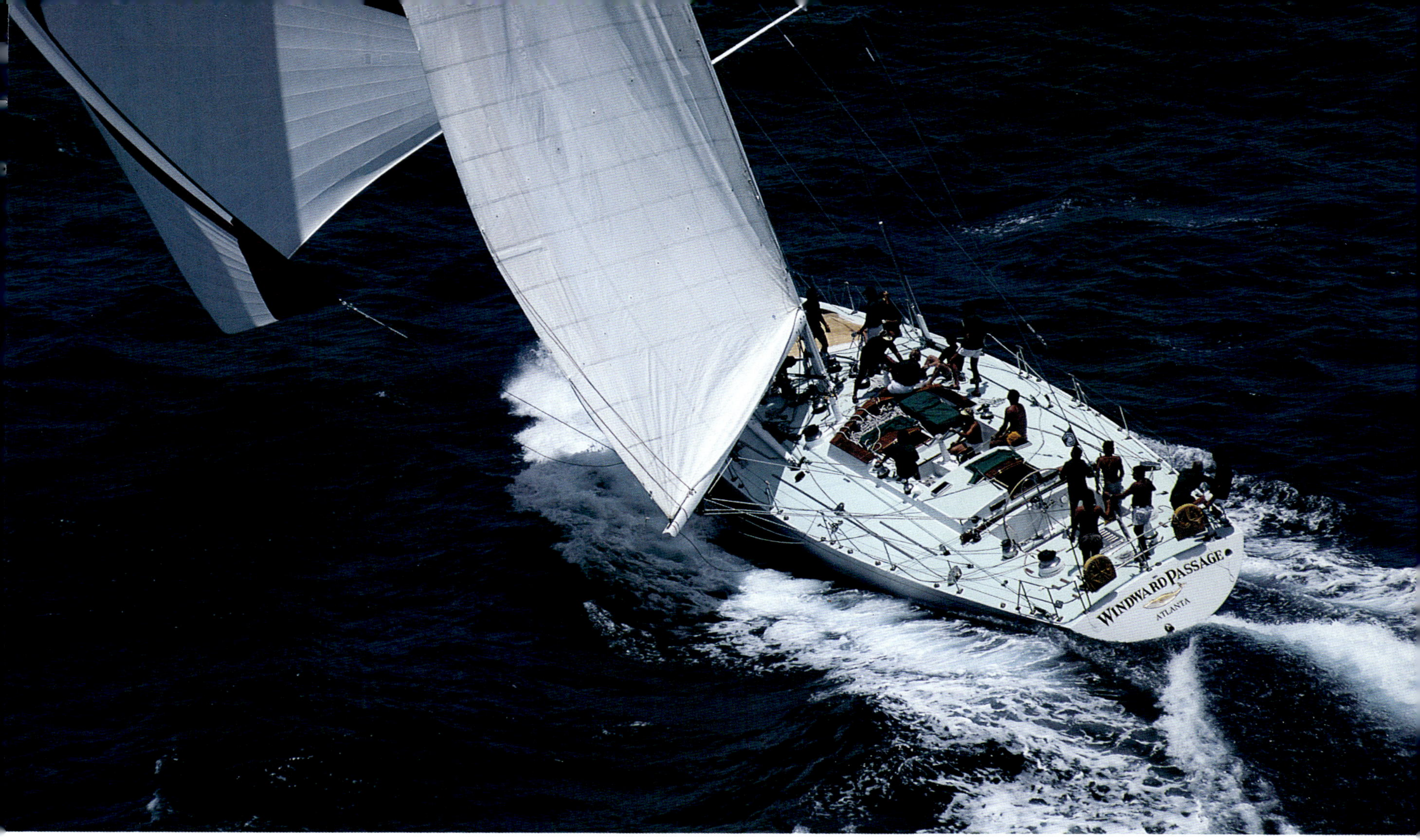
WINDWARD PASSAGE
ATLANTA

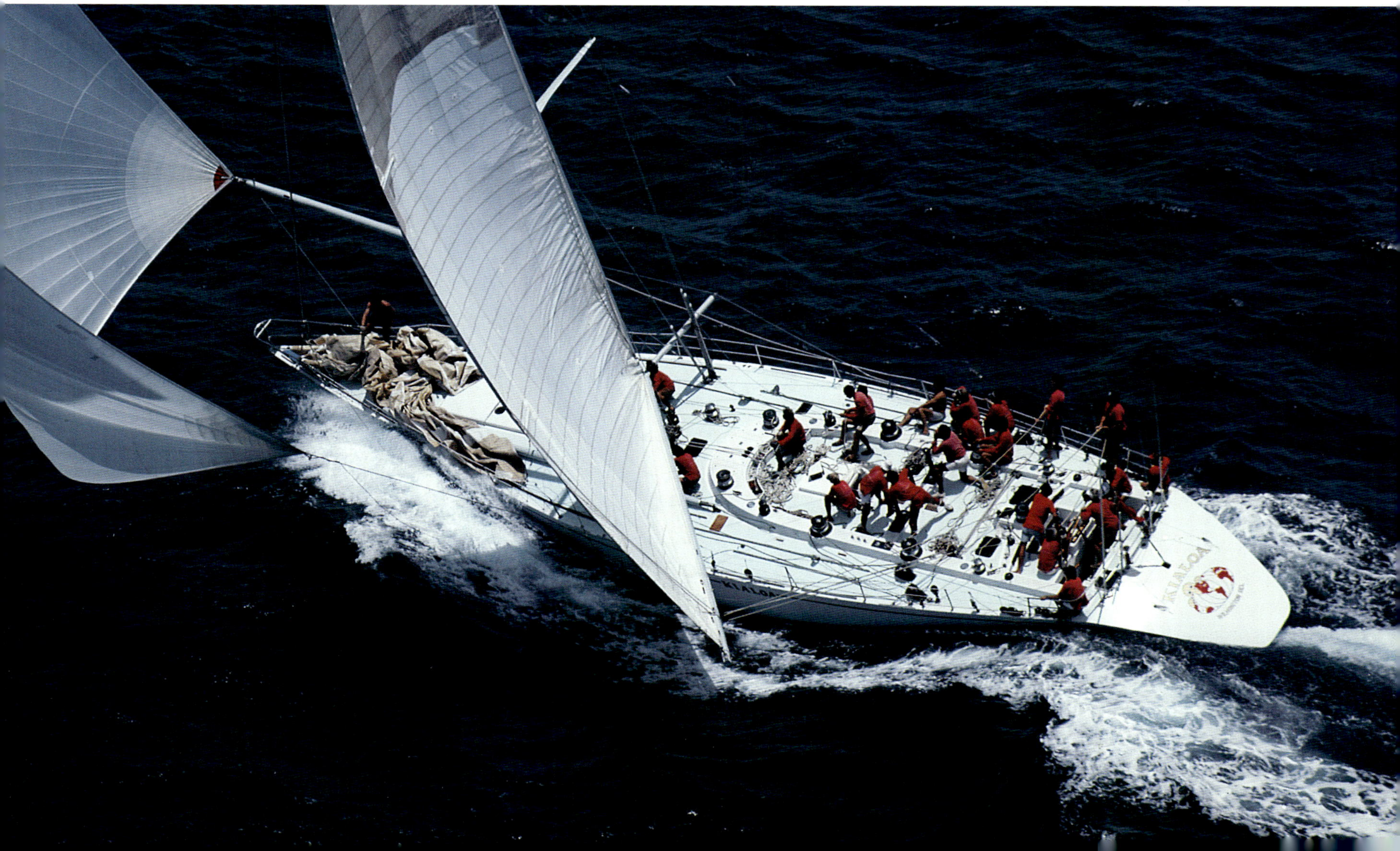
KIALOA

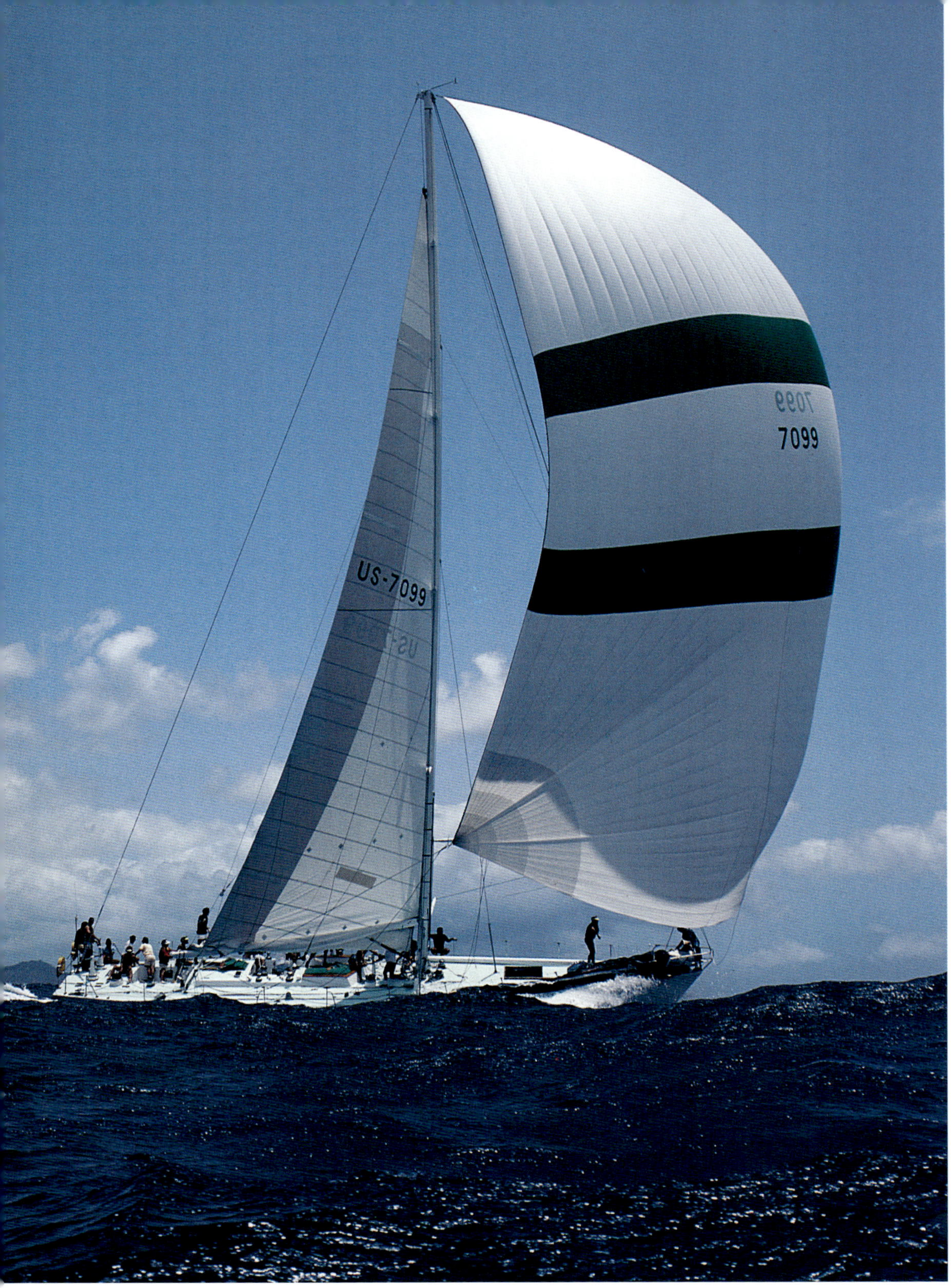

Downwind

In the first of a downwind sequence, *Windward Passage* drives along in a sparkling reach, spinnaker and main drawing beautifully.

Relaxed

The crew is scattered along the rail to weather. They are at ease, but — aware that the boat is moving at hull speed — no one sprawls. There is relaxed body tension to respond to the surging hull beneath. *Passage*'s owner, Bill Johnson, his left hand on the running backstay, stands along the windward rail outboard of the forward end of the cockpit. With a beautiful, surging craft underfoot, he savors the best of all possible worlds.

Mainsheet Eased

A more powerful burst of wind applies its pressure to the sails, and the hull heels and turns to weather. The mainsheet is eased to let the sail luff and prevent a knockdown. Some of the crew have been tending a reef in the main, but suddenly they, and everyone else aboard, lean to windward. The man in the red shirt at the wheel has his back arched as he feels the change in direction of the hull through its rudder. The mainsail is luffing, and the spinnaker pole shows a slight bend amidships as it flexes against the strain exerted by the spinnaker. It rests against the headstay. The hull is dipping as it accepts a bow-down attitude.

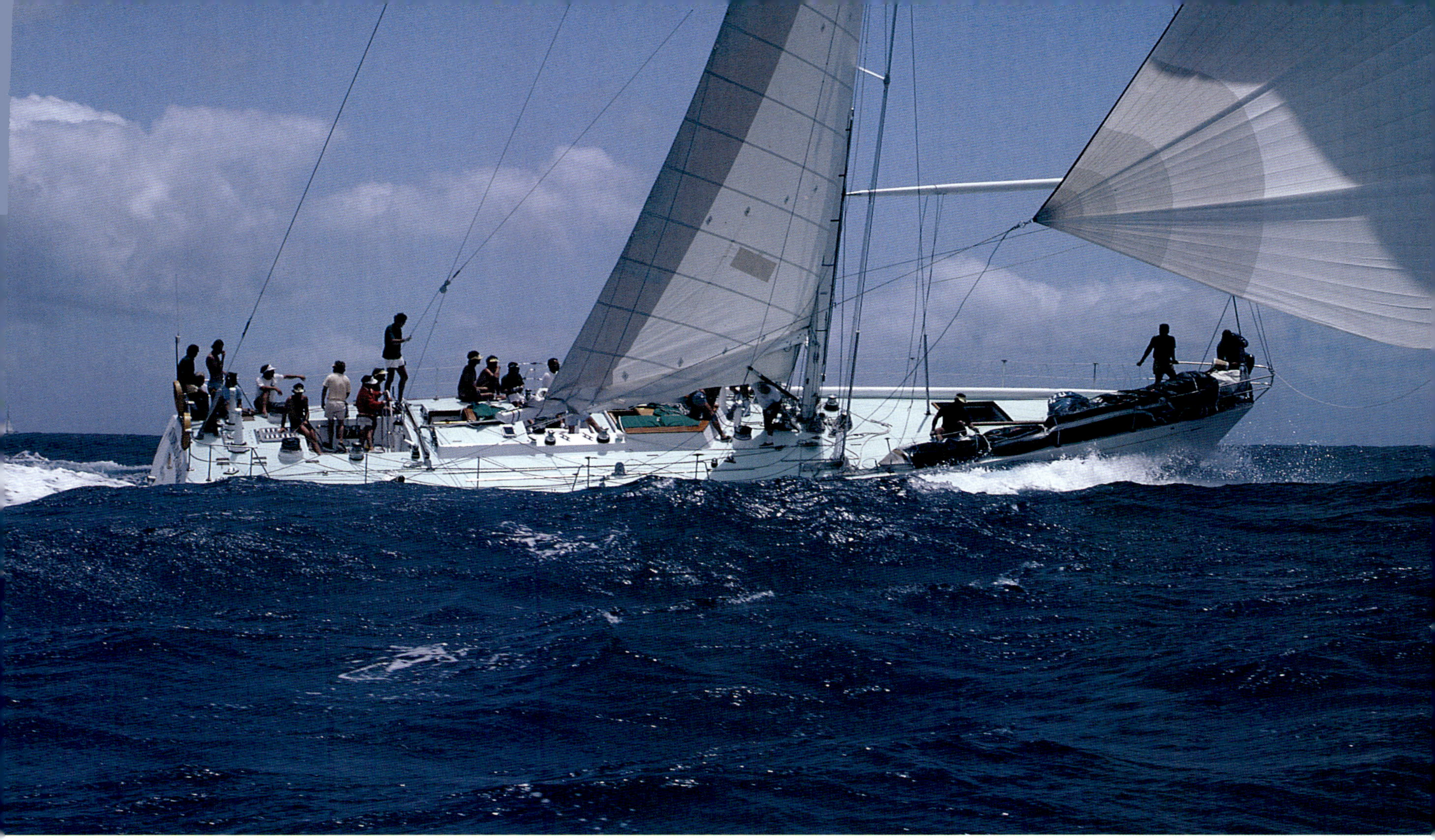

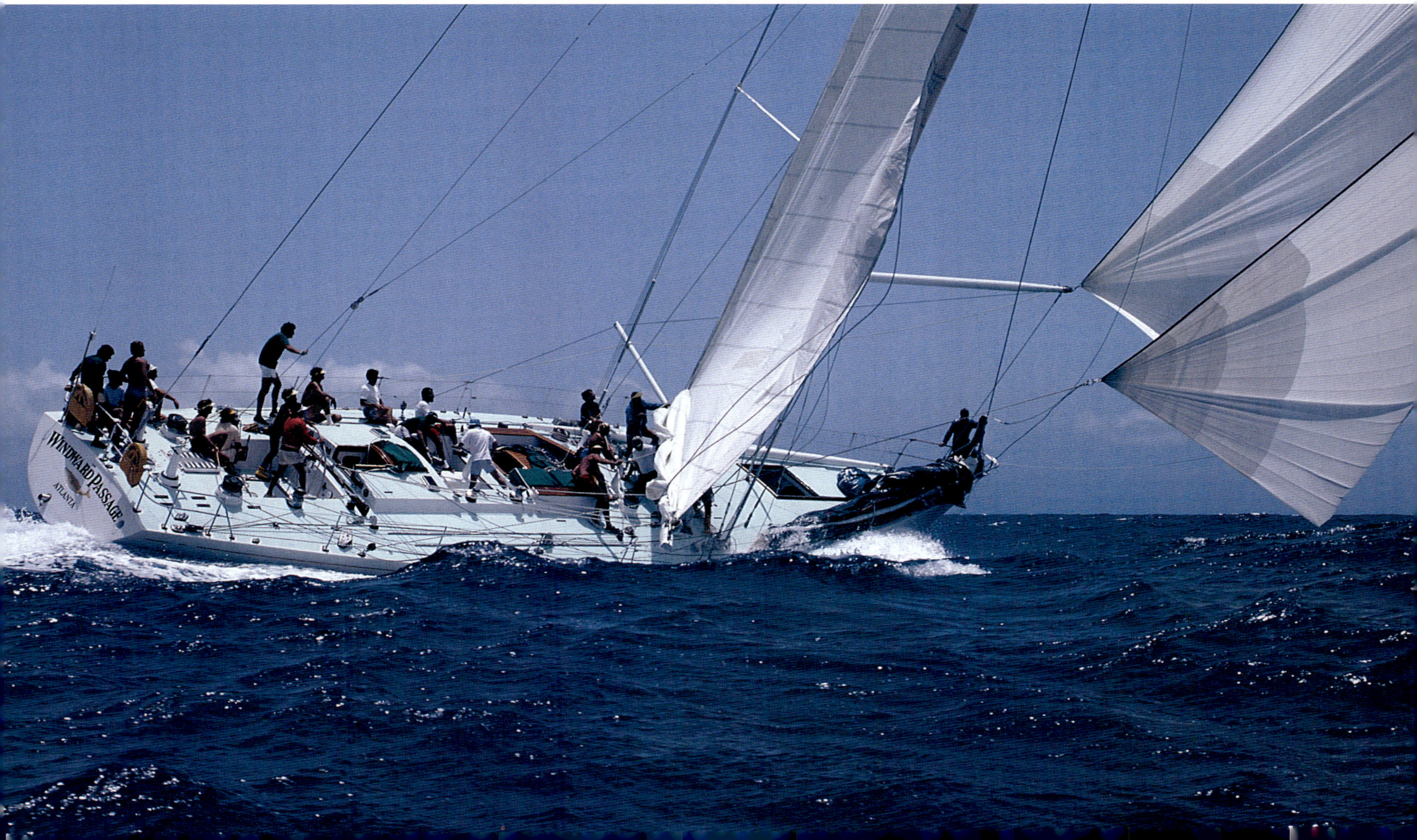
WINDWARD PASSAGE

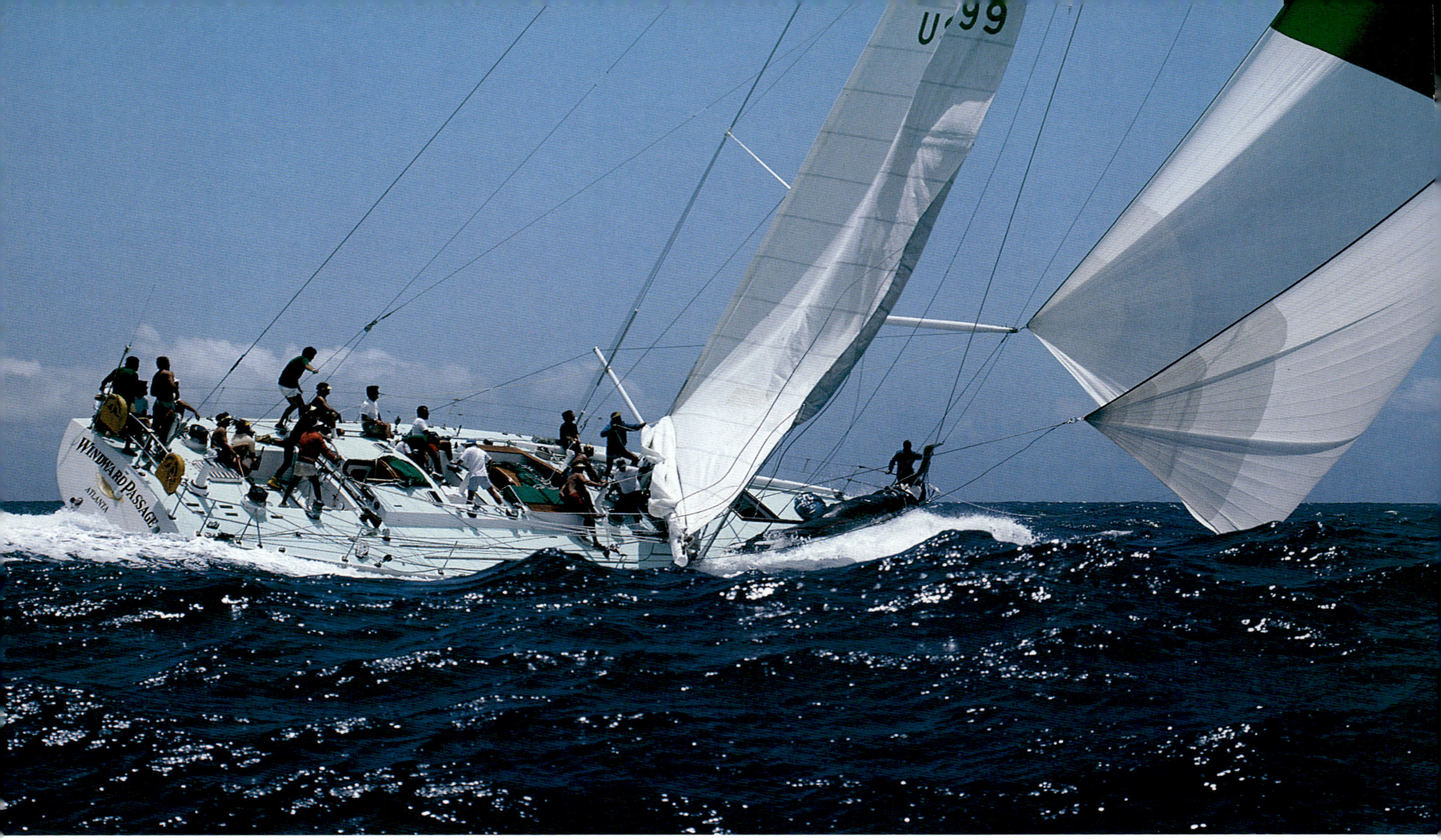

Pointing Higher

Now the distance between *Windward Passage* and the small photo boat I am on is just about equal to the trough on either side of the large swell that comes between us. *Windward Passage* continues to point higher, her mainsail luffs more violently, the boom end is dragging in the sea, and the crew amidships show more tension in the angle of their bodies. The red-shirted man at the helm thrusts down with his right hand as he moves the wheel to starboard to react to *Passage*'s broaching tendency. The bow on the other side of the wave crest seems to be digging in more, and owner Bill Johnson, in the green shirt and white shorts, standing at the backstay along the windward rail, flexes his knees to compensate for the boat's heel. The bend in the spinnaker pole moves forward toward the headstay.

Surging Spinnaker

Opposite above, *Windward Passage*'s bow lifts. The mainsail luffs more violently as the surging spinnaker has taken control, and the yacht points higher. I suddenly become aware that I must be reaching the end of the film in my camera and I read the film counter. I see that I have only three more exposures. My other cameras are wet and tucked under a tarp at my feet, so I dole out my three images carefully.

Spinnaker Collapse

Opposite below, *Windward Passage* is now over the edge of a knockdown, the spinnaker begins to collapse, the end of the boom creates its own wake, the mainsail luffs, the hull leans so the rail is under water, and all aboard lean to weather.

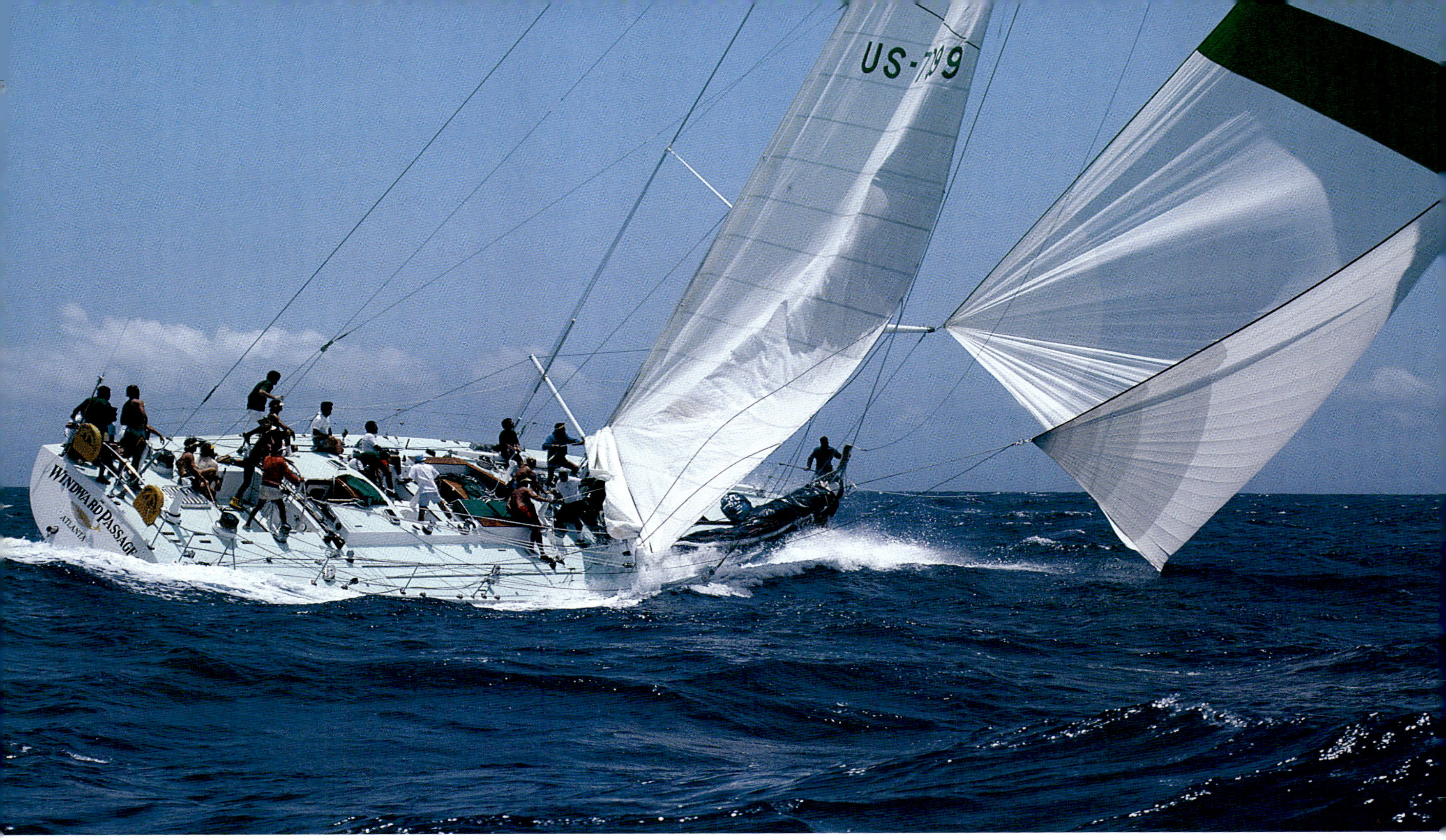
US-7099
WINDWARD PASSAGE

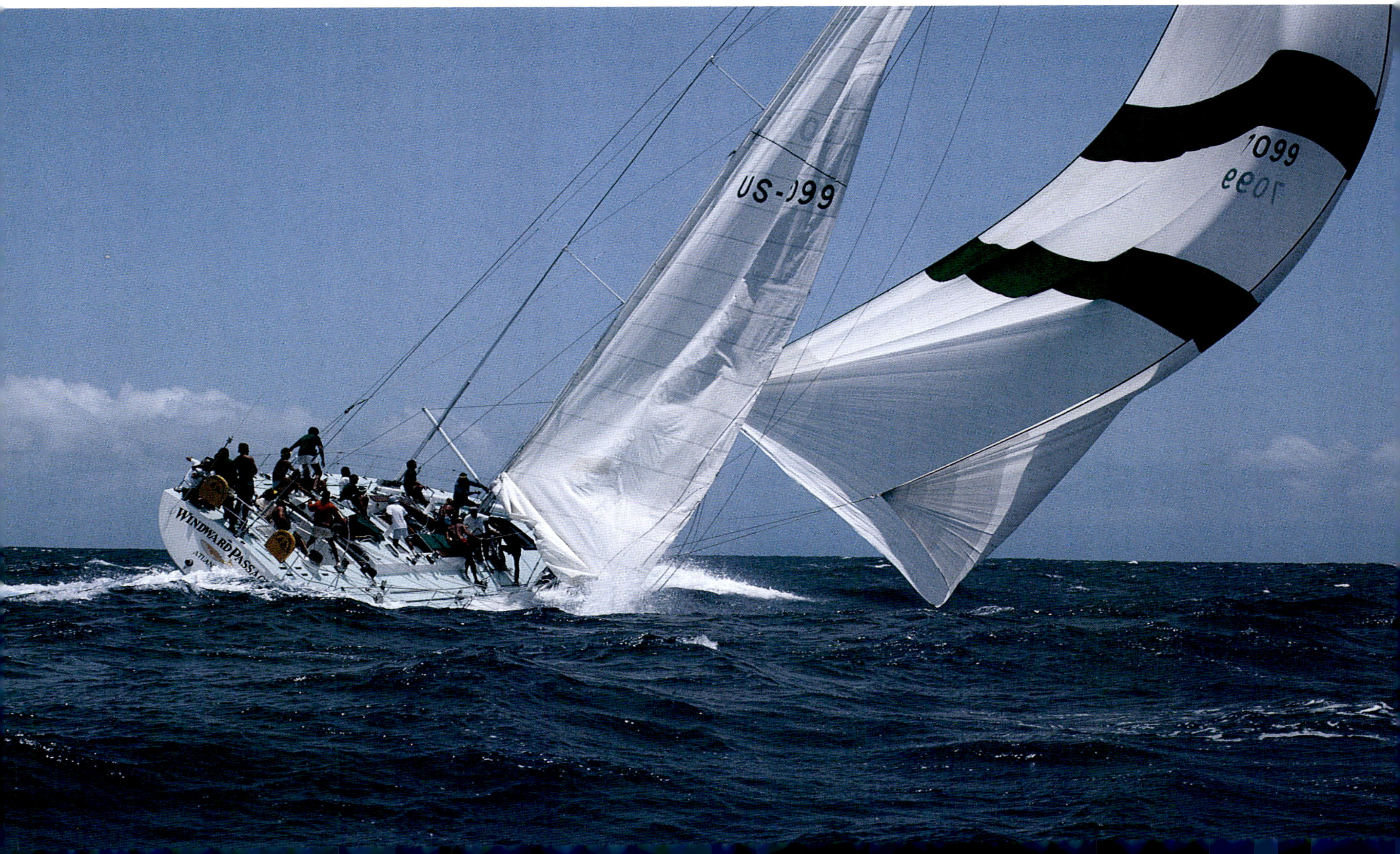
WINDWARD PASSAGE
7099

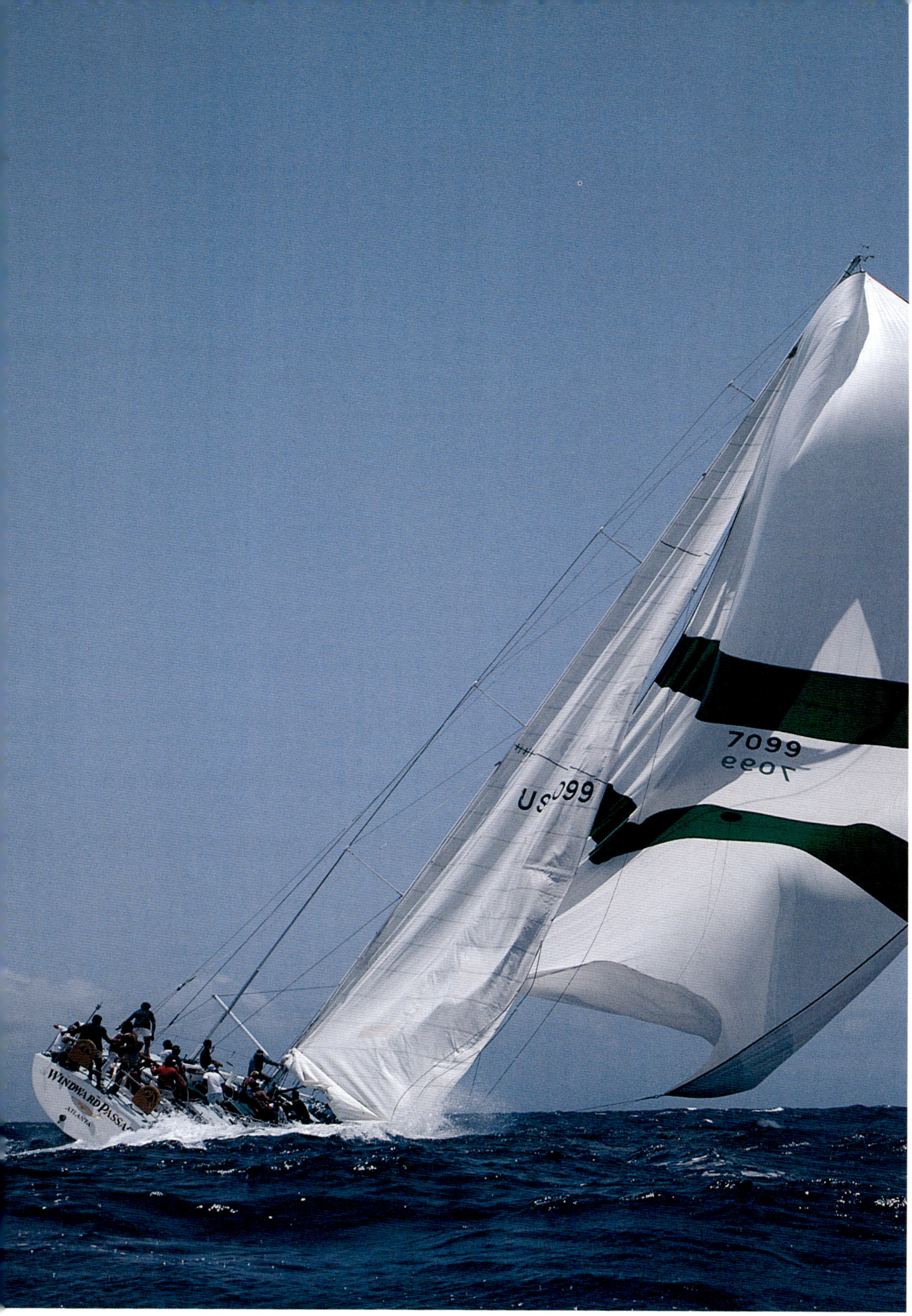

Control

I have turned the camera vertically to catch the collapsed spinnaker and luffing mainsail. The boom end splashes in the sea.

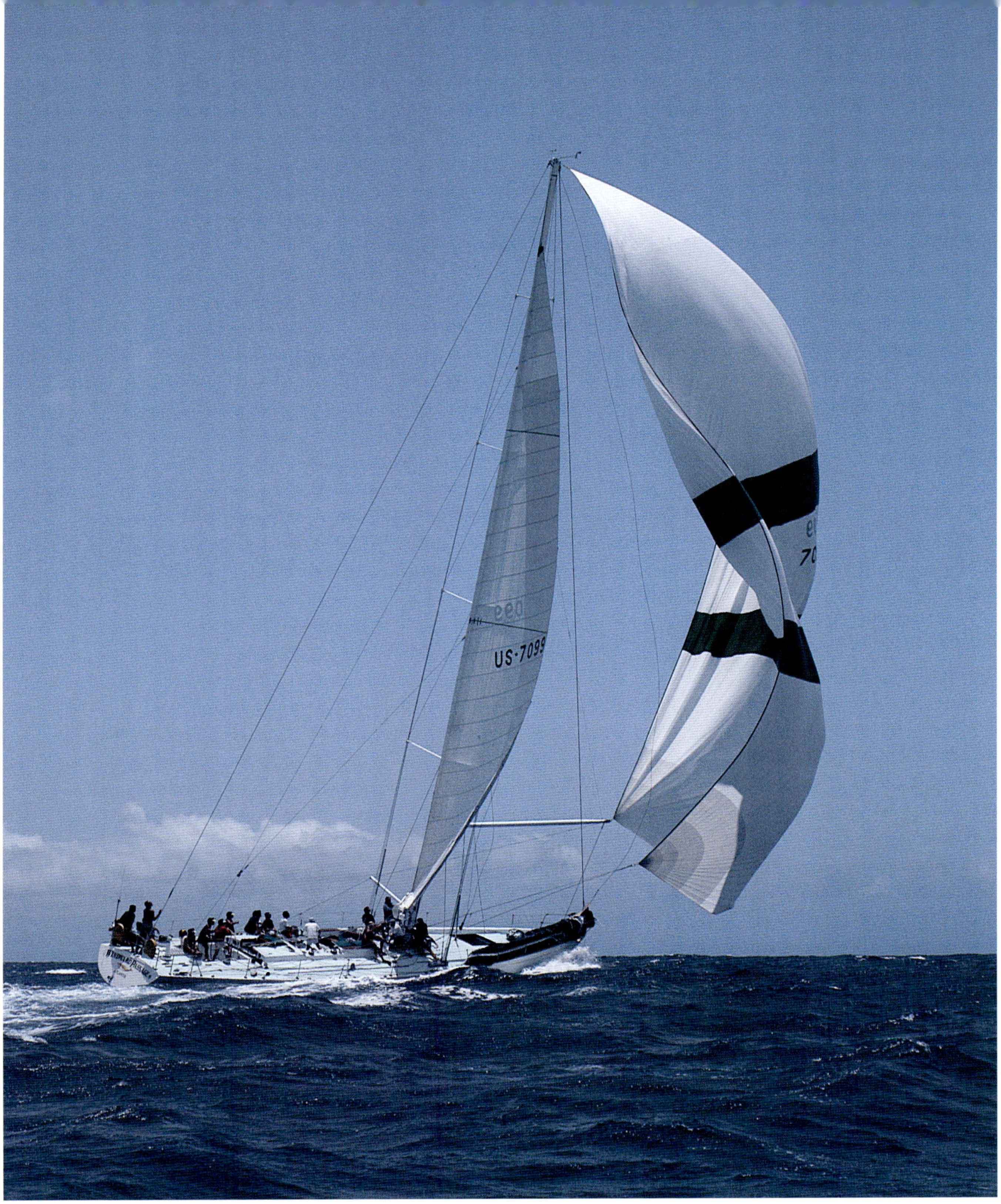

Back On Course

In my last exposure, the helmsman has *Passage* back on course, the mainsail drawing and the spinnaker unfurling, ready to fill again. The crew is back, with almost as much equanimity in their bodies as in the first image of this sequence. With another loud snap, the spinnaker will unfurl and fill and *Windward Passage* will resume her version of a Hawaiian sleighride.

Working in photography means communicating images in a language that is solely visual — a language confined to the sense of sight. If you can see an image, you can probably photograph it, but how to express the sensations, the feelings, so powerful or poignant that are inspired by the other senses? Afloat, I have felt the motion of the sea as it moves through the hull of a small boat and resounds inside me: through the flex of my arches, the thrust of calf, the bend of knee, the sway of hip, torso, and shoulders. I have known the lonely stretch to the horizon and the faint flush of inner power the distant horizon evokes. I have felt the damp wash of fog on my face and the chill of a small circle of visibility. I have seen the signs of shore in changing wave patterns, heard the sound of horn or whistle, and smelled the scent of grass reaching out to sea. Such sensory experiences may not actually leap off the photographic page. At times, however, their presence can be suggested in such a way that their essence clings. If anywhere in these pages that has been your perception, I feel rewarded.